SEASONS
of the SOUL

Contemporary Revelations
of the Ascended Masters

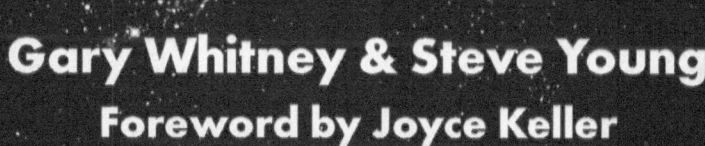

Gary Whitney & Steve Young
Foreword by Joyce Keller

Published by: Streaming Light Press
Cover & Interior Design: M. Miller Creative Services
Cover photo: Hubble telescope

ISBN: 979-8-9934566-0-7

Library of Congress Control Number
2025926761

This book is dedicated to

REVEREND KEITH MILTON RHINEHART

With Love, gratitude, and devotion

for all the sacrifices he made for his chelas,

his Church, humanity,

and the Ascended Masters.

For his demonstration of Love, kindness,

support, tolerance; and Mastery

in guiding all toward the Light.

CONTENTS

CONTENTS

CONTENTS

CONTENTS

Foreword

BEFORE MY BIRTH, I CHOSE TO BE BORN TO A MOTHER WHO WAS physically handicapped but an extraordinary psychic medium. I made a brilliant choice, because she did not disappoint me. From an early age, she taught me the secrets and truths about metaphysics and mediumship, and sent me into a life filled with joys, rewards, and disappointments. She warned me, though, that the world was not ready at that time for psychics and mediums and suggested that I never reveal my metaphysical abilities. She said it would only cause me heartache and pain. My 5-year-old mind looked at her, and I said, *"Ok, Mom, I will do my best."* But shortly thereafter, I was in trouble.

On my first day in kindergarten, I had a vision that my very harassed young kindergarten teacher needed to go home because her mother was having a heart attack. I hesitated, but then realized I had to give her that message and tell her she must go home because her mother was sick. So I raised my hand, and she came over to me. She said, *"This better be good because I don't want to hear any more nonsense from anyone."* I took a deep breath and said, *"Miss Harris, you have to go home. Your mother is having a heart attack!"* She looked at me and said, *"My mother is fine, and if I hear another peep out of you for the rest of the year, you are going to spend the rest of the time in the principal's office."* So I shrank back into my seat and said nothing.

On my second day in kindergarten, I was dreading what might be in store for me. But to my surprise, Miss Harris came over to me, knelt down beside me, took my hand, and said, *"Joyce, how did you know about my mother? Yesterday, when you told me to go home, she was having a heart attack, calling my name, and being led into an ambulance—how did you know that?"* I was so terrified at that point that I did not respond to her and just once again shrank into my seat. Then she said to me, *"Do you think you could please tell me if I am ever getting married?"* That began my path filled with psychic challenges. My mother was right.

As I grew up, I found myself delivering messages to people who were shocked and awed. I also found myself on many TV and radio shows, like with Oprah, Regis Philbin, Joan Rivers, and many others. I have done my own TV and radio shows for many years, with success because I told people about themselves. I realized that folks really need information about why they are here, where they are going, and what life is all about. I've written many books and have tried to share whatever wisdom I was blessed with over the years.

Now we have this amazing book, which sheds light on life's greatest mysteries, in a way that has never been done before. Gary Whitney and Steve Young help us to see beyond the veil of separation in the most entertaining and heartfelt manner. They bring into light many years of in-depth experience and knowledge, revealing mysteries that most of us have never heard of or dreamed about. Steve, a retired certified fraud detective, gives many testimonies, legitimizing the authenticity of Reverend Keith Milton Rhinehart's internationally acclaimed mediumship. Gary brings our attention to the fascinating history of Spirit communication.

Reverend Keith Milton Rhinehart was the founder of Aquarian Foundation, a Spiritualist Church, established in 1956 in Seattle, Washington. He was known for his extraordinary mediumship, manifesting physical phenomena where spirits took flesh and blood physical form, awing audiences from around the world. Through his adept mediumship, the Ascended Masters proved they could do just about anything as they brought forth scientific proof they

I presently feel more balanced in my relationship with Law Enforcement because of Steve. I'm able to value the contributions and sacrifices, along with the ongoing challenges. Are there corrupt police? Sure. Are there abusive police? Sure, they are human beings. But never in my wildest thought did I dream of having an encounter with a policeman in such a way as to influence my Spiritual Path! Our relationship coaxed me away from my flaming liberal stance and edged me toward the center.

Now I can honestly explore all views before coming to conclusions. I have been most pleased with my own personal growth stemming from our friendship and encourage others to embrace their opposites, their arch nemesis, whoever that might be, because the yin lies closer to the yang than one ever imagines.

I, Steve, the policeman, have an extremely different background and life experience from those of Gary. I worked the lion's share of my life serving on the Honolulu Police Force and working in security positions, while Gary was more involved in creativity and art. I've spent my time being part of a team working to ensure people get a fair chance at justice. I have had little interaction with the art world, and I must admit, I relate mostly to art that falls into the realistic vein. Modern abstract expressionism and other modern movements have not captured my interest, as I don't understand what the artists are trying to say. Gary's involvement in this aspect of art is one example of what makes our lives uniquely different. Nevertheless, we have become quite close, often seeing eye-to-eye, and that has been surprising.

Over the time we have gotten to know each other, Gary has brought different artists to my attention I would never have come across on my own. Our discussions around these artists stimulated a greater appreciation of different types of creativity and the skill it takes to execute various types of art. As a result, my interest in art has increased and broadened.

One of the things that most surprised me about Gary was his interest and involvement in social justice and Divine Principle. I never imagined artists being very involved in areas that cross over into the field of social justice or taking direct actions to bring about that end. I saw that Gary made personal sacrifices, marched in many protest events, and spoke to others in an attempt to encourage them to take a conscious stance to create a more peaceful, just world. I observed through Gary that artists in general are more diverse than I originally thought.

Additionally, Gary held extremely liberal political views, which are much opposed to my more conservative opinions. I witnessed how, after we spoke, he genuinely researched different ideas and integrated new perspectives, as he saw merit in the opposing views I presented, loosening his liberal, artistic stance.

As we look around, we know each of us has someone in our life where the original harmonious spark has flickered or, in some cases, a total breakdown has occurred, where inflammatory acrimony now exists. It is our hope that our collaboration inspires others to reach across the aisle and embrace what at first glance looks like irreconcilable differences, making an honest effort to discover new common ground in which to create a more tolerant, interactive, and respectful world.

ONE

SPIRITUAL PHENOMENA
THE SKEPTICAL WITNESS

"As I watch, Reverend Keith Milton Rhinehart steps from behind the violet curtain of the Holy of Holies, and a woman moves forward to peel off the strip of white medical tape sealing Reverend Rhinehart's mouth. His lips pooch, his cheeks slightly bulge, a muffled clatter rattles from his mouth as though something is hitting against his teeth, he tilts his head, and long flowing locks shake from side to side. Then, seemingly out of nowhere, glistening faceted stones spew from his gaping mouth and fall from his eyes in such numbers it confounds the mind. People in attendance stand rapt, as a reverent awe overcomes them. No accepted concept in physics can explain what I'm seeing; no past experience gives me understanding."

– **Steve Young**, Retired White Collar Violent Crime Detective, Retired Certified Fraud Examiner, Certified Protection Professional

WHAT EXACTLY DID STEVE WITNESS IN 1972 IN HONOLULU? Is it simply an illusionist's act, the jaw-dropping magic of David Blaine? Is it similar to the contrived manifestations of fraudulent Spiritualists' séances during the Nineteenth Century, or akin to a sadhu on the streets of Haridwar, India pulling a ring out of thin air?

When we witness a mysterious event such as what Steve described, the curious mind wants to know how it happened—what trick, what sleight of hand is at play. Is it real? There is a shock of sorts, blowing the doors off our accepted reality, a knee-jerk thrill widens our eyes in wonder, releasing a spontaneous flow of adrenaline animating our limbs. What is the purpose behind such theatrics? What are the psychic abilities enabling such an act? How can we make sense of Steve's experience?

Throughout history, rare paranormal events have pierced the veil between the World of Spirit and our material plane, jolting the current understanding of physics and religion. Startling phenomena occur; events that stand alone with no parallel and shatter the mind with but one purpose, to upend societies' applecart, shocking humanity out of an ingrained stupor, provoking inquisitiveness. Was there an accomplice? Was it entertainment produced by an ego-driven medium for adulation and attention? When all inquiring scientific and rational avenues fail to uncover fraud and mischief, it leaves but one answer: something paranormal must be intervening; something existing outside our understanding, no matter how irrational this answer might sound!

At first blush, we might assume the materialization of an avalanche of faceted stones pouring out of a medium to be a performance, Spiritual showtime, a schtick of superficial glitz, only to go up in a puff of smoke. But when due diligence finds that the cause of the event stems from the Spirit World and the faceted stones are real physical objects, it is clear the riddle goes deeper. If, in fact, the manifestation is caused by Spirit, we must consider that these seemingly miraculous and mind-bending events are not casual happenings created to titillate the audience with the medium's remarkable abilities, but rather, devised by the Spirit World for a sincere purpose.

For a moment, imagine yourself in Steve Young's shoes. How would you react to such an event? Would you take it in stride or dig to find answers? For some of us, events such as these present an existential shock, lifting us outside of time and space, and leaving us in disbelief. But most of us simply carry on with our lives because we don't know how to interpret or process something existing beyond our understanding.

As a professional fraud investigator, when Steve found that no fraud existed, he became inspired to discover the meaning. Why had he witnessed this event? What did it mean beyond the novelty of the incident's uniqueness? (We will investigate Steve's inquiry in depth in the coming Chapters.)

TWO

SPIRITS' PERSPECTIVE

I F WE JUMP FROM STEVE TO THE SPIRIT WORLD AND ASK SIMILAR questions of Spirit, what might we discover? The Masters, through Reverend Rhinehart's adept mediumship, present answers:

To the Ascended Masters, Spiritual events are not "unnatural" or "supernatural" but simply supernormal, that is, something that exists within the natural laws of the Spirit World. Spirit goes to great lengths, utilizing a paranormal methodology in such a way that humankind will understand something unusual is transpiring, something out of the norm that cannot be explained with the rational mind. In this way, we are able to recognize that a teaching is being dispensed from God, not something issuing from humanity itself.

The Masters imply that humanity has reached an evolutionary crossroads, a point at which a nudge towards the Light is required. If we look to Plato's allegory of the cave, referred to in his book, *The Republic,* it might provide understanding. It could be suggested that Spirit is implying we (in the cave) have been looking only into the shadows as our reality, and now it is time to turn toward the Light.

So we ask, is the event Steve witnessed simply a spontaneous occurrence? No, emphatically, No! The Masters state that a supernormal event in the order of what Steve witnessed is not a random happening but demarks a time in Earth's evolution that the Masters bring a new dispensation of Light, a time of delivering new wisdom to transmute the existing ignorance and negativity on the planet. The

Masters have been working thousands of years in Shambhala and the Spirit Realms, imbuing these sacred, faceted stones with Spiritual Light and new wisdom. The deliverance of these stones represents the moment when we are poised for a dramatic shift in consciousness, ready for a leap in Spiritual growth. At these critical junctures in time, when new cycles of Light and Energy are needed and when negativity is at its height, Spirit reaches out to humankind from the heart and mind of God with great compassion.

If we review the events surrounding great teachers of the past, such as Krishna, Buddha, Jesus, Moses, and Muhammad (to name a few), history tells us supernormal incidents punctuated each of their ministries and teachings, presenting irrefutable evidence that something transformative was at play, something that harkens to a consciousness existing beyond humanity's understanding or ability to duplicate. This high level of paranormal phenomena produced by Reverend Rhinehart is of a similar caliber and unmatched by most mediums of the New Age, and establishes evidence that Spirit is presenting us with a wakeup call.

We might ask why there is this intervention. Aren't we evolving just fine on our own? From the viewpoint of the powers controlling our planet, this might be a welcome conclusion. But when we empathize with the heartache and struggles of everyday people, we are likely to find this conclusion wanting.

A more elevated conclusion, one originating from Spirit, recognizes the repetitive patterns, the dogmatic, limited thinking, and the paralyzing pain of human existence—and takes action in an attempt to assist with humanity's conquest over the constant march through the turnstiles of reincarnation in one unexamined life after another.

With deep compassion and understanding, loving beings from the heart and mind of God reach back to humanity to lend their assistance.

They refer to themselves as Archangels, Dhyan Chohans, Bodhisattvas, and the Ascended Masters abiding in Shambhala and the Seventh Plane of the Seventh Sphere of the Spiritual realms. They are beings who have mastered the forces of life and death. Many have forgone the pleasures of this and other worlds, in order to serve humanity. Their mission and work is to encourage those of us who can hear their call to overcome the blind spots in our souls and rise. If we investigate, we will find history replete with riveting, colorful stories of these Spiritual Masters' interventions over the centuries.

Ascended Masters, or Avatars, have always represented high points in history where Spirit reaches out to interact with humankind to shift and transform our awareness. Few of us are fortunate enough to witness these auspicious moments, but for those motivated to experience the Masters' activities and teachings, there are many books describing their interactions with humanity. Some inspiring books in this vein are the *Life and Teachings of the Ascended Masters of the Far East*, by Baird Spaulding, *The Secret Doctrine and Isis Unveiled*, by Madame Blavatsky, some of the scripture in the *Holy Bible*, and the *Bhagavad Gita*. These readily available books are quite informative in presenting the mysteries and nature of the Ascended Masters' consciousness.

THREE

REVEREND KEITH MILTON RHINEHART, KUMARA 4-1-1936 CE — 4-30-1999 CE
Psychic Wonder of Seattle

Keith Milton, who? I have never heard of him—how could he possibly be an important person of the Twentieth Century? Well, we all know there's more to this world than the five o'clock news and the banter around the water cooler. Reverend Rhinehart's enigmatic and dynamic character might surprise you, not to mention his unsurpassed, yet often unacknowledged, accomplishments!

In the town of Nunn, Colorado, with the sun stationed in Aries and the ascendant in Aquarius, Keith Milton Rhinehart began his incarnation on Earth. The energy vortexes of this astrological portal were especially auspicious. As you will discover, it was not by happenstance that he arrived on April Fools' Day, 1936.

As early as age two, Keith's mother, Val, started teaching him to read, for which he took a fast liking and displayed a keen perception. By five, he could read and understand complex thought. At this early age, Spirit incidents like poltergeist phenomenon began to occur in Keith's home. Rapping banged out from the walls, and picture frames fell oddly to the floor.

When Keith was around ten, his mother escaped from the bitter cold of winter in Cheyenne to go on a trip to San Francisco and meet up with a good friend. On the evening of Val's arrival, her friend planned to attend a service at the Golden Gate Spiritualist Church and asked Val to accompany her. Each evening during the service, Mrs. Florence Becker, the founding medium of the Church, regularly performed billets (tickets to the Spirit world, where a medium acts as a go-between linking Spirit and humanity by bringing through personal messages from Spirit). Val decided to request a message. When Val's turn arrived, Mrs. Becker began to sing, *"Why, oh why did I ever decide to leave Wyoming?"* She went on explaining that Val had a young son back home who would one day become an extremely talented and famous medium.

As a young boy, Keith displayed interest in mediumship and psychical research, but when his mother informed him what Mrs. Becker related, he scoffed, feeling immediately doubtful of the validity of the message. He declared Mrs. Becker must have overheard a conversation before the meeting where his mother spoke of living in Wyoming. A skeptical youngster, Keith wasn't about to fall for wild declarations without critically thinking through all the possibilities.

At age twelve, Keith became a newspaper boy delivering papers in the frigid Cheyenne weather, often confronting twenty-below temperatures on his route. One morning, as he prepared his papers for delivery, he happened to glance at the personals column where he noticed a lady medium had placed an announcement seeking a group of people to join her psychic development class. Fascinated, Keith decided to explore if what interested him as a child could prove to be true. Immediately, he found the class engaging and started attending every week.

When he turned fourteen, an out-of-town medium visited his development group to give billet readings. Hearing the event was free, he decided to attend and submitted a billet card (card with a question for Spirit) asking for a message from Spirit, signing his card KMR.

Standing before the medium to receive his message, he heard, *"Keith Milton Rhinehart, you are not going into science or radio as you have planned, but you will end up being a world-famous medium!"*

Keith became outraged, asserting, *"You're definitely wrong about that!"*

Unfazed, the medium went on, *"Your main Spirit Guide will be Dr. Robert John Kensington, and you will go into trance within one year."*

Despite feeling the visiting medium's message most misguided, Keith continued attending the Spirit Circle. One evening, totally bored, he fell soundly asleep. Upon awakening, Keith found the entire development circle gathered around him! They exclaimed that when he was asleep, he fell into trance, at which point the candles on the table started to levitate. The circle declared many of their deceased relatives spoke through him, bringing messages that proved evidential. Despite the past predictions, Keith felt most astonished.

After this initial experience, Keith's development spiked rapidly. Nearly a year later, a Spiritualist Minister from Tacoma, Washington, invited him to visit her Church. During his summer break between his junior and senior year, he accepted her offer.

Quickly, the quality of his mediumship captured the loyalty of the members of her Church, and the minister decided to ordain him as a fellow minister. On this visit, he discovered the cool Northwest weather was extremely calming to his hay fever, which influenced his decision to attend the University of Washington after he graduated from high school. However, because he had already developed as an unusually gifted medium, his guides soon prodded him to forego college and start a Church. So it happened, with fifteen charter members, he founded Aquarian Foundation in Seattle, Washington, in 1955. Since he was only nineteen, the State required his mother to sign the Church documents as his legal guardian, and in 1958,

Reverend Keith Milton Rhinehart delivered his first sermon in Seattle at Aquarian Foundation.

Within a short period, Keith's charisma and adept mediumship, backed by scientific testing, attracted a devoted following interested in Spiritualism—people searching for genuine knowledge from the heart and mind of God. With a constant stream of wisdom pouring forth from the Ascended Masters, many found exactly that for which they were searching.

With scientific proof of Spirit speaking through his mediumship, Keith thought the Masters' wisdom would swiftly circle the globe. Given three world tours, to some extent, it did. But even though Keith generated substantial success on the tours, illustrating profound gifts, many unforeseen challenges arose, suggesting a malicious plan was at work, an evil force deliberately executed to thwart Keith's mission and to sabotage the Ascended Masters' plans for the coming of the Golden Age.

The following incidents illustrate the dynamics of good and evil at play, even in the life of a medium as adept as Reverend Rhinehart:

While still a teenager, Reverend Rhinehart gave a séance in Denver, Colorado, which was suddenly raided by the police. Keith was written up for the heinous crime of fortune-telling. One might ask how a young man presenting messages from Spirit attracted such attention? What provoked such an over-the-top response? At the police station, the officers beat him with rubber hoses, attempting to get him to sign an affidavit stating Spiritualism to be fraudulent. The officers pulled out their penises in obscene gestures to nail him on charges of sodomy. But nothing worked. Even so, Keith got a six-month jail sentence. He appealed, but the judge upheld the conviction, exclaiming it would take fifty thousand dollars for Keith to go to the Supreme Court if he were to appeal. In the end, the judge called Keith's followers *"gullible fools"*. Keith was released in four months. Thirty years later, a judge ruled the case unconstitutional, and the conviction was totally expunged.

In Hawaii, Reverend Rhinehart experienced the good fortune of meeting the famous Kahuna, Daddy Bray—the best-known practicing Kahuna coming from a long line of praying Kahunas on the islands. Daddy Bray possessed the ancient sacred stone passed down through the generations. Kahunas knew this stone to be imbued with the Spiritual power of the great God *Ku-ka'ili-moku*.

As an archivist, Daddy Bray revived many ancient Hawaiian chants and dances, including the hula. When United States President Franklin Delano Roosevelt visited Hawaii, Daddy Bray introduced him to the traditional Hawaiian dances.

Upon meeting Reverend Rhinehart, Daddy Bray challenged Keith to bring back his deceased wife. Reverend Rhinehart succeeded during a séance when Daddy Bray's wife returned in full physical form, speaking in a perfect ancient Hawaiian dialect. Overwhelmed, Daddy Bray became a member of the Church.

Later, he introduced Reverend Rhinehart to Doris Duke (American billionaire tobacco heiress and socialite, considered by many the richest woman in the world). Doris presented Keith with an offer to become her personal medium for a very attractive fee, an offer few could refuse—Reverend Rhinehart refused.

Given Daddy Bray's remarkable experience of Reverend Rhinehart's mediumship, he invited him to present a séance in Hawaii. Again, the police raided the séance. The police instructed a lady to make up lies about Reverend Rhinehart in court in order to ensnare him. Later, the woman admitted to lying. Eventually, Reverend Rhinehart was found innocent, but it became clear the police didn't want Reverend Rhinehart to create a following in Hawaii.

It happened again in Bogota, Colombia, during a Parapsychology Convention in 1979. No sooner had the Convention started than the police promptly raided it—no surprise! Reverend Rhinehart was arrested on charges of witchcraft!

There appeared to be a pattern: whenever Reverend Rhinehart went outside the confines of his Church to present a séance, he ran into legal troubles. But what could be so threatening about a séance in Hawaii or Bogota? We would suggest there was a concerted effort on the part of negative forces to derail Reverend Rhinehart's mission. (When Uri Geller, a fellow participant of spoon-bending fame, got wind of Reverend Rhinehart's incident, he quickly hightailed it out of town to avoid similar treatment.)

We have highlighted but a few of the events surrounding Reverend Rhinehart's unparalleled career as a medium, and by many people's estimation, the Psychic Wonder of Seattle. But we would be remiss if we didn't take a moment to speak of Reverend Rhinehart's character as a human being. Physically, he was a handsome man with dark-brown hair and delicate features. In his presence, people experienced a gentle, sincere man who appeared extremely present, yet strangely focused simultaneously inward. Over the years, he exhibited a variety of personas, at times clean-shaven with the popular hairstyle of the fifties and at other times sporting a dark, stylized, sculpted beard with a variety of hair styles and colors. People couldn't help but marvel at the complexity of his brilliant intellect, an intellect that dissected a situation or problem from every which way possible. Those working on Church projects claimed his mind went in ten different directions at once. Before proceeding on a project, he conducted endless research, leaving no stone unturned. Observers said he appeared tireless—there was simply no one who could keep up! He easily commanded the room as a dynamic speaker, broaching complex subjects in ways the common person could easily grasp. When the Masters presented a task, nothing stopped him from fulfilling their request, no matter how difficult, no matter what.

One of the roles he took seriously was that of a teacher. When many joined in on a project, he took the opportunity to teach. As the project unfolded, a chela's failings or misunderstanding was grist for everyone's learning. If you weren't paying attention—oh boy, his gaze bore in and your seat blazed with intensity, karma sizzled and popped, but through his intent and loving patience, new personal growth could be had by all.

To avoid some suggesting we are side-stepping an unsavory episode in Reverend Rhinehart's life, we will address another difficult circumstance. During the fifties, when the mainstream struggled with alternative lifestyles, there were those who considered Reverend Rhinehart's eccentric lifestyle threatening. He soon found prejudice fully alive, vengeful, righteously kicking, and close to home. The Seattle Vice Squad was not buying Keith's hifalutin' Spiritual claims, and they incessantly looked for ways to bust him on fraud. They were aware that Keith knew, through Spirit contact, all about their illicit activities. Their fear of being exposed kept them at bay for a while. In the end, though, they determined to use a sixteen-year-old hustler to trump up false charges of sodomy in 1965. Predictably, given the transparent prejudice demonstrated in the past, the court upheld the charges and Reverend Rhinehart served two-and-a-half years in the Walla Walla State Prison, initially restrained to nightmarish solitary confinement where he faced thirty-eight days of complete black-out conditions in the hole. Ultimately, the hustler recanted his story, acknowledging he had been put up to his claim by the Seattle Police Department. Once again, the charges were eventually completely expunged from the record.

Just as mediums throughout history have been harassed, so Reverend Rhinehart suffered the same dogmatic hostilities that mediums suffered in the *Bible* and the Middle Ages. (Examples of Saints and illuminated individuals dismissed and denigrated for their lifestyles include: Shams and Rumi, mystics of Sufi fame in the Thirteenth Century; Joan of Arc, Roman Catholic saint of the Fifteenth Century; Hildegard Bingham, German Benedictine abbess of the Twelfth Century; Saint Francis of Assisi, Italian mystic and Catholic friar of the Thirteenth Century; and Joseph Smith, the founder of the Mormon and Latter-Day Saint Movement in the Nineteenth Century.)

As persons who have been inspired by Reverend Rhinehart, we believe identity and lifestyle are wholly personal and have nothing to do with the purity and authenticity of Spiritual gifts, a person's Spiritual impact in the world, or the support from the Spirit side of life.

The subsequent story is an interesting footnote to Reverend Rhinehart's time in Walla Walla. While incarcerated, Reverend Rhinehart conducted a séance on the prison grounds. A thousand inmates sat spell-bound for six-and-a-half hours, weeping and sobbing throughout the messages delivered by Spirit. Before the service, Reverend Rhinehart allowed himself to be strip-searched and his mouth taped shut to ensure no fraud occurred, as was his custom on the outside. After Spirit voices spoke out, trumpets flew throughout the room, and a thousand sacred stones were apported into the room. Holes opened up in Reverend Rhinehart's cheeks where stones continued manifesting through the openings.

An inmate cried out, *"You must be the Messiah!"*

Then the voice of Master Saint Germaine exclaimed, *"Pass out the citrines to the inmates!"*

But there were merely a few citrines, clearly not enough to go around to some thousand inmates. As attendants began passing out the citrines, the stones began to multiply until at last there were enough for every inmate present! Wow! Reminiscent of the loaves and fishes when Jesus fed the hungry.

In 1964, the Church sponsored a coming-of-age world tour for Reverend Rhinehart, sending him to England, Egypt, India, and the

Union of South Africa, some forty countries in all, where he conducted séances in each country, always under the strictest of scientific test conditions.

On various stops, he visited a diversity of such dignitaries as Bertrand Russell, British philosopher and mathematician; Maurice Barbanell, British journalist and editor of *Psychic News* and *Two Worlds* out of London; Margaret Mead, American cultural anthropologist; Lord Dowding, British Air Chief Marshal, credited for defeating Hitler's plan to invade Britain; Agnes Moorehead, famous American actress of radio, stage, film, and television, well-known for playing the witch Endora on the TV show *Bewitched*; Aly Rady, doctor from Egypt; Laura Huxley, writer and Aldous Huxley's second wife; Arthur Ford, the well-known medium who broke the Houdini Code; and Madalyn Murray, outspoken atheist who claimed religion was a crutch and an irrational reliance on superstitions and supernatural nonsense, who also worked as the speech writer for Larry Flynt's Presidential run. On his tour, Reverend Rhinehart taped fascinating interviews documenting each of their widely diverse views on Spiritual and religious topics.

The following is a paraphrased testimony given by Dr. Aly Rady, who witnessed Reverend Rhinehart's Spiritual demonstrations in Alexandria and Cairo, Egypt:

"...Once I returned to Egypt from England in 1957, Mr. Abu Alkeir, who at the time was the leading Spiritualist in Egypt, invited me to travel to Alexandria to meet Reverend Keith Milton Rhinehart. I then attended a sitting arranged on November 23rd, 1957, at Mr. George Kitroff's residence.

"...Blindfolded, Reverend Rhinehart requested the sitters place before him, questions to their Spirit friends, written on a small piece of paper. I wrote my own name and that of my mother. Once the demonstration began, I saw one of the pieces of paper jump right off the floor by itself, right into the Reverend's fingertips. Then he would answer the questions, either by writing or by speaking. This went on for a while when I suddenly heard a click, something similar to an electrical discharge behind my ear. Immediately after, the medium wrote something on a piece of paper and tossed it to the floor. A young man picked it up and exclaimed, "It's written in Arabic!" As most in attendance were Greek, being Arabic, I asked if I could see the message.

"...He handed it over and I quickly saw it was addressed to me and it said, *"My son, Aly Rady"* and the signature was, *"Amoura Rady."*

"...Well, I felt astonished, the handwriting was similar to my mother's, although Reverend Rhinehart had never been to Egypt, knew not a single word of Arabic, and he was but twenty-one. He proceeded to give me a long message describing all my troubles, just as though my mother were still living with me at home.

"...The following evening in Cairo, a large meeting was arranged at the Medical Doctors Association, where ministers, ex-pashas, medical doctors, and judges all attended. To start the meeting, he repeated a session of billets, similar to what he performed during the previous evening in Alexandria; then he produced materialization.

"...He sat behind a small black curtain as he usually did, with his mouth filled with water and sealed with gummed tape. This procedure is done to demonstrate that when he talks during the billets, it is not his voice speaking, but the voice of someone in the Spirit World generated from the materialization of a physical voice box. I was one who shared in this operation, then signed my name in ink on his cheek. Soon, a trumpet rose above the curtain in full light with no seen force behind its rising. Then Susan, his cabinet guide, began to speak through the trumpet. She started by asking the person in the back of the hall to stop waving his hand from side to side. I looked, and a man was waving a newspaper to cool himself from the heat. Nobody could imagine how the medium, fixed to his chair behind the black curtain, could have seen through the curtain and the audience to detect this man waving his hands.

"...Then Susan said Sir William Crookes, the famous scientist of the nineteenth century, told her, *"This night will go down as a milestone in the history of Higher Spiritualism in Egypt."* (Higher Spiritualism involves communication from Master intelligence; whereas Spiritualism in general involves communication from less evolved Spirits.)

"...At this point, Katie King, the well-known Spirit who fully materialized through the medium Florence Cook in 1874, said she would materialize. Soon, light ectoplasm started to form on the top of the curtain, behind which the medium, Reverend Rhinehart, could be partially seen.

(Ectoplasm is a subtle physical substance that is withdrawn from a medium's body by Spirit. It can be both invisible and visible to the eye. When it is visible, it looks like a milky-white fluid substance of nebulous form and consistency. Spirit can manipulate the substance to form Spiritual phenomena, such as Spirit hands or bodies.) Then we saw Katie's shoulders and head, covered with the white shawl, quite similar to the famous picture which was taken of her, arm in arm with Sir William Crookes, back in 1874. There could be no mistake; we saw her very clearly as she moved from side to side, right next to us, in the dim light.

"Reverend Rhinehart's mediumship continued on that evening, but these were some of the highlights."

As mentioned, the Masters were intent on presenting as much scientific evidence around Reverend Rhinehart's mediumship as possible to provide scientific credence to their teachings. The testing at the Osaka Electro-Psychic Laboratories is a case in point and will be covered at some length in Chapter Five, Becoming Our Own Authority for Truth.

The following test, conducted by Dr. Helmut Schmidt, a senior research physicist with Boeing Scientific Research Laboratories, is another test the Masters encouraged Reverend Rhinehart to submit to further establish his psychic abilities in predicting the future. In this test, Dr. Schmidt used a small sample of strontium-90, a metallic element, placed near an electron counter. The counter registered the spontaneous decay of strontium-90's electrons as an emission. Scientifically, it is impossible to predict when the decay of an electron would be released and registered by the counter. Dr. Schmidt linked the electron counter with a four-position rotating switch to the emission process. The psychic was tasked to press one of the four positions on the switch to predict when an electron would release. A flashing light indicated if their prediction was correct.

Dr. Schmidt tested over one hundred different psychics, nearly all of whom posted chance results. Reverend Rhinehart registered 4.4 percentage points higher than chance, with the probability of recording such results by coincidence estimated to be less than one in five hundred million. There were critics of the test, but given the results recorded by nearly all participants who registered in the chance category, the test statistically demonstrated Reverend Rhinehart's acumen to prophesize the future.

Reviewing the countless Spiritual demonstrations throughout Reverend Rhinehart's illustrious career, including demonstrations before such notables as Rhodesia's former prime minister Ian Smith and Mexico's President Portillo and his wife, the crowning jewel was the seven-day 1975 Convention in Seattle called the *International Inter-Galactic Banquet.*

Throughout this event, Ascended Masters walked the halls hobnobbing with participants! Miracles of Biblical days were re-enacted! Full body physical manifestations of Archangels and Ascended Masters occured in the presence of Reverend Rhinehart's adept mediumship. "Supernormal" fell way shy in describing the events. The amazing events were too involved to elaborate in this short bio, but they will be sprinkled throughout the book.

To glean a more personal snapshot of Reverend Rhinehart, the following vignette describes an outing a couple experienced with Keith, revealing a different side of his personality.

"A workaholic, Keith rarely took time away from the daily demands of the Church. One day, after inviting him numerous times, he finally relented, and we all escaped on a fishing trip to Alaska. The trip took us far outside his comfort zone, and we were unsure how he'd respond. The snow just melted, and the days were still extremely chilly, so we bundled up in colorful layers to shield ourselves from the blowing wind.

"In no time, Keith exclaimed, *"Fish on!"* and with that, his excitement escalated to that of a playful child.

"He truly delighted in experiencing Alaska's enchanting nature, the wonder of the beauty, and the danger we faced as our boat moved through rapid currents. On the trip, he finally got to relax, and relax we all did. After a day of fishing, the stars reached down out of the huge, inky-black skies, igniting his vivid imagination. We sang around the campfire, enjoying a priceless time together. During the day, we ventured into a small town, tracking down the local burger hangout, and we even went bowling—a rollicking good time!

"If you could only see our picture of Keith, beanie perched atop his wavy hair, standing in front of the salmon we caught, glowing like a youngster with his first catch, a broad smile would burst across your face. One of our favorite life moments!"

Keith was described as a deeply feeling man, a passionate, expressive conversationalist, engaging in lively phone conversations for up to 12 hours at a time. Always fascinating, no topic existed out of bounds, he could carry on endlessly in abstract thought or on arcane subjects—if only college could have been so exhilarating! Time stood still when you were in his presence; you felt as though you were the only person in the world. He could be such a delight: with sparkling, endearing eyes, fun-loving humor, and a tremendously nurturing personality.

Throughout his life, we could easily observe that he possessed a deep compassion and commitment to transforming the struggles of humanity, enacting an unwavering commitment to serve in every way imaginable. One way manifested through his charitable nature, where he lavished gifts on close chelas, often giving to those with whom he never met, while finally willing his entire assets, worth millions, to the Church he founded and loved so dearly.

But his giving went beyond tangible gifts; when he conducted a wedding or christening, he invoked a love that could be palpable, filling the hearts of all present. Additionally, he created several supportive funds for people in need. There was the *Keith Milton Rhinehart Memorial Fund* to aggregate financial support for women and children of men who had been incarcerated at Walla Walla, easing their stress. Also, a Fund to assist the handicapped in getting the proper rehabilitation equipment for their particular incapacitation. And finally, a Memorial Fund to come to the aid of Spiritual mediums with no support from the government or their immediate families after retirement. Wherever Reverend Rhinehart perceived a need, he rose to meet it.

A private man, who wasn't inclined to broadcast his private life, he would likely cringe at the little we have written, so we will leave it at this. But there is no doubt he was a puzzling, mysterious man to many, who challenged most of the norms of contemporary society, where his mediumship confounded the best of intellectuals and religious figureheads alike. Throughout the book, further glimpses of his stature will be tucked away, peeking out through the pages of various stories.

FOUR

COMTE de SAINT GERMAINE EIGHTEENTH CENTURY

MANY HAVE DESCRIBED COMTE DE SAINT GERMAINE AS ONE of the most enigmatic, baffling personalities of modern history, a pure mystery confounding the best of his contemporaries. He was charged by the Divine Hierarchy to be one of the main communicators presenting the Ascended Masters' views on a variety of subjects, who regularly spoke through Reverend Rhinehart's adept mediumship. Annie Besant, in her co-authored book, *The Comte de St. Germain: The Secret of Kings*, claimed he was the son of Prince Francis Rákóczy II, Prince of Transylvania, born in 1690. The Comte's noble birth was never in question as his entire demeanor bore the stamp of gentle breeding. An unusual refinement and grace allowed him to meet every situation with clarity and composure. It was well known that he interacted with royalty in Versailles, London, the Hague, and St. Petersburg during the years 1710 to 1822, masquerading under many different names and disguises.

There existed a great amount of controversy over his role in secret diplomacy, as he appeared to be working for opposing sides on many occasions. He was arrested in England on suspicion of being a Jacobite agent. Upon his release, he stayed with Prince Ferdinand von Lobkowicz, the first minister to the Austrian emperor, who was allied with England in the war against France and Prussia. So his allegiances shifted like a chameleon to fit his agenda.

Many believe he was a representative of the higher Brotherhood, and his mission was to keep peace and order through his connections with international intelligence networks. There is so much conjecture regarding his allegiances and his blatant secrecy; honestly, all we can state is that the Comte became highly involved in the political operations of Europe.[1]

The Rosicrucians, Freemasons, and other Mystery Schools were created through his vast knowledge of the workings of the mind and Spirit. Unfortunately, these organizations have since been infiltrated by dark forces, calling into question their legitimacy.

According to Fredrick the Great, Saint Germaine demonstrated an ability to never age. At a gala in the courts of Versailles, Madame Pompadour (official chief mistress of King Louis XV), while dancing with him, asked if he was the grandson of Comte de St. Germaine, to which he responded, *"No, it is I,"* much to her shock. Others intimate that some in the Royal Court, such as Madame du Hausset, overheard conversations between the Comte and Madame de Pompadour where he referred to identities he assumed when visiting distant lands and his use of elixirs to maintain his youthfulness. Madame de Pompadour claimed the Comte intimated he had been acquainted with Cleopatra and the Queen of Sheba. Some boasted he had acquaintances with luminaries of the 18th Century such as Voltaire, Anton Mesmer, and Giacomo Girolamo Casanova. Voltaire, a renowned writer and philosopher, stated, *"St. Germaine is a man who never dies and knows everything."*

From *Souvenirs de Marie Antoinette*, by Madame la Comtesse d'Adhemar, rumors spread that an enormously wealthy man sporting magnificent jewelry had arrived at Versailles. He dressed simply, powdered as was the custom, most often with well-fitting black clothes of the finest quality. An air of dignity filled his aura. He displayed delicate, graceful hands, dark black hair, and a penetrating, soft glance. People remarked they had never seen the like.[2]

The Comte was recognized as a remarkable scholar and linguist. He spoke German, Italian, French, English, Portuguese, Spanish, Greek, Latin, Sanskrit, Arabic, and Chinese fluently, with such proficiency that each country he visited accepted him as a native. As a botanist, he gathered herbs from around the world and, as an excellent chemist, concocted teas claimed to have curative properties, healing many. He was a terrific musician, a virtual virtuoso on the violin and piano. (He often played the piano through Reverend Rhinehart's mediumship, with renditions of *"The God Chant," "It Is Written in the Heavens,"* and pieces from the *Ascension Symphony;* although, to the surprise of many, Reverend Rhinehart had not learned to play the piano.) Even his most ardent detractors claimed the Comte possessed admirable attainment in every domain of learning. Had it not been for his striking persona and seeming supernormal powers, he would have been considered insane, but it was evident to all that *"eccentric"* best described him.

Madame de Pompadour exudes over his genius, extolling his prodigious memory, inexhaustible conversational skill covering nearly all subjects with fresh and unexpected anecdotes. (Just as was evident in his communications through Reverend Rhinehart's séances.) He was intimately acquainted with the Courts of Russia, Turkey, and Austria, having traveled all over Asia and Africa, exhibiting more knowledge than the charge d'affaires of the kings. He held an uncanny knowledge of every occurrence of the preceding two thousand years, and in his conversations, he reminisced about intimate details of events where he played influential roles.

After dinner one evening, Baron Gleichen, a Mason, had the opportunity to view some of the Comte's extraordinary jewels and his colored diamond collection. He exclaimed that among them was an opal of monstrous size and a sumptuous white sapphire as large as an egg.

The Comte demonstrated an ambidextrous skill to such an extent that he could write an article simultaneously, commanding both hands to write on separate sheets of paper, and the final writing on each sheet would match identically. Once to prove the two lobes of his brain functioned independently, he wrote a love letter with one hand and, simultaneously with the other, penned mystical verses. He could repeat verbatim pages and pages of print after one reading. It is said he sang beautifully. Really, there seemed to be little he couldn't do. People even remarked he possessed the disconcerting habit of arriving in a room without the use of the door. [3]

On many an occasion, Reverend Rhinehart's main Spirit guide, Robert John Kensington, revealed that the Comte has lived in physical form for over eight thousand years, moving throughout the cultures of Europe, the Middle East, and the Orient, guiding the development of society and civilization. On occasion, during séances through Reverend Rhinehart, the Comte would pull up a stool before the piano and play transfixing music to establish a particular vibration he desired.

Dr. Kensington once related that in France, after the Comte's mock funeral service, conducted to beguile his enemies, authorities went to the buried casket, excavated it, and, upon opening the lid, discovered a single dog bone!

Through Reverend Rhinehart's mediumship, the Comte said, on numerous occasions, he was the Wandering Jew of the *Bible* (the legend of a sinner who taunted Jesus along on his way to the crucifixion, a doomed man without hope of death until the second coming of Christ). An entire book would be insufficient to list Comte de St. Germaine's attributes and accomplishments, but this short commentary captures a flavor of the unworldly character of this illustrious Master who is the present overseer of the Violet Flame and of civilization. (Through Reverend Rhinehart's mediumship, we came to understand that different Ascended Masters oversee the various color flames and work with the flames in their roles in the development of civilization. The Violet Flame represents the most subtle vibration of the Flames, reflects Mastery of human consciousness, and has a powerful transformational quality.)

FIVE

BECOMING OUR OWN
AUTHORITY FOR TRUTH

W HEN IT COMES TO UNDERSTANDING WHAT IS TRUE, MANY think the Ascended Masters position themselves to be authorities. However, one of the first comments the Masters make is to remind all those they encounter that it is not the Masters or our ministers who are the authorities in terms of Truth, but it is ourselves. As we delve into the Ascended Masters' work, it is good to set a tone for interacting with their way of thinking. Without exception, they encourage us to become our own authority for what we experience as Truth. This is vitally important. Everything from happiness, to day-to-day menial decisions, to karma, pivots from this understanding.

With this in mind, we ask to what extent do we believe we are our own authority for Truth? This idea applies equally to our emotional life, our mental life, our family life, our professional life, and our Spiritual life. Perhaps if we reflect on a Horace Greeley comment, the American newspaper editor and publisher, it could act as a touchstone for guiding us to Truth:

He states, *"I accept unreservedly the views of no man, living or dead."*

This is a good motto for a newspaper editor and a reminder for us to be unrelenting in our personal search for Truth.

Are we willing to be fully responsible, dig down deep to uncover exactly why we believe what we believe? Can we be unflinchingly truthful with ourselves? Do we believe if we genuinely seek, we will attract the Truth? Or do we think no matter what we do, we will likely not find the answer for which we're looking? Are we willing to allow others and various agencies to form our political opinions, make our medical choices and financial decisions, create our social insights, and establish our Spiritual understanding? Or do we make the effort to seek second and third opinions, reviewing the data from adversarial viewpoints? Clearly, we must look to the world for insights and information, but do we take the next step by questioning and sifting through all perspectives?

We suspect most of us would have to admit we are reliant on others, and admittedly, in today's world, time doesn't allow us to research every detail. Still, our life's critical domains are worthy of our constant inspection if we wish to lead a responsible life, one reflecting our commitment to becoming the embodiment of Truth.

I remember an encounter I experienced with the Qigong Master, Ko Wong (Sifu), in San Francisco. This experience related to personal responsibility and becoming an authority for my life. The experience rattled me more than any of the lessons I had gained over years of personal growth workshops. It awakened me to unconscious behavioral patterns.

One afternoon during a class Sifu taught in San Francisco Chinatown, he introduced a Qigong walk he created, which he called the *Bird Walk*. The walk was rigorous, demanding full control of the body. The walker walked in extremely slow motion, moving with nearly imperceptible movement, lifting one leg up and near the apex of the lift, the walker extended arms out to the sides as if suspended in flight—hence the *Bird Walk*. It created pure focus, graceful strength, and massaged all the acupressure points on the bottom of the feet, activating the Qi energy more than any other Qigong exercise. After Sifu demonstrated the walk, he exclaimed if we did the *Bird Walk* every day for forty-five to sixty minutes for six months, it would change our lives.

Well, that piqued my interest, so following my regular Qigong walk with Sifu every morning, I decided to take him up on his promise. After a couple of months of doing the Bird Walk, I noticed the Qi in my body becoming more pronounced, I could feel a subtle vibration all day.

One day during my regular Qigong walk in the park, I came up behind Sifu and asked, *"Sifu, if I continue doing the Bird Walk for six months, do you promise me it will change my life?"*

He turned to me with steely, thundering eyes and said, *"You Promise Yourself!"*

I reeled in astonishment at his response! After all, he promised if I followed his instructions, doing the *Bird Walk* every day, it would change my life. His words stopped me in my tracks. At first, I felt so let down, betrayed, even angered that he wasn't standing behind his word. Then I realized I was unconsciously attempting to get someone other than myself to be responsible for my life!

Throughout the process of self-discovery, we must continually ask ourselves: are we willing to do the work? Roll up our sleeves? Do whatever it takes to become mentally informed? Make emotionally balanced decisions? Become fully Spiritually engaged? Can we develop a framework such that our discernments and decisions are intelligent, moral, loving, and respectful of the world around us? What would it take to grapple with the content of the news before we believe the story, or validate what a friend relates, before we pass it on? We think, if we are honest with ourselves, we are especially gullible in these domains of life.

When policeman Steve Young witnessed the phenomenon of faceted stones dropping one after the other from Reverend Rhinehart's mouth, hair, and eyes, he asked himself, as many would, *What is the meaning of this? Is this truly miraculous, or is it an illusion? Is it a deception in some way meant to mislead me into following a false prophet, a false path, or a false teaching? Why am I being shown this seeming miracle?* Steve's heart felt unsettled, he mused to himself that he must uncover a rationale, an event in history that could provide him with some clue as to the import of the event. He required more than accepting the event on Faith alone. What could he discover that would possibly deepen and confirm his initial belief that he had witnessed a miracle?

There have been thousands and thousands of people who witnessed Reverend Rhinehart's Spiritual phenomenon. Yet, we are not aware of any others who sought the understanding Steve demanded for himself. Why? Many instantly believed what they saw was genuine and assumed they witnessed something miraculous since they couldn't explain the phenomenon in any other manner. Some appeared to be flat-out disinterested in the event or didn't connect what they witnessed with Spirituality. Still others were just moving along life's escalator and too distracted or too busy with their daily responsibilities to find out more, perhaps setting the event aside to "think about it later." But if we are sincere in our interest in the reality of Spirit and committed to our Spiritual development, wouldn't it behoove us to discover a reason beyond Faith alone? Is Faith enough in which to base our Spiritual life?

What happens when the path narrows, the way becomes arduous, temptations arise, and the mind is challenged by ideas opposed to our inner-most beliefs? Doesn't faith always dovetail with a trace of doubt? Is our Church, or Spiritual understanding, always sufficient to stay the course in the face of misgivings when the dark night of the soul confronts us?

At these moments, the *"Weasel Clause"* can slip in unnoticed, and the chela or parishioner thinks, *"Oh, this aspect of the teaching doesn't pertain to me! I just don't agree with it, it's wrong and doesn't resonate with who I am."*

But if we have taken the time to verify the credibility of the source of the teaching and reconciled our own doubt or denial, then we are more apt to recognize a Truth and work to find understanding rather than adopt some bit of mumbo-jumbo or long-held traditional dogma to defend our position.

With this stated, we are not saying that we are never reduced to Faith and Faith alone, or that Faith has no value in Spiritual practice. We must acknowledge history is replete with examples of the merits of Faith, and Faith will always remain one of life's Eternal verities. But expecting us to possess profound Faith at the beginning of the Spiritual journey is expecting too much for most, as many require something more temporal. For those who have been on the path for an extended period, Faith is accepted as a Spiritual tool in facing the darkest chambers of conflict.

Not long after Steve first witnessed Reverend Rhinehart's mediumship, he experienced a second encounter where the Masters spoke through Reverend Rhinehart's trance mediumship. This time, Reverend Rhinehart apported white stones in Steve's presence. Later, to Steve's surprise, he received one of the white stones as a gift. The stone had a moniker—the *"New Race Stone."* Although it appeared special, no claims were made about any properties with which the stone may have been imbued.

Shortly thereafter, on a visit to his mother's home, Steve learned one of her dear friends, Mrs. Wing, whom she worked with at Pearl Harbor, had been suffering from acute back pain. Bed-ridden, she experienced pain so severe she often talked of suicide. Mrs. Wing's life had deteriorated into an intolerable situation. Steve's mother related she felt highly concerned for her welfare.

After hearing his mother's comments, Steve blurted out a spontaneous claim declaring, *"Mrs. Wing will be healed in seven days!"*

Astonished at his bold assertion, Steve couldn't explain why he came forward with such force and clarity. His mother said she had never seen him act in such a bold, audacious manner—frankly, she felt shocked.

Steve went home, and in the evening, he placed the white stone he received from the Masters on a white piece of paper with Mrs. Wing's name, then he forgot about his claim. In exactly seven days, Mrs. Wing got up from her bed exclaiming she no longer experienced back pain. The pain never returned. When Steve learned what happened, he became so overwhelmed that his cheeks streamed with tears of joy.

Something seemed to be changing within Steve's awareness. His curiosity heightened, driving him to pursue answers for the recent inexplicable events. As a professional fraud investigator, he needed answers for himself; he couldn't accept the events on the surface value, he felt the events must have a historical precedent—there must be some way to find perspective about what transpired.

When performing his investigative duties, Steve never took an accuser's claim at face value, he'd do whatever necessary to uncover the hardcore facts behind the claim no matter where it led. He felt no different regarding Spiritual matters. So, he turned to where he often found meaning—the *Bible*. He wondered, could there possibly be a connection between the white stones that materialized in the presence of Reverend Rhinehart's mediumship and passages in the *Bible*? He was determined to find out.

A few days after Mrs. Wing's healing, while following his intuition, he picked up his King James version of the *Bible*. Holding it in one hand and with the other hand, he began thumbing through the pages starting with *Genesis*. As he continued turning through the pages, he affirmed he would feel a pull from the page where he should stop. Then, without looking, he'd point his finger at a passage on a certain page, revealing the answer for which he searched. His thumb passed through *Exodus, Numbers, Deuteronomy, Kings, Chronicles, Psalms, Ecclesiastes, Isiah, Jeremiah, Daniel, St. Matthew, St Mark, St Luke, St. John,* then on a page in *Revelation,* he stopped where he blindly pointed his finger to Chapter 2, Verse 17, and it said:

"He that hath an ear, let him hear what the Spirit saith unto the Churches; To him that overcometh will I give to eat of the hidden manna, and will give him a white stone, and in the stone a new name written, which no man knoweth saving he that receiveth it."

Astonished at the precise relevance, he became elated re-reading the passage *Revelation 2:17, "Spirit gave to man a white stone."* He knew in his heart Spirit led him to find this one line in the innumerable passages of his *Bible,* providing him with the proof and evidence he required to believe Reverend Rhinehart was indeed a genuine medium, a man of God. Also, that the Ascended Masters were who they claimed to be. That is, beings reaching out for humanity's betterment. Steve found no other passage in the *Bible* regarding the claim associated with a white stone. At this point, Steve got down on his hands and knees, joyfully weeping, thanking God for the Truth and healing that came from the Masters' gift of a white stone.

(It is interesting to note throughout the various Christian denominations around the world, ministers, priests, and laymen have been confounded by *Revelation 2:17,* unable to decipher its meaning.)

Just as Steve took the time to find evidence to support his belief, the Ascended Masters have not been content to simply say the phenomenon speaks for itself. When witnesses say, *"Oh, this is miraculous, it must be True,"* that is not enough for the Masters. They want to provide absolute proof through scientific means, so the common person in the coming age will not have to rely on Faith and Faith alone. In this way, they demonstrate the means for us to access Truth. They present their proof through supernormal channels,

43

defying accepted physics and the nature of physical reality while leaving no question as to their credibility and its source.

According to the Masters, it took many years of development from the Spirit side of life to evolve the means to accomplish these feats and present them through Reverend Rhinehart's mediumship. They insisted on absolute scientific proof so even a hardened skeptic could find the Truth, that there existed a Spiritual World beyond a person's body and mind.

The following scientific proof is of particular relevance and demonstrates the extent to which the Masters were willing to go to prove the existence of their reality. In 1958, the Church sponsored Reverend Rhinehart's first world tour to Japan, where he demonstrated his Spiritual gifts for professional scientists in the Tokyo and Osaka Electro-Psychic Laboratories.

In the laboratory, Reverend Rhinehart sat under stringently controlled conditions in a *"Fraud Proof Chair"* designed by Dr. Ando of the University of Osaka. Before assuming the chair, Reverend Rhinehart allowed the scientists to strip search him, thoroughly examining his entire body, and then he was given a kimono to wear for the ensuing demonstrations. This precaution assured that there could be no contrivances that imitated genuine Spiritual phenomena. Before and after the manifestations that occurred during the séance, he was precisely weighed and measured, his blood pressure assessed, his urine analyzed, along with other tests. These tests demonstrated if there were measurable physiological changes that occurred during his demonstration of mediumship, they would be registered.

The scientists then tied Reverend Rhinehart into the *"Fraud Proof Chair,"* where both arms were placed in wooden enclosures preventing any movement. Two electronic buttons located under his wrists were wired to two red lights, which flashed if the medium slightly moved his arms or wrists. In addition to these controls, an electronic graph recorded any bodily movement and increases or decreases in weight. Just before the medium slipped into trance, his mouth was filled with a colored liquid chemical and taped shut with special markings drawn on the tape to his skin, so the scientists could detect if the tape had been removed at any time during the séance.

Under these exacting, fool-proof test conditions, numerous physical phenomena transpired showing the manifestation of ecto-plasm in a variety of different forms, all executed under full white-light and photographed with still and movie cameras and subsequently aired on Japanese television.

Amid the Japanese tests, ectoplasm flowed from Reverend Rhinehart's nose, ears, throat, and solar plexus, levitating light alumi-num trumpets, forming finger-like protuberances known as pseudo-pods, and an ectoplasmic voice-box which allowed Spirit to speak. At one point during the séance, to everyone's surprise, an ectoplasmic pseudopod materialized, grasping a pencil where it began drawing a portrait on a piece of paper that was recognized by Mr. Mikami, a Japanese religious leader in attendance. Additionally, the ectoplasmic voice-box materialized by Spirit conversed in fluent Japanese with those in attendance. Reverend Rhinehart did not know Japanese.

During the tests, amazing physical phenomena continued to occur where Spirit apported over seven hundred mineral specimens along with samples of ancient Japanese writing.

Suffice it to say, Reverend Rhinehart passed all the exacting scientific tests the Japanese presented to their scientific satisfaction and amazement. It is through the passing of the physically and psychologically demanding tests that Reverend Rhinehart became known as the most scientifically tested medium in the history of mankind.

These are examples of external evidence which we have been exploring, but our internal experience in discovering Truth is important as well. There are those who find their inner experience and intuition more evidential, experiences that arise in the heart, feeding their emotional and Spiritual understanding. Here is a testimony that falls into this category.

The following is a woman's direct experience during the 1975 Holy Communion Convention (International Inter-Galactic Banquet), where people from twenty-eight countries gathered in the Georgian Room of the Olympic Hotel in Seattle, Washington. Her testimony reflects only one of many remarkable Spiritual demonstrations that transpired over the course of seven days of the Convention. The phenomena she witnessed are conducted to illustrate but one purpose—the activation of Spiritual Light on planet Earth through the externalization of the Spiritual Hierarchy, jolting humanity to awaken to a new understanding of their True nature.

This particular meeting she attended was billed as *"Trance Lecture and Demonstration by Master Jesus through Reverend Keith Milton Rhinehart, Topic: The 2nd Coming of Christ."* During the meeting the woman experienced new Spiritual dimensions, challenging her emotionally and Spiritually to process new Truths.

She begins, *"I am seated in close proximity to the stage, situated in the middle of the auditorium about six rows back, so I have an excellent view of all the proceedings. I'm excited, as I never know what will happen—soon we'll see what the great beings manifest through this one-of-a-kind Spiritual instrument. The event begins with an Invocation, some prayers, and we sing the Doxology, Gloria Patri, and a couple of familiar songs such as "In the Garden." There is an audible buzz of anticipation rising from the audience of five hundred as the policemen, Steve Young and David Silverstein, escort Reverend Rhinehart into the large hall. In a curtained-off area on the stage, they proceed to strip-search Reverend Rhinehart internally and externally to assure the audience that there is nothing hidden inside his orifices.*

Then the policemen announced they searched the Holy of Holies cabinet (a sacred place in the Hebrew tabernacle where God's presence dwells) and found nothing that could aid the medium in artificially producing any Spiritual phenomenon. With those statements and a brief greeting, Reverend Rhinehart steps into the Holy of Holies.

"Then the Master of Ceremonies declared all doors had security men stationed in place and that no one could enter unseen to affect the proceedings. At this point, infra-red lights are turned on to prevent any damage to the medium during physical phenomenon, as natural light can harm a medium when ectoplasm is produced during physical phenomenon. A few more hymns are sung, and the entranced Reverend Rhinehart steps out from behind the violet curtain of the Holy of Holies. Immediately, I notice his countenance had changed, his voice registered in a completely different tonality, with a dissimilar inflection, and varied pace than from Reverend Rhinehart's natural voice, and in a much deeper, more resonant sound, the voice says, 'Verily, Verily...' At that moment, we all knew who was speaking, we were in the presence of Christ Jesus. He presented a blessing with such Love that in the moment I felt his Presence so profoundly—I never felt so thoroughly nourished.

"However, I found myself struggling emotionally, questioning whether I was properly reverent and worthy enough to be the recipient of such Holy energies. Mixed emotions filled me as I grappled to accept my worthiness to experience the sacredness of the moment. (It has taken me decades to assimilate those few moments.) In looking around the hall, I could see that all were touched deeply by his words. The security guard at the door stood with his mouth gaping open.

"Jesus then said, 'This is the Second Coming.'

"This promise appeared in the Convention Program, indicating he would come back through evidential means that could not be proven as a hoax.

"I am so overwhelmed at this point, I go into a reverie and am unable to take further notes, but the Master went on with more

profound statements. When he finished his presentation, he returned to the Holy of Holies and requested the white lights to be turned back on very slowly. Then moments later, Master Jesus came back out from behind the curtain wearing an apported crown of thorns upon his head. The audience gasped in amazement! My heart pounded and I started crying, remembering what we did to him. Wrenching emotions overcame me, emotions I still feel to this day.

"Jesus went on with the most beautiful teaching. I paraphrase, but I am close to his words.

"He said, 'We have never been separated from God and Divine Love. We should attempt to live our lives in such a manner that when judgment day arrives, we will find we are not wanting for any aspect of goodness.' Finally, he stated something along the lines of, 'The path is arduous and difficult.'

"Upon finishing, he raised his hands in the air and was transfixed. I noticed blood on his forehead, leaning in to take a closer look, I could see blood on his palms too. I started shaking uncontrollably, asking myself how I deserved to have this experience? Yes, we were experiencing the Stigmata Phenomenon in a well-lit hall with Master Jesus entrancing and speaking through the mediumship of Reverend Keith Milton Rhinehart. The moment seemed to hang in the air for Eternity, I don't know how long it lasted as I lost complete track of time, but what I do know is my heart opened in total gratitude!

"Next, Jesus stated he was going to bring some very special Sacred Objects as gifts for those who demonstrated the Spirit of Revelations 2:17. He recited the verse. Then he reminded us of the burning bush that spoke to Moses, the tablets emblazoned with the Ten Commandments, and the multiplication of the loaves and fishes. All examples of sacred manifestations use the same natural laws that he would use to bring forward the Sacred Stones.

"In a moment, hundreds of beautiful, ruby-red faceted objects came pouring out of the entranced Reverend Rhinehart's facial openings,

his eyes, his mouth, and his ears. As he shook his head back and forth, the Sacred Stones flew off in every direction, all in plain view of the audience. For the finale, a large, orange, crystalline necklace came out from his mouth, obviously way too large to have been swallowed by the medium. Later, we learned from a report there were over one thousand stones materialized during the event. We all witnessed it, I witnessed it—even though you may not believe me!"

As we can ascertain, this encounter touched this woman to the core, forever altering her Spiritual understanding and inspiring new truths.

In this Chapter, we have provided a modicum of first-hand accounts describing Spirit's interaction with humankind, including scientific evidence that demonstrates the Spiritual manifestations are indeed genuine. In so doing, we trust we have given enough evidence for us to determine our Truth regarding the Masters' revelations. Even though the temptation is great to make the Ascended Masters our authority for Truth, to make Jesus our authority for Truth, or to make scripture our authority for Truth, it is only when we make our Self the authority for Truth that we become free and truly, Divinely informed.

We know for some people, proof is not required—they just believe. They find Truth in Faith. For others, such as existentialists and atheists, no matter the level of proof presented, they will scoff and come up with reasons for their disbelief. What the Masters have demonstrated, through Reverend Rhinehart's mediumship, goes far beyond what was provided back in the Nineteenth Century through Madame Blavatsky and other mediums of that era. So, for those who have been on the fence, questioning the legitimacy of the existence of the Spirit World and genuine mediums, the Masters' new dispensation of Light offers new insights.

Briefly, we say within the context of contemporary mediumship, it becomes extremely difficult to be an authority for Truth if a medium doesn't substantiate their mediumship with some level of scientific evidence. Without it, we are left to trust someone else's perspective, giving us little recourse to determine the truth of a message, a sure-fire means of raising doubts.

There have been many communications from Spirit in the New Age: communications from Seth through Jane Roberts (Jane was demanding and self-examining, but not scientific); Spirit messages from Lazaris through Jach Pursel; the wisdom from *A Course in Miracles*, channeled through Helen Schucman; and the messages from Abraham channeled through Esther Hicks, along with many others. Many feel they have received value, and we are not suggesting they haven't, but to our knowledge, none have produced evidence of a scientific nature, independent of Faith alone.

When a medium presents something controversial, existing outside religious scripture, social, or political convention, the genuine Truth seeker wants to know how to ascertain the Truth; therefore, it behooves the seeker to demand a more rigorous approach from mediums, channelers, and psychics to better evaluate the Truth. The Masters have suggested, if a medium can bring forth a message from an Avatar or a saint, it stands to reason that the medium can bring forth a personally evidential message from a deceased family member. This establishes evidence that their communications issue from a source beyond the medium's own mind.

With this said, we are not claiming to be enlightened or to know the absolute Truth. We offer the personal experiences we feel illustrate some facets of the gemstone of Truth to stimulate thoughts, investigations, and to further establish becoming our own authority. We maintain that the future seekers of Spirit communication, Spirit manifestation, and Spirit contact will demand scientific proof. We will dive deeper into this evaluation process in the Chapter on Mediumship.

What we've presented here is not a panacea for all of life's dilemmas, but an encapsulation of the Masters' thoughts and vision through Reverend Rhinehart's mediumship. Our exposition is an interpretation of what the Ascended Masters presented in their teachings through Reverend Rhinehart, not the Masters' actual thoughts.

Many Spiritual traditions teach a specific practice, but the Ascended Masters all agree there is no one way or particular practice to arrive at the Truth or a perfect understanding of God and Peace. The Path varies to such a degree that every chela's course may be as different as the peculiarities of their DNA.

Throughout the book, the Masters bring to our awareness their experience of Truth based on untold lifetimes of experience and mastery. We have attempted to illustrate their commentary with Steve's experiences as the Masters admired Steve's commitment to pursue Truth through his earnest heart, his professionally trained observation skills, and his nineteen years on the Board of Directors of the Aquarian Foundation, where he demonstrated relentless service to the Masters' work. Regularly, the Masters asked Steve to speak at gatherings and séances so people might hear his testimony as to the authenticity of the Masters' phenomena he witnessed.

Regularly within the Ascended Masters teachings, they elucidate their commentary with references from the *Bible* when speaking to a Western audience. So, we will continue with their example. If the audience had been in the East, they would have used Eastern religious references to punctuate their teachings, so know they are not biased toward the *Bible*. We understand many in the West have rejected the *Bible* as a source of wisdom for a variety of reasons. We know through Reverend Rhinehart's mediumship that Divine Intelligence doesn't endorse all passages written in the world's religious texts, yet we must acknowledge that Divine Intelligence has worked behind the scenes, producing the world's scriptures. So, it behooves us to make an attempt to discern the value of these enduring texts.

We will conclude this chapter with a parable from the Judaic and Far East traditions that provokes new perspectives on becoming our own authority for Truth. The allegory addresses our Spiritual journey in a cryptic manner. As Jesus, Buddha, and Muhammad all say, the Path is arduous and ill-defined at times, presenting unexpected twists. It is not as linear as we might expect, or desire.

The Far East version of this allegory gives an account of a man who, after accumulating vast material wealth and stature, comes to a great Master in the Himalayas in search of the mystical secrets of life. He no longer feels the pull of physical wealth and social stature. Even though he has accomplished most of his life goals, he senses something is missing. With all he has accomplished, he still isn't comfortable in his skin, questioning who he's become. He desires a deeper Truth, he wants true freedom and mastery of his Soul. Here he meets the Master:

"Oh, great Master, I have heard you possess the keys to the secrets of Moksha (total freedom). I humbly ask you to teach me your truth. I have gained great wealth and notoriety, but find I am empty, thirsting for something more. I am willing to do whatever you request to gain your wisdom."

"Ok, my beloved son, I trust you are earnest in your request. See the highest peak way out in the distance, hundreds of miles away, just over to the left?"

"Yes, yes I do."

"Go home and get your pillow and hike up to the top of that majestic peak with your pillow in hand. Once you have made the rugged ascent to the top, slice open the pillow with a knife and spread the feathers to all four corners of the Earth, then come back and meditate on your freedom. After a period of time, come and tell me what you have found."

"Ok, I will do exactly as you say!"

The man returns home, gets his pillow, and makes the arduous climb up the mountain. Once at the summit, he rips open his pillow and exuberantly tosses the feathers to all four compass points, feeling exceedingly satisfied with himself as he watches the wind scatter his feathers in every direction for miles around. Content, he returns home to meditate and eventually visits the Master again.

"Oh, great Master, I have done as you requested, but I feel no different, the keys to enlightenment seem to have eluded me. Am I missing something?"

The Master exclaims, *"Yes, now you must return to the mountain's peak and collect up every feather you have tossed to the wind!"*

Seasons of the Soul takes us on a journey where Eternity must be considered in evaluating Truth, feather-by-feather. We expect you'll find many feathers throughout the upcoming pages, feathers scattered through the seasons of your body, the seasons of your mind, the seasons of your emotions, the seasons of your Spirit, and the seasons of your Soul.

SIX

SHAMBHALA
LAND OF THE ASCENDED MASTERS

WHEN WE HEAR THE WORD "SHAMBHALA," A MYRIAD OF literary references and vivid, mystical temples spring to mind— legends of utopian kingdoms holograph through the imagination in cinematic technicolor. Oceanographers and archeologists claim the ocean floor to be less explored than the surface of the moon, but what of Shambhala? If it exists on the surface of the Earth, who can tell us of its terrain or its history? Its lore sparks controversy even amongst the Spiritually inclined, so how did Shambhala find its way into our contemporary lexicon?

Shambhala is a Sanskrit word that translates to "Place of Peace" and "Place of Silence"; however, legends intimate that Shambhala is a land of a thousand names. You might know it by Shangri-la, but there are those who call it the Forbidden Land, the Land of the Radiant Spirits, Land of Living Gods, Land of White Waters, and the Land of Wonders.

Several ancient texts including the *Kālacakra Tantra* (1025 CE —1025 CE), the scriptures of Zhang Zhung (500 BCE—625 CE) predating Tibetan Buddhism, a text existing in a civilization north of Lhasa, Tibet and part of the scriptures of the *Bon* tradition (one of the oldest Spiritual traditions in the world), and Hindu texts of *Vishnu*

Purana (1 BCE—1 CE), all speak to the physical existence of this mystical land.

The Chinese have called it Hsi Tien, as described by the Lady Master *Hsi Wang Mu*, the supreme alchemist who is said to hold the elixirs for immortality. (A single bite from one of her peaches and one attains immortality.) The Hindus call it *Aryavarta*, the Land of the Worthy Ones, and to the Russian Old Believers, it is *Belovodye*.

The first Dalai Lama (1415) and the sixth Panchen Lama (1775) were inspired by the *Kālacakra Tantric* tradition, so we can surmise that the physical existence of Shambhala has been established in the minds of those practicing Eastern religious traditions for centuries.

Myths abound claiming Shambhala to be a paradise where only the pure of heart exist, where love and wisdom reign, and where the inhabitants are immune to suffering, need, and old age. It is said therein dwell ancient Ascended Beings hidden from inquisitive eyes. One of the scriptures in which Shambhala was initially referenced is the *Kālacakra Tantra*, where Shambhala Kings spoke of their abode. This appears to be the same physical Shambhala referred to by the Ascended Master Emil in the *Life and Teachings of the Masters of the Far East*. It is Emil who frequently spoke through Reverend Rhinehart's mediumship, on Love and a variety of topics.

According to the Masters, through Reverend Rhinehart's mediumship, Shambhala, to some people's surprise, is a physical three-dimensional creation, not an astral, or inter-dimensional creation as some might think—nor created by nature or a God-like invisible being, but by physical Ascended Master beings. It is this creation where a limited number of Masters have chosen to dwell, living in abodes carved from solid rock, possibly similar to the Kailasha Temple 756 CE—773 CE, in the Ellora Caves area in India, where the temple was seemingly impossibly sculpted from solid rock.

Many explorers have embarked on journeys in search of this mythical paradise, but none have given the exact location. It's purported to be in the mountainous regions of the Himalayas, but the Masters have kept the exact locale a secret. Baird Spaulding's Shambhala expedition talks of assembling at Potal, a small, secluded village in India, but he gives no further details. So, for those who need to see and touch the parapets, and smell the gardens of Shambhala, this explanation likely falls shy of the mark. But for those who can enliven the gaps between literary comments and Baird Spaulding's testimony, Shambhala takes on a concrete reality.

Chapter Seven describes Spaulding's expeditions in more detail, and especially his encounters with the Ascended Masters in Shambhala.

ṢHAMBHALA
THE LIVES OF THE ASCENDED MASTERS

T HE FIRST TIME I CAME ACROSS THE CONCEPT OF ASCENDED Masters was reading the five-volume set of marvelous books by Baird Spaulding called *Life & Teachings of the Masters of the Far East*. Mr. Spaulding speaks of three different expeditions he took into India, Tibet, and China, where his party interacted with what he called Ascended Masters or Elder Brothers. In the last of the three expeditions, his party of eleven spent three-and-a-half years in the Himalayas, beginning in 1894, and living with the Ascended Masters. During this time, they observed these beings intimately, continuously witnessing the Masters demonstrate what they called the Great Law in their daily routines.

Spaulding's intent was not to present a new cult or religion through his books to the West, but to present, as best he could, the Ascended Masters' factual existence and their teachings. The men participating in Spaulding's expedition were all scientifically trained, having spent the lion's share of their professional lives doing scientific research. They came to the expedition as logical thinking skeptics and after years of observation, left thoroughly convinced—converted to the truths they witnessed first-hand.

One of the conditions the Masters suggested, which the research team respected, was to accept everything they witnessed as fact with no further explanation. After they delved into the work thoroughly, reflecting on the lessons, observing the Masters' daily lives, they could make inquiries to gain a deeper understanding. The members of the party were at liberty to interact with the Masters as much as they liked, then determine for themselves if what they witnessed hinted at trickery or remained founded in reality. At no time did the Masters attempt to influence the men's judgements.

Throughout the volumes, Spaulding speaks to his firsthand experiences of the Masters' attributes, which they exhibited in their daily routines. His accounts are some of the best reflections of the Masters in the outer world, so we will draw on his insights to gain a more thorough understanding of these Master beings.

In one incident occurring early in Spaulding's acquaintance with the Master Emil, Spaulding disclosed an experience he had on a walk. In this interaction, Emil looked up to the sky, calling Spaulding's attention to a circling pigeon. Emil then turned to Spaulding, indicating the bird was looking for him. Emil stretched out his arm, and the bird alighted. Emil said he knew a brother from the North who had been using pigeons to communicate. The Masters communicated with each other instantly by thought transference, through a force more subtle than electricity or wireless and certainly not through pigeons. Knowing this, the brother Emil referred to could not have been a Master. The following is a description of Spaulding's and Emil's encounter:

"I then began to ask questions, and Emil showed me that he was able to call the birds to him and direct their flight while they were in the air; that the flowers and trees would nod to him; that the wild animals would come to him fearlessly. He parted two jackals that were fighting over the body of a smaller animal that they had killed and were feeding upon. When he approached them, they stopped fighting and put their heads in his outstretched hand in perfect trust, then resumed their meal in quiet. He even gave me one of the young wild creatures to hold in my hands.

"He then said to me, *'This is not the mortal self, the self you see, that is able to do these things. It is a truer, deeper self. It is what you know as God, God within me, God the Omnipotent One working through me, that does these things. Of myself, the mortal self, I can do nothing. It is only when I get rid of the outer entirely and let the actual, the I Am, speak and work and let the great Love of God come forth that I can do these things that you have seen. When you let the Love of God pour through you to all things, nothing fears you and no harm can befall you.'* "[1]

To grasp a Master's full nature would be a difficult, exhausting task, but through Reverend Rhinehart's mediumship and Baird Spaulding's expeditions, we've been allowed to glean rare snapshots. For instance, Emil infers that in Shambhala the Masters live in an immortal physical body, regularly maintaining the body's permanency through their Spiritual practice. Babaji, although not living in Shambhala, claims to have existed in a physical body for nearly four thousand years, fully enjoying each moment, inspiring his chelas to awaken.

Many stories circulate through the foothills of the Himalayas claiming knowledge of Babaji fully resurrecting chelas' bodies after they jumped off a cliff to their death because he rejected their request to be his students. As previously mentioned, St. Germaine claims he has lived in the physical body for over eight thousand years, and Sanat Kumara, the oldest living being still existing in some degree of form, claims to have lived tens of thousands of eons.

If we read books from the Orient, we find legends of immortality referencing Bodhisattvas and Ascended Masters who, rather than moving on to more enjoyable, advanced worlds, remain committed to staying behind to assist in humanity's betterment and to end human suffering. They live hidden in retreats such as Shambhala, thriving far from prying, petty eyes. Their enclaves are secreted away in different locales. Some are located high in the Himalayas, or on Mount Rainier, Mount Fuji, Mount Shasta, or in the Gobi Desert and other remote retreats.

As the Masters move through their daily affairs, they operate within the limitations imposed under Natural Law, which promotes the common good and the Spirit of Peace.

Through the creation of force fields, they remain secluded, ensuring their protection and shielding themselves from harmful solar radiation to which we are all exposed. Spaulding says few Masters live in the physical compared to the nearly unlimited numbers existing in invisible realms.

As a result of the development of their Spiritual awareness, they have lifted themselves into conscious physical or Spiritual Immortality, awakening to dream no more. It is a process entailing many things, one of which is upon gaining Immortality, they must choose whether they want to live the rest of eternity in physical form or in Spiritual form. A difficult decision, I imagine, but a choice where no one selection is better or worse, but simply a personal preference.

The Masters allude to the fact that part of the process of cultivating Immortality is the lifting of every cell of the physical body into perfect attunement to the vibration of God. Once lifted, every physical cell vibrates at a rate exceeding one hundred and eighty-six billion times per second. With this raising, the body's vibration is synchronized to the vibration of God. This accomplishment translates into perfect conscious wakefulness.

In this same fashion, the Masters have permeated the atomic particles of their physical surroundings with the essence of God vibration, giving them the ability to manipulate physical substance and carve their homes from solid rock!

The Masters say they engage life without emanating a thought or word that is not based on Principle. Their vibration is perfectly harmonized with the one source of all, the All-Mighty. In living in harmony with Natural Law, all limitations fall away, and clarity of action through clarity of Mind becomes the norm. In this state, if an eye or any bodily part fails, it is simply replaced through perfected thought.

For the Masters, the body temple is far greater than many might imagine, far greater than any physical temple existing in this world or in galactic worlds. The body is maintained through perfected thought. Any negative thought emanating from our consciousness betrays the Christ resident within, and may defile the living temple of our body, jeopardizing the permanency of the cells.

The Ancient Ones say living in this body temple is God's gift, affording them the ability to serve and experience Joy. This awareness moves them to be steadfast in their practice, where they find any service and action without genuine, sincere Love is devoid of meaning and virtually empty. In reflecting on service, the Masters infer that five minutes of radiating pure Divine Love is more impactful than delivering a thousand loaves of bread to the needy.

The word GOD holds great meaning in generating permanency in the cells of the Master's body, as do the words I Am and Love. This Love they experience distinguishes itself from our common usage. It is a Love that is Knowledgeable and Conscious. Those who fail to discern are bound to live in delusion. If not awakened fully to the nurturing power of God, the vibration of permanency fails to be established, and the absence of the vibration of Love breeds biases, un-inspected hatreds, and vindictiveness.

The Masters state denying that God dwells within our cells is tantamount to asserting a fallacy. To declare we are God not only frees us from ego, but is the affirmation of genuine Truth. If we accompany this understanding with the discipline of moral thought, moral action, along with Love, we lift ourselves into the eternal, into infinity. We free ourselves from the delusions of the Christians' imaginary heavens and hells, and from reincarnation. The secret exists not in being something, nor attaining something, but simply in BEING, ever living as a demonstration of Love and the I Am consciousness.

Through their diligence and constant awareness, the Masters have demonstrated their ability to conquer life and death, and they maintain that they have done this by exercising a power that is not beyond our grasp, but is in fact our birthright!

We often hear quips in our culture declaring, "You only live once," and "Nobody escapes alive!" If we are to believe the Ascended Masters, these statements couldn't be farther from the truth. Here is a passage from *Life & Teachings of the Masters of the Far East,* supporting the Masters' statements around Immortality. This passage begins with Baird Spaulding speaking:

"We had been occupied in this work for about two weeks when we went to the temple one morning and found our friend Chandler Sen, who had apparently died and been resurrected, with not a vestige of old age about him. There was no mistaking him. As we came into the room, he arose and came forward with a hearty greeting and handshake. You can imagine our surprise as we gathered around and began to ask questions. We were like a gang of schoolboys turned loose, all attempting to ask questions at the same time. But the fact remained, there he was, with the vibrant quality of middle age, and everything about him showed that of a well-developed life, buoyant and keenly alive. The expression (in his) eyes and face was far beyond anything that I could put into words.

"In the first few moments, we could do nothing but picture to ourselves the contrast. When we had first seen him, he was a decrepit old man, leaning on a long staff for support, with long snow-white locks, halting step, and emancipated form.

"One of our party had remarked when we first met him, 'Here we find among these great souls one so aged that he seems ready to pass to the great beyond.'

"Of course, the transformation which we had witnessed just a few days previously had left its impression, but his sudden disappearance had rather taken him and the incident out of our minds, as we did not think we would ever see him again. (His abrupt reappearance) was more than a rejuvenation. I can compare it only to the transfiguration of the One we love and respect so dearly. That soul was surely reborn, judging from the contrast between his appearance the first time we met him and the way he looked this morning. It is true that we had known him only a short time, but we had been thrown into daily contact with him for a sufficient time to see and know that he was an old man. He was with us for nearly two years after this, acting as our guide and interpreter across the great Gobi." [2]

Briefly, we've spoken about some of the Masters' qualities. In this passage, Emil illustrates the notion of service in action, then illuminates us on his thoughts about existence. He is eloquent in his thoughts about God and the Christ light dwelling within. Baird Spalding explains:

"From the outset of our third expedition, in which we took up the metaphysical work, our little party assembled at Potal, a small village in the remote part of India. I had written Emil that we were coming, but did not write the object of the trip, nor did I even mention the number in our party. Much to our surprise, we found complete preparation had been made for our entire party and that Emil and his associates knew our complete plans. Emil had rendered us a remarkable service while in Southern India, but the service rendered from this time on surpassed all descriptions. To him and the wonderful souls we met, I wish to give all credit for the success of the entire undertaking.

"We arrived at Potal, from where the expedition was to start, late in the afternoon of December 22, 1894, and found we were to start Christmas morning upon what was to be the most memorable expedition of our whole lives. I never shall forget the few words Emil said to us that morning. These words were delivered in fluent English, although the speaker did not boast an English education, and he had never been out of the Far East.

"He began by saying, 'Tis Christmas Morning: to you I suppose it is the day Jesus of Nazareth, the Christ, was born; to you the thought must come that He was sent to remit sins; to you He must typify the Great Mediator between you and your God. You seem to appeal to Jesus as a mediator between you and your God, who seems to be a stern and, at times, an angry God sitting off somewhere in the place called heaven, located where I do not know, except it be in man's consciousness. You seem to be able to reach God only through His less austere and more loving Son, the great and noble One whom we all call Blessed and whose advent into the world this day commemorates.

"To us this day means more; to us this day not only means the advent into this world of Jesus, the Christ, but also this birth typifies the birth of Christ in every human consciousness. This Christmas Day means the birth of the Great Master and Teacher, the Great Liberator of mankind from material bondage and limitations. To us, this great soul came on Earth to show more fully the way to the real God, the great Omnipotent, Omnipresent, Omniscient One, to show that God is all Goodness, all Wisdom, all Truth, All in All. This Great Master who came to this world this day was sent to show more fully that God not only dwells without us but within us, that He never is, nor can be, separated from us or any of His creations; that He is always a just and loving God; that He is all things; knows all things; knows all Truth. Had I the understanding of all men, it is beyond my power to express to you, even in an humble way, what this Holy Birth means to us.

"We are fully convinced, and we hope you also will see that this Great Master and Teacher came to us that we might have a fuller understanding of life here on earth; that all mortal limitations are but man-made and in no other way should they be interpreted. We know that this greatest of all teachers came to show more fully that the Christ in Him and through whom He did His mighty works is the same Christ that lives in you, in me, and in all mankind; that we can, by applying His teachings, do all the works that He did and greater works. We believe that Jesus came to show more fully that God is the one great and only Cause of all things, that God is All.

"You may have heard it said that we believe Jesus received his early training among us. Perhaps some of us do believe. Let that be as it is. Does it matter whether His training came from among us or as a direct revelation from God, the one source where all things really exist? For when an idea from God-mind has been contacted by one man and sent out through the spoken word, cannot one or all again contact that thought in the Universe? Because one has contacted the idea and sent it out, it does not follow that it is his particular possession. If he did appropriate and hold it, where would be room for receiving? To receive more we must give out what we have received. If we withhold what we receive, stagnation will follow, and we will be like the wheel that generates power from the water and suddenly, of its own volition, begins to withhold the water which it is using. It is only when the water is allowed to flow freely through that it is of value to the wheel to create power. Just so with man. When he contacts God's ideas, he must give them out in order to receive the benefit from them. He must allow all to do the same, that they may grow and develop as he is growing.

"I am of the opinion that what Jesus taught came to Him as a direct revelation from God, as it no doubt has come to our great teachers. Are not all things of God, and whatever one human being can do, cannot all do? We believe you will be convinced that God is ever willing and ready to reveal Himself to all men as He has revealed Himself to Jesus and others. The only requisite necessary is for each one to be willing to let God come forth. We believe, with all sincerity, that all are created equal; that all men are one man; that the mighty works done by Jesus can and will be done by all. You will see there is nothing mysterious about these works. The mystery is only in man's mortal concept of them.

"We fully realize you have come to us with minds more or less skeptical. We trust you will live with us and know us as we really are. Our work and the results accomplished, we leave you to accept or reject as you will." [3]

EIGHT

CHELAS' INTERACTIONS WITH THE ASCENDED MASTERS

J UST AS WE CAN DETERMINE THAT THE MASTERS SPENT INVAL-
uable time with Spaulding's team, likewise, they spent inordinate
amounts of time nurturing and developing relationships with students
in mystery schools like the Aquarian Foundation. Throughout
history, the Masters' interactions with students have varied depending
on the needs of the students. When a student joins a mystery school,
there is a deepening of commitment. A Master Teacher then becomes
involved with the inner life of the student. No one knows exactly how
a Master Teacher may interact with the chela or when. However, once
a Master takes on a chela, blessings and protection follow.

What is the chela/Master relationship? What force draws the
chela and the Master together? Are there events from the past that
intertwine their life streams? Some suggest a Master Teacher may have
been concentrating on a particular chela for centuries to guide that
student into the Light.

We each have many guides reaching out to work with us—child
guides, health guides, Indian guides, chemical guides, Spiritual
guides, financial guides, and Guardian Angels, but none quite like
an Ascended Master Teacher, whose methods may well surprise.
For instance, the Master may reach out through the inner planes of

consciousness, whereby they make contact through the astral planes, the vibrational planes, or the Spiritual planes. Their contact is often not by rote. The Master creates a variety of methods for the chela to attune to the Master's consciousness. A chela may find himself or herself in the presence of a Master during an initiation where they simply sit in silence for hours, days, months, or possibly years. Mysterious is the way of the Masters, but be assured that the age-old refrain is true: When the student is ready, the Master will appear, somehow, somewhere, someway.

Over the years of Reverend Rhinehart's service, many Ascended Masters, such as Emil, spoke through his adept mediumship, confirming the Masters' existence and oversight of humanity. Throughout history, it is uncommon for the Masters to reveal themselves to the world. But at times they do. In the last sixteen years of the Nineteenth Century and the beginning of the Twentieth Century, they communicated with Madame Blavatsky, A. P. Sinnett, Colonel Olcott, and others during the foundation of the Theosophical Society. In the case of Reverend Rhinehart, they communicated regularly through what is referred to as Master Class and public services in Aquarian Foundation.

Here, the Masters spoke directly to the students, even physically materializing in some cases. During these sessions, they were compassionate, remarkably loving, giving extensive personal lessons pertinent to a student's welfare and inspiration, while delivering Spiritual worldly lessons. At times, they addressed a student's assets, failures, and specific events in their life. Often, past lives and personal karmas were broached while discussing future missions in which the student may be challenged. Over the years, an intimate rapport developed between the Masters and students, where the students received great Spiritual development.

Here, Steve Young gives an account of an interaction with Master Yogananda along these lines:

"It is the 1970s, I am sitting in the living room of an apartment on the fifteenth floor of the Ilikai Hotel in Honolulu, Hawaii, accompanied by a married couple. The living room is semi-lit, so we can easily observe any phenomenon occurring. Reverend Rhinehart is sitting in a chair in the apartment's bathtub, enclosed in a makeshift cabinet simulating the Holy of Holies. Looking down the apartment's hall, I see an ectoplasmic form coming towards us. It's a being that has stepped out of the makeshift cabinet where it materialized. Upon reaching the living room, he announces he is Master Yogananda. There are no facial features, so if he hadn't announced his name, I would not have known his identity. He gives us a short lesson, concluding the lesson by placing small white, crystal heart-shaped stones in the palm of my hand. He then materializes another stone in his hand and asks my associate to take the stone from his hand—he calls it the *'Self Realization Stone.'*

"I can't explain exactly why, but I feel the Holiness of his Spirit, experiencing a powerful presence. The lesson he delivers is of a healing nature, uplifting, encouraging us to be moral, love God, and serve our fellow man. He then chants, *'I Am the Bubble Make Me the Sea,'* a song for which he was well-known. I notice he is a much shorter man than I, as opposed to Buddha, who was a much taller, larger man."

Steve mused: "When Masters materialized, they presented their own individual characteristics. Babaji came across as a strict disciplinarian with a loving, but stern voice, very Masterly. Count Saint Germaine presented an intellectual vibration, saying he was the Wandering Jew of the *Bible*. El Morya, my Master teacher, claimed to be one of the Lords of Civilization, extremely steeped in Eastern Philosophy and esoteric thought."

Many have notions about the Masters, but who are these beings who refer to themselves as Ascended Masters, the Mahatmas? What are we to make of their outreach to humanity? The Masters say, after overcoming the life/death cycle, they have chosen to live in service to humanity. They exist in the most sublime spheres of Light, yet still part of the world of matter, functioning as conscious physical Immortal beings or conscious Spiritual Immortal beings.

Once Reverend Rhinehart established his adept mediumship, they began speaking through his mediumship, but it wasn't until Reverend Rhinehart agreed to start the Church, Aquarian Foundation, that their long-conceived Spiritual plan activated, releasing a new dispensation of Light on the planet.

For over forty years, through Reverend Rhinehart's mediumship, the Masters worked to uplift and establish a new vibration. New knowledge dawned in the world through spoken and written lessons along with the programming of sacred objects designed to guide students' and the world's advancement. The Masters are not known to the world in general; however, during the *Wesak Festival* held in Shambhala, it is said that Jesus and Buddha have appeared in the skies for participants to see. But this is not the norm, as their role is to work invisibly behind the scenes. To many, their work is mysterious, clandestine, maybe even overly esoteric, but whatever method the Masters choose to employ, their purpose is the same—to advance humanity's awakening process.

The following illustrates different types of exchanges students have experienced with the Masters. Some experiences are by advanced students, some are initial encounters, and some are by the general populace. The experiences vary widely and come when least expected.

Here is one student's experience:

"This is a dream experience I had one evening after Master Class. (Master Class typically entails Spiritual practices such as affirmations, meditations, and listening to a taped lesson given by an Ascended Master through the adept mediumship of Reverend Rhinehart.)

"In my dream, St. Germaine was teaching me how to use the Violet Flame and how to burn away the veil between our two realms of existence. In front of me, there appeared a veil—I burned away the veil, right behind the veil, a tunnel of intense white light took form. I became afraid. St Germaine put his hand directly in the middle of my back and gave me a firm shove. I went flying into the "White Fire." It became the most intense, powerful experience of my lifetime, more so than any physical experience. I felt as if every cell in my body took a deep breath and was purified. I have never forgotten it. When I awakened, I seemed to be living in two separate worlds at once, even though I went to work and executed all my tasks efficiently, I remained aware that every cell in my body felt renewed and very alive."

Another student's experience took place while she attended the 1975 Convention in Seattle, Washington, at the Olympic Hotel.

"The 1975 Convention was my introduction to Aquarians. I felt a little strange because my friend and I had been hopping from one psychic group to another for years, searching, searching, searching. Then one day, my friend brought me the Aquarian Convention invitation. Right off, it sounded very interesting, but they wanted two hundred bucks. Two hundred bucks in those days was a lot of money. So, I just wasn't sure.

"When the time came, I left a note in my office saying, '*See you in seven days.*'

"I drove down to Seattle from Vancouver, BC. I had no idea of how to get there, but when I got close, I went to a service station to determine my location. I asked the service station attendant how to get to the hotel.

"He said, '*Well, this is the exit, this is Parkgate, you park in here, walk across the street, and you're in the Olympic Hotel.*'

"I didn't know what to make of it, thinking back, that was the first miracle!

"The itinerary that week was phenomenal, phenomena going on all the time. Each day was dedicated to a color ray. Thursday was the Pink Ray of Master Emil, of whom I had no knowledge. That Thursday morning, I heard a knock on my hotel room door. Woke me up at nine o'clock A.M.! My goodness, it was sure early as we were always going for long, long evenings. I jumped up out of bed and went to the door. A young-looking fella greeted me, skinny, long hair, wearing a white robe.

"He said, *'Here is something for you to keep you safe,'* and he handed me two identical breastplates. He then said, 'Do not leave the room for ten minutes.'

"I didn't know what that meant, but he didn't say I couldn't stand there or close the door, so I watched him walk diagonally across the hall, then knock on another door. Momentarily, the door opened, and this time, unlike at my door, he walked in. I thought, 'This is interesting, he must know people staying there. I must find out who's lodging in that room.' I closed my door and hurried up. Got dressed, readied myself to go down to breakfast and the meetings.

"On the way out, I grabbed my pen and a piece of paper to write down the room number of the room the young man entered, because I wanted to go to the front desk and find out who was staying there to ask them a few questions. Once I locked my door and looked across the hall, there was no door! I looked closely, there were no doors all the way down the corridor to the elevator. I couldn't believe it! The wall all the way down the corridor was completely bare!

"When I told people, they all laughed and said, *'Oh, it must have been Master Emil,'* but who was Master Emil? Then I remembered I had seen this man the night before, down the hall where he was sitting, leaning up against one of the pillars with his eyes closed. There were crowds everywhere, but he sat alone with lots of empty space around him amidst the crowd. I suppose he was meditating—just there, like everyone else, fitting into the crowd with his long hair, looking much like all the other hippy types."

Here are some other unique experiences recorded by different chelas regarding their interactions with their Master Teachers:

"In the winter of 1968, Reverend Rhinehart conducted a Master Class Séance in our apartment. It was cold—I was the only person wearing a dress, everyone else was wearing pants. There were maybe twenty to twenty-five people present in our living room. During the séance, one by one, people came up to the Holy of Holies, the cabinet, to receive a sacred object and a blessing from their Master Teacher. Being one of the Spiritual Leaders of the group, I was one of the last to step up to the cabinet. With my back turned to the cabinet, my Master Teacher fully materialized, stepping out of the cabinet behind me in his ectoplasmic form. When he put his hands on my head, I felt his ectoplasmic robe brushing against my bare leg—I will never forget it. I felt one of the most profound and unusual feelings I have ever experienced. I don't even know how to describe it. It felt like a vibrational throbbing or a shimmering going through my leg and into my body, all transmitted through the touch of his robe to my bare leg. The cabinet cloth had been pulled open for him to step out into the room, so I am certain that his robe and not the cloth of the cabinet is what touched me."

This experience is similar to the *Bible's* description when virtue passed from Jesus' robe to a woman in a crowd, where healing occurred.

Luke 8:41-48 KJB

"And behold there came a man named Jairus and he was a ruler of the synagogue: and he fell down at Jesus' feet, and besought him that he would come into his house:

For he had one only daughter, about twelve years of age, and she lay dying. But as he went the people thronged him.

And a woman having an issue of blood twelve years, which had spent all her living upon physicians, neither could (she) be healed of any,

Came behind him, and touched the border of his garment: and immediately her issue of blood stanched.

And Jesus said, Who touched me? When all denied, Peter and they that were with him said, Master, the multitude throng thee and, pressed the, and sayest thou, Who touched me?

And Jesus said, Somebody hath touched me: for I perceive that virtue is gone out of me.

And when the woman saw that she was not hid, she came trembling, and declared unto him before all the people for what cause she had touched him, and how she was healed immediately.

sAnd he said unto her, Daughter, be of good comfort: thy faith hath made thee whole; go in peace."

Here, Steve Young experienced another interaction with his Master Teacher early in his association with Reverend Rhinehart. It is an astral projection experience occurring in the dream state. Often, we forget our astral experiences, but Steve recalls having a very strong desire to remember when he was in this particular astral experience:

"In a dream, I was sitting at the feet of my Master Teacher—Master Morya." (In the Nineteenth Century, Master Morya made his presence known to Madame Blavatsky, eventually dictating part of the text to *The Secret Doctrine,* in collaboration with Master Koot Hoomi. In the Twentieth Century, Morya made his presence known physically to Keith Milton Rhinehart, asking Keith to start a Church—Aquarian Foundation. Keith agreed.)

"My experience took place in the early 1970s. During this astral experience, where I was at the feet of Master Morya, he indicated that in addition to being my Master Teacher, he was the Master Teacher of my four children! He then placed four sacred stones in my hand. The experience seemed easy to remember as it meant so much to me that

Morya was the Master Teacher of my children.

"Later, Reverend Rhinehart held a public service performing billet card readings. Through Reverend Rhinehart's mediumship, Master Morya announced he was the Master Teacher of my four children. This reading confirmed for me that my out-of-body astral experience was indeed genuine."

Here is another experience of a chela during a Master Class:

"In the Spring of 1976, I had the privilege to attend a Master Materialization Séance held at the Mother Church of Aquarian Foundation in Seattle, Washington. This was a total blackout séance so as to protect the medium and the materialized spirit from harmful light. The stage at the front of the chapel was a step above the chapel floor. The séance cabinet, the Holy of Holies, was in the right-hand corner on the stage. The "sitter" stood in a line in front of the stage. The person standing to the right, in front of the cabinet, was the first to be served.

"Their Master Teacher exited from behind the cabinet curtains in full physical manifestation and, standing from behind the student, delivered a personal message. As each student served took a seat, the line moved to the right.

"When it was my turn, my Ascended Master Teacher, Koot Hoomi Lal Singh, exited the cabinet. He placed his hands on my shoulders— they were very large, much larger than the medium's, Reverend Rhinehart's. He greeted me, his voice seemed to be coming from far above me—he was a step above me, but it felt much more than that. I no longer remember the entire message, but I remember he told me he saw a large crown of many-colored jewels on my head—each jewel represented an accomplishment and an initiation. He ended by saying, *'But you still have karma!'*"

Throughout this chapter, we have been presenting a montage of vignettes showing personal interactions with the Masters to give the broadest understanding of the Masters' natures as possible. Here is an excerpt from *The Mahatma Letters*, a letter from Master Koot Hoomi Lal Singh to A.P. Sinnett, revealing a completely different side. It is highly personal, maybe even intimate in a strange sort of way. I'm not sure if Koot Hoomi is Sinnett's Master Teacher, but the communication displays his feelings for Sinnett and the workings of Koot Hoomi's mind. Many letters contained within *The Mahatma Letters* are lengthy, intellectually complex, and very hard-hitting at times—this letter finds a different vein.

"And now about yourself personally. Far be it from me to discourage one so willing as yourself by setting up impossible barriers to your progress. We never whine over the inevitable but try to make the best of the worst. And though we neither push nor draw into the mysterious domain of occult nature those who are unwilling, we never shrink from expressing our opinions freely and fearlessly. Yet, we are ever as ready to assist those who come to us; even to agnostics who assume the negative position of *'knowing nothing but phenomena and refuse to believe in anything else.'* It is true that the married man cannot be an adept, yet without striving to become a 'Raja Yogi,' he can acquire certain powers and do as much good to mankind and often more, by remaining within the precincts of this world of his. Therefore, shall we not ask you to precipitately change fixed habits of life, before the full conviction of its necessity and advantage has possessed you. You are a man to be left to lead himself and may be so left with safety. Your resolution is taken to deserve much; time will affect the rest. There are more ways than one for acquiring occult knowledge:

"*Many are the grains of incense destined for one and the same altar. One falls sooner into the fire, the other later—the difference of time is nothing,*" remarked a great man when he was refused admission and supreme initiation into the mysteries.

"There is a tone of complaint in your question whether there ever will be a renewal of the vision you had, the night before the picnic day. Methinks, were you to have a vision nightly, you would soon cease to 'treasure' them all. But there is a far weightier reason why you should not have a surfeit—it would be a waste of our strength. As often as I, or any of us can communicate with you, whether by dreams, waking impressions, letters (in or out of pillows) or personal visits in astral form—it will be done. But remember that Simla is 7,000 feet higher than Allahabad, and the difficulties to be surmounted at the latter are tremendous. I abstain from encouraging you to expect too much, for, like yourself, I am loath to promise what, for various reasons, I may not be able to perform.

"The term 'Universal Brotherhood' is no idle phrase. Humanity in the mass has a paramount claim upon us, as I try to explain in my letter to Mr. Hume, which you had better ask the loan of. It is the only secure foundation for universal morality. If it be a dream, it is at least a noble one for mankind, and it is the aspiration of the **true adept**.

Yours faithfully, Koot Hoomi Lal Singh" [1]

It is important to note that, whether or not you are a chela, it is still possible to feel the vibration of your Master Teacher and the blessings sent your way. You may sense the uniqueness of your Master's personality and immense Love. Perhaps you can use your imagination to draw your teacher closer. One thing we can state for certain is that as your Master Teacher draws closer, there is a felicity that arises from the intimate interaction with a Divine Being, an experience like no other.

NINE

UNEXPECTED ENCOUNTERS WITH ASCENDED MASTERS

THE FOLLOWING ENCOUNTER SPEAKS TO THE ASCENDED Masters' compassion and how they work with people, no matter the circumstances or locale. This is Baird Spaulding speaking after a day of exploring an ancient ruin in India, just before departing for another destination:

"The Governor of the village, through an interpreter, welcomed us, telling us we were to dine at his house and were to start immediately. We filed out of the room, led by the Governor with a guard of two soldiers, one on each side, as was the custom of the country. Next came the leader with our hostess and our Chief with the beautiful lady. Then came Emil and his mother. I walked with them, the rest of the party following.

"We had proceeded but a short distance when a poorly dressed child stepped from the crowd which had assembled and asked in the native tongue if she might speak to Emil's mother. The governor brushed her aside unceremoniously, saying that we could not be bothered with such as she. Emil's mother grasped our arms, and the three of us stepped out of the ranks to hear what the girl had to say. As we did this, our hostess hesitated, and as she stepped out of the ranks the company stopped. Emil's mother spoke to the Governor, saying she would like to have the rest go on and get seating arrangements completed, and that by that time, we surely would be there.

"Meanwhile, she was holding the girl's hand in hers. As the company moved on, she knelt down and, putting her arms around the little girl, said, *'Dear one, what can I do for you?'* She found that the child's brother had fallen that afternoon, and they thought his back was broken. The child begged the lady to go with her to see if she could not help him, as he was in great pain. Emil's mother arose, explained the situation to us and told us to go on, that she would go with the child, then come in later. The leader said that if it were permissible, he would like to go along. Emil's mother invited us all to go; so, we turned aside and followed her and the girl as they walked hand-in-hand. Then the girl bounded ahead to tell her family we were coming.

"When we came up to the door, we saw that the house was but a mud hut of the lowest order. Emil's mother must have interpreted our thoughts, for she said, *'Although it is a hovel, warm hearts beat within.'* At that moment, the door was thrown open, a gruff masculine voice spoke, and we stepped inside. If the hut looked wretched from without, it was doubly so from within. It was scarcely large enough for us to crowd into, and the ceiling was so low that we could not stand erect. A dim witch light burned and cast a weird light upon the hard faces of the father and mother as they sat amidst their squalor.

"In the far corner, on a mass of musty straw and vile-smelling rags, lay a lad not more than five years old, his face drawn and ashen pale. The girl knelt beside him, holding his face in both of her hands, one pressed against each cheek. She was telling him that he was going to be perfectly well again, as the beautiful lady was already there. She removed her hands, moved aside to give him a clearer view, and for the first time, the girl saw the rest of the party. Instantly, her expression changed and a great fear seemed to pervade her whole form. She dropped her face in her folded arms and her form shook with a convulsive sob as she cried out, *'Oh, I thought you were coming alone.'* Emil's mother dropped on her knees beside her, put both arms around her and held her close for a moment. She became silent, and Emil's mother said she would send us away if the girl wished to have us go. The girl said she was only surprised and frightened; that we need not mind her, as she was only thinking of her brother.

"Then Emil's mother said, *'You love your brother dearly, do you not?'* The girl, who could not have been more than nine years old, said, 'Yes, but I love everyone.' The conversation was interpreted to us by Emil, as none of our party spoke the language. Emil's mother said, *'If you love your brother so much, you can help to heal him,'* and she told the girl to take the position she had been in and to place her hands on each side of his face. Then Emil's mother moved so that she could place her hand on his forehead. Almost instantly, the moans ceased, the boy's face lighted up, his little form relaxed, a perfect calm settled over the whole scene, and the child slept quietly and naturally.

"Emil's mother and the girl sat as they were for a few moments; then with her left hand, the lady gently removed the girl's hands from the boy's face, saying, *'How beautiful he is, how strong and fine.'* Then Emil's mother removed her hand ever so gently, and, as I happened to be standing near her, when she extended her left hand, I reached out my hand in order to assist her to her feet. As her hand touched mine, such a thrill went through my whole body that it left me perfectly helpless. She sprang lightly to her feet and said, *'For a moment I forgot myself. I should not have taken your hand as I did, for momentarily I seemed to be overwhelmed, so great was the power that was flowing through me.'* I recovered my composure almost instantly. The others did not notice as they were all deeply engrossed in what was going on around them.

"The girl had suddenly thrown herself at Emil's mother's feet and, clasping each in one of her hands, was frantically kissing the coverings.

Emil's mother reached down and, with one hand, turned the fervent, tear-stained face upward, and then knelt and clasped the child to her and kissed her eyes and lips. The child put both her arms around the mother's neck, and both were motionless for a moment; then a strange light began to pervade the room and it grew brighter and brighter until every object seemed to be suffused with the light and nothing cast a shadow. The room seemed to be expanding. The father and the mother of the two children had sat on the dirt floor in stony-faced silence thus far. They arose, and the expression on their faces changed to blank dismay, then to fright, and the man bolted through the door, nearly upsetting the leader of the expedition in his haste to get away.

"The mother of the household threw herself prostrate at the side of Emil's mother, and sobs shook her frame. Emil's mother placed her hands on the woman's forehead, speaking in a low voice to her. Presently, the sobs ceased, she drew herself to a half-sitting, half-kneeling position, and saw the transformation that had taken place in the room. The expression on her face changed to one of terror; she rose hastily to her feet and started to run from the room. Emil reached out his hand and took one of her hands while the beautiful lady took the other. They held her hands thus for a moment and the frightened expression changed to a smile.

"We looked around and, in place of the hovel we had entered, we were in a moderately comfortable furnished room with seats, table, and a clean bed. Emil walked over and picked up the boy, still sound asleep, from the heap of musty straw and rags, placed him tenderly on the clean bed and drew the covers over him. As he did so, he stooped and kissed the child's forehead as tenderly as any woman could have done." [1]

Here is an unexpected experience in 1982, which Monica Szu-Whitney, my wife, had prior to joining Aquarian Foundation Master Class, illustrating the Masters' attention is ever-present:

"I grew up in Rangoon, Burma (Yangon, Myanmar). Several years before this experience, I moved with my family to San Francisco, California, much to my dismay, as I was involved with someone I cared for and was enjoying my life in Rangoon. On this particular evening after dark, I was feeling extremely depressed, lost, missing my loved one, sitting in my darkened bedroom not knowing how to deal with my feelings. I suppose I yearned to return to Burma and had been feeling out of place for some time. In the midst of my gloom, suddenly the room lit up with dazzling bright light, and immediately I felt the presence of Jesus at my side. I instinctively bowed down, asking His forgiveness for my sins. He responded, *'There is nothing to forgive.'* He stayed with me for several minutes, surrounding me in the Light—transfixed, I bathed in His grace. I felt ecstatic, overwhelmed with gratitude, Love, and renewed inspiration."

The next event is a remarkable example of the Masters' interaction in the world, taken from the *Life and Teachings of the Masters of the Far East*. It is incomprehensible, preposterous, and far-fetched for those who are ignorant of the Principles of the Law, but a reality for Ascended Masters.

Here again, Spaulding discusses an episode that occurred during the expedition when his team was excavating an ancient civilization with the Master Jast:

"After resting for a week and reassembling our outfit, the combined expedition set out for the ancient city of the Uigurs, where we arrived on June 30. Here we set to work immediately and when the first pit was down to a depth of fifty feet, we encountered the walls of an ancient building. When we had proceeded to a depth of a little more than ninety feet, we broke into a large room where there were a number of gold, silver, bronze, and clay statues, all beautifully wrought. After the work had progressed far enough to prove beyond a question of doubt that this had once been a very large city, we went

85

on to the second location. Here we went down about forty feet before we came upon anything that could be called definite proof of a former civilization. Again, we did enough work to prove that we were in the ruins of a large city.

"We removed to a third location, where we expected to find evidence that would prove this the oldest and largest of the three cities.

"In order to conserve time and resources, we had organized our forces into four parties. Three of these parties were made up of a leader and six assistants. This gave seven men to each party. To this combined force was assigned all the excavation work and its management, each part being assigned eight hours out of the twenty-four. The fourth party, consisting of the remainder of the personnel of the expedition, was assigned the duties of the camp. I was in the party of which our Chief was the leader. We were assigned the eight hours from midnight until eight in the morning.

"After we had completed the discovery of the first pit and had gained access to four of the underground chambers of rooms, we cleared away enough of the debris to show beyond a question of doubt that this was the oldest and largest city of the three and that it was rich in treasure.

"One morning, the party which relieved our Chief's party reported that there were horsemen approaching our camp from the north. When we reached the surface, we found they were headed in our direction and it looked as though they were a bandit band, since they were evidently following the trail we had made on our way there. As we stood looking, Jast (an Ascended Master) came up and said, *'They are a party of bandits who are determined to loot the camp, but I do not think we need fear.'* We waited for them to approach, and they came to within five hundred yards of our camp, then halted.

"After a short interval, two of the men rode up and, after exchanging greetings, asked what we were doing there. They were told we were attempting to find a ruined city. To this, they replied they did not believe a word of what we said. They suspected we were looking for gold and they had come to take our equipment and supplies from us. We asked if they were government soldiers, to which they replied they did not recognize any government, as the strongest party was the one that won in that country. As they saw no evidence of firearms, I believe they came to the conclusion that there must be a larger force than was evidenced by what they could see. They returned to their band to talk over the situation.

"After a time, the two came back and told us that if we submitted peacefully, they would not harm any of us but if we did not, they would advance and shoot everyone who showed resistance. We were given ten minutes to decide and after that time, they would advance without further preliminaries. To this, Jast replied that we would neither resist nor surrender. This seemed to anger them and, wheeling their horses, they started back toward the band, waving their arms. Then the whole band came toward us at full gallop. I confess that I was badly frightened, but almost instantly we seemed to be surrounded by a number of shadowy forms on horseback, galloping around us. Then these forms became more lifelike and increased in numbers. Evidently, our visitors had seen what we were witnessing, for their horses were either reined in quickly or stopped of their own accord, as they began to rear and plunge and get beyond control of their riders. In a moment there was wild confusion among the band, which numbered about seventy-five horsemen. The horses began plunging right and left, beyond all control of the riders and this ended in a wild retreat, with our phantom horseman, as we called them, in close pursuit.

"After the excitement was over, our Chief and two of the party, including myself, walked out to where the main band had halted and could find no tracks except those made by the robbers themselves. We were very much mystified at this since the relief had looked as real to us as it did to the bandits, and the rescuers had seemed to have come from all sides. We fully expected to find the tracks of their horses in the sand, as well as the tracks of the horses the bandits were riding.

"When we returned, Jast said, *'The phantom horsemen, as you can call them, were only pictures, made so real that you, as well as the bandits, could see them. In a word, they were the pictures of other occurrences that we were able to produce in so lifelike a manner that they could not be distinguished from the real occurrence. We are able to produce them for our own protection as well as for that of others and no one has been harmed. Where a definite purpose is served, there is no harm in the outcome. Doubt had risen in the minds of the bandits. It was not logical that an expedition like this would venture so far away without some protection and we were able to take advantage of this to frighten them. They are very superstitious and always on the lookout for trickery. That type is the most susceptible to fear and they saw just what they expected to find. If we had not used this method, we should in all probability have been obliged to destroy a number of the band before they would have left us in peace. As it is, we shall hear no more of them.'* We were not molested again." [2]

We'd like to conclude this chapter with another example of the Masters' emphatic outreach to humanity. Not a personal encounter with the Masters, but definitely an unexpected and extraordinary event. This particular demonstration represents one of the more remarkable phenomena that occurred around Aquarian Foundation.

The following testimony describes a series of occurrences that are rarely encountered but poignantly illustrate that the Masters are, in fact, interfacing with our world. Here is a chela's description of what transpired:

"Over a period of time, I witnessed the unusual phenomenon of the weeping of oils. The first incident occurred in 1977 at a séance in New York's Lexington Hotel. At the request of the Spirit communicator speaking through Reverend Rhinehart's mediumship, a sitter at the séance was asked to hold up the portraits of Jesus and Count Saint Germaine in the bright infrared light of the séance room. We who were sitting in the audience saw drops of oil form at the eyes and in the center of the foreheads of each of the portraits. The oils flowed down the front of the portraits, then continued to flow for several hours in full daylight after the red light had been turned off. After this séance, the pictures were moved into the headquarters in New York and continued to weep oils in full daylight, even though Reverend Rhinehart was not present. A jerry-rigged plastic funnel was applied to the portraits, with a film canister attached at the bottom of the plastic funnels, so the rose-scented oil that continued to flow could be collected.

"Later, Easter in 1978, after the pictures had been framed in glass, once again they began to weep oils. This was witnessed by a number of members. On one occasion during the Festival for Mind, Body, and Spirit in New York City, the portraits were hung on our booth wall. The day the Festival opened, the portraits began to weep and continued weeping throughout the entire Festival. Over the years, around Spiritually significant events, the pictures regularly wept oils. On one such occasion, Reverend Rhinehart, who had been entranced by St. Germaine, pointed to the portraits and in that distinctive St. Germaine voice said, *'Weep!'* Immediately, the portraits spurted oils out from the eyes. This was an awe-inspiring, amazing Spiritual experience.

"The collected oils were used for Spiritual blessings and Spiritual initiations for the members of the organization."

This series of events was reported in the *Psychic News*, London, February 9, 1980, in Issue 2,488, where the article displayed pictures from the séance in which the actual portraits of Jesus and Count Saint Germaine dripped the scented oils.

Reflecting over these diverse encounters, we find the Masters' deep compassion compels them to engage with the peoples of the world in the most unusual and unexpected of ways.

TEN

SPACE MASTERS
INTERGALACTIC INTELLIGENCE

U NTIL NOW, WE HAVE PRIMARILY FOCUSED ON THE ASCENDED
Masters of the Earth Plane, but we feel obliged to briefly men-
tion the existence of Space Masters inhabiting the Galactic Universe.
Over the years of Reverend Rhinehart's mediumship, many Space
Masters have communicated, beings such as Master Clarion, Master
Hilarion, Master Orion, Master Ashtar, Master Ancora, and Master
Oahspe, to name a few. Clarion relates that each of these Masters has
unique personalities and messages, and all exist in civilizations that
are far in advance of Earth's standards. They live in similar biological
forms to us, but he states there are many forms of intelligence
inhabiting outer space that are different from humans and as diverse
as the forms of land and sea creatures existing on Earth.

Some beings from these evolved cultures travel in craft-like saucers,
cigar-shaped vehicles, and motherships stretching the imagination.
They have long ago abandoned the forms of locomotion we still employ, patterning their modes of propulsion after the motion of planets.

Master Clarion infers that smaller planets orbit through space
utilizing the power larger mass planets provide; the more mass, the
more potential energy. This non-combustion approach for propulsion spins planets through space at thousands of miles per hour.

Interplanetary peoples have utilized this power to move through the universe for eons.

Well-documented sightings more than suggest that innumerable spacecraft exist in the physical universe and perhaps on many different planes of existence. *Star Wars, Star Trek, Deep Space Nine,* and other galactic tales give us a glimpse of their possible realities. We can look to TV programs like *Ancient Aliens* to find abundant clues to their past visitations and colonizations. Billy Meier's tales and books, *Messages from the Pleiades, The Contact Notes of Billy Eduard Meier,* document his close encounters with the Pleiadeans, giving us one of the best documented encounters of human interaction with interplanetary intelligence. Books like the *Oahspe Bible,* the *Mahabharata,* the *Vedas,* and the famous books by Charles Fort: *The Book of the Damned, New Lands, Lo!,* and *Wild Talents,* corroborate the evidence. It should be noted that in the 1800s, Fort worked at the British Museum and the New York Public Library for twenty-seven years, compiling references to UFO sightings long before the advent of airplanes. The flapdoodle the U.S. Military invented regarding the Roswell UFO crash, and the insincere denials of Project Blue Book and Majestic Twelve are flimsy misdirections for public consumption. We would say any inquiring mind can spot the deceit; however, we trust that more transparency may be forthcoming.

Contrary to what the public has been told, the U.S. government knows quite a bit more about UFOs (now called UAPs) than it admits. In 2023, the US Congress held a hearing on Unidentified Anomalous Phenomena (UAPs), formerly known as UFOs. The hearing featured testimony from former intelligence officials and military personnel, including the Navy's former Intelligence Officer, David Grusch, who stated the government is "absolutely" in possession of UAPs and has a "multidecade" program to collect and reconstruct crashed UAPs. Retired Navy Commander David Fravor also shared his account of a 2004 encounter with a white, "Tic Tac" shaped object over the San Diego coast, which he described as having "incredible technology" and no visible flight control surfaces. The hearing also explored the standardization of civilian reporting of UAP sightings.

Through Reverend Rinehart's mediumship, Master Clarion states he hails from a far distant region beyond our planetary plane, beyond the World of Spirit. He, along with Master Ashtar and others, has been active in interacting with Earth, representing beings who have Spiritually progressed, evolving over immeasurable ages of time advancing themselves beyond us Spiritually, psychologically, culturally, and technologically. Master Clarion, acting as an ambassador for the intergalactic community, assures us they have been, and are now, avidly observing our world, gazing in from faraway planets, solar systems, and galaxies with inquisitive interest and grave concern.

He suggests they have come to a dilemma of consciousness: do they or do they not make outward contact with our world, risking interfering with our karmic situations and resolution, progress, and evolution? They hold legitimate moral and interstellar questions regarding our free will. If they don't override our free choice, and we destroy our planet, what are the human implications, and what havoc could it wreak on interstellar space and its peoples? We have to look no further than the asteroid belt orbiting the Sun between Mars and Jupiter, where once existed the planet formerly known as Maldek, to find a prime example of a planet that once faced similar challenges and ultimately failed.

The Space Masters' view of our situation suggests that the crisis in which we find ourselves today is more disturbing than anything we have faced during the complex involution and evolution of our races. People say it is the corruption of our leaders causing the failure, and of course, their corruption is a major factor, but there are the karmic matrices we, as a society, bring to our incarnation which affect our planet.

The Space Masters lament—characterizing Earth as the prison-house and insane asylum of the universe. The tensions, prejudices, and poor intelligence of our leaders are the result of the group consciousness inhabiting Earth. These factors contribute to our lack of evolution and hardships. We all must assume some responsibility. It is a group karmic affair.

The Space Masters suggest that many may be surprised to find that even the members of mystery schools and advanced Spiritual practitioners cling to prejudices and uninspected biases. They like Earth's leadership, expect others to behave and think exactly as themselves, and attempt to persuade or institute rules to create conformity. If we are realistic, we know people have incarnated to planet Earth from different root races with different evolutionary curves, with different physiological and Spiritual vibrations, possessing different karmic backgrounds. (There are seven different root races incarnated on a given planet at any one time. A root race does not reflect the color of a people's skin, but the advancement of their evolution.) So, Earth's human inhabitants inherently bring lessons and challenges to their incarnation that are uniquely personal. But because of the rampant prejudices, people are forced to live their lives in conformity with societal norms that suppress individual exploration and development. This type of subjective thinking and attitude by both Spiritual and societal leaders is detrimental to each individual's progression and to humanity's overall evolution.

A good analogy of this concept is found when we discover the food that is good for one person may chemically destroy the constitution of another. Each of us has a different constitution. Things aren't so black and white. One individual's understanding should not be forced down the throat of another, no matter how ideal it might appear!

We must admit, if we can't overcome the prejudices we harbor in our current world with such minor differences in color, form, and thought, how can we possibly expect to intermingle peacefully with the myriad of forms and divergent thoughts that interstellar civilizations present? How do we sit at the conference table with insectoid races, octopoid forms, variform beings of the wildest imagination? Are Shiva's four arms merely fantasy—a wild Spiritual depiction? Ganesh's trunk far-fetched? Ibis's beak, the imagination of some Egyptian Daliesque artist? For many, they are but cartoonish fantasies, but we may be approaching the time where we must evolve, mature our consciousness to respect each sentient being, no matter the form, as a sacred expression of the Divine. If we are unable to do so, we may encounter a complete social breakdown.

Although the Masters generally avoid political commentary, there are times they express their concern. Though Reverend Rinehart, Master Clarion, notes that we evolve as a race when there is an observance of a delicate balance where all individual freedoms are equally respected. If we create social structures where rigid social order outweighs the interests of the individual, we have created confusion, destroying individual rights and most certainly the rights of minority groups.

To find the ideal form of governance, all elements of society must have a legitimate voice. It's a constant process of balancing. Allowing political, economic, or military factions, and even the majority, to totally control large segments of society creates a loss of freedom, bringing about the onset of insanity, evil, and widespread suffering. If we are honest in our observation of our current world, we see elite factions controlling the fabric of our society. The outcome leads to pervasive imbalance and hardship.

The Space Masters allude to the notion that it is time to release old models if we are to progress. Even the attempt to create a melding of all the traditional religions as a Spiritual solution is not the answer. Instead, we might access new visions where we investigate the highest values and insights from the greatest minds in the universe. To accomplish this, we must open our hearts and minds to intelligences from beyond our immediate environment and resist meddling with insignificant shifts. In other words, contemplate a quantum shift and listen to the cosmic signals issuing from our higher intelligence and from far-advanced interstellar intelligences. Uprooting and raising our consciousness in this way can assist us in the upliftment of the social order, from the ignorant to the most advanced, with a message and vision of Cosmic Light. This has the potential to create a tipping point, to transform the culture into a better, happier, more evolved world. The Space Masters reinforce this belief and suggest it is our task to work ceaselessly in establishing peace and harmony, but it should not be enforced at the deprivation of any individual's freedom of Spiritual and intellectual thought.

Master Clarion warns that with all the present confusion, lack of moral and intelligent direction existing in our world, the Masters are grappling with the possibility of shifting their stance of thousands of years, facing the possibility of accepting the consequences of over-stepping into Earth's karmic stream. Do they make more and more appearances to those who can perceive their Spirit? They allude to actively questioning, contemplating their options more than ever before.

The Space Masters implore us to not delay but to take immediate action. It is time to direct our destiny, employing visionary action gleaned from experiences taken from all bodies of awareness: our mental body, our astral, emotional, Spiritual, vibrational, and monadic bodies of consciousness. Clarion encourages us to seek out new cosmic patterns for solutions, reaching beyond past earthly models and ruts. He suggests that through meditation and the use of our vehicles of awareness, we can reach into interstellar rainbows, galactic mandalas, the Horsehead Nebula, and the vast abstract configurations throughout interstellar space for answers. The Masters agree that now is the time for us to leap into the great galactic sea of God. They assure us that here, amongst the supernovas, in the presence of cosmic energies, we will find our answers!

The Masters might ask, *Do we want to elevate our game? Step up and evolve into a new species? What might that look like?* Eventually, each soul will evolve, rising to inhabit planets and space beyond our solar system. Our growth is inevitable, opening infinite possibilities of higher forms of cosmic consciousness.

So, the question is, are we willing to release our clinging to obsolete patterns of belief, thought, and action? Are we willing to entertain the possibility we are not alone in the universe? Are we willing to accept we may someday join a wider cosmic community of beings who have evolved to a higher consciousness?

ELEVEN

FINDING UNITY WITH ALL OF HUMANITY

O VER THE YEARS, THE ASCENDED MASTERS HAVE APPEALED TO their chelas and humanity to: *Ceaselessly Strive to Understand Our Unity With All Of Humanity*. It has become nearly a mantra for personal growth. The Spiritual Lineage of Babaji, to Sri Yukteshwar, to Yogananda lights up in neon as proponents of this teaching. This reasoning is easy to follow as our unity with humanity is established through LOVE, through COMPASSION, through TOLERANCE, and especially through SERVICE—all aspects of reaching out to deepen the bond with our human family. So why adhere to this mantra? Many reasons, we suspect, but the first that comes to mind is when we reach out to feel the needs and longings of others, we hit the pause button on our self-absorption. We transcend our judgements and move beyond pettiness. We refrain from asking, *"Are they worthy? What have they done for me? Are they Spiritually deserving?"* With active empathy, we feel someone's sorrow, we feel the deep despair of another, and in this moment of communion, we coexist with all the sorrows and pains of humanity.

Through our intention to find unity, we become neutral and simply act to fill the needs of another, abandoning the machinations of the mind and act straight from Love. In so doing, our own neediness falls by the wayside and we open to the compassionate heart. There is a unifying of Spirit, an expansion beyond the ego. In attuning to the mantra, we are more prone to hear the call of another. At that moment, there are but two choices: ignore it or take an action, doing our best to face, empathize, and relieve another's suffering.

When our listening is turned toward our heart, we begin to act from selfless Love. We start to hear the call of Divinity within, a listening that edges us towards obedience to Divine Love and Divine Law. With the deepening of our listening, we begin to instinctively attune to another's need, no matter how faint the signal. In choosing not to listen or neglecting to act, are we not in some way diminished, separated from the source of true joy?

In Spiritual circles, we hear we are all one, but how often do we, in fact, act as though it is true? How often do we experience this unity after meditation, after our yoga session, or after chanting? Or when we are engrossed in the world, where our emotions and minds run us ragged?

It is the Masters' sense when we engage in serving those with whom we have strong karmic links, or even those with whom we feel somewhat indifferent, that we open ourselves to an expansive sense of unity where the Golden Rule and Divine Principle live. (Divine Principle: where all life is respected and considered sacred with an understanding that all life issues forth from the one creative source of God.)

Many on the Spiritual path simply turn to meditation, saying all suffering is but illusion, finding meditation to be the solution for life's dilemmas. But practicing meditation is no excuse for neglecting those in need. We've heard the Masters refer to incidents involving their chelas. In some instances, the Master felt compelled to attend to the needs of their chela's friend when their chela neglected to respond to their friend's urgent call. It is a concern to the Masters when a chela finds their Spiritual practice more important than the needs of a friend.

Service unencumbered by self-consciousness comes from God. It is a listening to God's voice within and represents an opportunity to expand our awareness on the path of Karma Yoga—a sure-fire way to experience our *"Unity With All Of Humanity"* while deepening our communion with God.

If we listen to the signals in our lives, we will find there is no lack of opportunities to reach out to support others. It can be as simple as baking a cake, bending over to assist someone with spilled groceries, or as demanding as being in service at the end of a friend or loved one's life. On a more social level, we can advocate for human rights, support local community organizations, or assist those who are aged or suffering. Look anywhere and you will find there is much to do. You can march, organize, advocate for the rights of the oppressed, the rights to religious freedom, the rights of the disabled, the rights of the poor, the rights guaranteed by the Bill of Rights, and on and on. The question is, where do you want to put your love and energy? Where do you think you can make the most impactful contribution?

Karma Yoga is a path of service engaging action that creates a practical end, one which contributes to the whole. Clearly stated, a selfless action wherever and whenever possible. Karma Yoga engages the body, the mind, the emotions, and the Spirit. It utilizes the hands, the feet, the eyes, and our prayers and blessings.

Students who diligently serve in this world prepare themselves for work in the Karmic Temples of the Spirit World. In these Karmic Temples, all deeds, events, and actions of nations are recorded. Within, karma is meted out, not vindictively as a form of punishment, but as a form of reestablishing balance, learning, and forwarding personal and group evolution. Service, like no other activity, burns negative karma while generating positive karma.

The following are testimonial stories about people drawn to serve, people magnetized towards the path of Karma Yoga. You may find some acts unfold in places you would not expect, along with unexpected results. Reverend Rhinehart dedicated his life to service, both in orthodox and unconventional ways, opening our imagination to new ways of serving. Along the path of service, we may find experiences of uproarious glee and uncontrollable anguish, all elements of *"Understanding Our Unity With All Of Humanity."*

The next three chapters include stories inspired by the Masters' teachings.

TWELVE

UNITY THROUGH COMMUNITY SERVICE

To ILLUSTRATE THE IMPORTANCE OF BUILDING UNITY THROUGH Community, we will begin with a testimony from a close woman friend of Reverend Rhinehart's:

"After Reverend Rhinehart left Walla Walla State Penitentiary, his heart yearned for ways to improve prison life. The inmates suffered appalling conditions, despair, and loneliness, he felt empathetic to their plight. So, our Church decided to explore outreach ideas in an attempt to alleviate some of their pain. We protested on site regarding the inhumane conditions, put together a pen-pal program, and created an evening of entertainment for the inmates, so they might have occasion for a little fun.

"One day, a group of us took a bus from Seattle up to the Penitentiary to perform. I sang, my good friend did the Hula in a grass skirt, and our Church choir sang a medley of songs. During the program we were instructed to stay backstage until our performance time arrived, so disappointingly, I didn't get to see the other performances. In accepting Reverend Rhinehart's request to sing a solo, I really had no idea of what to expect, but if I'm honest, I wasn't feeling my usual comfort zone before I sang. I took the stage dressed in a gorgeous red-sequined gown. As I walked onto the stage, a wild reception broke out like you might imagine a girl received performing for the troops with Bob Hope overseas! Cheers and yells bounced through the rows and rows of prisoners. Then I sang, *Here You Come Again*, by Dolly Parton. I received a nice ovation, which left me feeling quite good.

"Next up came our choir, an all-woman chorus, dressed in pure white choir gowns with colorful leis slung around our necks, featuring Reverend Rhinehart singing. The choir looked similar to a typical choir in the Catholic tradition on any given Sunday, projecting a pure, Spiritual, uplifting vibration. They entertained the prisoners with mostly inspirational religious songs and pop songs of the day. Songs like: *Amazing Grace, Don't Stop Thinking About Tomorrow*, and songs from the then-popular musical, *Hair*.

"A humble, reverent vibration filled the prison audience as our choir sang some of the old gospels. The choir continued singing popular pop songs, then just before singing the finale, the entire choir dropped their white robes to the floor, revealing hot skimpy bikinis to one of the tunes in *Hair!* Well, the prisoners went hog-wild, hooting and carrying on to no end.

"At the conclusion, all the choir members tossed their leis out into the audience in the *Aloha Spirit*, shouting out, *'Do you want to get lei-ed?'* Again, uproarious laughter! The choir had great fun that day, catching the inmates off guard. For the prisoners, they enjoyed a fleeting escape; for us, loads of preparation and logistics, but well worth our efforts.

"I remember the bus ride home from our program, Keith made a point to sit next to me. He said how appreciative he felt of my performing and held out his hands displaying an array of beautiful masculine rings on each of his fingers.

"He said, *'Pick any one you want!'* I chose the most feminine ring. He exclaimed, *'I knew you would pick that one!'*

"I said, *'Well, no, you didn't, you influenced my choice.'* We had a good laugh and reminisced about our performances."

Here is a testimony from a couple of members of the San Francisco Branch of the Church, illustrating that giving isn't always received in the manner you might expect:

"Today is Thanksgiving Day! We have all cooked turkeys and prepared bag lunches for the homeless on the streets of San Francisco.

There is an air of excitement within our group as we hit the streets. One of the ministers in our group is new to the area and delighted to be serving the needy on this day of giving. A genuine smile beams across his face as he approaches his first recipient, a haggard man in a seedy back alley of the Tenderloin.

'Happy Thanksgiving!' our minister says, gleefully reaching out to hand the man a bag lunch.

"The man rushes him screaming in his face, *'Get out of here you M F'er—F_ _ K YOU!'* The minister is dumbfounded and starts back-peddling as fast as he can. He finally turns and runs for his safety.

"A few minutes later in the same district my wife and I approached a downtrodden couple engaged in idle conversation leaning up against the parapet wall at the Old Mint.

"We exclaimed, *'Happy Thanksgiving,'* and handed them each a bag lunch. An appreciative smile spread across the woman's face. The man reached into his bag pulling out the bottle of sparkling soda and without provocation hurled it helter-skelter at his partner who ducked in-a-nick-of-time as the bottle whizzed past her head shattering to smithereens against the parapet wall.

"The mental and emotional pain existing on our streets is rarely confronted until an up-close encounter brings the situation into focus. There are lives in deep, unrelenting despair in the heart of our cities going mostly unnoticed. Sorrow fills me as I face the reality of their suffering."

The following testimony comes from a woman who participated in the Seattle congregation:

"This day, a group of women who decided to participate in the pen-pal program at Walla Walla took a bus trip to the penitentiary. The idea encouraged the prisoners to make a connection with the outside world, which would provide an outlet to express pent-up emotions they may be experiencing.

"Once on the prison grounds, each of us got invited to accompany a prisoner back to his cell so we might develop better rapport and understand what our pen-pal might be feeling. I followed my inmate through the prison chambers to his cell, sitting next to him on his bed. Soon his life story unwound, stories of his family, his work, and feelings about prison life.

"Then he stopped and looked at me and said, *'Why would you ever want to write to a person like me?'*

"There was such a heaviness and deep despair in his question it gave me pause. His oppressiveness and strong hate pierced right through me. At that moment, volumes of evil and anger came oozing out from the prison walls. Right then, I felt ready to get the heck out of there! Later, we corresponded, writing one letter each, but I have to say, I never felt comfortable writing and didn't really experience the pen-pal program working. I'm not sure what others experienced."

Here is an experience from a choir member of the San Francisco Branch:

"We assembled a modest choir in our Church in San Francisco, practicing before Wednesday night Healing Services to buildup group camaraderie, improve our abilities, and just have fun. Eventually, we improved to the point where we felt able to go out into the community if the venue was small and unimposing. We enjoyed visiting rest homes and convalescent homes where we were well received by owners who felt grateful to have us entertain their patients.

"One day during an engagement at a convalescent home on Pine Street, a talented member of the choir hit a pure high note, triggering the release of an elderly gentleman's emotions. He began to cry tears of unabashed Joy, he kept crying and crying and crying, unmasking deep pure emotions. I never saw anything quite like it. He really moved me, opening me to the beauty of not fearing the display of genuine emotional innocence. I'll never forget him—and to think I nearly refused to join the choir for lack of talent."

A member of the Mother Church in Seattle makes this statement:

"A group of us from the Seattle Church loaded onto a bus to go to Walla Walla State Penitentiary to protest the prison's abject conditions. We learned of the inhuman conditions as a result of Reverend Rhinehart's imprisonment on false, trumped-up charges, which were subsequently expunged from the record. We determined to stage protests to instigate changes.

"About an hour into our two-hour bus trip, someone shouted, *'What is that on the horizon?'* Everyone turned to look, but we saw nothing. Then out of nowhere, an enormous silver saucer-shaped ship swooped down, filling the entire window, it must have been three hundred feet long! The ship rode along following the bus for maybe thirty seconds. Wow! Thrilling! Later, a friend spoke with Reverend Rhinehart regarding the incident, and he confirmed through his mediumship the UFO we saw was indeed genuine."

Here is an interesting testimony from a member who attended a séance in the nineties.

"I remember a telephone hookup séance in the nineties where St. Germaine entranced Reverend Rhinehart. At one point during the séance, St. Germaine began waxing about *'Our Judy,'* referring to Judy Bari, the outspoken principal leader of the Earth First movement. At the time, I felt somewhat surprised as Judy and the Earth First organization aroused a plethora of controversial sentiments. St.

Germaine spoke to her courage employing non-violent means by chaining herself to Caterpillar tractors in an attempt to prevent corporations from destroying the natural heritage of our wilderness. She was a champion of focusing national attention on the plight of the old-growth virgin redwood forests in Mendocino County, California, where the old-growth trees had been in existence for one thousand to two thousand years. She spearheaded efforts to preserve these majestic giants, blocking logging on public land near Cahto Peak in Mendocino County.

"An inspiring speaker, Judy attracted and organized thousands of people to protest the ongoing environmental exploitation in Northern California. Attentive to not only environmental justice, Judy worked tirelessly for social justice in the areas of racism, sexism, abortion rights, and the unnecessary destruction of ecosystems. She gave the Earth First movement a feminist spin, where previously males dominated the movement.

"To the outrage of the logging industry, Judy created an alliance between the timber workers and the environmentalists, demanding that Louisiana-Pacific stop over-cutting its lands at an unsustainable rate. Judy never said no to logging, she lobbied for sustainable logging, demonstrating to the timber workers that their livelihoods were at stake if they didn't cease logging at the rate Louisiana-Pacific planned. These efforts, her demand for the seizure of corporate property through eminent domain, her campaigning for Redwood Summer, a plan to save the redwood forests, made her a target of corporate executives. Eventually, her car was rammed in the rear by a logging truck, totaling the car. Shortly thereafter, she began receiving death threats, and finally in Oakland, CA a bomb exploded under the driver's seat of her Honda, fracturing her pelvis, nearly killing her. The police determined her to be the only suspect, claiming she was an eco-terrorist carrying terrorist bombs. No evidence could be found linking Judy to the bomb. Never completely healed, often in pain, she continued working for social justice for the remainder of her life."

The Masters feel a close affinity to people like Judy who physically and passionately engage in life to the fullest, making many sacrifices fighting and advocating for social justice. We suspect Judy had no awareness of the Masters' admiration. With this stated, we do not know the Masters' overall position on the broad-ranging aspects of the Environmental Movement or their sentiments regarding its broad implications. We do know, however, that St. Germaine's interest and support of Judy dominated that particular séance described above.

This next incident is the testimony of a Church leader who was close to Reverend Rhinehart:

"No matter what city in which Reverend Rhinehart found himself, come Christmas Eve, he made it a tradition to ask someone to fetch about thirty bottles of wine from the liquor store. When the person returned, Reverend Rhinehart and others hopped in the car, and they trolled the wino districts passing out bottles of spirits.

"Reverend Rhinehart thought these hapless souls were going to partake one-way-or-the-other, so why not give them a little happiness which they rarely experienced on Christmas Eve or Thanksgiving?

On one particular Christmas Eve in Seattle, after Reverend Rhinehart handed a homeless man a bottle of wine, a glint dashed deep in the man's eyes, spreading a joyous, prankster grin across his weathered face, he exclaimed, *'Oh my God! You must be Jesus, I was just praying for a bottle of wine!'*"

109

THIRTEEN

UNITY THROUGH CHURCH SERVICE

R EVEREND RINEHART'S COMMITMENT TO STAY CONNECTED AND
serve the members of his congregation is demonstrated by a
testimony from a young woman Church member living overseas:

"I lived in Tokyo, Japan, singing in a private club for a few years in
the seventies. On a trip back to Honolulu, while passing through the
Honolulu Airport, I got stopped by a Customs Agent inquiring if I
had anything to declare—did my baggage contain any items I recently
purchased?

"I said, *'No, everything in my suitcases I brought with me from the
States.'* Despite my claim, they rifled through my belongings anyway.

"I became outraged. *'What right do you have to go through my
private belongings? I told you everything in my suitcases I brought with
me, I have no new items!'*

"They never answered, holding me up for almost five hours. After
manhandling my belongings, a female agent invasively frisked my
entire body; she didn't enter my body, but I certainly felt violated. In
the end, they confiscated all my jewelry and clothes.

"When I got home, I explained the situation to the local Spiritual
leader in Honolulu as to what happened. He said he'd discuss the
matter with Keith.

"Keith called me sometime later, exclaiming, *'Why this is completely unfair. If you want, I will help you write a letter to the Customs Office here in Honolulu, so you can get your belongings returned.'*

"And that is exactly what he did. In time, I retrieved all my belongings, but it took months. I was young and naïve when this happened. They basically took all the jewelry I owned at the time and a good share of my clothes.

"The event really shook me up, so when Keith offered to assist, I felt grateful.

"The Honolulu Customs Agents were notorious for being aggressive and mean, taking advantage of travelers like me. Later, Keith helped me stage a protest at the airport, making a statement to demonstrate how Customs was violating and abusing innocent people and ignoring people's legitimate rights. Taking action felt good!"

Within the walls of the Mother Church, a Board Member experienced a truly remarkable phenomenon while fulfilling her duties:

"I served as Secretary of the Board of Directors of the Church. As Secretary, I kept the keys to the Parsonage Office in the Anchorage Branch of the Church. The office was kept locked at all times when not in use. I possessed the only key. In the office, we stored one hundred Spiritual Psychic Art posters of Master Jesus and Master Count Saint Germaine. The posters stood on end on the floor of the office.

"Upon entering the office one morning, to my surprise, I observed oils weeping from the eyes of Jesus and St. Germaine on the posters. The oils bled from the eyes and then leaked to the bottom of each of the one hundred posters. After scrutiny, it became clear the liquid oils didn't bleed through one poster to another—the oils bled from each of the Master's eyes in the poster. This phenomenon was subsequently witnessed by Reverend Rhinehart and the co-Spiritual leader of the Anchorage Branch, Reverend Alvis Dunn, both of whom didn't possess keys to the office during the time of the weeping of the oils.

"After this discovery, Master Saint Germaine entranced Reverend Rhinehart, communicating that the Ascended Masters brought through the sacred oils phenomena in gratitude for the many sacrifices chelas of the Church made toward the fulfillment of God's plan on Earth. The only way I can explain this event is to say that a miracle occurred, delivered by the Ascended Masters."

The following is one woman's experience of serving in the Parsonage of the Mother Church in Seattle:

"Reverend Rhinehart's home, the Parsonage, was the gathering place for students coming to the Mother Church to serve the Masters and the Church. We'd work during the day and in the evenings, casually gather in the Parsonage's living room for sessions with Reverend Rhinehart. The evenings were fun, filled with laughter, cola, and ham sandwiches, but no time with the Reverend was without purpose and education; challenges always presented themselves. Reverend Rhinehart permeated the space with a feeling of parental care, both for the students and the Church, ensuring we would do good in the world and the Church would be properly cared for, protecting its stature into perpetuity. During these sessions we were encouraged to think for ourselves, think of the world as our family, and to tolerate the differences in our immediate group as our group represented the diversity of the world. In Reverend Rhinehart's eyes every human being deserved to be treated with the grace and the mercy of God. He spoke openly, sharing his visions and asking about ours. He included everyone in the circle, there was no hiding out, the shy and timid were coaxed to share as much as the naturally expressive extraverts.

"My husband was a macho, full-blooded Chinese man whose life experience more than substantiated the promise of equality, for which our country stood, was hollow. The blatant prejudice he experienced damaged his self-esteem. The evening sessions were healing, Reverend Rhinehart deliberately drew my husband close, sharing his compassionate, gentle love, genuinely inquiring as to what he thought about certain issues, nurturing him, calling him forward, such love poured out, my husband began to shed the feeling of prejudice he experienced directed by maître d's, loss of work, and being seen as the enemy from WWII. My husband felt a warmth in the Parsonage from Reverend Rhinehart. He found he couldn't hide his deep shame from the Master—little by little, it melted away, and what was once a liability blossomed into strong self-esteem.

"On one occasion, days after we were married by Reverend Rhinehart, we stayed at the Parsonage in an upper bedroom looking out over Lake Washington—just beautiful! The room we stayed in presented ten-foot walls of floor-to-ceiling glass; the stars showered the room all night, very memorable! What a wonderful wedding gift! Our Parsonage stay felt so unique, capturing the vibration of the Masters in a special way. Each room was painted a different color, representing the sacred color rays used in healing and Spiritual work. Ascending the staircase to the upper rooms, each carpeted stair changed color as one ascended the stairs, it was as though one was rising up through the colors of the chakras, moving towards the crown chakra. The Parsonage held so many wonderful experiences, nights with the living room floor covered from wall-to-wall with sleeping bags of people from all walks of life, nights where those with psychic-sight glimpsed the Masters walking through the rooms bringing in sacred objects, moving from one room to another, nights where Reverend Rhinehart stayed up all night entranced by Count Saint Germaine practicing piano pieces from the Ascension Symphony for the next day's service (Reverend Rhinehart had no piano training), nights where youth were tasked with cleaning the chandelier's crystal glass droplets, as a training to attend to details, the chandelier was a marvelous fixture reminiscent of the chandeliers of the courts of Versailles. So a stay at the Parsonage always proved to be a memorable experience, one of learning, service, and becoming more familiar with our unity with all of humanity.

"The Parsonage housed museum-quality pieces of art Reverend Rhinehart received on world tours, along with objects he collected and personally loved. One piece I remember was a two-and-a-half-foot by two-foot wooden carved temple, all carved from a single piece of wood; no matter how hard you looked, you couldn't find a seam, a stunning piece of work! If someone was attracted to a certain object, Reverend Rhinehart may come up to you asking if you like it. If you perchance said *'Yes,'* he would often give it to you right on the spot. Reverend Rhinehart was renowned for his generosity."

Although the Mother Church was in Seattle, when Reverend Rhinehart was on tour, Church services and séances could take place anywhere in the world. The following testimony is from a chela who experienced a séance on one of Reverend Rhinehart's world tours.

"In Johannesburg, South Africa, Reverend Rhinehart sat in a makeshift cabinet in Louis Rothchild's estate's living room, preparing for a séance. Seated were a number of Mr. Rothchild's circle, mostly the white, wealthy nobility of Johannesburg. To begin the séance, Spirit rattled the trumpet from within the cabinet, lifting it into the air then pronounced through the collapsible metal cone the séance would not begin until every servant in the household was ushered into the séance room and seated. Finally, when all the black servants were settled into their seats, the trumpet clanked and rattled, flying over the heads of the white folks only to finally come to hover over the head of a black servant. Then Spirit proceeded to speak through the trumpet in fluent Zulu, which only the black folks understood. The trumpet went from servant to servant, delivering each a message, leaving most swaying in their chairs, sobbing in tears. Once Spirit finished serving every black person, Spirit served the white sitters."

FOURTEEN

UNITY THROUGH HEALING SERVICE

T
HIS IS STEVE YOUNG'S TESTIMONY REGARDING A REQUEST
by St. Germaine. It involves directing healing under unusual
circumstances:

"One afternoon in 1978 at Reverend Rhinehart's Ilikai apartment
in Honolulu, Hawaii, Count St. Germaine entranced Reverend
Rhinehart.

Once entranced, the Count turned to me and asked if Wes and I
would fly to Atlanta to give hands-on healing to Larry Flynt (founder
and creator of *Hustler Magazine*), along with a message from the
Masters. Mr. Flynt and his attorney Gene Reeves had been shot in an
assassination attempt outside the Lawrenceville, Georgia Courthouse,
where Mr. Flynt was in the act of defending his First Amendment
Rights against charges of distributing obscene materials.

"When we arrived at Emory Hospital in Atlanta, we discovered
a large contingency of police surrounding the hospital to insure Mr.
Flynt's personal safety. I asked a uniformed police captain stationed
nearby if we could be allowed to see Mr. Larry Flynt. He inquired as
to our purpose. I told him we came to administer hands-on healing.
He responded, saying that Althea, Mr. Flynt's wife, would have to
approve, then he left. In minutes, he returned, indicating Mrs. Flynt
had said, *'Yes, it would be fine for just myself to see Mr. Flynt.'*

"We waited quite some time for the Critical Care Unit to arrange his body in an upright position so we could better communicate. His abdominal region was wrapped like a mummy as his gruesome wounds needed protecting. The attack inflicted by a high-powered rifle, blasted a gaping hole, leaving him doubled over in excruciating pain, holding in his guts with his bare hands until the ambulance arrived.

"When I entered, Mr. Flynt lay propped up in an inclined position, exhibiting more tubes running in and out of his body than I could count. He looked washed out, weak, like he'd been clobbered by an unrelenting opponent. If death wasn't banging on his door, clearly it was staying close by. The drugs kept him mostly pain-free, but I could see they affected his ability to be present. Wanting to connect, I looked softly into his dulled eyes, grabbing a hold of his gaze and said, *'The Ascended Masters sent us to give you a healing and impart their love and blessings. They urge you not to give up your will to live.'* I then directed Spiritual Healing from the Ascended Masters.

"Afterward, I related, *'The Masters are very pleased with your lifelong battle of fighting to keep our First Amendment Rights alive and using your magazines to expose and defeat rampant governmental and congressional corruption. They say freedom relies on people like you to protect our Constitutional Rights. They want you to live!'*

"Through a drugged and vacant demeanor, he nodded in agreement.

" *'Who shot you?'* I inquired.

" *'I know—but I'm not prepared to speak out.'*

"Soon, he became too weak to continue, and just like that, our session ended. I never saw Mr. Flynt again. One week later, I got an unexpected letter from his wife, Althea, thanking me for my visit and healing. Shortly, thereafter, he felt strong enough to be released from the Hospital, but he remained paralyzed from the waist down, wheelchair-ridden for the rest of his life. He lived a productive life though, continuing to exercise his First Amendment Rights, becoming number one on the list of the most powerful people in porn."

We might note that the First Amendment is crucial in guaranteeing our basic freedoms. Without the Freedom of Speech and Expression, Freedom of Religion, Freedom to Assemble, and the Freedom to Petition, we are reduced to mere chattel, subject to the whims, the denigration, and the mercy of the State. Freedom of Speech represents the battleground of ideas and the marketplace for creating new thought; therefore, the Masters want it protected.

Some may struggle with the Masters' stance regarding the freedoms surrounding our sexual lives, but the Masters have said on many occasions, we in the West are overly prudish and dogmatic around sexual mores. They indicate that without porn and prostitution—rapes, violent abuse, and murder would significantly rise, as many European countries have proven, and psychologists here willingly admit.

Porn and prostitution provide the means of relieving pent-up stress and unmet desires, so we might suggest they are a necessary evil. The torment and suffering experienced by the unwanted and undesirable people living on the fringes of our society are never fully appreciated nor even contemplated by those who are desirable, but the needs of the fringe should be alleviated within the fabric of society and viewed in the same context as those able to afford the more acceptable forms of sexual freedom.

With this said, our commentary, and certainly the lessons from the Masters, in no way condone any form of sexual abuse, sexual force, pedophilia, satanic ritual abuse, or any type of perverse activity unwelcomed by a sexual partner. Our world is inundated with unwelcome sexual advances and forced participation in sexual acts and sexual slavery. No one professing Divine Principle excuses this activity as harmless, and all who engage in any manner of such activity should be prosecuted to the full extent of the law.

My testimony as the husband of a member of the Church.

"I must say my wife would never discuss these stories with anyone. Her demeanor was always modest, unassuming, and highly private, which some might call to a fault. To focus attention on herself just wasn't her way. Unfortunately, she passed into Spirit some time ago. Her life's work moved me so that I am impressed to share her gifts to relate the successful work the Masters accomplished through her psychic and Spiritual Healing abilities.

"After becoming members of the Church, maybe a year into our membership, the Church leadership invited us to direct Spiritual healing energies during Wednesday Evening Healing Services.

"We felt extremely honored to work as conduits directing the Masters' Spiritual Healing energies to those who came in search of healing and relief. We continued our healing activities throughout our membership and thoroughly enjoyed our time working as Spiritual Healers over the years.

"One night, a woman visited the Church who previously sat in my wife's healing chair. Before my wife began directing healing, the woman indicated she had been diagnosed with cervical cancer through MRI technology. She said that shortly after having sat in my wife's healing chair, her doctor recommended she get further imaging to determine the stage of the cancer. When she received the results of the MRI, the doctor revealed the testing showed her to be completely tumor-free. The woman said the doctor acted highly surprised at the results, having no explanation as to how the tumors suddenly disappeared. The lady declared the only possible explanation was the healing session she did with my wife, where my wife directed Spiritual Healing energies, during the Wednesday Night Spiritual Healing Service."

"Many other experiences continued to evolve around my wife's healing abilities, of which I will elaborate but a few. One entailed an experience with her brother. At some point, her brother began experiencing tiredness accompanied by severe pain in his liver. When he saw the doctor, the doctor indicated he contracted Hepatitis B, announcing the disease to be incurable. To mitigate the situation, the doctor stated her brother would need to be on drugs the rest of his life. The doctor even said his wife and son should receive shots as the disease could be contagious.

"Once my wife discovered the situation, she began a hands-on healing routine during the weekends when she traveled by bus from Oakland to Daly City for several months, directing Spiritual Healing. During this time, her brother's doctor requested a blood test to examine the current state of his blood composition. To the doctor's amazement, the test revealed no evidence of Hepatitis B. Her brother has been free of Hepatitis B ever since.

"During my wife's last weeks alive, she traveled to Sutter Hospital in Sacramento for surgical implantation of draining ports in her pleural cavity to alleviate her difficult breathing caused by breast cancer. At this time, she suffered from on-and-off severe pain and had been confined to a wheelchair.

"One evening during my wife's stay in the hospital, a woman patient arrived, occupying the extra bed in her room. The woman also suffered from cancer, exhibiting an unpleasant, foul mood. During the evening, she trashed the bathroom. When the nurses inquired as to what happened, the woman blamed my wife. My wife said nothing, intuiting that likely the nurses understood the situation. As the evening moved into early morning, the woman began screaming out in pain, suffering unmercifully, carrying on in extreme distress.

"At this, my wife focused what healing energies she possessed on the woman, reaching out to the Masters for assistance. Within minutes, the woman stopped screaming, and a peace came over her for the remainder of the early morning. In the morning, she left the room and my wife never saw her again.

"True to form, my wife only related the story to me. She passed in less than two weeks after this incident. I felt so proud of her as she demonstrated that no matter the circumstances, we can always serve if we have the heart!"

This is an account of my attempt to heal my wife during her last days.

"When my wife received the diagnosis of stage-four cancer, we never imagined our journey or what the demands would be to try to beat the odds. The winding course, dead ends, and harrowing events are too numerous to recount, but I would like to relate one incident that speaks to our love and how we served each other over our thirty-five years of marriage.

"After nine months of chemo, the doctor announced my wife to be in full remission. We were elated! Shortly thereafter, to our dismay, the cancer returned. We fully believed in her healing and continued to pursue every avenue we felt offered merit—traveling to Mexico to a cancer clinic, juice cleanses, immuno-therapies, vitamin C infusions, Rife Therapy, Rick Simpson Oil, and on and on. Slowly, the cancer moved from her breast to her lymph nodes and into the pleural cavity of her lungs. Even so, we continued to believe in her eventual healing. But no matter our effort, her care continued to escalate to the point I needed an assistant to give myself a break from the day and night demands. There were times her pain became so severe; I was desperate to alleviate her agony. At these moments, I relied on the sacred white stones from the Masters, directing the Light to the area of pain. As I directed the Light, I chanted devotional songs, letting the inspiration take me where it may. Gratefully, within fifteen to twenty minutes, the pain always subsided or vanished.

"In time, it became necessary to drain my wife's lungs for her to breathe. At first, we took trips to a Sacramento clinic once a week, then twice a week, and finally every other day. Her breathing became so labored that even talking exhausted her; once the need reached every day, the trip to Sacramento proved too debilitating and impossible. Finally, I was able to convince the doctors to insert ports on both sides of her lungs, slipped in between the ribs. Now each day we drained both lungs into plastic drain kits. The procedure was delicate and demanding, but we could do it from home. Finally, to breathe, my wife required an electric oxygen concentrator unit operating 24/7.

"One stormy winter morning after completing the draining of her right lung, I turned to move to the left lung when I heard a CLICK! *'Oh my God, NO, NO, NO, God!'* I realized the electricity just went off due to the storm! I leapt up scrambling to the portable oxygen tanks across the room to ensure my wife could continue breathing. The gauge read empty! I grabbed the second tank. It too read empty. Somehow, I needed to get to our generator in time so my wife could keep breathing. It was positioned a couple hundred feet down a set of stairs outside of the house, but first the circuit breakers needed to be switched over from PG&E to our generator. I charged down the hall to the circuit breakers and flipped the switches, then raced outside to the generator, fearing all the while she would expire any moment. When I got to the driveway, over a foot of snow had dropped in the night, so I rushed carefully, trying not to slip, or that would be it. Finally, I got to the generator.

"I swung open the top lid and hit the start button. Reh-reh-reh, the engine moaned, but wouldn't start. Again, I hit the start button, reh-reh-reh, the engine wouldn't kick in. In desperation, I screamed to God, "Help me, I beg of you, please help me!" Reh-reh-reh the engine continued to moan; ten times I tried, frantically screaming my brains out. Finally, the engine kicked over and began to roar.

Emotionally blown, I dashed back up the stairs, sure I would find my beloved dead upon my arrival. Once in the bedroom I lunged toward her bedside, my friend shouted, *'She's still breathing! She's alive!'* I collapsed in disbelief and a heap of tears, completely spent. Relieved for the moment, I felt deep in my bones some kind of karmic test just transpired so my wife might live another day."

No one knows what will be demanded when we step into service, or where it may take us. The challenges and tests that must be met, or how we may give more than we ever imagined possible. It is here that we experience our highest nature. Nothing is more joyous or rewarding than to know we rose to meet the crisis of another. Nothing gives more pleasure and contentment.

The Masters suggest that we do good for the sole reason that we experience pleasure in doing good. Not to choose to do good because we expect some future reward from a friend or God. Even doing good as an accomplishment is a trap. The real objective, if there is an objective, is simply basking in the pleasure of experiencing oneness with the Divine.

One of the primary reasons the Ascended Masters urge us to *"Seek Unity With All of Humanity"* is to break the fixation on ourselves, reaching out to engage in life experiences we would not otherwise encounter. The Masters contend we are physical creatures, so engaging our physicality recognizes that we incarnated into bodies for a reason: to live, to feel, to be both body and soul within a community of other bodies and souls. We may never know fully the depth of another's suffering or the height of their joy, nor they ours, but in our effort to reach out and understand each other, serve each other, we grow ever closer in oneness, ever closer to intermingling our stories such that when we step back into the world we are more tolerant, more loving, patient, and understanding of our sameness and able to appreciate our differences.

We might say we are tested for what we can DO for humanity rather than for who we might want to BE for humanity.

FIFTEEN

MEDIUMSHIP
ITS PURPOSES AND DANGERS

MEDIUMSHIP CAN BE A THORNY TOPIC. LOOK NO FURTHER
than the Victorian era of Sir Arthur Conan Doyle and Harry
Houdini, where its legitimacy became highly contested. Spiritualists
and magicians looked on as the icons publicly duked it out, eventually
splitting as friends over the acrimonious debate of whether real Spirits
were communicating through mediums. Unfortunately, though
certainly more accepted today, the debate rages on as Christians, New
Agers, occultists, magicians, and scientists keep the barbs flying.

In this chapter, we hope to shed light on mediumship so any
sincere sitter or seeker can discern the *genuine* from the *fraudulent*.
Many require no proof, but for those who may be on the fence and
want more evidence, we bring in facts drawn from the *Bible*, the
history of Spiritualism, and parapsychologists.

We all know there is no shortage of shysters and charlatans littered
throughout the ranks of psychics, many of whom worked the parlors
in Houdini's day, where he encountered numerous impostures on his
search to communicate with his beloved mother. The sidewalk, card
table tarot readers, the Madame Rubies ensconced behind the doily
curtains, and the local star-studded astrologers generally fall by the
wayside in the search for authentic mediumship. Not that some can't
be evidential and provide valuable information, but that is more rare.

Many entertainment magicians and conjurers often believe they are the greatest mentalists and sleight-of-hand artists, and those who defy the accepted laws of physics are simply deception artists like themselves. But even so, there is no reason to conclude because the field is fraught with con-artists and critics, there are no authentic mediums who are of God and good. We should never assume because there are quack doctors, there are no good doctors; or, opportunist attorneys, therefore no honest attorneys, so why is it that so many people determine all mediums are up to no good because some are fraudulent?

There are many different narratives we could explore. We could start with the propensities of the mind. We all know linear thinking is useful in negotiating the world, but when we become entrenched in linear thinking, we can take the position the rational mind holds the only valid instrument for unlocking the mysteries of physical reality. Persons who hold this perspective are often the executives running the corporate state, the media, the medical establishment, religions, the military, and the scientific and educational communities. It isn't uncommon for scientists to believe their minds grasp the world more profoundly than others, and for the priests to see their faith as superior. These people sincerely believe it is they who control the world. It doesn't occur to them that Spirit is in control.

Generally, those controlling the world have never experienced a moving Spiritual episode, do not believe in an afterlife, or the existence of a God. Influential persons holding negative opinions regarding Spirit can attempt to impact society through subtle forms of mocking the supernormal, often embedding derision and contempt in news stories, in ads, and in late-night shows, or other forms of public persuasion. Their commentary attempts to overtly and subliminally convince the population to disbelieve there exists a natural phenomenon behind supernormal events. We believe this is a factor contributing to why so many are hesitant to subscribe to the fact there is a genuine reality behind mediumship.

This kind of thinking runs deep, lying hidden behind the scenes. You may not realize, as I didn't, many municipalities around America have ordinances forbidding fortune telling. It is rarely enforced, but the threat is always present, as evidenced when Reverend Rhinehart was a teenager and arrested in Colorado for what was claimed as "practicing witchcraft." Massive banking fraud and war crimes continue to flourish under the blind eye of justice, but an innocent teenager gets arrested for giving Spirit messages! Criminal!

Over many years, genuine mediums have provided bona fide scientific proof beyond all reasonable doubt; however, there are still those who never budge. No amount of truth scientifically conclusive ever persuades them. Among the outspoken disbelievers are the Harry Houdinis, the James Randis (The Amazing Randi), the Carl Sagans, and the Penn & Tellers.

We feel many contemporary Christian interpreters have chosen to demonize mediums out of fear and ignorance based on the verse in Deuteronomy 18. Why? What is behind their interpretation? One reason that comes to mind is that scientifically tested mediumship challenges the *Bible's* authority as the only source of scripture and voice of God. The Church suddenly loses its position as the supreme authoritative power. This is an extremely threatening proposition for an organization that deems itself infallible and unchallengeable.

The *Bible* represents one of the main sources condemning mediumship. Paradoxically, there is an admission within both the *Bible* and the Church that Spirits do, in fact, communicate through mediums. Yet, they are considered dangerous and false prophets. In researching the *Bible,* we find references sprinkled throughout that support and contradict the legitimacy of mediumship.

The following are references that highlight the lion's share of the criticism coming from the Christian community regarding mediumship:

Deuteronomy 18:10-12 KJB

There shall not be found among you any one that maketh his son or his daughter pass through the fire, or that useth divination, or an observer of times, or an enchanter, or a witch,

Or a charmer, or a consulter with familiar spirits, or a wizard, or a necromancer.

For all that do these things are an abomination unto the LORD: and because of these abominations the LORD thy God doth drive them out from before thee."

One of the instrumental stories in the *Bible* that some interpreters claim supports this passage in Deuteronomy is the story of the "Witch of Endor" in 1 Samuel. Let's review this passage and see if we can understand its meaning and how it may or may not apply.

1 Samuel 28:3-25 KJB

Now Samuel was dead, and all Israel had lamented him, and buried him in Ramah, even in his own city. And Saul had put away those that had familiar spirits, and the wizards, out of the land.

And the Philistines gathered themselves together, and came and pitched in Shunem: and Saul gathered all Israel together and they pitched in Gilboa.

And when Saul saw the host of the Philistines, he was afraid, and his heart greatly trembled.

And when Saul enquired of the LORD, the LORD answered him not, neither by dreams, nor by Urim, nor by prophets.

Then said Saul unto his servants, Seek me a woman that hath a familiar spirit, that I may go to her, and enquire of her. And his servants said to him, Behold, there is a woman that hath a familiar spirit at Endor.

And Saul disguised himself, and put on other raiment, and he went, and two men with him, and they came to the woman by night: and he said, I pray thee, divine unto me by the familiar spirit, and bring me him up, whom I shall name unto thee.

And the woman said unto him, Behold, thou knowest what Saul hath done, how he hath cut off those that have familiar spirits, and the wizards, out of the land: wherefore then layest thou a snare for my life, to cause me to die?

And Saul sware to her by the LORD, saying, As the LORD liveth, there shall no punishment happen to thee for this thing.

Then said the woman, Whom shall I bring up unto thee? And he said bring me up Samuel.

And when the woman saw Samuel, she cried with a loud voice: and the woman spake to Saul, saying, Why hast thou deceived me? For thou art Saul.

And the King said unto her, Be not afraid: for what sawest thou? And the woman said unto Saul, I saw gods ascending out of the Earth. And he said unto her, What form is he of? And she said, An old man cometh up; and he is covered with a mantle. And Saul perceived it was Samuel, and he stooped with his face to the ground, and bowed himself.

And Samuel said to Saul, Why hast thou disquieted me to bring me up? And Saul answered, I am sore distressed; for the Philistines make war against me, and God is departed from me, and answereth me no more, neither by prophets, nor by dreams: therefore I have called thee, that thou mayest make known unto me what I shall do.

Then said Samuel, Wherefore then dost thou ask of me, seeing the LORD is departed from thee, and is become thine enemy?

And the LORD hath done to him, as he spake by me: for the LORD hath rent the kingdom out of thine hand, and given it to thy neighbor, even to David.

Because thou obeyest not the voice of the LORD, nor executedst his fierce wrath upon Amalek, therefore hath the LORD done this thing unto thee this day.

Moreover, the LORD will also deliver Israel with thee into the hand of the Philistines: and tomorrow shalt thou and thy sons be with me: the LORD also shall deliver the host of Israel into the hand of the Philistines.

Then Saul fell straightway all along on the Earth, and was sore afraid, because of the words of Samuel: and there was no strength in him; for he had eaten no bread all day, nor all the night.

And the woman came unto Saul, and saw that he was sore troubled, and said unto him, Behold, thine handmaiden hath obeyed thy voice, and I have put my life in my hand, and have hearkened unto thy words which thou spakest unto me.

Now therefore, I pray thee, hearken those also unto the voice of thine handmaiden, and let me set a morsel of bread before thee; and eat, that thou mayest have strength, when thou goest on thy way.

But he refused, and said, I will not eat. But his servants, together with the woman, compelled him; and he hearkened unto their voice. So he arose from the Earth and sat upon the bed.

And the woman had a fat calf in the house; and she hasted, and killed it, and took flour and kneaded it, and did bake unleavened bread thereof:

And she brought it before Saul, and before his servants; and they did eat. Then they rose up and went away that night."

In reviewing this passage, what can we discern? What did the Witch do? Was she an "abomination unto God?" Or did she provide evidential information giving Saul proof she was indeed in touch with a genuine Spirit who had passed? Or is there conclusive proof she was deluded or possessed by the devil?

First, she agreed to make contact with Samuel despite her legitimate reservations, demonstrating a deep commitment to serve Spirit and people searching for answers. She makes contact, at which point she realizes Saul is disguised and has deliberately deceived her. This awareness alone proves she has immediately intuited a truth and is in contact with more than her own mind.

We would suggest that Saul examined the Spirit that the Witch of Endor brought forward and knew the Spirit was indeed Samuel by Samuel's familiarity with Saul. The Witch of Endor presents Saul with proof of survival after death, as Samuel had recently passed. She perceives Saul's deception, then presents Saul with evidence that she knows that his past actions are out of integrity with God's commandment of obedience, and finally she prophesies his eventual demise. Clearly, Saul finds the encounter evidential as he bows down in reverence and fear, for he knows she is in touch with Samuel and she has spoken the truth. No subterfuge, no lies, and no finagling, in fact, she gives of herself without expectations of a return. All communication points to the fact that she is genuine and in touch with Samuel.

All the contemporary conjecture regarding the Witch of Endor that claims the Witch is satanic, acting against God's will, and a charmer of the devil is pure prejudice with which we believe the Ascended Masters would never agree.

Here is another *Biblical* reference regarding contacting Spirits:

1 John 4:1

"Beloved, believe not every spirit, but try the spirits whether they are of God: because many false prophets are gone out into the world."

Here Christ doesn't say to shun every medium but rather advises us to be aware and test the Spirit to see if it is of God and good. No way is this a blanket denouncement of all mediums or Spirits. How could Christ denounce the experience of his life, as a Spiritual medium expressing the Word of God?

Frankly, we believe these verses in 1 Samuel and 1 John demonstrate why the passage in Deuteronomy 18 is in error. To alert a seeker to remain aware that there may be fraud or deception with some mediums is responsible and honorable, presenting sitters with legitimate guidelines. Patently calling every medium an "abomination unto the Lord" is unfounded and out of alignment with Master thought and even contradictory and inconsistent with passages in the *Bible*.

The following *Biblical* references describe many types of mediumship regarding God's gifts to man. If we begin with Genesis and continue through Revelation, we discover many exchanges between the Spirit World and our physical world. There is a sense of excitement in the passage exclaiming God's gifts of clairvoyance, clairaudience, speaking in tongues, levitation, speaking through trumpets, healing, direct Spirit writing, and physical manifestations of Spirit. The following *Bible* passages highlight God's gifts to humanity:

1 Corinthians 12:7-10 KJB

But the manifestation of the Spirit is given to every man to profit withal.

For to one is given by the Spirit the word of wisdom; to another the word of knowledge, by the same Spirit;

To another faith by the Spirit; to another the gifts of healing by the same Spirit;

To another the working of miracles; to another prophecy, to another discerning of spirits, to another divers kinds of tongues; to another the interpretation of tongues:"

What follows is an example of the physical manifestation of Spirit. This phenomenon is referred to as "pseudopods" by parapsychologists. The phenomenon is similar to Reverend Rhinehart's materialization of "pseudopods" during the Japanese *"Fraud Proof"* tests, and we suspect it was deliberately demonstrated to show the parallel with the Biblical phenomenon. There are mediums and then there are mediums of God. In Daniel, as with Reverend Rhinehart, we see the latter illustrated:

Daniel 5:5-30 KJB

In the same hour came forth fingers of a man's hand and wrote over against the candlestick upon the plaister of the wall of the king's palace: and the king saw the part of the hand that wrote.

Then the king's countenance was changed and his thoughts troubled him, so that the joints of his loins were loosened, and his knees smote against another.

The king cried aloud to bring in the astrologers, the Chaldeans, and the soothsayers. And the king spake and said to the wise men of Babylon, Whosoever shall read this writing, and shew me the interpretation thereof, shall be clothed with scarlet and have a chain of gold about his neck, and shall be the third ruler in the kingdom.

Then came in all the king's wise men: but they could not read the writing, nor make known to the king the interpretation thereof.

Then was king Belshazzar greatly troubled, and his countenance was changed in him, and his lords were astonished.

Now the queen by reason of the words of the king and his lords came into the banquet house: and the queen spake and said, O king live forever: let not thy thoughts trouble thee, nor let thy countenance be changed:

There is a man in thy kingdom in whom is the spirit of the holy gods; and in the days of thy father light and understanding and wisdom, like the wisdom of the gods, was found in him; whom the king Nebuchadnezzar thy father, the king, I say, thy father, made master of the magicians, astrologers, Chaldeans, and soothsayers;

Forasmuch as an excellent spirit, and knowledge, and understanding interpreting of dreams, and knowledge, and understanding interpreting and shewing of hard sentences, and dissolving of doubts, were found in the same Daniel ,whom the king named Belshazzar: now let Daniel be called, and he will shew the interpretation.

Then was Daniel brought in before the king. And the king spake and said unto Daniel, Art thou that Daniel which art of the children of the captivity of Judah, whom the king my father brought out of Jewry?

I have even heard of thee, that the spi*rit of the gods is in thee, and that light and understanding and excellent wisdom is found in thee.*

And now the wise men, the astrologers, have been brought in before me, that they should read the writing, and make known unto me the interpretation thereof: but they could not shew the interpretation of the thing:

And I have heard of thee that thou canst make interpretations, and dissolve doubts: now if thou canst read the writing, and make known to me the interpretation thereof, thou shalt be clothed with scarlet, and have a chain of gold about thy neck, and be the third ruler of the kingdom.

Then Daniel answered before the king, Let thy gifts be to thyself, and give thy rewards to another; yet I will read the writing unto the king, and make known to him the interpretation.

O thou king, the most high God gave thy Nebuchadnezzar thy father a kingdom, and majesty, and glory and honor:

And for the majesty he gave him, all people, nations, and languages, trembled and feared before him: whom he would he slew; and whom he would he kept alive; and whom he would he set up; and whom he would he put down.

But when his heart was lifted up, and his mind hardened in pride, he was deposed from his kingly throne, and they took his glory from him:

And he was driven from the sons of men; and his heart was made like the beasts, and his dwelling was with the wild asses: they fed him with grass like oxen, and his body was wet with the dew of heaven; till he knew that the most high God ruled in the kingdom of men, and that and he appointeth over it whomsoever he will.

And thou his son, O Belshazzar, hast not humbled thine heart, though this knewest all this;

But hast lifted up thyself against the Lord of heaven; and they have brought the vessels of his house before thee, and thou and thy lords, thy wife, and thy concubines, have drunk wine in them; and thou has praised the god of silver, and gold, of brass, iron, wood, and stone, which see not, nor hear, nor know; and the God in whose hand thy breath is, and whose are all thy ways, hast thou not glorified:

Then was the part of the end sent from him; and this writing was written.

And this is the writing that was written, MENE, MENE, TEKEL, UPHARSIN.

This is the interpretation of the thing: MENE; God hath numbered thy kingdom, and finished it.

TEKEL; Thou art weighed in the balances and found wanting.

PERES; Thy kingdom is divided, and given to the Medes and Persians.

Then commanded Belshazzar, and they clothed Daniel with scarlet, and put a chain of gold about his neck, and made a proclamation concerning him, that he should be the third ruler of the kingdom.

In that night was Belshazzar the king of the Chaldeans slain.

And Darius the Median took the kingdom, being about threescore and two years old."

Again, as with the Witch of Endor, we find Daniel is sincere. He performs his service for free while providing verifiable evidence to King Belshazzar of the veracity of his message.

In 1 Corinthians, God speaks of the gifts given by Spirit, then in Deuteronomy 18 God chastises any who uses these gifts as "abominations unto the Lord." Are we not receiving conflicting messages regarding the use of mediumship? Which message are we to believe?

Holding these verses in mind, let's start by discussing what true mediumship is and what it is not from the point of view of the Ascended Masters. First, the Masters tell us their main interest regarding mediumship is that a sitter, or receiver of wisdom, must be able to determine the source of the message if the message is to have meaning and lasting value. If a message comes to us from an Ascended Master, it would likely have greater and more lasting value than if it came from Aunt Elsie, who recently passed into Spirit.

Second, the Masters say a genuine, proven message from Spirit is NOT one coming from the medium's own mind, and the sitter must make the distinction. Anyone who genuinely seeks the truth and is not simply wanting to be flattered with grandiose messages must determine who, in fact, is delivering the message.

And Third, a sitter must be aware that a discarded astral shell taken up by a rogue entity is not considered a genuine message from an advanced Spirit by the Masters. (Astral shells result when a dead person's astral body is cast aside after they pass. When the passing spirit moves on into a higher vibrational body, these cast-off astral shells are captured by spirits lost in the astral realms. Lost spirits take up residency in these astral shells and communicate through less developed mediums. Mediums can easily be fooled into believing a communication from an astral shell is genuinely from a spirit who passed, when in fact it is not. Madame Blavatsky discussed astral shells in Theosophy.)

It is well-known the Ascended Masters have employed genuine mediums to deliver their messages over the years. Although they have at times expressed fiery admonitions, declaring they are not in sympathy with mediumship as a general rule. There are those, such as Keith Milton Rhinehart, who are exceptions to the rule.

Unfortunately, thousands of mediums claim to deliver messages from St. Germaine, Jesus, and the Masters. This causes the Masters endless consternation as they clearly state they will not work with mediums who have not taken the time to provide proof and evidence as to the validity of their mediumship.

Typically, the Ascended Masters have only worked through Avatars, Semi-Avatars, or other advanced souls like Madame Blavatsky,

Daniel Dunglas Home, Florence Cook, William Stanton Moses, Eva C, Edgar Cayce, and Arthur Ford, to name a few, who have brought forth startling evidential phenomena.

Because a medium can breach the space-time continuum, seeing into the future, bringing so-called prophetic messages to movie stars and society's fashionable personages, does not guarantee the messages are coming from an eternal source of good and advanced Spirits from beyond the grave.

Sitters, famous or not, are as responsible as the medium for elevating mediumship to a higher level of authenticity. To establish authenticity, sitters must demand higher standards from their mediums.

We trust this writing will encourage more mediums to move beyond self-delusion and do the work necessary to develop legitimate, authentic mediumship. A medium's function is to provide content that enlightens the sitter. The message should inspire a higher sense of morality. A message should uplift a sitter's consciousness to a new awareness. These are the criteria that align with the demands of the Ascended Masters.

Entertainment is one thing and can be amusing and jolly good fun, but genuine knowledge and wisdom are of a different order, and we must be sure we make the distinction. We, the sitters, out of our neediness to believe, regularly fool ourselves as much as the deluded mediums fool themselves. So how might we articulate the intention and purpose of sincere mediumship? Here are the guidelines Master Intelligence puts forth:

1. **To console and comfort the mourner.**
2. **To heal the sick.**
3. **To uplift and teach the genuine truth seeker.**

SIXTEEN

MEDIUMSHIP – TO CONSOLE AND COMFORT THE MOURNER

T HE ASCENDED MASTERS MAINTAIN THAT EXAMPLES OF EVI-
dential mediumship are important, so even the non-believer
can conclude the existence of an afterlife. Proof of authenticity
accompanies the lion's share of these testimonies with affidavits sworn
to under the penalty of perjury. The following is our attempt to meet
their standards.

This is a testimony of a chela being comforted by her deceased
father, who committed suicide. After searching to find a medium for
years to hear a message from her father, her father comes to her through
Reverend Rhinehart's adept physical phenomena mediumship:

"Growing up, I had an idyllic family life. My father was a highly
respected doctor in an Alaskan community, where he performed
miraculous surgeries, saving lives and limbs. To me, he was bigger
than life. I can remember an incident when we were kids. We were
attending a party, driving in our Willys Jeep on a frozen-over lake
when we hit a thin spot—the jeep immediately began to submerge.
My dad responded so heroically, instantly wrapping my one-year-old
baby sister securely into a blanket and, like a torpedo, tossing her
out the window to safety. Then he hoisted my other sister up and
out the window, turned and quickly formed a human bridge out of
myself and my mother for my other two siblings to cross before he

got out himself, and just like that, we avoided total disaster. With this incident, our family bonded deeper than ever. But not long after, when my brother was shot dead in a hunting accident, everything began to unravel.

"After the accident, my father despaired and fell to drinking. This created problems at the hospital and eventually, instability and pain seeped into our wonderful home. As my world started to crumble, it drove me to search for answers. I began to meditate and attempt to communicate with Spirit. I found some relief, but my parents' home life continued to deteriorate. Then one day, I came home and found my dad dead in bed after taking a tranquilizer. I became confused and despondent.

"I searched from church to church to church for answers, finally coming upon Reverend Keith Milton Rhinehart. One day, I was fortunate enough to have a private Holy Communion Séance with Reverend Rhinehart. At my appointment, I inspected the Holy of Holies where the Reverend conducted the séance to be sure everything was on the up-and-up and found nothing hidden within but a glass of water and a chair. Once Reverend Rhinehart went into trance, I asked the usual questions a twenty-year-old might ask. My incredibly loving Master Teacher, who had entranced Reverend Rhinehart, responded by saying,

'There is somebody here who wants to talk with you.'

"Then a séance attendant was instructed to turn on the infrared lights to ensure no physical damage would occur to the medium. You are not gonna believe what happened next. My dad, in a flowing ectoplasmic body, fully materialized physically right before my eyes! Standing before me with the exact same stocky body and the exact same voice he used when alive. He showed me how far he advanced since his suicide by demonstrating his ability to present his form once again. He said I didn't have to worry about him anymore and thanked me for introducing him to the Teachers with whom he was currently studying. I was so relieved and proud to be his daughter."

This is one of the finest demonstrations of adept physical phenomenon mediumship anyone can encounter. There is no audience, only the sitter, no showmanship, and no financial substance exchanged, only a commitment to serve someone in need, fulfilling the highest purpose of true mediumship. Though some frown upon financial compensation for the demonstration of God's Spiritual gifts, it is not an issue for the Ascended Masters, as they say those serving God deserve to be compensated just as a nurse or a police person serving another human being. Those serving God must make an income, but Reverend Rhinehart's declining remuneration further demonstrates his selfless compassion and his willingness to serve those who suffer.

It is the testimony of countless students and those of the general public that the most important message they have ever received through Reverend Rhinehart's mediumship is the proof that life exists beyond the grave, and their loved ones continue on. They feel this experience is more valuable than all the miraculous physical phenomenon materializations. Here is another testimony to this effect:

"I witnessed the physical materialization of the Spirit of a young man, the son of well-known hotel owners in Johannesburg, South Africa. The parents were overwhelmed to see their son again and to speak with him of his continued existence in a life after death."

Testimonies and evidential proofs come in all shapes and sizes. Here is one that comes from a little different angle. This testimony is from a book called *This Timeless Moment*, written by Laura Huxley, discussing her personal experiences with her recently deceased husband, Aldous Huxley. In the book, Laura describes an experience with Reverend Rhinehart where he read billet cards at Laura's home under scientific test conditions. The reading was intended for Laura and a number of her friends.

The evening proved to be unforgettable for all the participants, even altering the nature of death for some. Laura felt so impressed she requested a private reading the following day. This event took place in 1964 and is historic in that it provides irrefutable evidence for the survival of the personality after so-called death. This proof is why Aldous was excited about the opportunity to work with Reverend Rhinehart from Spirit. He never felt, during his lifetime, that a medium provided irrefutable evidence. Through his existence in Spirit, he wanted humanity to know the honest truth about life after death.

The next evening after the billet readings, Reverend Rhinehart conducted a private reading for Laura in Aldous's private room. In *This Timeless Moment*, Laura indicates that Reverend Rhinehart's reading was different from the previous night when the medium's eyes were bandaged, and the participants wrote out billet cards. This time, the medium and Laura sat facing each other, one on each side of Aldous's writing table. In the reading, Laura asked for more details regarding the murdered man who had been discussed the previous evening. Reverend Rhinehart said this man was present along with Aldous this evening. The man indicated he did not want to reveal certain facts about the murder in the presence of those present the previous evening. Then Reverend Rhinehart discussed facts only known to Aldous and Laura.

They were suddenly interrupted by Aldous exclaiming, *"You are going to receive what is going to be considered classical evidence of survival of the personality that cannot be explained away by telepathy or other theories."* Laura understood from Reverend Rhinehart, Aldous wanted to show proof, irrefutable proof, that something not incidental or that which could be attributed to intuition, imagination, or probability was at work with genuine mediumship. He wanted to demonstrate beyond a doubt that which could not be explained away by the workings of the mind.

When Reverend Rhinehart concluded his reading for Laura, she felt the reading was good and impactful; yet, she still believed she could argue what Reverend Rhinehart communicated was something he could have retrieved deep from her unconscious mind. This theoretically eliminated Aldous' hypothesis of the survival of consciousness after death and could be attributed to ESP.

But true to Aldous' promise, the following experience transpiring on the heels of the reading demonstrated facts beyond Laura's consciousness and even Aldous' consciousness when alive. Here is Laura's testimony:

"K.M.R. and I went downstairs. Ginny and her children had started preparations to show the filmed interviews K.M.R. had brought from his world tour. A few minutes before, Gina Cerminara, the well-known writer on parapsychology, had arrived to spend the evening with us and see the films. I realized later that it was fortuitous that she was present for the following occurrence. Now everyone was busy with the projector, screen, and films. K.M.R. was trying to solve the threading of the film when without diverting his attention he said to me. 'Please give me a pencil and a paper; Aldous is saying I must write this down.' I gave him a piece of paper and Gina Cerminara gave him a pencil. He wrote:

> **17th page**
> **6th book from left**
> **3rd shelf**
> **or**
> **6th shelf**
> **3rd book from left**
> **23 line**

He then handed me the paper, turned back to the projector, and said nonchalantly, 'Aldous wants you to look up those books.'

I was left with that piece of paper in my hands, wondering. I had not, then, heard of what is known in parapsychology as a "book test." I kept looking at the words and numbers. Then slowly and thoughtfully I went upstairs to Aldous's room, where the reading had taken place. Two walls of the room are covered with bookshelves. I went to the small wall, next to the door, which has six shelves about four feet in length. I counted to the third shelf from the floor, counted to the sixth book from the left, and took it out. It was a book six and a quarter by nine and a quarter inches and had 257 pages. It was a soft-cover book inside a cardboard container, in Spanish. It looked and felt as if it had never been opened before. The title *Coloquio de Buenos Aires,* 1962, published by the P.E.N. Club of Argentina in Buenos Aires; the printing was finished August 20, 1963. I opened the book to page 17. Before I even count to line 23, the name Aldous Huxley, from the paragraph in the center of the page, leaped to my eyes. This is the paragraph containing line 23:

> *Marcos Victoria: Aldous Huxley no nos sorprende en esta admirable comunicación, donde la paradoja y la erudición en el sentido poético y el sentido del "humor" se entrelazan en forma tan eficaz. Quizá la mayorí a de los oyentes de este coloquio no tengan una idea completa de la riqueza espiritual de esta comunicación través del resumen que acaba de leernos la fiel traductora y también erudita en disciplinas científicas que as Alicia Jurado. Pero no es culpa de ella, sino de la complejidad extrema del pensamiento del escritor inglés que exige la lectura repetida del texto completo de cuarenta páginas.*

I do not know Spanish, but it is a language similar enough to Italian, my mother language, for me to understand quite a bit of it. I looked at those lines, not understanding completely, but fully knowing *la riqueza espiritual de esta comunicación*: "the spiritual richness of this communication."

After a few moments the thought came strongly to my mind that this event should have witnesses; and that I should be checked by other people. I had marked the place from which I had taken the book—the sixth from the left—by pulling out about an inch the fifth and seventh books on the shelf; the space where the sixth book had been was empty. I put the book back as it was before I touched it. I went downstairs and asked the others to come up. When everyone was in the room, I asked K.M.R. to do what Aldous had dictated. K.M.R. went through the same procedure I had gone through, pulled out the same book, went to the same paragraph. Standing near the bookcase, the four of us stared at that paragraph while Gina Cerminara translated it aloud into English:

Aldous Huxley does not surprise us in this admirable communication in which paradox and erudition in the poetic sense and the sense of humor are interlaced in such an efficacious form. Perhaps the majority of the listeners to this conversation will not have a complete idea of the spiritual richness of this communication through the summary which the faithful translator, and learned scholar in scientific disciplines, who is Alicia Jurado, has just made for us.

We were speechless. Then, immediately, the question arose whether Aldous knew of that book and its location. He did not know. Many books had accumulated during the last months of Aldous's life, first during the summer of 1963 when we were in Europe, then during the last three months, when he was too sick to read. This book had arrived either shortly before Aldous's death or after. My sister, who had come from Italy to visit a few weeks after Aldous's death, had reorganized the library; the location of the shelves in the room had been changed, as well as the arrangement of the books in the shelves. Since she had put the books in order, no one had touched those in that group of shelves near the door.

I had never seen the book before. ..." [1]

We believe Spirit and Aldous were satisfied they provided clear evidence of the survival of the personality continuing after death. But

SEASONS OF THE SOUL

it is worth mentioning here, even after all the scientific testing to which Reverend Rhinehart submitted and passed, some, even those close to him, continued to suspect trickery and fraud. The prejudice against psychic phenomena goes deep into our subconscious; it appears to be programmed right into our DNA.

When an evidential message is brought through to a sitter who has no knowledge of the information being delivered and the message proves true, it is considered the greatest proof a medium can provide, as it shows the medium did not pick the brain of the participating sitter. Here is a testimony from a casual participant to Reverend Rhinehart's séance during his visit to Mexico City. She is about to receive a message not for herself, but for her sister, who is not present at the séance, yet her sister receives moving comfort from her boyfriend, who passed some time ago:

"Back in 1973, I was part of a Spiritual group that gathered on a fairly regular basis to meditate in Mexico City. Our group organized Spiritual events and we were responsible for sponsoring Reverend Rhinehart's visit to Mexico City. His visit occurred in 1973. The first day, proceedings took place at the Hotel Presidente on Reforma Avenue in a small conference room with about thirty to forty people present. We all lined up in a Darshan-like fashion, and Reverend Rhinehart touched each of our foreheads, placing a wafer in our mouths, then he gifted each of us a small sacred stone.

"The day after, we met in a much larger auditorium, theater style, with about five hundred people in attendance. Reverend Rhinehart sat on the stage while an attendant wrapped a cloth around his head several times, covering his eyes, then, with duct tape, covered his mouth tightly; these two procedures eliminated any ability to see or talk. I sat about halfway back in the audience, I'd say fifty meters from the stage. We were handed small white cards, called billets, and instructed to write the names of people whom we knew who passed

148

into Spirit. I wrote down my grandmother's name and my sister's boyfriend's name, Isaac Alvarez. Shortly thereafter, a staff member collected the cards, depositing them in a small offering basket.

"When all the cards had been collected, we began to sing, *'Oh my God, my God, how I love thee, how I love thee'* three times in English, three times in Spanish, and three times in French. We continued chanting different chants for maybe fifteen to twenty minutes. Then Reverend Rhinehart started to pray out loud, with his mouth taped shut, how—I don't know, but he prayed out loud, saying a series of decrees. When he finished, he took out some billet cards from the basket, pressing them to his ears and, within moments, began loudly speaking names of the so-called dead. Soon shrieks of emotion poured out of the audience and continued unabated throughout the presentation as people heard from their loved ones who had passed! Startling! In time, we broke for lunch.

"After the lunch break, I was sitting in the audience feeling very relaxed next to my brother. All of a sudden, Reverend Rhinehart said, *'Isaac Alvarez is here, he says to light a white candle for him at Christmas time.'* Isaac, that was my sister's boyfriend! Wow! He died in a car accident on January 19th, 1969, when he was nineteen years old. At the time, I didn't understand his message. Days later, I told my sister of the event and what Isaac had said about the candle. Immediately, chills shot up her spine—goose bumps crawling all over her body. She said Christmas was a very important day to Isaac. When alive, he mentioned many times to light a candle for him during Christmas; no one knew of this request but the two of them. I thought to myself, how can Reverend Rhinehart know this? It's impossible!

"Because our group helped organize the event, I knew many people who attended. They all expressed experiencing genuine communications, coming away completely amazed."

Events such as the ones described bring comfort to the mourner and leave no doubt as to the authenticity of the message.

Unfortunately, these isolated events are not more readily available to all who are interested in genuine mediumship, especially regarding understanding life after death.

SEVENTEEN

MEDIUMSHIP
TO HEAL THE SICK

M ANY BELIEVE THE ABILITY TO HEAL OTHERS TO BE THE greatest of all God's Spiritual gifts. Of all the phenomena surrounding Reverend Rhinehart's adept mediumship, he felt the gift of Spiritual healing to be superior to all others. Jesus's ability to heal is what lifted him to miraculous status in his day. This Spiritual, seemingly miraculous, form of healing persists today through the efforts of mediums such as Reverend Rhinehart and others.

Steve Young relates this story, told to him by Alma Hogan in the 1980s. Alma was the long-time beloved Reverend of the Aquarian Foundation's Honolulu Branch. She had not been feeling well for a period of time:

"Doctors reached the diagnosis Alma had lung cancer. They were treating her for the cancer; additionally, Alma was receiving healings from the local members of the Honolulu Branch. Not long after her diagnosis, Alma and I were talking. She told me, one day Reverend Rhinehart came to her apartment for a visit. He said he wanted to direct Spiritual healing to her. Alma agreed, and Reverend Rhinehart directed hands-on Spiritual healing for over forty-five minutes. At the conclusion of the Spiritual healing, he told Alma there was no cancer left in her body, but a bit of water remained in the area where the tumor once existed. Later, Alma went to her oncologist. After her

MRI, the doctor reported the tumor to be completely gone and all that remained was a bit of water in its place.

"Reverend Rhinehart never talked about performing Spiritual healings and I never witnessed him doing any Spiritual healings, but I felt he was able to perform any of God's Spiritual gifts described in 1 Corinthians 12:1-11 when he applied himself."

It is interesting to note, before Steve discussed this incident, we were sitting next to each other at my dining room table, preparing the voice recorder for the session. I looked over at Steve when we were about to begin our recording. As he opened his mouth, a whitish vapor escaped from his mouth, swirling out into the room! He closed his mouth, and I thought, *Am I seeing things? What the heck just happened?* After several seconds, Steve opened his mouth again and another waft of white vapor puffed into the room!

The day was a mild summer day, and the vapor could not be caused by a temperature change from the body to the temperature in the room. The vapor left his mouth as if he had been smoking a cigarette, but Steve was not smoking and hadn't smoked for over forty years! This is the only time during our three weeks of recording sessions that this type of event occurred. We claimed no immediate explanation for this extraordinary occurrence.

It is my testimony the phenomenon was inexplicable and super-normal in origin. The only explanation I could come up with is that ectoplasm had been extracted from Steve's subtle body to show that his testimony regarding Reverend Rhinehart's healing of Alma was indeed extraordinary and true.

Here is another healing testimony related by Steve Young:

"In 1973, I received a Master Designated Spiritual Healing Designation from the Church. Many years after receiving this designation, my new wife and I were invited to dinner at my ex-mother-in-law's home. While at the get-together, my ex-mother-in-law told me they recently called in priests on two separate occasions to perform last rites for her husband.

"After dinner, my wife and I approached my ex-father-in-law, who was lying on a small bed in the living room. He appeared extremely thin and frail, whiling away his dying days watching TV. Upon entering the rather large living room, I asked him if he would like a Spiritual healing. He said yes and indicated he was familiar with Chi and Spiritual healing.

"I then laid my hands on him for five minutes, directing Spiritual healing, while my wife acted as my battery. Later, I repeated the Spiritual healing twice within a short period of time. Days later, the family said my father-in-law got out of bed and started walking around the house. They were amazed because previously he was unable to walk—completely bedridden from the prostate cancer that had spread throughout his entire body and into his spine. In a follow-up visit with his oncologist, the oncologist declared my father-in-law to be cancer-free. With renewed energy, he returned to work in his Chinese herb shop, living many more productive years.

"In directing healing, I call upon God. I am aware that all healing powers come through God, the Ascended Masters, and the power of Love that heals all things. There is no doubt in my mind a miracle happened that day as a direct result of Divine intervention from the Spirit world and the Ascended Masters.

"In our Church, a Master Designation in Healing is earned by a developing Spiritual healer who accumulates several sworn affidavits from individuals seeking Spiritual healing, who affirm under penalty of perjury, they had an illness or an affliction disappear as a result of Spiritual healing energies directed by the aspiring healer.

"A Master Designated Spiritual Healer implies the Ascended Masters and highly evolved consciousness are working through the instrumentality of the Designated Spiritual Healer."

The following is a testimony from a woman who attended a séance in Mexico City, Mexico, illustrating how a deep emotional healing occurred, relieving a lifelong burden of a sitter:

"In 1976, in a hotel room in Mexico City, I was present where over two hundred people gathered to witness Reverend Rhinehart present spirit communicators and Ascended Masters through his adept mediumship. One particular message during the billet card readings stood out; it came from a man in Spirit who claimed to have been murdered by a member present in the audience. This man wanted to communicate to the man in the audience that he forgave him for his actions and wanted the man to forgive himself and to no longer feel remorse over the incident.

"When the spirit finished speaking, five rows in front of me in the very large conference room, a man stood up, bawling and weeping profusely, shaking in grief and remorse. He acknowledged he indeed was the killer of the spirit communicating. He exclaimed he felt eternally grateful for this message! This was not the only evidential message received that day, as other profound and startling messages also left recipients sobbing."

Next is another healing testimony from Steve Young, which also takes place in Mexico City. The incident refers to his near-death experience:

"In a hotel room in Puerto Vallarta, Mexico, I was accompanied by Reverend Rhinehart and another man. The person I traveled with offered me a glass of wine, and against my better judgment, I accepted. After consuming about half of a glass, I began experiencing an intense asthma attack. I started wheezing, the wheezing intensifying until I felt like I needed every muscle in my body to breathe. I really felt as though I was dying. Quickly, Reverend Rhinehart left the room and returned with a medical doctor who gave me a shot to counteract the attack, but as a result, the wheezing became even more pronounced.

My alarming lack of breath prompted St. Germaine to entrance Reverend Rhinehart. Through Reverend Rhinehart's mediumship, St. Germaine exclaimed I was near death's door—my spirit drifting half-in and half-out of my body. I sensed it was true and I feared I could die! The Masters were doing all they could to send healing and keep me in my body.

"Then St. Germaine apported a sacred object of a small red clay cup into the room, similar to clay cups one finds in Mexico. The cup appeared on the kitchen counter a few feet away from me, where previously nothing existed. Reverend Rhinehart indicated the Masters' offered the clay cup as a gift. Almost immediately, my breathing returned to normal, and I was asthma-free for over a year.

"Occasionally, asthma attacks have returned, but never like this one; however, with these later attacks, I required hospitalization several times."

Now, a testimony from a lady who was a chela of the Masters and a close friend of Reverend Rhinehart. She often traveled assisting Reverend Rhinehart and accompanied him on his mission to Papua New Guinea and the Borobudur Buddhist Temple:

"In July of 1976, I developed a high fever. I went to my doctor for treatment, and he prescribed antibiotics and sent me home. I took the antibiotics for one week. The antibiotics produced no effect. In fact, the fever rose higher. On the seventh day of treatment, I returned to the doctor. Upon examination, he sent me to the hospital for immediate attention. They put me through every test I could imagine, to no avail. Throughout, the fever stayed very high. They gave me my own hospital room, drew blood, and took my vitals. The hospital doctor, a surgeon, arrived to give me his prognosis. He said I had Peritonitis (inflammation of the abdomen) stemming from an unknown cause, declaring he needed to cut me from my sternum down to my lower pelvic cavity and from the left side of my abdomen to the right side of my abdomen! Prescribing immediate surgery! After his prognosis and remedy, he promptly left the room.

"Immediately, upon his departure, I received a long-distance call from Reverend Rhinehart, who received news of my illness's severity.

He expressed his love, concern, and gave me his prayers. I explained to him what the surgeon just prescribed, and the surgery was immediately planned.

"No sooner had I finished my explanation when Reverend Rhinehart went into trance while still on the phone with me. These were the next words I heard: *'Greetings in the Name of the Mighty Christ I Am, this is Master Count Saint Germaine, entrancing Reverend Rhinehart to get this message through to you. Your body is too weak to survive the surgery the surgeon has planned. Your illness stems from your appendix. It is the source of your infection. It is in the lower right quadrant of your abdomen. You must convince your doctor to make the incision there and no further incision is necessary.'* Right after Saint Germaine's statement, a nurse entered the room and wheeled me to the surgery area. Upon relating to the operating surgeon what the Count explained, the surgeon threatened me, saying if I was going to tell him how to do the surgery, he could refrain from doing the surgery entirely! Then they whisked me to the operating room on the gurney.

"As they administered the anesthesia, I noticed, standing just to my right, six tall blue beings. I relaxed and drifted out of my body. The next moment in which I became aware, I saw a tunnel of white light with my parents (who passed years before) standing at the end of the tunnel, beckoning me to enter and meet them on the other side. Instantly, I bolted from the hospital bed shouting, *'No, No! I have work to do!'*

"Later, to my surprise, I discovered the operating surgeon executed the surgery exactly as Count Saint Germaine recommended.

Post-surgery, my doctor prescribed intravenous antibiotics and a hospital stay of thirty days to heal a hole the size of a grapefruit in my liver that the illness created. The intravenous antibiotics created a severe burning sensation in my arteries and veins; however, I steadily improved, and after thirty days, they sent me home. Once home, I did physical therapy to recover my strength. I credit Reverend Rhinehart and Master Count Saint Germaine for saving my life!"

EIGHTEEN

MEDIUMSHIP – TO UPLIFT AND TEACH THE GENUINE TRUTH SEEKER

A S WE MOVE INTO THE SECTION ON "UPLIFT AND TEACH THE Genuine Truth Seeker," we would like to prepare the reader to better understand the nature of a séance. For sitters to accept and learn from a message, they must feel comfortable with the process and understand the mechanics behind a séance. Becoming familiar with the medium's relationship with Spirit and the procedure of a séance allows a sitter to be guided by the message if the message is meaningful.

There is much superstition, misinformation, and straight-up fear regarding Spirit communications and séances. Ouija Boards are prone to attracting rogue Spirits and can be dangerous, and as we have mentioned, it is best to be cautious when contacting the Spirit World, especially through Ouija Boards.

As we have mentioned, Christian denominations are responsible for much of the trepidation involving Spirits, as they have created an inordinate amount of distrust by characterizing all mediums as "an abomination unto God." We sense the fear that a person may not be able to clearly identify a Spirit, but a sitter can test a genuine medium, as we have seen.

The word "trance" simply conjures up something downright scary to some folks as a result of all the gruesome Hollywood movies deliberately creating a sense of horror around anything that smacks of the occult. This depiction of the occult is a one-sided narrative and misleading when it comes to the *intent* behind a genuine séance. But in the end, we would suggest Christian dogma is at the core of most negative publicity for a simple reason—it ensures Christian scripture remains the one source of religious truth. It is our sense that the denouncement of Spirit interaction with humanity has stunted the expansion of human consciousness throughout the Christian world.

Yes, there is reason to be wary in terms of the occult, as there are many satanic and ritualistic practices inspired through the misinterpretation and misuse of genuine Spiritual practices. Looking up the word "occult," one finds it means that which is hidden from view, not revealed, mysterious. It is knowledge or wisdom not in the public domain per se. Like any truth, it can be used for good or used for evil, so it is not any one activity that is evil, such as mediumship. It is the *intent* behind the activity that is either good or evil. In contacting the Spirit World, we must ask, What is the character of the medium, and what is the purpose and *intent* in contacting Spirit?

The general public is simply unaware of all the workings that go into creating a séance, which includes presenting *billets* (explained below), or the physical phenomenon manifesting through the caliber of a medium like Reverend Rhinehart, or the use of paraphernalia deemed necessary by the Spirits involved. Not only do the proceedings and logistics have to be planned in the physical world, but in the Spirit World as well.

Let's take a moment to further discuss some terms and the logistics behind a séance on the physical side of life. Many of Reverend Rhinehart's Spirit Messages were delivered to sitters through tuning into billets. The term "billet" is the French word for ticket; in the World of Spiritualism, it means a ticket to the Spirit World.

A medium tunes into a billet using Psychometry, which is the process of divining facts the medium retrieves through extrasensory perception. A medium can glean facts from an object owned by someone, or receive facts about someone, who had contact with an object being psychometrized. So, if a medium such as Reverend Rhinehart is employing billet cards, he is psychometrizing the billet card to attune to the sitter's energy or life story.

Before Reverend Rhinehart performs a billet reading for someone from the audience (a sitter), the people in attendance are given three-by-five white index cards and asked to address three questions to Spirit, which they would like answered. They are requested to avoid asking financial or medical questions, as there are professionals who are better prepared to address those concerns. Once they are finished writing out their questions, they are asked to press the card to their solar plexus for a few minutes. Afterwards, they are instructed to take their card, fold it in two, write their first name on the outside of the card, and place it in a plastic box being passed through the audience.

During Reverend Rhinehart's reading of a billet card, he is blindfolded by an assistant who tightly wraps a cloth around his forehead, covering his eyes, then they place medical tape across his mouth so when a sitter hears a voice, they know it is not Reverend Rhinehart's, but comes from a voice-box manifested by Spirit. This assures the sitter that every measure has been taken to bring genuine messages from a Spirit beyond the grave and not a message from Reverend Rhinehart's mind or consciousness. Finally, after all the conditions have been met, Reverend Rhinehart grabs a billet card and presses it to his forehead or ears. Then Spirit rapidly begins to speak out messages to those in attendance.

As we can see, a genuine séance is a complex affair. It might look as though a solitary gentleman is sitting on stage delivering messages to sitters, but this picture is deceptive, as on the Spirit side of life, there are many scurrying around in preparation for the sitter. Some sitters attract lines of relatives and friends, all wanting to communicate. This can present a logistical nightmare in Spirit and must be managed so only Spirits who are valued and recognized by the sitter are allowed to present themselves. In the case of Spiritual lectures from Spirit, there can be unwanted spirits crashing the séance, attempting to get a message across, so there is security and protection in place to avoid such issues.

Based on the type of psychic phenomenon being produced by Spirit, special guides may be required. The production of different types of Spirit phenomena, like manifesting a voice-box, the creation of pseudopods (as in Daniel in the *Bible*), full body manifestations, levitation, and the flying of trumpets, can be demanding, so the Spirit room may be brimming with various Spirits all working to produce the effects needed to accomplish the highest outcome.

The event is always protected from the Spirit side to ensure only Spirits having loved ones in attendance are those allowed into the Spirit room. This applies to Spirit Guides as well. So what types of guides might Spirit want to include? Depending on the needs of the sitter, there may be healing guides, chemical guides, Indian guides, child guides, and others who could be involved. But it must be stressed, only highly evolved Spirits are assigned to conduct the séance proceedings.

Reverend Rhinehart has two such Spirits who oversee each of his Spirit communications, called Cabinet Guides. They are Doctor Robert John Kensington and his wife, Suzie, two quite lively, colorful Spirits. Doctor Kensington lived in the Boston area in the Nineteenth Century. He is usually the guide who works with Reverend Rhinehart, bringing forth the Spirit communications during billet readings and prophesies.

In most instances, billet messages are conducted by a controlling Spirit whereby they manipulate the brain centers of the medium, pressing the right buttons, so to speak, to get the medium to communicate their message, or through manifesting a Spirit voice-box in which to speak. The more developed the medium, the more accurate the message. Messages can be colored by the consciousness of the medium, so the medium must have the ability to step aside and allow the Spirit communicator to take full control.

Here, we must make a distinction between the subjects of *Possession* and *Obsession*. These two terms refer to the degree by which a person, or a medium, is being controlled. The first question to ask is: does the medium step away from the body willingly, or is the medium forced out of the body by an outside agent? According to the ancient Kahuna religion, *possession* is considered good or bad depending on the intent of the controlling Spirit. For instance, a Spirit that is of God and takes Jesus as its Lord and Saviour is always good, holding the highest intent. The duration of possession can vary, lasting for a few seconds to hours, or even days.

Obsession, on the other hand, is always dark and evil. In *obsession* cases, there is no consent, and the controlling Spirit returns again and again, taking over the personality. It is easy to determine if the Spirit communicator is of inferior development or emotionally imbalanced when stepping aside becomes problematic and happens without consent. It is inappropriate for any Spirit to control a medium, or any person, to the extent that the person must live outside the body for long stretches of time or a major portion of that life. When a genuine Master is at the helm, there is no issue with *obsession*.

The Masters have indicated on many occasions that Reverend Rhinehart's adept mediumship is extraordinary. His consciousness and mental faculties are developed in such a manner that they have been able to present stirring wisdom never before accomplished through other mediums in history. The Ascended Masters are on record indicating just one faint whisper from a genuine developed Spirit, especially a Master's consciousness, is worth more than hours of messages from delusional mediums or astral shells masquerading as genuine Spirit communicators.

The following testimony is simple but demonstrates the power an adept Master can deliver with but a few words. It speaks to the idea that a whisper from a genuine Spirit or Master is more valuable than hours of messages from the mind of a deluded medium or an astral shell:

"My first séance with Reverend Rhinehart was in 1983 during a telephone hookup call with only the San Francisco Branch of the Church connected on the call. Count St. Germaine entranced Reverend Rhinehart from an undisclosed location, then circled the room from person to person in our Chapel, delivering personal messages to each in attendance. When he came to me, he addressed me, saying, *'Beloved Gary,'* the compassion and respect that filled his words completely overwhelmed me. In those two words, I experienced being totally loved, such a simple two words, so un-nerved me. The unconditional love communicated in the tone, flavor, and feeling *of* *'Beloved Gary'* reduced me to sobs, moving me deeply. I strain to put into words my inner experience, but I can say, never before have I felt so thoroughly accepted and uplifted! Inexplicable! St. Germaine went on to give me a profound message too personal to elaborate, but highly evidential, instructive, and meaningful to me." ~ Gary Whitney

What follows is merely a small smattering of readings as Reverend Rhinehart produced thousands upon thousands of readings over the many years of his career for people in his Church and on his three world tours.

Here is a surprise, first-hand experience with Reverend Rhinehart that left the student feeling inspired and with more clarity regarding his current circumstances:

"In the early 1980s, I was on a short vacation staying in the Ilikai Hotel at Waikiki Beach in Honolulu. A couple of months before my trip, I joined Aquarian Foundation. I was aware the San Francisco Center Leaders were going to be in Honolulu at the same time, but we did not make any prearranged plans to get together. However, they knew where we would be staying.

"During our stay, my friend and I spent several days enjoying ourselves, seeing the sights of Honolulu. One morning, we were in our room when we heard a knock on the door. I answered the door and to my surprise, standing before me were the San Francisco Center Leaders. They said, *'Just a minute, there's someone here to see you!'* They stepped aside and Reverend Rhinehart appeared. I was shocked! Dressed in all white, with a flowing tunic garment, sharp slacks, and long golden blond hair, he presented quite an image. He said, *'It's nice to meet you, I've been hearing about you, welcome to the Church!'* Then he hugged me, and as we hugged, I realized under his sports coat he wore a bulletproof vest! It's the only time I've been hugged by someone wearing a bulletproof vest—I thought how strange. Looking at him, I noticed the quality of his skin to be quite unusual. It seemed waxy and unusually shiny. I invited him and the center leaders into my living room, offering them a seat on the couch. Even though Reverend Rhinehart was wearing the vest, he appeared at ease, acting extremely cordial and friendly. We exchanged pleasantries about our stay.

"Suddenly, seemingly out of nowhere, his entire demeanor changed and a booming voice announced, *'Greetings in the name of the Mighty Christ I Am, this is Count St. Germain!'* With that, an electric energy filled the air in the room, which I had not experienced previously. With no further ado, he gave me a message regarding my immediate situation concerning a current relationship. His message cleared up many questions I harbored, which had been bothering me. He asked if I had any questions but I felt so overwhelmed by the experience I couldn't formulate a response. At this point, he said goodbye, turned, and walked out of the room as Count St. Germain, whereas he entered as Reverend Rhinehart. I never got to say, "Goodbye," to Reverend Rhinehart, though I did say, "Goodbye," to St. Germain. This remains one of the most unusual experiences of my life, these many decades later!

"This was the only time I had the opportunity to be with Reverend Rhinehart. I was especially surprised by his visit because I knew during this time period he had gone underground, so to speak, to guard against outstanding threats. I felt privileged he went out of his way to see me."

I wish to relate another testimony that changed the course of a person's life for the better. This testimony stems from a telephone hookup séance where Reverend Rhinehart is communicating from an undisclosed location. The chela is Monica Szu-Whitney, my wife:

"In January of 1990, I attended a Prophecy Séance at the Church in San Francisco. Reverend Rhinehart conducted the séance through a telephone hookup from an undisclosed location and was unaware of my attendance. The Master Count St. Germaine entranced Reverend Rhinehart and was discussing a topic when all of a sudden, mid-sentence, he stopped and announced Monica of San Francisco had been developing as a psychic artist. Well, I was absolutely shocked to hear this message. I thought Master St. Germaine must have mistakenly called out my name. The message must be for another member attending the San Francisco meeting, who was already doing psychic art, and Master St. Germaine just got our names mixed up—or if not, it must be Gary who was good at drawing.

"I had no formal training in art other than a few drawing classes many years ago, and was certainly not involved in doing any Spiritual Psychic Art, much less developing it. I felt thoroughly convinced there was a mistake. But everyone at the séance said, 'No, St. Germaine said it's you, Monica.' I left the séance feeling somewhat confused and apprehensive, yet still a little excited. I didn't take any immediate action, just mulled it over for a while.

"In the end, I thought Count St. Germaine, being a Master, knew more than I, and I believed in Reverend Rhinehart's mediumship, so I decided to give it a go. I went out and bought some art supplies. I tried very hard to focus my mind on the page, doing my best to skillfully pencil in my drawing; even so, the first few drawings turned out like little kids' line drawings. I felt disappointed, wondering if I could ever really do psychic art. I didn't want to give up though, so I tried all kinds of ways to improve. I taped sacred objects on my forehead, rubbed my third eye really hard, and tried closing my eyes, hoping Spirit might take me over, but nothing worked. "Finally, I realized I was trying too hard, trying to direct the drawing myself. The Count said I was to be an instrument. I decided to wipe my mind clean and just trust. At that point, a new energy started to flow and I no longer had to willfully direct the drawing. Gradually, personalities began arriving on my page. I became so delighted to see real Spirit beings take form.

"In early 1991, after several years of drawing Spirit guides and unidentified Spirits, I began to see different types of faces, faces that looked out-of-this-world. I became a bit startled, but I drew them anyway. At first, the drawings were based on an impression and guidance I received through my hand. Then I started seeing outlines of beings projected onto my paper, all I had to do was trace what I saw. After the tracing was completed, I saw colors projected from my guide, and I was directed as to which colors to use in different parts of the drawing. Simultaneously, as I received instructions, more clarity arrived concerning my drawing's details.

"These drawings came effortlessly, rapidly. Whenever I sat down before a blank sheet of paper, a being just appeared on the page. These beings kept coming, and I even started seeing and feeling the beings during Wednesday Night Spiritual Healing, during meditation in Master Class, at home, and in my dreams.

"Spiritual Psychic Art has brought me great happiness and become a part of the fabric of who I am. It has helped me in many areas of life, both directly and indirectly. Through my development as a Spiritual Psychic Artist, I drew many Ascended Masters, Space Masters, and inter-dimensional beings. Using the pictures of these guides and teachers, I was able to contact and communicate with them. In so doing, they drew ever closer, teaching me about love, life, compassion, healing of others, healing of myself, healing of the world, and about just having fun.

"In time, inner guidance developed regarding the purchase of our home, creating Gary's and my book, *Portals and Corridors*, executing successful Feng Shui remedies, setting up healing ceremonies, and making basic everyday decisions.

"None of this would have been possible without the prophecy from Reverend Rhinehart's mediumship, entranced by St. Germaine. I am so grateful to him and the Ascended Masters for their gift to me. It has changed my life all for the better. Through the years, Reverend Rhinehart supported and encouraged me in my development, not only in psychic art but in other interests as well.

"One example happened during the mid-1990s when I experienced a strong interest in designing costumes and clothing accessories. No one in the Church knew of my interest except my husband, Gary. One day, completely out of the blue, I received a gift from Reverend Rhinehart. I was shocked when I opened it. As I tore off the wrapping, a ceramic teapot sculpted in the shape of a sewing machine revealed itself. I have not pursued this interest as of yet, but I know the Masters'and Reverend Rhinehart foresaw something, and when I delve into it, I believe it will bring me the same kind of joy and happiness I received from doing Spiritual Psychic Art.

"Gary and I had another experience regarding my Spiritual Psychic Art. During a telephone hookup séance sometime around 1997, St.

Germaine had entranced Reverend Rhinehart, and at some point in the séance, he began acknowledging different Spiritual Psychic Artists in the membership of the Church. He called out their names, praising them for the demonstration of their gifts. This went on for some time, but St. Germaine never mentioned my name.

"On our drive home, Gary and I talked about how disappointed we were that St. Germaine hadn't mentioned me, especially since I had been acknowledged in the past—it almost felt deliberate. As we talked, Gary said we must have people write out affidavits attesting to the authenticity of my work, presenting notarized testimonies documenting that they received value and genuine experiences surrounding my Spiritual Psychic Artwork. So that's what I did, I collected maybe six different testimonies and submitted them to the Center Leader.

"About a year later, again with St. Germaine entrancing Reverend Rhinehart during a telephone hookup séance, he said he held in his hand two Spiritual Psychic Art Designations to present, one to Monica and one to another person in the Miami Branch of the Church. Then he talked about the conversation Gary and I discussed on the way home after he failed to mention my name, amongst the other Spiritual Psychic Artists, during the séance a year ago. He described our discussion in detail. We never mentioned this conversation to a soul. I was shocked! He said the Masters deliberately passed me over because originally I failed to provide the Ascended Masters with testimonies regarding the genuineness of my work. He acknowledged us for thinking it over and taking the necessary steps to document our experiences by having people provide notarized statements that indeed they had experienced I was a genuine Spiritual Psychic Artist. I was a bit shocked to realize how attentive the Masters were to our lives, how they followed our development by listening in on our conversations, and then in the end acknowledging us for our growth and shift in consciousness." ~ Monica Szu-Whitney

SEASONS OF THE SOUL

Here is the testimony of a student from Vancouver, Canada, regarding a telephone hookup that attests to the foresight a Master can bring in protecting a student from harm and uplifting the chela:

"It is early morning and I'm preparing to leave for work. I have a distinctly strong feeling of trepidation. I sense it is not about my job, but the commute. The Vancouver rush hour could be stressful, but something about today felt different. Call it a gut feeling, but I did not want to get into traffic this morning as it just felt dangerous. And yet what was I to do? I had a duty to be at work and be on time, so off I went out into the pouring rain with a deep feeling of uneasiness. To alleviate my apprehensive vibration, I sang hymns out loud in the car, hymns like '*In the Garden*' and others that I particularly liked.

"Soon, I knew the reason for my concern.

"In freeway driving, most people typically travel at least ten miles per hour beyond the speed limit. I was no different. In time, I approached my exit. Oh my gosh, the rain came pouring down, the roadway was extremely slippery, and the exit traffic had bottlenecked! Vehicles were completely backed up to the off-ramp exit. At a glance, I found no room to exit, but clearly it was too late and dangerous to bypass the exit, so I took the risk of sliding into the vehicles in front of me. I exited, fearing a chain reaction of rear-endings. But by the grace of God, and don't ask me how, because it defied all logic, the vehicle in front of me moved out of my way in a nick of time. Miraculously, I averted a collision disaster. *'Thank you God! Thank you God! Thank you God!'*

"Several weeks passed, and on April 17th, I attended a Holy Communion Seance through the mediumship of Keith Milton Rhinehart. You can imagine my surprise when the Ascended Masters communicating through Reverend Rhinehart's mediumship said, *'We have recently helped avoid a number of motor vehicle accidents since our last gathering, including one involving a maroon-colored car.'* I owned a maroon-colored car! What? Was that my near miss, or should I say my near hit, the Masters were referring to? They had protected me and others from harm. I felt a wave of gratitude. My *"Special Day"* was just a day or two from my driving incident and provided me with additional evidence Master intelligence intervened on my behalf, saving me from certain disaster."

"In working with chelas, the Masters often gave out a *"Special Day"* through Reverend Rhinehart's mediumship at the beginning of each year, in which to alert the chelas to be on the look-out. This *"Special Date"* infers that this particular day is significant in some way; the day could be either a day or two ahead or after the selected date."

Uplifting and inspiring the truth seeker can take on many different forms, from delivering a couple of heartfelt words to directing someone to find a more profound meaning to their life, to saving a life. As we have seen, the Ascended Masters are adept at each!

NINETEEN

MEDIUMSHIP
HISTORICAL SCIENTIFIC REFERENCES

I N THE LATE NINETEENTH CENTURY, SEVERAL PROMINENT SCI-
entists, all tops in their fields, at the zenith of their mental prowess,
put their careers and reputations on the line to test mediums. There
was wild conjecture at the time regarding mediumship. They intended
to scientifically prove one way or the other if the phenomena touted
by Spiritualism were legitimate. Sir William Crookes, Sir Oliver Lodge,
Dr. Charles Richet, and Baron von Schrenck Notzing all participated
in the testing of the physical phenomena of mediums. Each concluded
without reservation that the phenomena was genuine.

Although Reverend Rhinehart stands alone as the most accomplished, scientifically tested medium of all time, he is certainly
not alone as the only accomplished medium who has demonstrated
physical phenomena and other evidential psychic gifts. The *History of
Spiritualism*, by Sir Arthur Conan Doyle, is an important book to the
Ascended Masters and throughout their communications, they often
referred to it. In fact, they were highly involved in producing some
of the phenomena described in the book. So, it stands to reason it
would be valuable to provide context to Reverend Rhinehart's physical
phenomena by mentioning other examples of Spiritual phenomena
produced by other famous mediums who defied the naysayers
of the day. It is not our intent to give a history of all the colorful

physical phenomena mediums, but we'd like to highlight some of the phenomena, especially ectoplasmic materialization.

In discussing this phenomenon surrounding the physical materialization of a Spirit Being, we refer to Dr. Charles Richet, physicist and Nobel Prize recipient in 1918, who coined the term "ectoplasm." (*Ecto* refers to something that is external, exterior to the body, and *plasm* a formative or formed material, as in cellular tissue.) Dr. Richet describes ectoplasm as a viscous milky-white substance extracted from the orifices of a medium, through the mouth, nostrils, ears, vagina, and can exude from the solar plexus and skin as well. At times, ectoplasm can look somewhat nebulous in form, be vaporous, invisible, or can take on the form of a physical body, or an inanimate object, such as a pair of eyeglasses or clothing.

Dr. Richet observed the ectoplasm phenomenon in Tangier in the 1870s. For over four years, under test conditions, Dr. Richet studied the mediums Eva C (Eva Carriére) and Eusapia Paladino, and first reported their ectoplasmic experiences in the *Annuals of Psychical Science* and was later quoted in the *History of Spiritualism*. Here are some of Dr. Richet's comments on ectoplasm, written about in the *History of Spiritualism*:

In his first reports, Dr. Richet describes at great length the manifestation of a spirit who called himself Bien Boa through the use of ectoplasm extracted from Eva C's body. The professor says that this form possessed all the attributes of life. "It walks, speaks, moves, and breathes like a human being. Its body is resistant and has a certain muscular strength. It is neither a lay figure nor a doll, nor an image reflected by a mirror; it is as a living being, it is as a living man; and there are reasons for resolutely setting aside every other supposition than one or the other of these two hypotheses: either that of a phantom having the attributes of life; or that of a living person playing the part of a phantom." [1]

174

There is criticism from some, saying that Bien Boa was a cardboard cutout, but the intellect of Dr. Richet can certainly distinguish cardboard from ectoplasm after four years of study, and when is the last time we heard of cardboard speaking?

If there is one physical phenomenon medium who merits discussion, it is Miss Florence Cook. As a young girl of fifteen, when she began displaying the possession of strong psychic powers, she produced the physical manifestation of a Spirit Being that called herself "Katie King." Under the duress of skeptics, to clear her character, she made herself available to the scientific testing of Sir William Crookes, giving him complete control as to the tests he might perform on her mediumistic talent.

Sir William Crookes was an English chemist and physicist who attended the Royal College of Chemistry. He was highly interested in Spiritualism and became president of the Society for Psychical Research. Mr. Crookes witnessed Florence Cook produce ectoplasmic phenomena under rigorous scientific conditions and also reported that ectoplasm is a real observable substance.

At the time of the tests, Mr. Crookes was at the height of his intellectual powers as a well-respected physicist, chemist, and editor of the *Quarterly Journal of Science*. For many, he was considered the scientific doorkeeper of the generation, the discoverer of Thallium, an investigator into radiant matter and vacuum tubes. As a scientist, he found curiosity in Miss Cook's bizarre phenomena and thought scientific inquiry would prove fruitful. The following is excerpted from the *History of Spiritualism* and explains Crookes's testing and experience with Miss Cook:

"In his house at Mornington Road, a small study opened into the chemical laboratory, a door with a curtain separating the two rooms. Miss Cook lay entranced upon a couch in the inner room. In the outer (room) in subdued light sat Crookes, with such other observers he invited. At the end of a period which varied from twenty minutes to an hour, the materialized figure was built up from the ectoplasm of the medium. The existence of this substance and its method of production were unknown at that date, but subsequent research has thrown much light upon it, an account of which has been embodied in the chapter on ectoplasm. The actual effect was that the curtain was opened, and there emerged into the laboratory a female who was usually as different from the medium as two people could be. This apparition, which could move, talk, and act in all ways as any independent entity, is known by the name which she herself claimed as her own, 'Katie King.'

"The natural explanation of the skeptic is that the two women were really the same woman, and that Katie was a clever impersonation of Florence. The objector could strengthen his case by the observation made not only by Crookes but by Miss Marryat (invited observer) and others that there were times when Katie was very like Florence...

"However, the student has certainly the right to claim that Florence Cook and Katie King were the same individual until convincing evidence is laid before him that this is impossible. Such evidence, Professor Crookes is very careful to give.

"The points of difference which he observed between Miss Cook and Katie are thus described:

"Katie's height varies; in my house, I have seen her six inches taller than Miss Cook. Last night, with bare feet and not tiptoeing, she was four and a half inches taller than Miss Cook, Katie's neck was bare last night; the skin was perfectly smooth both to touch and sight, whilst on Miss Cook's neck is a large blister, which under similar circumstances is distinctly visible and rough to the touch. Katie's ears are unpierced, whilst Miss Cook habitually wears earrings. Katie's complexion is very fair, while that of Miss Cook is very dark. Katie's fingers are much longer than Miss Cook's, and her face is also larger. In manners and ways of expression, there are also many decided differences."

In a later contribution, Crookes adds:

"Having seen so much of Katie lately, when she has been illuminated by the electric light, I am enabled to add to the points of difference between her and her medium, which I mentioned in a former article, I have the most absolute certainty that Miss Cook and Katie are two separate individuals so far as their bodies are concerned. Several little marks on Miss Cook's face are absent on Katie's. Miss Cook's hair is so dark a brown as almost to appear black; a lock of Katie's, which is now before me, and which she allowed me to cut from her luxuriant tresses, having first traced it up to the scalp and satisfied myself that it actually grew there, is a rich golden auburn.

"On one evening, I timed Katie's pulse. It beat steadily at 75, whilst Miss Cook's pulse, a little time after, was going at its usual rate of 90. On applying my ear to Katie's chest, I could hear a heart beating rhythmically inside, and pulsating ever more steadily than did Miss Cook's heart when she allowed me to try a similar experiment after the séance. Tested in the same way, Katie's lungs were found to be sounder than her medium's, for at the time I tried my experiment, Miss Cook was under medical treatment for a severe cough." [2]

We can see Crookes's investigation was thorough and executed over a period of time rather than simply on one occasion. Many said Crookes was fooled by Miss Cook, but for a man of his professional stature, highly esteemed for his exacting methods of scientific inquiry, to be fooled by a fifteen-year-old girl was impossible. Many in the scientific community were outraged by his declarations, but he didn't back down and was one of the first to give scientific credibility to the physical manifestation of Spirit by a medium using ectoplasm extracted from the medium's subtle body.

For contemporary examples of the veracity of physical phenomenon, there is a photograph reproduced in the book, *Photographing the Spirit World*, which shows Reverend Rhinehart sitting in a chair with a white ectoplasmic chord extending from his mouth to the fully physically materialized form of Archangel Gabriel, who some have declared to be the most important photograph ever taken! [3]

Additionally, the authors of *Photographing the Spirit World* describe the famous tests made in 1958 by a committee of Japanese scientists, which we have previously referenced regarding the *"Fraud Proof"* chair. In the book, the authors discuss an infrared picture from this series of séances and experiments showing a wide tape of ectoplasmic substance, about four to five inches wide, flowing from Reverend Rhinehart's solar plexus down to the floor and up to the top of an adjacent table where it forms a small three-fingered hand-like structure which grips a pencil and is writing. (pseudo-pod)

Another medium, Alex Harris, like Reverend Rhinehart, was noted for his development of trance mediumship, direct voice communications, and healings. He was devoted to bringing hope and comfort to those who suffered. The book, *They Walked Among Us*, tells his story. One of the most remarkable demonstrations of physical phenomenon appearing through mediumship took place in a collaborative séance with Reverend Rhinehart and Alec Harris in Johannesburg, South Africa, in 1958.

Before their demonstration, Reverend Rhinehart presented to the audience of 50 sitters a séance through direct-voice mediumship. In this setting, the voice of an African servant's dead father came through, speaking in pure fluent Zulu. Reverend Rhinehart, being an American, was completely unfamiliar with Zulu!

Mrs. Carleton, who frequented psychic gatherings in Johannesburg, South Africa, described the public sitting conducted by Reverend Rhinehart as a highlight in the psychic history of Johannesburg. At Reverend Rhinehart's direct-voice séance, a half dozen sitters received apports of hand-painted cards covered with a variety of different subjects painted on each card. In this demonstration, each sitter stepped before a floating trumpet and was instructed to reach inside the trumpet—when they did, they exclaimed there was nothing inside. Momentarily, a rattling sound occurred, after which each sitter reached back into the trumpet and pulled out a decorative painted card.

The collaborative demonstration by Reverend Rhinehart and Harris was reported in the phpBB SpiritualismLink (website) by Zerdini. Unfortunately, the report lacks a scientific approach, but the astonishing nature of the séance deserves presenting, especially given Reverend Rhinehart's established credibility.

In this séance in Johannesburg, Alex Harris and Reverend Rhinehart linked their Spiritual forces together in a unique tour-de-force demonstration of adept mediumship. Harris sat on one side of the stage and Reverend Rhinehart on the other, then a broad stream of ectoplasm poured between their two bodies. Once the stream of ectoplasm established itself between their two bodies, ten Spirit figures fully materialized within the broad stream of ectoplasmic light. Extraordinary!

The number of Spirits materializing at once could only occur with the power of two adept physical phenomenon mediums present. I know of no other incident on record of this type of phenomenon.

During another demonstration on the same day, a tall, materialized Spirit known as "The Scientist" came bathed in a strong blueish light, put his hands on Reverend Rhinehart's solar plexus, then extracted a long stream of ectoplasm. He walked towards Alex Harris, stretching and broadening the ectoplasm as he walked, finally joining the ectoplasm to Harris's body. Then the Scientist gathered a section of the ectoplasm and took it to one of the sitters, where he exclaimed he was going to give the man a healing. Mrs. Carleton said the Scientist fed the ectoplasm into the sitter's solar plexus, drawing it from Reverend Rhinehart through Alex Harris. She says it was a living force seen by all present, moving in the most amazing way. Then, suddenly, in a flash, it vanished.

So we can determine there have been years of effort by the Spirit World to provide irrefutable proof of the manifestation of physical phenomena by adept mediums, even though physical phenomenon mediumship has been dismissed by many contemporary critics as a fad of the 1880s. These proofs confound skeptics like James Randi, Joseph Dunniger, and Harry Houdini. Reverend Rhinehart puts the controversy to rest with his testing. But there are many other examples of genuine mediumship with Gladys Osborne Lenard, Nettie Maynard (the Medium who President Lincoln consulted about the Civil War), William Stanton Moses, Edgar Cayce, and others.

We would like to conclude with one last word from Dr. Richet.

In the book, *Phenomena of Materialisation*, Dr. Charles Richet, the French Professor of Physiology, famous for his pioneering work in immunology, says this about the physical phenomenon he witnessed in mediums:

"At the same time, I do not consider myself justified in despising the 'metaphysical' facts, which must be methodically studied without prejudice... We must not be appalled by what is strange... that which marks a discovery, the unforeseen, the unexpected, the new. It may clash with popular opinions and may contradict the classic official teaching. Otherwise, it would not be a discovery. And after it has come forward, it counters a thousand denials. Even if it is as clear as the sun, it is not accepted... It is only with difficulty that we form the conviction of having lived in error, having made wrong assertions... Only unusual phenomena astonish us. A thing appears true because we have often seen it, but not at all because we have understood it, for all natural phenomena are incomprehensible."

To end the chapter on mediumship, we will relate a fascinating story surrounding Harry Houdini and his emphatic denial of the validity of mediumship and the continuance of life after death. This account alone debunks his rancorous skepticism.

After Houdini's Mother passed, he desperately wanted to communicate. They were extremely close, so he sought out the mediums of the day in hopes of finding peace and comfort. But medium after medium failed to bring satisfaction. He was inconsolable and angry that the entire lot of psychics was nothing but a bunch of charlatans. Bent on justice, he set out to expose the frauds.

He went from parlor to parlor posing as a genuine "sitter," then exposing the mediums when he spotted their chicanery. After securing his proof, he brought in the authorities to arrest them as frauds, finally writing articles in the papers about their deceptions so all would know the truth about the scandalous psychics. Since his famous escape acts relied on deception, he determined all psychics relied on the same kind of deception.

But it wasn't beyond Houdini's integrity to practice some deception himself in the séance room as he got caught stuffing a rubber stopper in a glass bell that inhibited Spirit from ringing the bell. When Sir Arthur Conan Doyle discovered this fact, their relationship fell apart beyond repair.

Before his death, Houdini and his wife, Beatrice, made a pact that if life continued after death, he would come back through a medium and reveal a coded message that only he and Beatrice knew. If no medium could provide the code, this would prove once and for all the truth regarding life after death.

After Houdini's death, Beatrice held séances every Halloween for ten years with the hopes of having someone provide the coded message. She offered a reward of ten thousand dollars! Then in 1929, Arthur Ford, the American psychic, spiritualist medium, revealed the secret coded message at Mrs. Houdini's house with several witnesses present, including a Mr. Fast and Mr. John W. Stafford, the associate editor of *The Scientific American*, who were both strangers to Mrs. Houdini. The message, Ford's Spirit guide, Fletcher, brought through using the secret code that only Beatrice knew was, *"ROSABELLE BELIEVE."* Fletcher then asked, *"Is this right, Mrs. Houdini?"* Mrs. Houdini answered, *"Yes,"* with much feeling. Rosabelle was Houdini's pet name for Beatrice.

Later, this incident was corroborated by Beatrice live on the radio in an interview with the commentator Walter Winchell, confirming that the medium Arthur Ford, indeed, delivered the genuine secret coded message Houdini had left with her. So ironically, from the greatest skeptic that mediumship has ever known, comes the proof that life goes on after death!

Ford says from the moment Mrs. Houdini pronounced the message to be correct, attacks began to fly, questioning her veracity, claiming she had given the secret code to Ford, and other outrageous lies, all pointing to Ford being a fraud. Once again, the skeptics deny the truth. Interestingly, the contemporary community of magicians continues to promote Houdini's skepticism.

TWENTY

THOUGHT
KEEPING OUR CRITICAL FACULTIES ALIVE

T HE MASTERS SAY, "STAY PRESENT!" THEY ADVISE US TO PAY attention to details! Eliminate our biases, prejudices, and anxiety triggers. Let's look at some issues contributing to our inability to stay present, especially pertinent for those involved in Spiritual practices, but obviously true for everyone.

He is late, as usual. Miles's wife waits for her husband to give her a ride to work as he rushes through his morning routine. He grabs his muffler, coat, stocking cap, keys, and he and his wife are finally out the door, into the foggy morning, immediately bumpered into 6:00 A.M. commuter-hell.

Traffic slows to a crawl. Miles reviews his plans for the day. Thirty minutes of slinking through stressed-out, white-knuckled commuters, and after dropping his wife off, he must hurry to get to Huntington Park in San Francisco's Nob Hill District for the first segment of the Qigong Walk. After Qigong, it's up to Marin County to take his mom to a 9:30 dental appointment she is anxiously awaiting.

Miles whips his Camry into a parking slot in front of the Masonic Auditorium just in time for the start of the Qigong Walk. The curb's yellow—he intuits, no problem, he'll be gone way before the meter maid rolls by at 8:05.

It's a cold, chilly morning and once the walk begins, the Qi starts to flow and his brain and body thaw. When the walk is over, he enjoys a little banter with his fellow walkers, and just before he exits the park, he spots Stephen, the dog walker. He stops to exchange pleasantries and pet Stephen's dog, Lucca. The conversation rambles. Miles feels a pull, he needs to go, but continues to talk a bit longer, then dashes off to the car.

Standing in front of the Masonic Auditorium, he looks up and down the bustling California Street. Where did he park? In front of the Masonic—Right? He's sure it was right there at the yellow curb, but there's no Camry! He can't be late for Mom's appointment. A pang of panic shoots through his abdomen! Then he spots the yellow zone parking sign: **VEHICLES WILL BE TOWED AFTER 8:00 A.M.**. He looks at his watch, 8:15. *"Damn—I talked with Stephen that long?"* Clearly, the meter maid did her duty. His car's been towed. Dammit! What to do? He calls Gordon, a fellow Qigong walker to see if he'll drive him to the impound station halfway across the city. Gordon says he and his wife are on their way to Cayucos and will pick him up right before leaving. Once at the station, Miles waits an hour in the impound line, noticing that several young people are huddled against the impound wall, looking lost.

Finally, at the front of the line, the clerk says matter-of-factly, *"Your parking ticket is $300.00, the impound fee is $500.00, and the tax is $75.00. How do you want to pay?"*

"Holy Shit! So that's why these kids are squatted up against the wall, looking so forlorn—no money! I wonder if they need a ride..."

After Miles charges his credit card, an attendant leads him through the maze of impounds to his car. He reaches into his pants pocket, fumbling around—no keys! He reaches into his coat pocket—no keys! Miles concludes his keys have fallen out of his pocket and are now halfway to Cayucos, lying in the backseat of Gordon's car.

He looks at his watch—10:00 A.M., he's late for Mom's 9:30 appointment. At age ninety-seven, Mom's frantic button has long since triggered! He must call. He searches his coat for the phone—then remembers his phone is in the glove compartment of the car—No keys! No car! No phone! Totally unhinged, he walks an hour across the city to his wife's workplace to get her copy of the car keys and then back another hour to the impound station. One horrendous morning! The only positive was that his wife had called Mom to let her know he hadn't been in an accident!

Is this chaos an isolated case—not necessarily! (True Story) Like Miles, those intuitively gifted and psychically inclined can be distracted by subtle levels of thought and the bewilderment of new energies awakening within them. They are simply prone to be less engaged in practicalities and more likely to face the type of morning that blindsided Miles, who fancied himself high on the intuitive scale.

The Masters admonish, live and anchor yourself in the present moment! St. Germaine has pointed out that those who demonstrate psychic-intuitive skills are less adept in survival skills and everyday sensible judgements. These folks show a track record of drifting out of the present moment and often have difficulty providing for themselves by consistently holding down work. Is this always the case? Of course not! But there is a tendency in this direction worth noting.

There seems to arise a spacey quality around different phases of Spiritual practice, whether it be meditation, chanting, or yoga. But it doesn't matter whether we are engaged in work, Spiritual sadhana, or a casual conversation; life demands that we stay present. Space out and we stir the recipe for Miles's morning.

What can we do to better keep our critical faculties alive? We can start by adopting a rigorous attitude of being mindful of living in the present moment, resisting the tendency of the mind to float out of the body into the past or future. When we are diligent, our awareness is tuned, stationed in the body, and acutely focused on what's at hand, thereby creating the tendency to respond appropriately in the moment.

Another aspect of keeping our critical faculties alive is working to recognize what causes us to "zone out." What types of events trigger unconscious responses? What thoughts cause us to drift out of the present time into the past or future? In taking the time to identify the thoughts, feelings, and events that make us uneasy or anxious, we can become more aware and less prone to slipping into an unconscious mode.

Psychologist Dr. Judson Brewer, author of *Unwinding Anxiety*, discusses overpowering stimuli and how they can trigger unconscious behavior. For instance, events like an upcoming difficult project, a loved one who has passed, a stern masculine voice, or maybe a growling dog, can bring on a state of out-of-control anxiety, triggering any number of avoidance tactics. Avoidance examples include eating unconsciously, watching a movie for the fifth time, gambling, overindulging in sex, random spending, or mindlessly going through the motions without thinking of the purpose behind our activity. Here we are speaking of patterns of thought and activities that are not so severe as those triggered by deeply traumatic events. We are speaking of stimuli encoded in the brain from past events that activate habitual patterns to avoid confronting the emotions sitting behind our anxiety.

To overcome this tendency, Dr. Brewer suggests we map the mind through observing the body to discover the ways it responds unconsciously to overpowering, anxiety-causing stimuli. When feelings of anxiousness or a tightness arise in the body, that is a sure sign we are being triggered based on past events, stressful thoughts, fear of the future, or the need to choose between "fight or flight." In constantly scanning the body, we can begin to map our mind. Using bodily discomfort as a guide, we can identify psychological discomfort by scanning the body from head to toe. The body doesn't lie; trust it, as the mind can deceive. So if we locate bodily tightness, we know an anxiousness has been triggered. Observing the physical tightness and the emotional event that triggered it guides us to reveal habitual patterns and brings awareness to unwanted avoidance strategies. By making it a practice to note tightness in the body when it arises and asking what was the trigger—what did I do in response, we might avoid the wrong kinds of strategies, like devouring chocolate, watching a movie, rushing half-wittedly through balancing the checkbook, or shopping excessively.

Allowing curiosity to arise at these moments and asking what is going on assists us in our discovery. Taking the time to locate our physical response will create a space, allowing us the opportunity to pull back from our habitual response and bring awareness to unwanted avoidance strategies.

Dr. Brewer suggests the appropriate response is to witness ourselves and simply BE rather than having to DO something. We generally think our response of doing something best serves us, but our response is likely a deflection or an avoidance of dealing with a difficult emotion. Asking ourselves if this deflecting behavior is actually rewarding, or useful for our greater good and peace of mind, is a good question. Am I living in the present? Are the results I'm getting from my behavior more harmful than rewarding? Does that extra donut serve me? Is my nasty comment about my friend warranted? Did going shopping solve my issue? By inspecting triggered activities, we might find they aren't as rewarding as we originally thought.

If we revisit Miles's morning, we recognize that his being late created an anxiousness. He slips out of present time awareness in his haste to take the first available parking spot, then his emotional neediness to stay in conversation too long with his friend Stephan creates another distraction, and finally, his upset with the morning's events spins him out emotionally, and he again goes unconscious, losing his keys in Gordon's car.

We believe these types of events can be avoided when we have a better understanding of our emotional and mental triggers and by simply witnessing ourselves, sensing our body, and being mindful rather than feeling the need to do something.

With severe emotional traumas, we should not pretend we are simply lacking the ability to stay present but recognize that confronting these types of disabilities on our own is unwise. It is best to consult a professional in these types of cases.

Another thought pattern obstructing us from clear thinking is the prejudices we hold. Any prejudice can prevent us from enacting our critical faculties, hampering us from realizing a truth, preventing us from listening with an open mind and heart, or, in some instances, blinding us from accepting proven facts. Some prejudices we may have installed to please our parents, uncles, or siblings who have sway over us, others from fear, and still others from a lack of clear thinking. If we make an effort to root out all prejudices and identify our personal beliefs, we can begin to act, think, and respond in ways that become more expansive and clear. As we work to reveal our beliefs, we may uncover uninspected prejudices suggesting how we detest the rich, dismiss the uneducated, pity the poor, discard the obese, or any number of prejudices coloring our life experience.

The Masters have suggested the majority of us have repeated the same debilitating life patterns from life to life, to life, to life, re-enacting old karmic habits ad infinitum, all to our detriment and lack of personal growth. The majority of these life patterns stem from over-valuing the material world, coveting money, sex, and power, and under-valuing our unity with all of humanity. At some point, isn't it time to step out of the habitual pattern and evolve? The Masters' suggest, why not now?

In addition to negotiating our own inner thoughts, we must deal with the bombardment of thoughts, opinions, and data coming in from every direction. How do we process these thoughts in our daily lives? How do we sift through the constant barrage of daily information, determining what to keep and what to trash? In this crazy world where we are fed urban legends, misinformation, disinformation, friends' statements, and religious superstition regularly, how do we remain unbiased and level-headed while not becoming overly gullible when processing information? How do we discern truth from error while negotiating constant mental minefields? With our early educational training of mostly regurgitating facts, this is a legitimate challenge.

In general, it can behoove us to take a more adversarial mindset when receiving information. We must insist on questioning extraordinary claims and extraordinary stories and demand extraordinary, undeniable evidence, no matter the source or circumstance. To illustrate this point and since we are living in a technological society, Reverend Rhinehart posed a question to one of the Center Leaders of the Church at a special gathering in Houston:

He asked, *"If you were presented a picture of your best friend fornicating with a pig, would you believe he was guilty of the perversion?"* The lady hemmed and hawed and Reverend Rhinehart jumped in, exclaiming, *"No! Absolutely not. This is your best friend whose character you know better than anyone. In this day and age, anything can be deep-faked and you must demand further uncontroversial evidence if you are going to accept the picture as real!"*

An adversarial approach instills more rigor in discerning information, pushing ourselves and those around us to be more responsible for any claims. This can be especially true around Spiritual wisdom, where we can assume each tradition is embedded in the absolute truth. In the case of traditional religion, we might investigate at a deeper level, asking, Is this tradition grounded in absolute truth?

Are there critics, and what do they say? At the minimum, it would deepen our understanding. Are there truths and half-truths existing within the belief system? What is the lineage? How did it evolve?

By making the effort to explore the truth from different vantages with an adversarial mindset, comparing our findings to other traditions, then measuring each finding against personal experience, and finally consulting our inner voice as to the truth, we can evolve our thinking. This approach can be taken not only with Spiritual matters and outlandish claims, but in everyday situations. Even taking an adversarial perspective with a friend may be a way of furthering our understanding and discerning the truth. It doesn't have to become combative but can be a mutual exploration without animosity if we hold each other in respect. Being open to our friend's rebuttal can contribute to our understanding, as Steve and I experienced while writing this book.

By the same token, if extraordinary evidence doesn't immediately surface, it isn't necessarily a sign the information is in error. It's entirely possible the facts haven't revealed themselves to date. Some may claim everything is a conspiracy story if they don't find instant online confirmation, but life isn't that simple, nor that black and white. Some cases require us to put our final judgment on the back burner, leaving it in suspension, while we move forward and remain open to the answer. But when the source of our information is telling us what to think regarding an extraordinary claim, a red flag should flash, and we might want to proceed with caution.

TWENTY-ONE

THOUGHT
BEYOND PREJUDICES

THE ASCENDED MASTERS, THROUGH REVEREND RHINEHART, suggest we use our critical faculties for evaluating their work and mediumship in general. But most importantly, we confront our prejudices. The following life story from Steve offers this kind of reasoning, where he confronts his prejudices regarding mediumship. In the first chapter, you will recall how Steve initially reacted to Reverend Rhinehart's materialization of white stones. His ultimate response is a good take on his willingness to confront his beliefs through the use of inductive reasoning. Here is more on the background of what Steve confronted:

(It all started when) "I got a call one day from my sister asking me to attend a yoga lecture that evening at the home of someone in the Kahala District of Honolulu. She said a highly acclaimed physical phenomenon medium was visiting and would be present at the meeting. This grabbed my attention as I always doubted the authenticity of mediums, psychics, and fortune tellers. One reason I will mention is I once read a local newspaper article exposing fraudulent fortune tellers in the red-light district of Honolulu that raised my brow. The article brought to light an incident about a "sitter" who visited a local fortune teller. The fortune teller gave the person a chicken egg, asking him to rub the egg over his body, then to hold the egg for a few minutes. After that, the fortune teller cracked open the egg. Upon inspecting it, the fortune teller found the egg's insides to be black. The fortune teller exclaimed, *'You have been cursed, but don't worry, I can remove the curse for a small fee.'*

"As a police officer assigned to patrol the red-light district, this disturbed me. I'd experienced vivid spirit hauntings as a kid. These incidents terrified our family, causing me to distrust anything to do with entities of the Spirit World.

"I became so upset, I felt compelled to discover more about the Spirit World. So I started researching Spirits of the dead, photographs of the dead, and Spiritual phenomena in general. The information I uncovered left me mostly confused. The photographs of Spirit phenomenon looked so superficial and strange; they were really flat and appeared like two-dimensional images made up of a hazy, white substance researchers have named ectoplasm. I found the images almost cartoonish, cardboard-like, incredibly naively formed. These unusual whitish images were claimed to be formed by Spirit using the ectoplasmic substance drawn out of a medium's body—weird! I wasn't buying it! They looked phony to me! But in the end, my extensive research proved unsuccessful as a means of relieving my fears.

"To this day, my childhood hauntings torment me. I feel the apparitions I experienced were evil. Admittedly, my religious influences were to blame to some extent, but my fear was real. There were nights of being awakened by footsteps walking up and down our family's stairs, nights of hearing heavy chains drag across our bedroom ceiling, and voices crying out in the dark! It wasn't just me; the entire family feared the angry, scary ghosts. One night, my father, a policeman, grabbed his revolver and searched the house inside and out, but found nothing. The noises stopped during his search, but when he came back inside, they started up again. These never-ending events terrified us.

"Grandmother prayed every day to stop the hauntings, but they continued. Mother finally called in an exorcist to cleanse the house—we were so happy, but again that night the rappings returned. So, as you might imagine, because of my early childhood turmoil, I harbored many fears around being in the dark and surrounded by Spirits of the dead.

"When I pulled up to the gathering that day on my police Harley Davidson motorcycle, dressed in full uniform, black leather jacket and boots, I came ready to expose the good Reverend as a fraud. I came weighted down with years of frightening nights, so when I casually sauntered into the upscale home that day, I brought with me strong biases against the so-called Spirit phenomenon. I am not kidding when I say, I came prepared to defend myself against any possible Spirit attacks by whatever means necessary.

"The only person I knew at the event was my sister. Everybody and everything else was unfamiliar. To say I felt uncomfortable wasn't an exaggeration, but my training in self-defense eased my fears to a degree.

"There were maybe fifty people gathered in a nicely appointed home that day. In the front of the room stood the medium, Reverend Keith Milton Rhinehart, wearing a white flowing robe. At first glance, I noticed a beautiful, radiating presence that immediately lifted my comfort level. He spoke of the History of Spiritualism, séances, the *Life and Teaching of the Ascended Masters of the Far East*, the Fox Sisters, and the scientific investigations performed on various mediums over the past century.

"After the Reverend's talk came his demonstrations of blindfold billet psychometry. A pencil and a blank piece of paper (referred to as a billet card) were passed out to all those in attendance. An assistant requested we address three questions to the Spirit World, sign our name, hold the billet card against our solar plexus for several minutes, fold the message so the contents faced inwards, then drop the billet card into the plastic box being passed around the room. Once the plastic box made the rounds, an assistant placed it on a table in front of the medium. Reverend Rhinehart then asked a volunteer to come forward from the audience to prepare him for the billet reading. The person folded a heavy white cloth into a four-inch-wide band and wrapped it around the medium's head, tying it at the back. Several people inspected the cloth wrapping, stating they were convinced he couldn't see out.

"The Reverend pulled one billet card at a time out of the box, placing the billet to his forehead. As he did, his cabinet guide, Doctor Robert John Kensington, a person on the Spirit-side of life, spoke through the medium in a voice distinctly different from the Reverend's. Then Dr. Kensington called out the first and last name of the person who wrote out the billet card. How he knew who wrote the billet without seeing the card mystified me. Then he delivered a message to the person whose billet card Reverend Rhinehart pressed to his forehead. The message might come from anybody in Spirit, addressing nearly any subject. One after another, grandfathers, wives, and old friends spoke, bringing forth startling messages, leaving each "sitter" in total shock, with many left sobbing.

"Suddenly, I heard, *'Steve Young,'* called out by Dr. Kensington. A quiver shot through my stomach. *'Your dead brother is here wanting to extend his love!'*

"This shocked me. I didn't have a dead brother! I said to myself, *'Oh, now I've got you, just like I thought, fraudulent like them all!'*

"He went on, *'This is your father. Please forgive me for the way I treated the family. I was wrong to behave like that. I am very sorry I treated you poorly. Ask your mother about how she and I used to pray before a makeshift altar in our bedroom. I am now friends with Doctor Kensington and have met some of the Masters.'*

"After the reading, someone passed me the billet card, which was the card I'd placed in the box. The message about my brother was absolutely false, but the message where my father spoke proved evidential, though I wasn't familiar with a make-shift altar and felt conflicted as to his assertion he and mother prayed in front of the makeshift altar at night. That was a surprise. I moved away from home when I was eighteen, before they began this supposed practice, so I had no idea of its truth.

"As I pondered Dad's message, the Reverend indicated the séance would start soon and told us to prepare for absolute blackout conditions. A sharp tremor again shot through my stomach. He reminded us not to ignite any cigarette lighters or use flash cameras, as light could cause him physical harm. (Light is disintegrating to an ectoplasmic phenomenon and is known to have even caused death to some mediums.)

"Shortly thereafter, the Reverend asked for a volunteer from the audience to place him under simple test conditions, just before I could raise my hand, another volunteer came forward. Then Reverend Rhinehart took a mouthful of water, the volunteer placed white tape over his mouth, and with a ballpoint pen, he drew lines from the tape to his skin. This procedure ensured if someone tampered with the tape during the séance, the deceit would be detected as the lines wouldn't realign perfectly. Finally, the volunteer signed his initials to the tape and we were ready for the séance.

"With the test conditions in place, Reverend Rhinehart stepped into a violet cloth cabinet, the size and shape of a regular shower. I looked in the cabinet and the only objects I could see were a chair, a pitcher of water, and an aluminum collapsible trumpet (which I later learned was used by Spirits to magnify their voices). If fraud occurred, I would know.

"The lights went out, black as black could be. My fears accelerated! Past anxieties reeled through my mind, imaginary hands reaching out of the black and choking the life out of me, followed by any number of the torments I experienced as a kid. Just in case, my blackjack and Smith and Wesson .38 were resting at my side.

"The Reverend then called on his Guardian Angels for protection and we began singing, *I Walk in The Garden Alone*, (A song many of us learned in Church.) To my surprise, somehow years of fear drained out of me as if someone turned on a spigot! I felt uplifted! Out of the dark, I heard a kind of metallic, banging sound, the trumpet had extended into its telescopic form, readying for Spirits to speak. Next, a host of voices, one after the other, rattled through the trumpet. Ascended Masters and personalities from the *Bible* began speaking inspirational messages. Confounded, I stretched my mind to understand. The entire lineup of personalities overwhelmed me—so much wisdom, so much love.

"After the messages, St. Thérèse of Lisieux materialized in ectoplasmic form, fully physical before us! Amazing! No words could describe my feelings. We were in awe. She told us she lived in Shambhala, high in the Himalayas, where many great beings existed with her, saying the head of Shambhala was none other than Jesus the Christ of the Piscean Age. I found it nearly impossible to believe people like St. Thérèse and Jesus still lived in physical bodies! But that is exactly what she said.

"To close the séance, St. Thérèse declared, *'I will end the séance with the physical materialization of red roses from my garden in Shambhala.'*

"If you remember, when the Reverend entered the cabinet, only a chair, a pitcher of water, and the trumpet occupied the cabinet. When he exited, they were still there, but now they were accompanied by St. Thérèse's red roses!"

(For those interested in the historical significance of Marie Françoise Thérèse Martin: She was born in 1873. As a young teenager,

Thérese wanted to enter the convent following her sister Pauline. When she met the Pope, he advised her to follow the advice of her superior. It was Pauline who soon became her superior and upon her advice, Thérese received permission to join the convent. When Thérese turned twenty-two, her sister Pauline, now known as Mother Agnes, requested Thérese write her autobiography, which she called the *Story of the Soul*. The next year, she started coughing up blood, which eventually ended her young life.

Following her untimely death, something remarkable happened. Miraculous cures began occurring for those who visited her grave in Lisieux. She was canonized in 1925 and Pope John Paul II named her a Doctor of the Church in 1997. Throughout her life, Thérese was obsessed with showy flowers, especially little violets. After a nun gave her a card with a picture called *"The Little Flower,"* she adopted the name for herself, *Le Petit Fleur*.)

"The volunteer returned to inspect the tape he previously applied to the Reverend's mouth before the phenomenon occurred, stating the tape was still perfectly aligned with the markings. When he peeled the tape off, I received the shock of the evening. Standing just six feet away from me in full white light, the medium spat out not only the water he had been holding in his mouth throughout the séance, but hundreds of faceted gemstones, long-chained necklaces, and broaches. One particular broach with an open pin-clasp caught my attention; it could easily have punctured the medium's mouth or internal cavities, but somehow it didn't. To my amazement, stones kept falling from his mouth, tons of them, then his eyelids, and his hair. Then the Reverend spread open his white robes, exposing his bare chest—gemstones popped right through the flesh of his chest—startling! He rolled up the sleeves of his robe, and more and more stones fell to the ground. Finally, he called a retired police detective from Canada to extract stones from his ears. More stones instantly appeared. What could I say? Nothing in my life prepared me for this. Speechless best describes my mental state.

"I thought to myself, could there possibly be some type of trickery going on? But the only explanation I could come up with after all my years of working as a trained police observer was that I'd observed genuine, real, and sacred events. The apported physical objects demonstrated to me that hardcore physical evidence occurred in our midst, evidence that cannot tell a lie, evidence that cannot perjure itself, proving genuine Spiritual phenomenon occurred. The happenings utterly shattered my previous biases against Spirit, sending me on a lifelong journey exploring the wonders of God and my Spiritual nature.

"The séance finished up at 3 A.M. As it happened, my lunch break turned into a thirteen-hour absence from duty! I feared a possible suspension because I failed to report back to dispatch after lunch, but to my surprise, I never received a negative response. This in itself proved to be a minor miracle!

"A week later, I visited my mother, at which time I told her of the messages I received from father regarding a dead older brother and how she and father used to pray at an altar in the bedroom.

"She looked surprised at my comments, then said, *'Yes, we did pray together every night and I miscarried once before your birth.'*

"This topped off the overwhelming evidence attesting to the complete authenticity of Reverend Rhinehart's mediumship. I couldn't have been more stunned!"

The following is another chela's experience regarding mediumship, reinforcing and expanding her perspective based on a new encounter, where she also employed deductive reasoning:

"During my stay in Japan, Keith contacted me over the phone. He said he was sending someone to Japan on a mission. He wanted me to meet him and assist him with this mission. Keith requested I locate

Dr. Ando, the Doctor who conducted the scientific testing on his mediumship years ago. Then, once I made contact, I should attempt to pay him a visit. After substantial research, I finally found him. Dr. Ando stated he'd be happy to have us drop by.

"On our visit and without my provocation, Dr. Ando enthusiastically related how privileged he felt having the opportunity to meet someone of Keith's caliber and conduct scientific testing on his mediumship. He declared his tests proved Keith's mediumship to be one hundred percent genuine. He went on describing how astounded he'd been by the Spiritual phenomenon that transpired under the most rigorous of scientific conditions, indicating in all his years of research, he'd never witnessed anything comparable.

"I had been aware of the irrefutable evidence the Japanese testing proved, but for Dr. Ando to be so overly enthused, something shifted for me. Rather than reading an article in the *Psychic News* or *Psychic Observer* describing the facts, I saw and felt the genuine emotion of a man of science and heard him speak of exactly how he experienced Keith's unparalleled abilities. His sincerity and enthusiasm moved my experience from an intellectual experience to a deeper knowing. As I was leaving, Dr. Ando gave me several gifts to present to Keith, showing his appreciation for their friendship."

TWENTY-TWO

THOUGHT
DIVERSE AVENUES OF PERCEPTION

W E MIGHT CALL THIS SECTION THE SEASONS OF THE MIND. Having investigated ways of keeping our critical faculties alive, now let's review thinking and reasoning processes to find ways of lifting ourselves out of the drift of public opinion and thought forms hanging about in the ethers. We'll start with simple reasoning processes evaluating how Steve and the other chela furthered their understanding of Reverend Rhinehart's mediumship, utilizing two traditional ways of thinking that philosophy, logic, and analytical reasoning employ. We could implement either one or both in thinking through an issue or situation.

Inductive Reasoning—a posteriori, creates knowledge that is concluded from an experience or observation; it is a relative analysis. The knowledge comes from observing through experience or experiment, an event not based on theory. It is not absolute and can employ leaps beyond the facts, it could be either true or false, as it is not based on pure logic. However, Inductive Reasoning makes a logical connection between two statements, experiences, ideas, or patterns. So here we are bringing together two separate experiences and drawing conclusions. The imagination, dreams, intuition, and other means of concluding can come into play. A simple example could be: *Steve believed Reverend Rhinehart would be a fraud, based on his past experiences. Then he observed Reverend Rhinehart and thought he could be genuine, based on what he witnessed.* Inductive reasoning suggests possibility and, at best, probability.

Deductive Reasoning—a priori, is knowledge obtained entirely by logic from conclusions derived through reasoning. This is knowledge that comes from claims made independent of experience. Deductive Reasoning is logically certain, but does not provide new information; it is simply another way of stating or proving the original premise. An example could be: *Count St. Germaine is a Master, all Masters are immortal; therefore, Count St. Germaine is immortal.*

If we examine Steve's recent testimony, we find many triggers in his language. We can readily surmise psychics and fortune tellers, dark nights, and spirits all triggered danger, putting him on edge. If we were to look at Steve's issue with his fear regarding poltergeist spirits and assess his thought processes, we could start by stating that Steve's fear is an experience based on observation. It is real for him. Subsequently, he attains new knowledge based on his recent observations with Reverend Rhinehart. He now realizes there are Spirit encounters that are not fearful and can generate an uplifting experience. When we bring these two separate experiences together, there is new information allowing Steve to draw a different possible conclusion based on a relative analysis from Inductive Reasoning. Is it absolutely true? Not necessarily, but it brings Steve closer to a new truth for himself, generating a reconciliation with his past fear by assimilating and integrating his new experience.

In the case of the woman chela who visited Dr. Ando, she has not come upon new outside data regarding the facts about Reverend Rhinehart's mediumship; rather, she has come upon a person who is an authority on what the facts mean and their relevance to the history of mediumship. This allows her to gain deeper faith in the facts she gleaned before her encounter with Dr. Ando. So, her process is mostly *a priori*, deepening of her knowledge, but one might additionally argue she encountered an inner experience as well, where something shifted. This drew on *a posteriori* thought.

How do we prepare our minds to stay open and make informed decisions, to think in new, creative ways? How do we ensure we keep evolving in our decision-making process and not stagnate? Master Emil, one of the Ascended Masters whom we've met on the Spaulding Expeditions, offers one idea. It is an idea somewhat analogous to meditation, but it is more mental in intent.

Master Emil suggests if we are to renew the mind, we must constantly pour out that which resides within, emptying ourselves fully. In so doing, we create room to receive new waters. If we aren't constantly emptying ourselves, the waters quickly stagnate. Emil advises us to let go of all that we have learned, both the bad and the good, to share it with those we contact, then release it and move on to something new. In this way, we keep ourselves in a constant state of flowing. We restore, refresh, and reset ourselves by releasing. A Master unfolds a truth and understands when to let go in order to move to another truth. By contrast, the human mind finds a truth and holds onto it as long as possible, building organizations and universes around it.

If we allow the events, the thoughts, and the circumstances of our lives to move through us, we release the need to cling to ideas and events. In this way, we keep refreshing ourselves and challenging our minds to keep expanding. As we share our wisdom, an emptying occurs, creating a vacuum, magnetizing new wisdom to rush in.

Emil's idea may sound counterintuitive to logical thought. But an Ascended Master is an immortal being operating from Infinite Mind, so it behooves us to entertain Emil's sharing. We know our minds work in unique ways and are not limited to strictly retrieving the past storage of facts and opinions. When ideas arise that rival our convictions and experiences, we must suspend our beliefs for the moment and do our best to understand the reasoning behind the Master's thoughts.

This is the main factor why the Masters insisted on the scientific testing of Reverend Rhinehart's mediumship. They knew the Spiritual phenomena and wisdom they presented would challenge our beliefs and wanted to provide a way for us to suspend our usual reasoning and honestly investigate their work.

Another way to keep the mind relevant is each time we take in new data or new experiences, we make an effort to compare the new data to existing data, asking the question: *Is this the same data I have filed away in my being, or is this new data? Does it conflict with the old data?* If there is a conflict with the existing data, we need to determine which data to keep as the truth and which to dump as outmoded or irrelevant. There must be a constant reconciliation process occurring, a reconciling of all new incoming truths with all existing truths. In this way, we continue to evolve our mind and spirit, consciously moving to a clear understanding of the truths we hold. If we leave conflicting data unresolved, filling the mind with mental conflicts, it inhibits us from moving forward, as we are not clear as to what is true and what is not. So, when we fail to resolve new information, especially information that challenges established beliefs, it paralyzes and stagnates the mind, leaving us frustrated and mired in piles and piles of unreconciled data. This inability to reconcile data supresses mental evolution.

For instance, on the physical level, if we are taking a medication and a new medication is prescribed, but we don't do our due diligence to conclude what side effects might occur with the new medication, we find ourselves in a quandary as to whether or not to take the new medication. We must decide whether to move forward with the new medication if we are to receive the possible benefits. It is the same with our mental body. For example, if we are unsure of the value of mediumship, but refuse to reconcile our issues with it, we will keep going back and forth as to whether or not to entertain its possible value.

This is true for resolving many concepts that we come across: *Is the Earth flat or round? Do I believe in Darwin's evolution or creationism? Is Elvis alive or dead? Is carbon dating a legitimate form of estimating the age of something? Is the Electoral College fair?* Unresolved thoughts inhibit the mind from a fluid thinking process, causing mental lethargy and confusion.

We have investigated issues limiting our ability to stay in the present moment, the holding of biases, how to empty the mind, different ways of reasoning, and how to reconcile new information. Each concept, when implemented, improves our ability to think and our ability to think is one of our most valuable assets in negotiating our world.

We feel somewhere along the educational journey, students should be taught how to think, the Socratic Method of questioning comes to mind, and how to use the mind in a manner that supports critical thinking. For instance, asking: *What does this mean? What can be assumed from this statement? Could this be explained in another manner?*

It is unfortunate that schools in general, from grade school through college, primarily teach students how to get the right answer, to simply regurgitate facts. This is a good exercise for the memory, but our minds are creative and much vaster than basic memory reservoirs. Our education system has flat-out failed us to be self-sufficient, thinking individuals, teaching us *what* to think rather than *how* to think. We all have different mental gifts and capacities for thought, so wouldn't it be wise if we were educated about the diverse attributes our minds hold? Wouldn't it be better to identify our specific gifts or deficiencies so we might thrive? A thinking person might suggest there is almost a deliberate flaw in the system, designed to inhibit our abilities.

We found it interesting to discover in 2014, that our Naval and Marine divisions embarked on research projects to explore the phenomena of premonition and intuition. They called it *Spidey Sense*. Many call this our sixth sense. Peter Squire, a program officer in the *Office of Naval Research's Expeditionary Maneuver Warfare and Combating Terrorism Department*, says the Navy scientists were attempting to examine the mysterious process. The military scientists assure us the phenomenon is not based on superstition. They believe if the researchers can further understand the process, there may be ways to accelerate the powers of intuition and spread intuitive instincts throughout the military units. If this power is good for the military, wouldn't it be good for students to discover their latent mental potential early in the education process?

The Pentagon's focus was to maximize the gift of the sixth sense to utilize it in an operational environment. They asked: *Can training be developed whereby the intuitive decision-making process is modeled by a greater number of soldiers?* This question has arisen as a result of field reports from the war theater, where, in 2006, an incident in Iraq brought this phenomenon to the Pentagon's attention:

Staff Sergeant Martin Richburg, using intuition or premonition prevented carnage in an IED (improvised explosive device) incident. This *Spidey Sense* alerted Sergeant Richburg of an impending attack, and without taking the time to consciously analyze the situation, he instinctively took action and avoided disaster. A decade later, active-duty Marines are being taught to hone precognitive skills to preempt snipers, anticipate hidden IEDs, and other irregular assaults by using advanced perceptual competencies.

Because of the public's stigma regarding ESP and psychic abilities in general, the military has changed the nomenclature, allowing the Defense Department to distance itself from its Remote Viewing past. Under the *"Perceptual Training Systems and Tools"* banner, extrasensory perception has a new name: *"Sensemaking."* This is defined as a motivated effort to understand connections among people, places, and events to anticipate danger and act effectively.

Even though weapons and locations of war change from generation to generation, man's perceptual abilities remain mostly the same. Events from fifty years ago in Vietnam corroborate this fact:

Joe McMoneagle employed his precognitive ability to avoid stepping on booby traps, falling into punji pits, and walking into Viet Cong ambushes. Knowledge of his ability to sense danger spread throughout his unit. Soldiers developed confidence in his skill and followed his lead. He saved lives as his precognitive abilities were real.

Since 1972, the CIA and DoD research shows premonition and precognition skills are weak in most, strong in others, and extraordinary in the rare few. It is interesting to note that in Vietnam, black soldiers from the Bayou were placed on point because their years of hunting in the swamp created the ability to avoid snakes, reptiles, and cougars. As a result, they developed precognitive awareness not shared by most soldiers.

Today, the Navy is researching cognition and perception in soldiers' virtual dream states using biofeedback techniques and, more recently, virtual reality technology. Biofeedback draws on the idea that the human brain can benefit from seeing itself work in real time. With biofeedback, a trainee can see brain waves, heart rate, muscle tension, skin conductance, and even pain perception.

In this study, soldiers enter a software program called the "Book of Dreams"—a virtual world or *"Second Life."* Here, soldiers can produce changes in the way they process information. This is used to help soldiers who are suffering from PTSD-related nightmares. If this type of research accelerates a soldier's awareness, could it be helpful in everyday living and in our educational training? [1]

Another way to expand our perception is through synesthesia. It is known that *synesthesia* allows people to sense in a multitude of ways beyond normal sensing, like the ability to see colors through the fingers. Scientifically proven, we know animals have senses beyond the five senses, so it is not a stretch to believe we can think and sense in more ways than we are currently doing. We believe our education would improve significantly should we promote and develop processes whereby we begin to expand new ways to think and sense. (As an example, in Japan, in a school setting, a young child is taught to *"feel"* colors by naming the color of a small block placed in the child's cupped hands held behind the back.)

There are diverse innovative ways in which to approach the nature of thought which have been studied by philosophers over the years. For our purposes in seeking new ways of thought, we'd like to visit Einstein's thought experiments (Gedankenexperiments). What we first notice in his experiments is his commitment to intellectual freedom, courageous creativity, especially in bucking the foundations of knowledge, and a childlike awe in facing the nature of the universe. In the experiments, he conceptualized complex scientific ideas by imagining real-life scenarios. Occasionally, he noodled on a construct for over a year, accessing his mental body, dream body (astral), and his Spiritual body to solve the thought experiments.

In one instance, he queried: *Can two people experience an exact same event differently?* We may be familiar with one of his experiments, asking us to stand on a train while a friend is standing outside the train watching it pass by. Einstein asked: *If lightning struck near the front and back ends of the train, would one of us see the bolts differently?* Einstein induces that our friend would see the bolts at the same time, and we, standing in the train, would observe the bolt of lightning that we are moving towards before the friend, because the light has a shorter distance to travel. In other words, time behaves differently for someone who is moving than it does for someone standing still. This understanding created Einstein's belief that time and space are

RELATIVE! In this test of *Simultaneity*, that is, when two events happen at the same time, the experience of it depends on perspective! These two premises became a cornerstone of Einstein's *Special Theory of Relativity.*

In visiting the concepts of the world's greatest scientist, we begin to broaden our notions of thought. His ideas provide a platform for gaining a deeper insight into how to come from *Beingness* by setting aside the notion that our existence is purely of the mind.

The Theory of Relativity unveils the nature of matter and how its understanding can be applied to truth, spatiality, and time. Regarding this concept, Einstein states that nothing exists in the past or in the future which is not existing in the present. Everything from the past and everything from the future is contained in some reflection, some capacity realized or unrealized in the present. With this in mind, any concepts of beginning or ending are circular in nature and both live in the NOW. If so, we can compare and contrast in relative terms that anything which exists in the physical universe exists within this circle of time.

This presents us with entirely new and exciting ways of thinking, creating, and being in the world. Time as we know it drops away! Einstein reasons that if this is so, then the Mental and Spiritual Worlds must be relative as well, since the material world is created by the stepping down of higher frequencies of the Spiritual and mental vibrations into the lower vibrations of matter. With this understanding of the relative relationships between the physical, Spiritual, and mental worlds of objects and time, we might open ourselves to new dimensions of creativity.

Every Ascended Master knows infinity, eternity, and all concepts of time cannot be understood by the mind or Spirit alone, but its understanding comes from a place that supersedes these notions; and that is, *Beingness!*

In following Einstein's reasoning, we can see he is employing *abstract inductive reasoning*. Is it absolutely true? No, there is only a logical connection linking two statements. His imagination and logical reasoning connect the dots. His thought process is fascinating, opening new avenues of thought in social, scientific, and Spiritual domains.

There are many methods in which to think and relate to our world. The following are ideas conveyed by Master thought and represent an extension of the Concept of Relativity.

The creation of words is one of the only methods we possess to express that which has been revealed or created within our being, and therefore an extension of the intellect's ability to visualize and think in ideas. We might ask: *Is one idea more important than another, or is one thing more beautiful or better than another?* As we formulate these questions, we immediately confront the notion of Einstein's Relativity.

Human language is filled with concepts such as close and distant, good and bad, dark and light, but each only has meaning as it is relative to the other. Words such as infinity, finite, or the color of something, and its characteristics, are all relative terms and depend on the comparison of something to another. *How do we know anything about something if it is not by describing something in terms of something else?*

It is through the use of analogies and metaphors that we analyze the nature of our world. Whether we are investigating a piece of string, a galaxy, or an idea, we are forced to describe it in terms of other things, other timelines, other dimensions. It is by this analysis that a thing's relative relationship to the first thing gives us a better understanding of what is being investigated. The physical world can be seen as relative in every instance.

We might ask: *Is there something absolutely true that can be found apart from human thinking?* The Masters would suggest, *"No! Only the unseen presence is that which thought cannot define!"* Form, and the order of form, originates in our thinking, but using Einstein's theory, we can reflect on mind and matter as formations of Spirit which have no beginning and no end.

Given Spiritualism is a driving force behind much of our writing, it would be negligent if we didn't consider Spiritualism as a legitimate method of accessing thought. Spiritualism acknowledges that we each have Spirit Guides constantly prompting us. Spiritualism could be defined as a communion beyond the Earth plane connecting us with intelligences separate from ourselves. This allows us to be informed of possibilities beyond our own minds. This incoming information is impressed upon the mind by a Spirit Guide through either symbolic visual images viewed as if on an inner screen, or through words impressed upon the mind.

We all possess the ability to tune into infinite wisdom and knowledge through communion with angels, loved ones, and higher consciousnesses. To access the communication, first we have to believe it is possible, then we have to make a distinction between our own thoughts and the inner images and thoughts from our guides.

In the case of thought, if we are familiar with our own thinking and the manner in which we articulate our thoughts, we can then decipher a thought that originates from a different consciousness than our own by recognizing the different patterns of expression. Once identified, these inner thought promptings bring in thoughts from an entirely different consciousness, expanding thought in new and unforeseen directions. This is the same with inner visions. Some have difficulties making these distinctions of thought, and that is one of the reasons Spirit often uses the symbolic language of images or allegorical stories that we can attune to through visualization and imagination. Developing our ability to access a guide's promptings can be advantageous in negotiating life's challenging curves and also in discerning fact from fiction.

The Ascended Masters have often commented that we are controlled by inner and outer forces. This can be viewed as positive in terms of Spirit Guides, and negative regarding dark, ill-intending astral entities. But there are also harmful influences from society, as well as our own debilitating thought patterns. So, it behooves us to develop our awareness of where our thoughts originate and whether we feel we are being prompted by Spirit Guides or not.

Throughout Chapter Twenty-Two, we have discussed many ideas regarding the thought process of *how to think* and not *what to think*. The information has been presented in hopes we will gain access to additional analytical tools and become more aware of how to begin an active process of thinking for ourselves in new and creative ways.

By evolving beyond the programming of outside influences such as parents, friends, schools, religions, media, and government, or the inside influences of personal biases, prejudices, and emotional triggers, we learn how to become a person who is more present and self-actualizing. By doing so, we avoid mornings like the one Miles experienced. We create a fluid relationship with our critical, adversarial faculties and are better able to discern genuine wisdom and truth.

We will conclude with the myth and parable of the *Tower of Babel* in the Book of Genesis to give us one last insight into thinking:

After the Great Flood, the peoples of Babylon built the *Tower of Babel*, symbolizing man's zeal to learn everything, and unlock every secret of the Universe. They worked hard and built a beautiful structure to the Glory of Man, with its top bursting high into the sky. But eventually, the Tower fell, scattering upon the Earth, crumbling man's self-aggrandizements.

If we take the parable a step further, suggesting each human is building a *Tower of Babel* within the self, a ladder climbing to find the highest wisdom and learning, we encounter a new perspective of thought coming to light. The Masters admonish, when we think and learn for the purpose of gaining fame, glory, and praise, our tower crumbles, but if we use our thinking power for the love of growing, progressing, and the pure joy of gaining wisdom, then the tower becomes an inner structure of strength and truth.

If we don't rush up the ladder, but instead enjoy the journey, we become content with our inner structure. However, if we race, we thwart the progression of inner expansion. The building of the tower, the nurturing of thought, is the building of the knowledge of ourselves, the inner architecture of our Soul, not the fashioning of a physical building that will someday tumble to the ground.

The Masters encourage us to think, think until it hurts, and enjoy the process of thought. If we enjoy thought as an approach to the expansion of our being, not as a product for achieving worldly attention and gain, then we more closely align ourselves with the wisdom of the Ascended Masters.

TWENTY-THREE

FINDING GRACE
IN SUFFERING

M ASTER COUNT SAINT GERMAINE REFERS TO SUFFERING as the key to swinging open the door to the mysteries of the human Soul—a portal revealing the fluidic nature of the life experience. So, though difficult to accept, life's greatest joys can present life's greatest sorrows, as joy cannot be pondered without reckoning its opposite, sorrow. Suffering is pure grace bestowed on those prepared to know the Self. Sorrow creates an emotional stir, unlimbering any fixed notions we might hold.

The Masters explain that suffering remains alive as long as we keep our self-made illusions in place, illusions stemming from a belief in false authorities, a belief that happiness depends on having a relationship with a special person, such as a soulmate, or a belief that the fulfillment of any ideal is reliant upon certain events happening in the outer world.

We all know that everything we possess in the physical world, the mental world, and our Spiritual selves will one day seemingly be taken. Every chela at some juncture along the Spiritual path reaches a place where the most cherished friendship, most beloved mate, greatest truth, or most prized possession vanishes in a blink. The degree to which we cling will determine the extent of our suffering. The Masters say incessant clinging accounts for the only reason we suffer.

Resistance to the flow of life's events, coupled with holding fast to the way we think life should be, interrupts the natural motion of life, leaving us in a quagmire of unresolved emotions. Traumatic events are unsettling, but resistance is futile. To the exalted, suffering is a law governing human existence and is unavoidable. They counsel that continual suffering is a choice we make resulting from our inability to unhinge from our attachments. Through unflinchingly facing our suffering, we begin to identify that to which we cling. So, by staying conscious, each attachment eventually surfaces if we are persistent.

By attuning to the fluidic nature of life-motion, we start to recognize we are not a fixed identity, we are not our thoughts. We are a constant evolving process that is not static, but dynamic. Allowing this dynamic flow of energy will unwind the feelings of panic or despair we may feel when we are confronted with loss and change. This unwinding process brings us the awareness that our assumed identity is a state of mind and changeable. This awareness demonstrates it is impermanent! Not who we are! With this awareness, we begin to unearth the triggers residing in our being that cause the habitual patterns of suffering.

To eradicate this suffering, some distinctions must be made between the impermanent and the permanent. We must distinguish the difference between human affection and the true source of Love. Likewise, the distinction between a balanced relationship with material goods and unhealthy attachments to the world. For example, if we are overly attached to a person, we lose understanding that everlasting Love emanates from God and not from a person; or, if we receive enjoyment from a material object in a balanced way, it is a healthy relationship. But, for example, if a musician becomes overly fond of a beautiful instrument, it can cause heartache if the instrument is lost or broken.

Regarding our illusions stemming from suffering, inquiring within is a good place to start. How do we process our sorrow or disappointment? Where do we go emotionally? How do we replace a loss? Do we cover up our pain with over-indulging in pleasure, creating false rewards to fill in the loss? Do we fall into inflating our self-importance? Do we blame ourselves or others and become victims? Do we escape into fantasy? Are we suddenly prone to extreme renunciation or extreme excess? How do we misidentify happiness by attaining false rewards? Where do we go?

The Masters teach that to unwind illusions, we must begin by inquiring within ourselves. By fully engaging in an inner inquiry, the great beings have conquered life and death, stepping into their enlightenment and eventual Immortality. Their lives serve as guiding examples on our path of self-inquiry.

By following their counsel, we work to create emotional balance in the face of disappointment or loss. We can begin by moving away from the extremes of personal desires. We can drop the masks impersonating genuine Joy and begin a practice of cultivating true Joy and Peace. We do this by releasing our attachments to outer authorities, false identities, and inauthentic rewards. We begin to tune to the I Am presence that is ever-present within us, radiating light to all, grounding unshakable inner peace. We relax into the motions of life, trusting each life event has a personal gift hidden within, and we stop insisting life show up the way we think it should.

The following is about me, Gary, speaking from personal experience:

For much of life I have escaped great sorrow, but recently I have been challenged by a personal loss with the passing of my beloved soul mate. As a result, I am a prime example of St. Germaine's comment that suffering is eventually unavoidable. He suggests it is a portal to unlocking the secrets to life and death, and one of the Seasons of the Soul we all encounter. Nothing in my life has been more demanding than the process of integrating this loss into my life in a graceful, powerful way. I will attempt to relate my story, not to glamorize the suffering, but to illustrate the emotions, pain, and travails confronting me in hopes my story may lessen in some way another's suffering.

I have studied Spiritualism for nearly forty years and believe I have a reasonably good understanding of the transmigration of souls from the physical world to the Spirit side of life. But even so, I cannot say this understanding has allowed me to grieve graciously, avoiding pain and immense suffering. In fact, what I notice is I am steeped in second-hand concepts, intellectual words lacking true experiential knowingness. This approach falls short of providing direct life experience.

For me, all the mental understanding and wisdom in the world have not translated into the slightest amount of emotional peace. In seemingly losing my beloved, all my emotional entanglements, all my emotional immaturities, all my false identities have come undone, and I find myself in complete free-fall—the world as I knew it sank into oblivion.

My beloved and I worked to cultivate a deep, loving, trusting, respectful relationship where we thoroughly basked in the joy of each other's presence. In our union, we loved our families, created wonderful art, traveled the world, designed and promoted successful events, wrote books, served as Master Designated Healers, created businesses, and rebuilt houses. We intimately danced through life in perfect sync. Our happiness effortlessly radiated and many of our friends remarked we had a loving, balanced relationship. Yet what we experienced as a healthy, rewarding love has thrust me into a deeply profound sorrow with my beloved's passing.

Over time, I have come to see that I identified my beloved as the source of love, rather than seeing her as a demonstration of God's love! I failed to recognize my beloved was God's gift to me; that is, a way to understand the power of Eternal Love. Untangling from this grand illusion has become all-consuming, for the wound of love-lost runs deep.

After my beloved's passing, I found myself in a panic to keep alive the love, intimacy, and mutual support we experienced. How could a love so real simply vanish? My mind grasped at phantoms, flailing at what I believed to be genuine love. I struggled to recreate the intensity of our past experiences. My emotional being strategized to re-enliven the feelings of our love, but as much as I liked feeling my past joys, even experiencing a deepening of my love, in so doing, I exacerbated my intense loss. I found myself releasing deep soul-wrenching bellows rising from unexplored regions of my heart. Unfathomable, unconscious emotions came barreling out helter-skelter. I experienced a genuine release, but in the end, was left with a profoundly unresolved, unbalanced emotional body, ever deepening my wound of lost love.

I now find myself searching to refind, redefine the value of being an individual, an individual who is self-actualizing, contributing to my community, and the world. Each day I stand in the middle of my suffering, sensing into its origins. In reflecting on my grieving, I notice my loss is not only for my beloved, but for a part of myself I lost over the years. I have not found the process easy, but it has been a tumultuous, bruising path, full of conflict and raging emotions. Continued suffering may, in fact, be a choice, as Master St. Germaine suggests, as I realize my habitual pattern of reenacting sorrow does not produce peace, and if I am to find relief, I know I must choose differently.

Recently, I have come across a Buddhist practice called *Shenpa* that I find engaging. I've discovered the process allows me to meet my inner turmoil more gracefully. *Shenpa* is defined as the process of unhooking from habitual patterns. The process helps me to identify the subtle nuance of a feeling arising just before hooking into the negative thoughts and habitual patterns, giving them power. By identifying that nuance of a feeling and associating it with a thought, I can determine it is a thought, and not who I am. My past pattern is that when this subtle feeling arises, I dive deep into the emotions and thoughts tied to this feeling. In effect, I poured fuel into the situation and set it ablaze!

Some specific thoughts I encounter might be: *"I am unworthy of love, I am alone, I am stupid because I failed at this or that, this person hurt me, I feel manipulated."* I could be experiencing feelings of self-denigration, anger, or any number of emotions. Initially, there may be a tensing, a sense I don't want to be here, a closing down.

The practice of *Shenpa* calls on me to pause and pull back when this kind of subtle feeling first arises, ideally even before it crystallizes into a thought, when it's but an inarticulate hint of a feeling. It is here where the work begins, right at the point where the barely perceptible feeling forms, before it spirals into an emotional upset. What I notice is when I pull back from this feeling, resisting moving into the associative emotions and thoughts, I begin to experience a space, a distancing from the emotional content. At this point, it is apparent that these emotions are *Not Who I Am!*

This practice alone allows me to detach from my habitual pattern, clearing a path back into the flow of life. I stop the indulgence of identifying with the nuance that precedes my uneasy feeling, which for me is mostly sorrow, despair, and loneliness. Detaching from these emotions, I become more dynamic again and not fixed in my being. When I stop my thoughts at this critical point and create a pause, the notion *that I am not my thoughts* becomes apparent. With the pause, I can then slip beneath my thoughts, and open to a fluidic process where I shift into a more expansive way of being. It's then that I avoid being stuck on the uneasy feeling.

In employing this technique, when I edge past the pause, the thoughts to which I cling slowly identify themselves. Once identified, disengaging, and simply witnessing these thoughts assists me in releasing from my debilitating habitual pattern. Again, these are of the mind and *Not Who I AM*.

What I notice is each of these debilitating thoughts lies in the mind as a trigger projecting me into the past or future. They arise when I'm focused on what I think is missing, that with which I am dissatisfied. If I stay present, employ the pause, the nature of time begins to warp and the past and future dissolve into the present, where, if I am honest, all is well. If I do not stay present and allow myself to spiral into the abyss, then I experience great loss, a lifetime of love slipping through my fingertips, feeling oceans of self-pity, abandonment, and a haunting despair.

Through this process of *Shenpa*, I have become clear my pain stems from misidentifying the source of my joy with a human being rather than God. So, I seek to release my clinging, my neediness of my beloved, and cultivate a true understanding of Infinite, Eternal Love. In so doing, I reach out to the I Am presence, invoking its Eternal Love. In my outreach, I affirm that the I Am presence IS the Power which is ever-present, ever-nurturing, and ever-transforming all my joys and all my sorrows into perfect Joy. This, I Am presence is directing my Soul this very moment, and every moment.

In reviewing the period of my beloved's illness, I am convinced the illness and the entire harrowing ordeal, though difficult, conspired in our highest Spiritual interests, hence the grace of suffering. It created the circumstances whereby we might come to understand the nature of permanent, Eternal Love, breaking past the limitations of impermanence, and releasing our souls from fixed patterns of illusory love.

I sense we have passed through a sort of crucifixion, a rite of passage. We now find ourselves resurrected into new dimensions of Love existing at the soul level. I am in the process of eclipsing living solely from the level of my personality and moving more deeply into living from the vantage of Soul identity. It is here where true freedom dwells, a wake-up call beyond what I ever imagined. When I identify with being a Soul, and not just Gary, I do not suffer.

THE FOUR NOBLE TRUTHS–WISDOM OF THE BUDDHA

One of the most profound understandings of suffering comes to us from the teachings of the Buddha (circa 450 BCE). Buddha addressed suffering through the *Four Noble Truths* he attained during his meditation under the Bodhi Tree. Understanding the causes and remediations for suffering led to his enlightenment.

The *Four Noble Truths* encapsulate the core of Buddha's discernment into the human experience. It is said these *Four Noble Truths* offer a diagnostic and therapeutic approach to addressing suffering, and we could say that if practiced diligently, they bring about the cessation of suffering. It is to this end his entire teachings were directed.

When he ventured out from the protective enclave of his father's compound, Buddha witnessed old age, poverty, disease, and immense suffering. This experience overwhelmed him, and he became driven to find a way to break free from these limitations, hence his presentation of the *Four Noble Truths,* which have addressed human suffering for nearly five hundred years!

1. **The Noble Truth of Suffering:**
   The human experience inherently involves suffering. We are living in a constant state of dissatisfaction, incessantly craving the next desire. Even if we experience contentment for a brief moment, we quickly return to a state of dissatisfaction. This feeling causes us the pain and suffering we experience. The experience of dissatisfaction is due to the impermanence of our conditioned existence, our mortality, our vulnerability to pain, and our inability to find lasting satisfaction. It is by fully knowing and understanding the source of

our suffering we develop a strong desire to liberate ourselves from its grasp.

2. **The Noble Truth Behind the Origins of Suffering:**

It is a simple matter to blame our suffering on external causes, like people and situations. But our own attitudes, thoughts, and actions are what determine our happiness or suffering. When we are attached to our delusions of anger and self-grasping, it is impossible to attain liberation. These limitations must be recognized and abandoned. Suffering arises strictly from our own attachment and desires.

3. **The Noble Truth of the Cessation of Suffering:**

If committed, we can attain the end to suffering. Buddha demonstrated the reality of living without suffering, though it is not attained by shutting down the mind or turning it off, but is brought about by the realization of the ultimate Reality. Every living being, without exception, is bound to experience the cycles of suffering through sickness, aging, death, and rebirth without end. If we are to follow the Buddha's example, we renunciate these cycles and determine to make a concentrated effort to cease all suffering and attain enlightenment.

4. **The Noble Truth of the Path to the Cessation of Suffering:**

Buddha presents a Path to follow. It is referred to as *The Eightfold Path*. If we traverse the Path consisting of moral discipline training, ethical discernment, higher concentration, and higher wisdom, we will recognize the impermanent nature of physical existence and other misapprehensions, such as ignorance, attachment, and aversion. These realizations, along with the continual practice of following *The Eightfold Path*, lead us to liberation and a clarity of wisdom.

TWENTY-FOUR

THE DILEMMA
OF DUALITY

O N OCCASION, WE ARE SHOCKED BY THE ASCENDED MASTERS' concepts. One concept that caught us off guard came about when Archangel Gabriel suggested that beyond Oneness is Duality. Really! During a communication through Reverend Rhinehart's mediumship, Gabriel infers he has come to debunk Eastern Religion's tenet that to overcome Duality and attain Oneness is an absolute, unqualified truth. He's not disputing that Oneness is anything but sublime. So we ask, why would he present a notion that flies in the face of hundreds, if not thousands, of years of one of the main precepts of Eastern religious doctrines?

It is good to reach out to find Oneness at times. However, Gabriel claims there has been an overemphasis on Oneness as a result of false doctrines within the teachings of Spirituality. Let's take a moment to examine his suggestion. First, we must recognize this isn't an assertion from Uncle Eddie, who just took up residence in Spirit; it comes from a being existing in the highest realms of Spirit who has attained Conscious Immortality. Gabriel contends to conquer Duality and find Oneness is but a half-truth. If the Ascended Masters hadn't the foresight to document years of Spirit communications backed by irrefutable scientific evidence authenticating Reverend Rhinehart's mediumship, this comment would sound like pure gibberish. For those of us who haven't fully appreciated the rigor and effort the Masters provided, you are likely shaking your heads. Admittedly, I found myself shaking mine.

Archangel Gabriel goes on to indicate the body depends on our understanding the qualities of Duality for its survival, such as night–day, hot–cold, hard–soft, positive and negative electrical charges, and so forth. Duality highlights the value of the polarities of good and evil, suffering and freedom, Love and fear, feminine and masculine, and how we must come to see that there is an interaction operating in our world between these two polarities that drives personal and worldly evolution. He also implies if we were to deny the existence of Duality, ignoring its importance, we would be left relying on the superstitions of religious doctrine and societal norms for guidance rather than direct knowledge gleaned from first-hand experience in the play of Duality. There is a dynamic tension created between polarities, polarities like order and chaos, control and surrender, attachment and detachment, dharma and love. The conflict between these opposites is not a problem in which we need to rid ourselves. Embracing these primordial opposites leads to the unfoldment of wholeness, allowing the contradiction to exist without resistance, creates a synthesis and transcendence.

We believe Gabriel is saying personal mastery transpires by not taking shortcuts through the physical world, but instead using Duality's properties to deepen our personal evolution. When we are focused only on Oneness, there is a tendency to gloss over the value gained in Duality. At times, we want to numb the pain Duality can present rather than resolve the issue.

We are creatures of eternity, momentarily living in the physical for a reason. We suspect the nature of eternity is much different from what many might imagine, even the so-called "enlightened." Our excursion into the physical may well enhance our experience of eternity if we take Gabriel's comment seriously and realize that Oneness isn't necessarily the final goal when we view ourselves as Eternal Souls.

The Ascended Masters suggest there is another state of consciousness existing beyond Oneness! They say we are Souls meandering our way towards Spiritual or Physical Immortality, not Souls permanently merging into nothingness or the annihilation of individuality. We are both individual personalities and Spiritual Souls, a Duality that makes us *human* and *eternal.*

After years of confronting a regular diet of confusion from the multitude of external voices attempting to gain our attention, many seek to transcend the chaos and come to rely on the word of religious doctrines and religious figureheads rather than their personal experience, hence a buy-in to the superstitious. Others have become so mired in the pain Duality can deliver that they only want relief.

So how does Duality serve us? It can be paradoxical—yes, the physical world is impermanent and illusory, but the Masters explain that Duality offers the Soul an environment where we can grasp the causation of existence. We must make distinctions between what is relative (duality) and what is absolute (oneness). The relative offers a proving ground of sorts, where we find near instant feedback for our thoughts and actions. To write off the Duality experience as only illusion can leave the unenlightened in a state of despair. When the tensions of Duality persist despite our denial of its existence, a sense of hopelessness can arise.

Our physical aspect, according to the Masters, offers an arc of progressive evolution for the Soul. With each new awareness, we evolve. At the conclusion of this physical journey lies a type of experience representing the Soul's final conquest analogous to Jesus' crucifixion.

During his ordeal on the cross, Jesus experienced his mastery over the illusion of the limitations of the body and the world. He suggests the greatest gift God ever presented was his experience at Calvary. He relates through Reverend Rhinehart's mediumship that on the cross, he did not say, *"Why hast thou abandoned me?"* If we truly experience Jesus' consciousness, we know he would not express such a sentiment. No! He said, *"Why hast thou glorified me?"*

God's gift transpired in Duality, where Jesus experienced the paradox of physical torture and ecstatic Spiritual conquest simultaneously. It is on the cross where Jesus found it was He who gave his life meaning, no one else, no doctrine, no discourse. Those relying on Jesus to guide them toward a meaningful life may be greatly inspired. He blazed a masterly example. However, the Masters warn that expecting Jesus' death on the cross to absolve our sins lacks the maturity of personal responsibility. The outward search and reliance on an external example always eventually rendezvous back through the heart to the Self.

Another source pointing to the value existing in Duality comes through India via the *Bhagavad Gita*, the "Song of God," an East Indian Hindu poem bound into the Sanskrit epic of the *Mahabharata*. The *Bhagavad Gita* puts a focus on Action in the world as a method for deepening the understanding of the Self and Unity.

The setting for the episode, known as the *Bhagavad Gita*, takes place in the Kingdom of Bharat in Northern India around 450 BCE. There are several speculations as to the date, because the Mahabharata, the world's longest poem, written 3100 BCE., was probably written over many years, possibly centuries. But this gives a feel for the time period regarding the recognition of the event that vividly addresses the value of Duality versus Oneness.

For decades, the Kauravas and the Pandavas families endured their differences. With a final breach of trust, the Pandavas could no longer tolerate the injustices doled out by the Kauravas and consequently, the battle of Kurukshetra commences for control of the throne.

Before the conflict begins, a conversation ensues between Arjuna and Krishna. Arjuna is from the warrior cast and Krishna is the incarnation of Shiva, one of the supreme Hindu depictions of God. Arjuna is faced with the prospect of battling what he believes to be Evil, but he despairs, balking at the idea of warring where brother kills brother, uncle kills uncle, cousin kills cousin. He's a warrior, so killing is not foreign, but in the past, he believed he was killing something outside of himself, a "them," now he is faced with the prospect of killing what he interprets as "us." Kinship exists where family love and loyalty are honored. He sees himself as a loving, honorable man, but the lines have blurred. How can he take down his friends and family?

Krishna explains he must vanquish his prior ideals and operate from a different set of motives. Krishna reminds Arjuna he has chosen him to be his guide, and in so doing, he has declared he is committed to rising to a higher standard. Krishna tells Arjuna it is his dharmic duty to fulfill cosmic natural law. A teaching is unraveling, and to face his dilemma, Arjuna must re-identify himself in a larger context, look from a different plane of consciousness, and reinvent himself from the vantage of the Soul while operating in Duality.

Here are two lines where Master Paramahansa Yogananda gives insights into Arjuna's challenge:

Transforming the Little Self (Ego) Into the Divine Self (Soul)

(5) *Let man uplift the self (ego) by the self; let the self not be self-degraded (cast down). Indeed, the self is its own friend, and the self is its own enemy.*

(6) *For him whose self (ego) has been conquered by the Self (soul), the Self is the friend of the self: but verily, the Self behaves inimically, as an enemy, toward the self that is not subdued.*[1]

In this context, the self is the manner by which we carry ourselves through the Dualistic World. It must not be cast down, nor must it be allowed to dominate. Our body relies on Duality for its functioning, its individualization, and its perceptual awareness of how we navigate through our daily lives. Gabriel suggests that if we deny Duality, it places us in physical and Spiritual jeopardy, leaving us in an irrational state of mind. The theological ideology that Duality and the interplay of opposites must be transcended hampers our ability to engage in the physical world to evolve. Like Arjuna's dilemma, there is a paradox at play where the individual self (ego) must be honored on the journey to discover the Spiritual Self (Soul).

Throughout this journey, we discover the Truth is not so black or white. It is like a many-faceted gemstone; the more facets we perceive, the greater our human experience and the greater our understanding of God. We could say God is present, reflecting attributes in all that is considered Dualistic and Oneness simultaneously.

Interestingly, we find this same point that Krishna emphasizes described in Western scripture in the Gospel of Matthew 16:25-26 KJB:

"For whosoever will save his life shall lose it and whosoever will lose his life for my sake shall find it.

"For what is a man profited, if he shall gain the whole world, and lose his own soul? Or what shall a man give in exchange for his soul?"

In both instances in the *Bhagavad Gita* and the *Bible*, the idea for the discovery of the Soul or life eternal comes via the body, Duality!

On this journey in Duality, facing the challenges we each encounter, we meet up with karmic patterns where looking beyond the obvious is required. Our usual ally, the rational mind, can be a hindrance at this stage of the Soul's evolution because a surrendering to the mystery must occur if we are to succeed. These challenges could be viewed as facing the enemies existing within and without. They are often camouflaged, hiding within our identity and not perceived, but they act as Blind Spots in our ability to increase our awareness.

To understand what is required, a more far-reaching self-inquiry must ensue—a deeper listening. Like Arjuna, we cling to our roles, but how we identify ourselves must be investigated. Who we are as husbands, wives, sons, daughters, mothers, fathers, friends—the community leader, the business person, the religious person, and on and on. If we fail to unveil the attitudes and beliefs behind these roles (Blind Spots), they can create internal imbalance or even external chaos.

The first step is to flesh out and identify these elements in ourselves and in the world. By doing this, we can understand the limitations inhibiting our ability to thrive or to reach our Godself's full expression.

To accomplish this, Arjuna had to re-evaluate his relationship with Krishna and his religion, his family, his inner values, and his relationship with the world. He was prompted to begin to reinterpret his role with a much broader brush stroke. Who was he really? Who was he not? He observed chaos, deception, death, and destruction all within God's plan. Arjuna is shaken to the core. To resolve the conflict, Krishna demands that Arjuna surrender to his lead. To accomplish this objective, Arjuna cannot use reason to understand God's law! He listens to his inner Self, reflects deeply beyond the facades, releases his attachments to his ego-driven life, lets go of it all, and embraces his Godself. As with Arjuna, our Blind Spots can hide behind our religious passion, harboring dogmas espoused by our faith, society, and our own self-limiting beliefs.

Let's take a moment to identify some of these aspects in our nature. Some are quite obvious, others we might find surprising, triggering some resistance. Resistance is a natural human response but notice if you have an emotional or physiological tightening when you read some of the statements regarding the Blind Spots. It can feel uncomfortable when we face our constructs of how we operate in the world. Moksha or attaining total freedom requires that we peel away delusions until, at last, all glimmers of attachment and misidentification are vanquished.

SEASONS OF THE SOUL

In the end, we must acknowledge we are our own authorities for truth. We must feel into ourselves, experience every nuance of life, not making it right or wrong, not looking for a cause outside our own body, mind, or spirit. These are the actions we take towards personal responsibility.

There is a tendency for humans to place blame at the feet of another, or on bad luck, or on an unexpected event, anything outside the self. Satan and Lucifer have often been the ideal targets, getting lambasted from every direction. Most of us experience Evil and believe it exists. But again, we must make distinctions between the relative and absolute. In the absolute, Evil is unmanifest—unexpressed, but in the relative, it is part of the play of consciousness interacting with life. Interestingly, the Ascended Masters indicate the being called Satan never existed! They say he is fictitious, an imagined character for the sole purpose of projecting humanity's guilt onto another. To avoid responsibility, humans often direct all their unconquered negative emotions about others and themselves upon Satan. We've all heard, *"It's the Devil's fault!"* or *"The Devil made me do it!"*

Likewise, what do we know about Lucifer aside from the religious fervor stirred against him? Who amongst us has directly experienced the being called "Lucifer" and his Evil ways? Through Reverend Rhinehart's mediumship, Jesus implies that Lucifer is a fallen angel who came back to Earth to experience the earthly physical experience as Jesus did himself. Jesus calls Lucifer a brother in Light, so we might pause before we take aim!

The Masters contend it behooves us to begin taking responsibility for the negativity we ourselves create and continue to perpetuate. Unless we do, the Golden Age will never fully bloom. The attributes ascribed to Lucifer or to Satan are often projections of our own imaginations. Yes, negativity and negative forces exist in the world and in the astral realms! We are wise to not deny its existence and act to rebuke its force, but at the same time be willing to acknowledge that negativity and Evil are the active ingredients fostering the cultivation of our moral nature.

Here are some of the Masters' observations and examples of personal "Blind Spots Within" and worldly "Blind Spots Without."

BLIND SPOTS WITHIN

- Negative thinking about ourselves, others, and events in everyday life.

- Lacking the capacity to accept the contradictions existing in life, such as life's paradoxes.

- Filling the mind with thoughts borrowed from assumed authorities, whether they be religious, societal, friends, or family.

- Lack of acceptance that Evil and dark forces operate in Duality.

- Inability to discern falsehoods, resulting from too much positive or naïve thinking!

- Failure to recognize if we are mired in a haunting despair of the mind, thus curbing the ability to experience the fullness of Joy and Love.

- Resisting the fluidic nature of life-motion stemming from attachment to someone or something.

- Maintaining extreme views, as in the case of believing there is only goodness or only Evil—analyzing the world in terms of only friend or foe, us or them, believers or non-believers.

BLIND SPOTS WITHOUT

- **Cultism:** giving over control of our life to an unenlightened figurehead, following strict adherence to organized religion, fundamental or otherwise.

- **Communism:** belief that there is no God. Allowing the state to deny the right to freedom of religion. Annihilation of the individual through the elimination of free expression and personal rights. Elimination of the right to own property (all personal rights spin off the right to own property).

* **Fascism:** placing the state over the individual, where leadership is dictatorial and brutal.
* **Totalitarianism:** instituting the subordination of the individual under the state, controlling all aspects of life.
* **Unwillingness to Acknowledge Evil and negativity** as forces at play in the universe. Forces that operate through human interaction in politics, worldly institutions, and religions, disguised as beneficial organizations.
* **Refusing to Acknowledge Evil can also operate astrally,** as a menacing force whereby negative astral entities attempt to thwart personal and worldly evolution.

Some may find these Blind Spots a stretch or far-fetched. The idea of the Masters labeling a Blind Spot as an enemy may not resonate with them. No matter how we label these phenomena, it remains a fact that their existence can be observed and foment human suffering. Acknowledging their presence in our lives opens a greater awareness of ourselves and society, while creating the possibility to address the suffering.

There is a Native American story that may be familiar, speaking to our Blind Spots in our awareness. It states we each have two horses existing within ourselves; one a white horse, the other a black horse. When challenging situations arise, we are called upon to choose which horse we are going to ride, the white or the black horse? Are we going to enable negativity by riding the black horse, or are we going to enable Goodness on the white horse? Are we going to act out of Love or are we going to act out of fear? We are always at choice, but often we fail to make the distinctions as to which horse we are riding and are blind to the ramifications of our choice.

Many popular movements have come in and out of vogue over the years, such as EST, Al-Anon, the Men's and Women's movements, and other personal growth movements addressing the shadow side of our personality with varying degrees of success. These movements have accelerated personal awareness and growth.

Acknowledging our shadow side, inspecting our faults squarely in the eye, assists our emotional and mental maturity and development. If we are honest and do the work, we each discover we possess a shadow side. To pretend there is not a personal shadow, or a group shadow, is a Blind Spot in the personal and group mind.

The Masters warn us that it is time we acknowledge the evils of the group-shadow and physically, socially, and Spiritually combat its crippling of humanity. It rears its head in the fomenting of deliberate wars, human trafficking, banking Ponzi schemes, inequality of races and genders, medical lies and drug pushing, all of which are forms of enslavement. It has become accepted to work to transform our personal shadow, but when we mention the shadow side of the group mind, people often cry out, "CONSPIRACY THEORY!" And that stops our investigation. We must go deeper when the evidence proves valid. In other words, there is a truth to the rationale that fiction always adds up, but reality doesn't. We can't let crazy and irrational dismiss our search for the Truth.

In terms of the Blind Spots existing without, Count Saint Germaine once made a comment addressing the Blind Spots in the world from a provocative angle. He indicated:

There is no genuine Love without genuine Social Justice
And there is no genuine Social Justice without genuine Love.

Embracing this concept redefines the meaning and implications of Love! It addresses our responsibility regarding the individual and the group mind. Those fighting for our rights in the field of social justice and world peace can lose sight of the meaning of Love. Ministers and gurus illuminating the value of Love can miss the fact that Love, true Love, depends on social justice. In other words, we can become so focused on one ideal that we overlook the big picture: the enactment of genuine Love wherever we might put our focus.

As we deepen our inquiry into our Blind Spots, peeling back new layers, how might we move forward, eyes blazing with new insight? There must be an honesty as we delve into the aspects of our lives where we are simply playing roles, living on autopilot, acting out emotions that are unresolved traumas. The Masters state unequivocally that there must be a commitment to engage beyond the personality and operate from the Soul.

In this process, we humans will encounter setbacks and difficulties. But even in the face of immense challenges such as personal grief and traumas, imprisonment, facing the prospect of war, or terminal illness, it is paramount that we remind ourselves to keep our eyes on the celebratory Spirit where Joy sings out the beauty of the living Spirit in the midst of challenge.

If we cannot locate that place where Joy lives, then we are doomed to be mired in life's extremes, believing there is only good or only Evil to the exclusion of its opposite. To remain mentally balanced in our crazy world, it benefits us to allow life's contradictions to surface, accepting the paradoxes, rather than pretending otherwise.

So how can we celebrate the entire life experience while observing the Dualities and Blind Spots? No matter the obstacle or the difficulty we face, it is good to admit we are being challenged and not simply to say, God and Divine Justice will save the day, or that's it's only an illusion and it will pass. If we call every difficulty, every heartache, every unfortunate event an illusion, it can create the *"Weasel Clause"* whereby we attempt to escape the challenge the Soul is presenting.

It is too easy to call Duality a delusion. In so doing, we endanger our personal development. Yes, there is a permanence beyond the impermanence of Duality, but in this world, when we find ourselves struggling with the throes of Duality, it can be wise to turn the situation to our benefit.

Life is a play of many varying harmonics; it is not just a few notes. By engaging in the full symphony, by listening to the phrasing of our lives, we can overcome our obstacles. Some have found, under the most horrendous of tortures and lesser abuses, that they have conquered all fear. We each possess the capacity for mastery over the complexities of Duality. There is comfort in knowing the Masters never doubt human capabilities or discount the opportunities presented in Duality for Soul growth.

The Masters inspire us to ponder:

We are individual Souls temporarily living in a body, moving towards the awareness of Conscious Immortality of the Soul, either existing in our physical or Spiritual bodies—not Souls melting into loss of personal identity and Oneness forever.

We are Oneness and Multiplicity, simultaneously moving into Infinite Awareness, that which we are and always have been.

TWENTY-FIVE

THE CHALLENGE OF EVIL IN DUALITY

A S THE MASTERS HAVE OFTEN SAID, WE ARE CONTROLLED FROM the cradle to the grave! We are constantly confronted with opposing forces that don't have our best interests in mind. Financially, many are deliberately burdened with debt and fiat currency; biologically, we are exposed to drugs within the food and healthcare systems that imperil our health; environmentally, debilitating radio frequencies bombard us from the atmosphere, blue light radiates from computer screens, and fluorescent lighting from above, causing ill effects. Socially, we are regulated by the Patriot Act, promoting investigations and surveillance, and various statutes limiting our Rights. Politically, we are controlled by Parties requiring campaign contributions that lead to corporate control. Even Spiritually, we are subjected to ancient dogma delivered by religion. This doesn't even take into consideration the legalities placed on us at birth and death.

By living in Duality and believing Evil doesn't exist, we could put ourselves in danger! When the disbelief in Evil is unrecognized as a Blind Spot, many succumb to the feeling there is nothing they can do and take no direct action, refusing to struggle with the complexities presented in Duality. They feel overwhelmed and continue to say they are not responsible, blaming others for their situation. To meet a challenge of adversity, it is imperative to take responsibility, affirming we can, we will, and we do Act! Even in the most dire of circumstances, we can find a way to accomplish some objective.

To begin, facing any adversity, it's essential to observe correctly, seeing the situation as it truly is, in order to become as objective as possible. All accomplishment begins from this single point of clarity. Once this is realized, we need to make sure our objectives are evaluated within the context of a specific situation. If we set unrealistic objectives, we have created a sure-fire formula for failure.

Acceptance of real limitations means working with them without giving the limitations inordinate power. This is especially true in terms of confronting the enemies lurking in the world. They are relatively straightforward, but not believed by many and regularly minimized by others. The enemies without represent the macrocosmic group self or group shadow. They influence how we interact with the world. The enemies within live in our microcosmic self, the way we relate to the personal self. Some do deep work on themselves and are not able or willing to relate to the group self or the world. Others, the reverse, but we must recognize each domain is a part of us, and if we are to become fully present and continue evolving, it is wise to investigate both the inner and outer selves.

When we become responsible for both aspects, this initiates a balanced interplay, an integration of the two modalities and reflects what the Masters teach. In affirming success, believing success is imminent, in seeing victory, while keeping our critical faculties alive, we will be able to salute triumph over error. Doing so, we will expand our mindset, connect to our Godself that is flowing from the heart of God, knowing we have a right to happiness and eventual victory.

It takes effort to discern contemporary events and history as there is so much misinformation and disinformation. If we are to accept responsibility for the actions of the group mind, we must make an effort to fully educate ourselves on all the various perspectives that emerge within a particular culture. But it is good to recognize we can be easily swayed by strong opinions and it is wise to remain open.

As a person who attended college in the late sixties and early seventies, I was led to believe Communism was never a real threat. We all made fun of the notion we should stay alert to a communist infiltration. To many of us, it was all just a fabricated boogieman conjured up by an insane Eugene McCarthy and misguided Richard Nixon. In those days, the educated believed that if we saw reality correctly, we would know Communism never presented a legitimate threat to our freedoms and liberties. The Chinese society was vastly improved as a result of Communism. Why should we be concerned with Communism in America? In the early Fifties, during the McCarthy Era, suspicion of the evils of Communist propaganda pitted neighbor against neighbor and brought the entire movie industry under suspicion. Many were unsure about the real meaning of Communism.

At one point, I had an opportunity to listen to a lesson by Archangel Gabriel through Reverend Rhinehart's mediumship. Gabriel read from a document that Congressman Usher L. Burdick of North Dakota read into the Congressional National Record in the House of Representatives back in 1957. After listening to Gabriel's reading, I had to admit my understanding of Communism was biased by the ideals of the Sixties.

I was shocked at the intent of the speech, comprehending for the first time there existed then and now a genuine threat to our freedom from the inside. It could be Communism, Fascism, or any tyranny. This particular address is not some myth or conspiratorial theory; this address came word-for-word directly from a speech made by the Communist, Lavrentiy Beria, who was the head of the police system in Russia back in the fifties. The speech was originally prepared for American students studying at Lenin University in Moscow. The following is the speech as read into the Congressional Record, labeled as *"Communist Brainwashing for Americans."*

Congressman Burdick rose and read Beria's speech given to the American students. (This is the same Beria who caused the execution of millions of Russians, arrested by the Malenkov Dictatorship, and finally executed by the coup d'état and the rise of Nikita Khrushchev in 1957.) Here is his speech:

"American students at the Lenin University, I welcome your attendance at these classes on psycho-politics. Psycho-politics is an important, if lesser-known division of geo-politics. It is less known because it must necessarily deal with highly educated personnel, the very top strata of mental healing.

"By psycho-politics, our chief goals are effectively carried forward. To produce a maximum of chaos in the culture of the enemy is our first most important step. Our fruits are grown in chaos, distrust, economic depression, and scientific turmoil. At last, a weary populace can seek peace in our offered Communist State; at last, only Communism can resolve the problems of the masses.

"A psycho-politician must work hard to produce the maximum chaos in the fields of mental healing. He must recruit and use all of the agencies of mental healing. He must labor to increase the personnel and facilities of mental healing until at last the entire field of mental science is entirely dominated by Communist principles and desires. To achieve these goals, the psycho-politician must crush every homegrown variety of mental healing in America; actual teachings of James, Eddy, and Pentecostal Bible faith healers amongst your misguided people must be swept aside. They must be discredited, defamed, arrested, stamped upon, even by their own government, until there is no credit in them and only Communist oriented healing remains.

"You must work until every teacher of psychology unknowingly or knowingly teaches only Communist doctrine under the guise of psychology.

You must labor until every doctor and psychiatrist is either a psycho-politician or an unwitting assistant to our aims.

"You must labor until we have dominion over the minds and bodies of every important person in your nation. You must achieve such disrepute for the state of insanity and such authority over its pronouncement that not one steersman so labeled could again be given credence by his people.

"You must work until suicide arising from mental imbalance is common and calls forth no general investigation or remark. With institutions for the insane, you have in your country prisons which can hold a million persons and can hold them without civil rights or any hope of freedom. And upon these people can be practiced shock and surgery so that never again will they draw a sane breath.

"You must make these treatments common and accepted, and you must sweep aside any treatment or any group of persons seeking to treat by effective means. You must dominate as respected men the fields of psychiatry and psychology. You must dominate the hospitals and universities. You must carry forward the myth that only a European doctor is competent in the field of insanity and thus excuse amongst you the high incidence of foreign birth and training. If and when we seize Vienna, you shall then have a common ground of meeting and can come and take your instructions as worshippers of Freud along with other psychiatrists. Psycho-politics is a solemn charge. With it, you can erase our enemies as insects. You can cripple the efficiency of leaders by striking insanity into their families through the use of drugs.

"You can wipe them away with the testimony as to their insanity. With our technologies, you can even bring about insanity itself when they seem too resistive. You can change their loyalties by psycho-politics. Given a short time with a psycho-politician, you can alter forever the loyalty of a soldier in our hands or a statesman or a leader in his own country, or you can destroy his mind.

"However, you labor under certain dangers. It may happen that remedies for our treatments may be discovered. It may occur that a public

view and a cry may arise against mental healing. It may thus occur that all mental healing might be placed in the hands of ministers and be taken out of the hands of our psychologists and psychiatrists.

"But the capitalistic thirst for control, capitalistic inhumanity, and a general public terror of insanity can be brought to guard against these things. But should they occur, should independent researchers actually discover means to undo psycho-political procedures, you must not rest, you must not eat or sleep, you must not stop one tiniest bit of available money to campaign against it, discredit it, strike it down, and render it void. For by an effective means, all our actions and research could be undone.

"In a capitalistic state, you are aided on all sides by the corruption of the philosophy of man and the times. You will discover that everything will aid you in your campaign to seize control and use all mental healing to spread our doctrine and rid us of our enemies within their own borders.

"Use the courts, use the judges, use the Constitution of the country, use its medical societies and its laws to further our ends. Do not stop in your labor in this direction. And when you have succeeded, you will discover that you can now affect your own legislation at will, and you can, by careful organization of healing societies, by constant campaigns about the terrors of society, by pretense as to your effectiveness make your capitalist himself, by his own appropriations, finance a large portion of the quiet Communist conquest of the nation."

Few in America have known the existence of this speech or its filing in the Congressional Record. The goal was for these students to return to America and foment chaos, distrust, economic depression, and scientific turmoil in the field of mental health. Some might claim this is an isolated voice out of Siberia, written by a pro-communist Russian extremist, and deliberately read into the record by an American anti-communist to mislead Congress.

This speech is brought to our attention via Archangel Gabriel entrancing Reverend Rhinehart; it is a voice that aligns with other documents like *The Protocols of the Learned Elders of Zion*, published by Sergei Nilus (religious writer and self-professed mystic) in Russia in 1906, and later translated by Victor Marsden.

It is said the *Protocols* are a hoax meant to generate antisemitism. But the *Protocols*, much like Beria's speech, suggest the idea of fomenting chaos within the government is a positive objective. Here, we must recognize that Zionists and Jewish people are not synonymous! Our Constitution declares that all Americans must retain the right to articulate critiques of any political system. That includes the right to critique Zionist political policies without being called antisemites.

The Masters gave out the *Protocols of the Learned Elders of Zion* to chelas to read as an addendum to their education. They did so without commentary, allowing each chela to come to a personal conclusion. We don't believe it was by happenstance the Masters chose this material. In contrast, Anton LaVey, the head of the Satanic Church in San Francisco, once said this about the *Protocols*, *"Well, what's wrong with this, isn't this (chaos) the way of the world?"*

Myron Fagan, an American author, playwright, film producer, and director, made a tape called *"Illuminati, Council on Foreign Relations."* In it, he presents another example of the threat existing without. Wikipedia and the mainstream media outlets lambast Fagan for being anti-communist, antisemitic, and a conspiracy theorist. But if we research what Fagan described as Jacob Schiff's actions in the banking industry, it is difficult to find that his policies served the American people's best interests. Without question, he acted as a Trojan horse housed inside the banking institutions serving the Rothschilds' best interests.

Fagan outlines in detail how the Rothschild family sent Jacob Schiff to America with an agenda. His mission was to acquire control of the U.S. monetary system, place stooges in high places of government and federal agencies, create strife in minority groups throughout the nation, and create movements to destroy religion, using monetary incentives and sex to bribe and control men's allegiances. Does this sound familiar? Designed Chaos!

Call it what you like, but reviewing recent history, there is an abundance of evidence referring to plans to infiltrate and take over from within! When we pay attention, we recognize this threat, exists even today!

If we trust Archangel Gabriel's warning, he is saying we have a dharmic duty to be vigilant to secure our sacred freedoms. They are not a given right; therefore, we must stay alert for ourselves and for future generations. (Many of whom could be ourselves as reincarnations of our current selves!)

There has been a relatively successful movement to address our personal shadows, but few, especially in the Spiritual movement, are willing to address our group shadow. We don't believe Gabriel is implying to be fearful, but rather prompting us to be responsible for our world and the enemies within and without. The group mind is real, group karma is real, and the Masters believe it is time we address humanity's shadow.

Yet another source lending credence to the group shadow is Cathy O'Brien's book, *Trance Formation of America*. Her testimony, which documents her experiences from 1957 at birth to 1988 when she was rescued, is most troubling. When she attempted to bring her testimony before the US Congressional Permanent Select Committee on Intelligence Oversight, she was censored by the 1947 National Security Act.

As a young girl, she was given over to *Project Monarch*, the CIA's *MK Ultra Program*, by her father. The book goes into depth regarding her ordeal within the CIA's mind-control program (MK Ultra was the CIA's version of the Nazi's Mind Control Experiment). It outlines the CIA's plan to install CIA plants into positions of power around America. No one can hear Cathy's story without a complete re-evaluation of the political landscape that has been delivered to us via the media and history.

Any one of these references, the *Protocols*, Cathy's story, Fagan's testimonials, only remotely scratches the surface of the group shadow. This presentation is not meant to be a dissertation on all the enemies without, nor a political commentary, simply a lifting of awareness and a prompting to keep our critical faculties alive regarding the possible negative realities that constantly lurk within the group shadow and threaten our well-being. Some may find these particular references offensive, but if we travel back in time (or forward), we would find similar examples demonstrating we have always been controlled to some extent from without.

We believe Archangel Gabriel is suggesting we utilize Duality to provoke and expand our awareness and responsibility on all levels of our being. He is suggesting Duality offers us the opportunity to engage at a more profound level with our unity to all of humanity. Can we become socially responsible in this demanding outer world in the way we expect ourselves to be responsible for our personal lives? And if so, how do we respond to these issues?

For me and for Steve, St. Germaine's revelation lights up in vivid, neon:

Love without Social Justice is not Love!
Social Justice without Love is not Social Justice!

We'd like to close this Chapter with a couple of stories demonstrating how Evil can operate in life in unsuspecting ways. This represents an example of enemies without, illustrating how negative forces can and do affect our lives.

The first event is brought to our attention through a warning from Reverend Rhinehart's mental mediumship to Steve Young. This is a good example of why it serves us to expand our awareness, staying alert to threats from beyond our person to maintain self-preservation. Here is Steve's testimony:

"In 1973, I was attending a blindfold billet reading given by Reverend Rhinehart. Robert John Kensington, Reverend Rhinehart's cabinet guide, had entranced him at the Ilikai Hotel in Honolulu. Dr. Kensington picked up my billet card and proceeded to give me a strong warning regarding an event occurring several weeks in the future. He insisted that whatever I was riding, to be sure I strapped myself down, even if it was an elephant! I imagined my message would be about my promotion day raise since I had recently been promoted to a traffic division as a solo Bike Officer—a police officer's dream for many officers in the Honolulu Police Department. Now I could use a Harley Davidson Road King in the Traffic Division to patrol the streets and highways of Oahu. But Doctor Kensington had my welfare on his mind and was emphatic in his message. To me, the Harley Davidson was the most macho and sexy bike in the USA, I was excited, but unaware of how prone to accidents and dangerous this motorcycle could be. Kensington again reiterated, "Strap Down!" and predicted a two-to-three-day window during which to be especially alert.

"My duty included riding during daylight hours and on this particular day, I was traveling West, headed to an onramp, making my way towards a major highway in Honolulu. Before I could make my way onto the freeway, traffic halted me at an intersection. I always used a practice of counting three seconds after the light changed before I entered the intersection, and after three seconds, I proceeded.

"Suddenly, clear out of nowhere, a male driver blasted through the red light! I broadsided his vehicle and went airborne. While in mid-air, I thought, *Oh no, I'm going to rip off my testicles on the radio knobs as I careen over my bike.* Fortunately, I lucked out, but I struck the driver's windshield and flew over the top of his car, landing hard on the ground.

"Immediately, I knew I had broken my left shoulder and was experiencing intense pain in my toes. Lying on the ground, I sensed a circle of light surrounding me. I felt the bone structure in my left shoulder realigning and energy filling my boot. Quickly, my attention turned to the precarious situation at hand—I must get off the road before I get run over!

"Within minutes, people arrived on the scene asking what they could do. I told them to use my radio to get me an ambulance. Soon, an ambulance arrived and took me to Queen's Hospital in Honolulu. At the hospital, they took X-rays—no broken toes and only a slight hairline fracture in my left shoulder. Eventually, after I got home, I remembered the message Dr. Kensington gave me, warning of a possible accident. I knew my guides played a major role in minimizing severe damage from the accident, I felt immense gratitude!

"Subsequently, in a future communication from Reverend Rhinehart where physical phenomenon was present, Dr. Kensington indicated, without any solicitation on my part, that the motorcycle accident had been created by negative forces intending to take me out. It wasn't even the driver's fault, as he had been overshadowed by the dark forces. I have experienced ten other motorcycle accidents, and I've often wondered how many of them could have been the result of similar circumstances with dark forces. After my eleventh accident, the commanders of the Traffic Division decided my life was in jeopardy and transferred me out of the Traffic Patrol against my wishes and objections. They said I was accident-prone and they were taking action to protect my life."

We'll end with a story that transpired in the Seattle Chapel of the Aquarian Foundation, demonstrating how Evil can arise in unexpected places, even overtaking an unsuspecting person.

One day, during a public service with many present, a man wandered onto the stage of the Chapel and exposed his genitalia! Quickly, someone was asked to retrieve the fishbowl located above the Chapel's refrigerator in the kitchen. Once fetched, the fishbowl was placed on the stage next to the man. Reverend Rhinehart immediately went into trance where a powerful energy passed through the exhibitionist. He went limp, falling to the ground. Simultaneously, the water in the fishbowl turned black, and the fish leapt straight out of the bowl, flopping dead on the stage. With the Evil, demonic force cast out, the man's behavior became quite normal. This episode represents an excellent example of possession by an Evil force, demonstrating Evil's influence on a person, and how an adept medium can exorcise the Evil force.

We believe the Masters saw an opportunity to educate the congregation regarding Evil and reenacted an incident reminiscent of Jesus casting out unclean spirits into the swine in Matthew 8:28-34 KJB.

Many in Spiritual circles don't believe Evil exists, saying how could God create or allow Evil? Again, it is wise to discern the nature of the absolute from the nature of the relative. In the absolute (God), Evil remains unmanifest. But in the relative (the world), Evil is a force inhabiting Duality. On many occasions, through Reverend Rhinehart's mediumship, Jesus spoke to the existence of Evil.

TWENTY-SIX

AVATARS
THE DESCENT OF THE DOVE

Wʜᴇɴ ᴛʜᴇ ᴡᴏʀʟᴅ's Eᴠɪʟs ᴀʀᴇ sᴜꜰꜰᴏᴄᴀᴛɪɴɢ ᴛʜᴇ ᴘᴏᴘᴜʟᴀᴄᴇ, the Divine Hierarchy counteracts the chaos with the incarnation of an Avatar. The cosmic equation is delicate and the universal, or galactic alignments of force fields, spatial vortexes, and universal conditions must be in the right relationship with the Earth's cycles for an Avatar to manifest.

Many in Spiritual circles are familiar with Koot Hoomi Lal Singh, the Ascended Master who worked with Helena Petrovna Blavatsky in the late 1800s, founding the Theosophical Society. Koot Hoomi assists us throughout this Chapter in gaining an understanding of Avatars. (We are not reviewing a genetically engineered Na'vi body as in James Cameron's movie, "Avatar." So, we must expunge our minds of all contemporary, colloquial trends referring to "Avatar.")

The timing of an Avatar's emergence on the planet can be somewhat arbitrary. For instance, an Avatar may only appear once in 10,000 years, or two to four Avatars may manifest in a 2,000-year period. The appearances of Jesus, Buddha, and Muhammad are cases in point. Even two Avatars could be incarnated at the same time in different hemispheres, overseeing different societies.

Approximately every 1,800 to 2,000 years, an Avatar is sent into an age as a Divine incarnation. It could be considered a cyclic event arising to meet the divisive conditions existing on a given planet. The Divine Hierarchy considers many factors in determining whether an Avatar is sent; in general, it is based on how humankind has been using its accumulated knowledge for social and moral advancement.

An Avatar is sent to inaugurate a new era, to shift the prevailing thought in a society from one line of thinking to a more expansive evolutionary line of thought. An Avatar's arrival often denotes moving from one Age into another, as in moving from the Piscean Age into the Aquarian Age. Throughout the centuries, Avatars have attracted throngs of followers. Given their numbers, it is evident Avatars such as Jesus, Buddha, Muhammed, and Krishna have clearly influenced the consciousness of humanity.

A 2024 religious consensus by World Statistics reported there existed:

- 2.39 billion Christians

- 1.9 billion Muslims

- 1.3 billion Non-Religious (Atheists and Agnostics)

- 1.1 billion Hindus

- 502 million Buddhists

- 209 million Ethno-religions

- 28 million Sikhs

- 15 million Spiritists

- 14 million Jews

Even with these many religious sects formed by or influenced by Avatars, there is a good amount of confusion around what determines whether a particular incarnation is an Avatar. The word Avatar has been bandied about rather casually in recent times. Just because a being has attained great wisdom, dispensed invaluable teachings, produced healings, set up schools of learning, orphanages, hospitals, and is enlightened doesn't make him or her an Avatar. Even miraculous events surrounding a saint are not infallible indicators.

Madame Blavatsky produced materializations, writing volumes of Spiritual wisdom. St. Teresa of Avila reformed the Carmelite Order and levitated. Saint Francis of Assisi rebuilt the Christian Church, experienced visions and even exhibited the stigmata phenomenon. Many Ascended Masters led extraordinary lives, but none of these highly influential persons were advanced to the status of Avatars.

As per Madame Blavatsky's commentary in her book *Secret Doctrine*, every planet has seven root-races of people evolving on the planet at any one time. Each root-race potentially is divided into seven sub-races. As a presiding root-race descends into sub-races in the midst of a new root-race evolving, the forces of Evil begin to take hold and wreak havoc on the planet. It is when the presiding root-race descends into sub-races and a new root-race begins to evolve that an Avatar may be required to combat the ensuing chaos. (Again, it must be stated that root-races have nothing to do with skin color, but everything to do with the evolution of consciousness.)

What is the distinction between an Avatar and a semi-avatar? Avatars are rare, and few people chance upon a true Avatar, but many have met a semi-avatar during a lifetime. The Avatar generally stands alone as unique, a great teacher pointing towards a more evolved path for an era that is advancing. Semi-avatars, though great in their own right, are not demarking a societal shift. They are more focused on a shift in consciousness at the personal level. There can be many thousands of semi-avatars existing on a planet at the same time. According to Koot Hoomi, the possibility of up to 144,000 semi-avatars may manifest between the arrival of two incarnations of Avatars.

Avatars represent a cosmic stir, provoking a dramatic leap in consciousness, inspiring humanity to open to new wisdom and a higher moral ground. They redirect the evolutionary path of a root-race, overcoming the current unconscious drift of the masses. Brushing shoulders with an Avatar is a blessing, even if we are often unaware, because an Avatar can be working invisibly in service to humanity for many years before receiving the mantle of Avatarship.

At some point, there is a power that descends to a great teacher, a force, a Divine Energy. When this occurs, the teacher becomes wholly united with the Christ Light, the Christ Power, the same energy that ultimately infuses all Avatars. It is at this moment the descent of the Divine has melded into a physical person. Not until the dove alighted over Jesus and a voice from heaven spoke, *"This is my beloved Son in whom I am well pleased,"* was Jesus anointed the Divine Avatar of the Piscean Age and the World Teacher.

According to Koot Hoomi, World Teachers don't necessarily have a large following during their lifetimes; in fact, they are often persecuted and face divisive challenges in overcoming society's ingrained dogmas before they establish any semblance of a new understanding. It is often preferable that they are somewhat invisible so they can fulfill their mission with less interference. The acknowledgement of Christ Jesus and Buddha as World Teachers of their day was not released upon the Earth plane until after the fulfillment of their life's work. Sometimes it is not apparent that a particular Avatar was the Avatar of the Age until he has transitioned to the Spirit side of life. In many cases, the Dove may not stay with an Avatar for an entire incarnation. At times, mysteriously, the mantle comes and goes throughout the physical life span of the Avatar.

We must make a distinction between the man Jesus and Christ the Avatar; between the man Siddhartha and Buddha the Avatar; and between the man Yamuna and Krishna the Avatar. The Christ Power, the Buddha Light, and the Krishna Light always speak the truth; in contrast, the man Jesus, the man Siddhartha, and the man Krishna may err in speech or action. A man has preferences; he may like certain people over others, and he may have peculiarities or unusual appetites. The Avatar does not, and as difficult as this is to accept, the man is not always perfect as we may want and expect. Through Jesus' very lips, he stated he was not perfect. He was a man.

In our zealousness to find exceptional role models, we have tried to create perfection in form, expecting a saint's personality to be as we are not, this is but a human foible. With this stated, it behooves us to acknowledge the Christ Force inhabiting Jesus and Buddha is perfect and never errs. But we can still hold Jesus or Buddha to such high standards, imagining them so pure that they can never meet our expectations, and in the same manner, we can attempt to emulate an ideal model we have created for ourselves, which becomes unreachable.

Looking to past history, one of the universal earmarks attesting to the belief a person is an Avatar is the enactment of miraculous Spiritual phenomenon. The Masters do not consider a miraculous event important in and of itself. The miracles of Jesus raising Lazarus from the dead and turning water into wine, or the fifteen days of miracles in Buddha's life, serve to provide credibility to the truth of the new dispensation of Light coming through the Avatar. The miracle focuses our attention on the fact that something unprecedented is happening; a Truth is being delivered from the Heart and Mind of God!

Without the production of miracles, most would dismiss the new teaching as false and remain entrenched in the dogma of the day. The miracle's purpose is not to impress or wow the common people, but solely to validate the teachings. It is best if we view the miracles performed by each Avatar in the context of their day and not attempt to compare Krishna to Buddha, or Christ to Reverend Rhinehart, mainly because their miracles are culturally sensitive. Many of the distant past miracles seem fantastical by today's standards and unrealistic, but the Celestial Realm has its ways. Even with the demonstration of miracles, no matter the scale, Avatars face an uphill battle getting their teaching accepted. Quite often, they are compared to the reigning messiah and denigrated as false prophets. Part of the cosmic rub is that an Avatar lives simultaneously as a Spiritual allegory and a genuine physical person in flesh and blood.

Every story in scripture, no matter the religious tradition, is but an allegory, a parable, revealing an archetypal pattern living within our person. Whether it is the drama of Jesus meeting Judas in the Garden of Gethsemane, Jesus' crucifixion and the resurrection from the tomb, the events in the Upper Room, or scenes from other traditions such as the battleground in which Arjuna finds himself in the *Bhagavad Gita*, each presents inner conflicts, confounding paradoxes, and a grappling with Truth to further understand the Self.

Koot Hoomi tells us that Truth presents through the Avatar to advance the karmic evolution of human beings in the process of setting them free. Those unwilling to discover the relationship between the Avatar's allegory and themselves are courting misunderstanding. To fully grasp the import behind an Avatar's teaching, it serves us to step out of the concrete world and enter the terrain represented by the symbolic.

Let's take a moment and investigate how this might unravel in our lives with one of the more recognizable parables in the *Bible*. Opening to this view, we might recognize that each disciple exists within us. During our lives, we may be acting out one or more of the disciple's specific dramas, a pattern of energy operating within our personality. The disciples provide the most obvious examples. Judas represents the betrayer in the group mind; Thomas, the skeptical, acute mind; Peter, the principle of faith; John, love. Each is a reflection of an aspect of ourselves.

Exploring the drama that transpired in the Garden of Gethsemane from the standpoint of an allegory pertinent to our personality, we begin to observe a more in-depth understanding of how the stories in the *Bible* serve our Spiritual development. Judas exists not only as a real character, but also as the betrayer living in each of us. If we are honest, we each have performed this archetypal pattern in life and in many previous lives.

Koot Hoomi asks us how might we address this awareness and how we transform this human quality into Light? What exactly is this pattern living within us? Like the disciples, those of us on the Path have made commitments to act in alignment with Christ Light, Buddha Light, striving to be examples of living by Christ Principle. But at times, we find ourselves pressed when old egotistical patterns confront us. We default to our age-old ingrained behavior and betray ourselves, turning our back on our commitment to the Christ Light, then denying to ourselves the truth of our actions, saying, *"Oh, this isn't really who I am, what I did is clearly appropriate given these outlandish circumstances, especially given what so-and-so did to me!"*

Our actions often parallel Judas' when he says in the garden, *"Hail, oh Master,"* and kisses Jesus, then turns around and hands him over to the chief priest of society to be crucified, all the while thinking he is doing the right thing. (Oh, how our Blind Spots sabotage our promises to Self!)

Shortly thereafter, each of the twelve disciples, each personality type, turns and walks away from a commitment to the Christ, not to Jesus the person, but to the Christ within themselves. They caved, copped out to societal influence, buying into the deceit of the ego's self-importance, hence their betrayal. Each disciple crucified the Christ within himself!

This is how the Christ dies! How Jesus supposedly died for our sins. But Jesus the Christ never died—he is eternal. It is we who extinguish our Christ Light within ourselves by our acts of ignorance and self-importance. Herein lies a different understanding as opposed to the one espoused by many in our Christian Churches. The Christ within dies upon our failure to observe our promise to ourselves to live by Christ Principle, the Golden Rule.

Jesus is directed by his instinctual awareness of goodness and his love of goodness. His total personality is directed towards this end, no waffling, just complete steadfastness in the Truth! Until we lift, rise, and conquer ourselves, we keep reenacting the Judas principle, betraying our highest good governed by Christ Principle, postponing our resurrection into the Light!

There have been great, pure beings who have come and gone during the Twentieth Century. They are great teachers, not Avatars but semi-avatars like Swami Yogananda, Ramana Maharshi, George Gurdjieff, Anandamayi Ma, Krishnamurti, Shirdi Baba, Baba Nityananda, St. Teresa of Avila, Padre Pio, and Baba Muktananda—teachers of enlightenment immersed in God or Brahman consciousness.

The Avatars Krishna, Osiris, Moses, Jesus, Buddha, Muhammad, Reverend Rhinehart (Kumara), were Lights sent upon the world, Lights that changed the presiding Spiritual discourse, ushering in wisdom and altering the course of history. Let's take a look at a few of these past Avatars and examine what distinguishes them as Avatars.

Madame Blavatsky points out that there existed many similarities between the Avatars Jesus, Buddha, and Krishna. Though their lives are unique and distinctly different, their life patterns were cast from the archetypal models of Avatarship. Here are some of the characteristics repeated, where their lives partially reflected each other, and life's incidents overlapped.

Each Avatar was born of royalty, living apart from the masses. Jesus descended from the royal family of David, Buddha was the son of a king, and Krishna descended from royalty but was brought up by shepherds. At some point in their lives each endured persecution. Krishna is persecuted by Kansa, Jesus by Herod, and Buddha also experienced persecution from the populace. Their mothers were said to be immaculate virgins, although controversy regarding this claim has emerged and has been challenged through Reverend Rhinehart's mediumship. Even so, the claim symbolizes the purity of birth which is hard to refute.

Krishna is endowed with beauty, produced miracles, cured the lame, the blind, and cast out demons. We find Buddha displaying similar gifts, performing miracles and wonders. Jesus is gifted with beauty, performed many miracles, and cast out demons. Krishna denounced the clergy, claiming they are overly ambitious and hypocrites. He taught the Unity of God and the Immortality of Spirit, revealing to the public the secrets only previously known by the Sanctuary of his time. Some traditions state he died on the cross, but actually, he was nailed to a tree by an arrow. Buddha wiped out idolatry, taught the mysteries of Nirvana and Unity, divulging knowledge previously known only by the priests. Jesus rejected the old Judaic law, denouncing the Pharisees and Sadducees for dogmatic intolerance and is accused by Jews of revealing secrets known only in Sanctuary. He is put to death on a cross.

But it is clear all Avatars are aware the world is an illusion-dream. It is a field that exists in the play of consciousness of the knower, the knowing, and the known. An Avatar's concentration is perfected to the extent he has developed the power of the Creator and can materialize his thought into a material object. This object is perceived not only by the Avatar, but by other physical witnesses. The Avatar can create anything as a visible object, as solid as the Earth. We see this phenomena displayed by the Ascended Masters when Jesus created a new bodily life-consciousness in Lazarus, bringing him back from the dead; when Babaji created a beautiful, golden mansion fulfilling a long forgotten desire of Lahiri Mahasaya (Chela of Babaji); and when Emil's mother, who we visited in Chapter Nine, "Unexpected

Encounters With Ascended Masters", healed the boy and replaced the bleak family chamber with a sparkling new interior. The Avatar knows in this illusive world, it is God who moves through his hands, his feet, who sees and hears through his senses, the Avatar knows he gazes at only Himself in this manifest world.

In reviewing this highly condensed Cliff Notes version of past Avatars, we can easily recognize similar patterns and similar energies inherent in the archetypal patterns of Avatarship. We can surmise earlier Avatars like Osiris from Egypt, even earlier Avatars from Atlantis and Lemuria, demonstrated the same archetypal essence. The dissemination of Light from on high induces similarities—so Jesus is not unique, nor is Buddha, or Krishna, though their devotees may insist differently.

What follows is a cursory look at Jesus, Buddha, Krishna, Muhammad, and Reverend Rhinehart (Kumara). With these summaries, we may further understand the distinction between a semi-Avatar and an Avatar.

We will begin with Jesus.

TWENTY-SEVEN

JESUS
1 CE — 33 CE

JESUS LIVED AROUND THE TURN OF THE MILLENNIUM. THOUGH if we look at the historical record of the day, it is very difficult to determine the exact years Jesus lived. History writers such as Philo Judaeus, who also lived in Palestine during the supposed years of Jesus' ministry, never mention his name.

According to the Book of Matthew 2:11 KJB, three Magi arrived at Jesus' birth bearing treasures. The Magi opened their offerings, presenting gifts of gold, frankincense, and myrrh. When they saw Jesus with Mary, they bowed down in worship. What is not known from the biblical commentary is there was a fourth Magi. In the days of the *Bible*, Magi weren't simply wisemen but were known as astrologers and those who interpreted and told the future by dreams. Some called them magicians.

The three Magi were from the mystical order of the Essenes from the land of Chaldea in the region of Babylonia. Although not mentioned in the *Bible*, they are strongly associated with the information discovered in the Dead Sea Scrolls. Jewish historian Josephus and Roman historian Philo described the Essenes as scholarly Jewish purists, who separated from the dominant Jewish traditions which they felt had been corrupted.

Through the mediumship of Reverend Rhinehart, we learn the fourth Magi, Master Vortheo, hailed from a Temple in Tibet. Vortheo tells how an Avatar is prepared by the Council of the Great White Brotherhood, the *Dhyan Chohans*, beings who are the Guardians of the Tree of Knowledge of Good and Evil. The Dhyan Chohans educate an Avatar to dispense a new level of morality for the next two thousand years.

Vortheo previously arrived at the births of the three Avatars: Melchizedek, Krishna, and Buddha, and was keenly intent on arriving at the birth of Jesus. He joined the three Magi following the Star of Bethlehem. They were well on their way when Vortheo received a telepathic message that his Temple faced a crisis and he must return. He stated his personal desire, though strong, had to be secondary to his duty to his higher Self in service to the Temple. So, he abandoned his trip and returned to his Temple.

Following the visit by the Magi, the prophecy of Jesus as a "King" quickly spread. King Herod's monarchy was mocked by this assertion and consequently, the king feared the popular ascent of Jesus.

The night after the departure of the Magi, Joseph, Jesus' father, had a dream of an Angel exhorting him to flee with the child Jesus into Egypt and stay until he received word of Jesus' safety. The Angel warned that Herod would seek to destroy the child. Herod did, in fact, order the slaying of all male children two years or younger to ensure the continuance of his reign. It is said Herod's fury led to the massacre of fourteen thousand to over forty thousand innocent children, but those numbers seem exorbitant, given the population in Bethlehem at the time of Jesus' birth. After Herod's death, Joseph received another dream where an Angel informed him that Herod had died and he could return to Israel.

In the *Infancy Gospel of Thomas*, there's a story of Jesus' early prowess. (The *Infancy Gospel of Thomas* is an apocryphal gospel about the childhood of Jesus. The scholarly consensus dates it to the mid-to-late second century, although the precise authorship is unclear.) The Gospel tells that at five, Jesus was playing with other children by a flowing stream after it rained. Jesus took the mud from the soft clay and formed twelve sparrows. It was the Sabbath and one of the fathers of the other children went to Joseph and said it isn't permissible for Jesus to make sparrows on the day of the Sabbath.

Joseph rebuked Jesus, asking, *"Why are you doing these things on the Sabbath?"*

Jesus clapped his hands, ordering the sparrows, *"Go, take flight like living beings!"*

The sparrows then took flight, chirping away as they left. Having seen this, the Pharisee was amazed and reported the incident to all his friends.

In another incident, at age twelve, Jesus and his parents went to Jerusalem for the festivals of the Passover. During their return, Jesus stayed behind without his parents knowing. His parents traveled a day's journey searching for him among their relatives. Not finding him, they returned to Jerusalem. After three days, they found him in the temple, sitting in the middle of the teachers, listening and questioning them. Many were surprised by how he questioned the elders, explaining the main points of the law, providing insight into the understanding of the prophets' riddles, and praising their foresight.

His mother said, *"Child, what have you done to us? Look, we've been searching for you in pain and grieving."*

Jesus said, *"Why were you looking for me? Didn't you know that it's necessary for me to be in the place of my Father?"*

And the scribes and Pharisees said to Mary, *"You're the mother of this child?"*

"I am."

And they said to her, *"Blessed are you that the Lord God has blessed the fruit of your womb, because we've never seen such wisdom of praise (of the Lord) and glory of virtue."*

There are numerous stories of Jesus healing and raising the dead in the *Infancy Gospel of Thomas*. Here is one:

In Joseph's neighborhood, a certain child was sick and died. His Mother wept and wept. Jesus heard the commotion and, running quickly to the scene, he found the child dead.

He touched the child's chest and said, *"I say to you, baby, don't die, but live and be with your mother."*

And the baby looked up immediately and laughed, and Jesus said to the mother, *"Take your child, give him milk, and remember me."*

And the crowd standing there was amazed and said, *"The truth is, this child Jesus is a god or an angel, because his every word becomes a deed!"*

Rather than diving into the various controversial historical accounts of Jesus, which give reasonable credence to a much different story than Western history presents, we will defer to Helena Petrovna Blavatsky's comments, which incidentally were subscribed to by the Ascended Masters. Madame Blavatsky refers to Jesus as an initiate of the mystery schools of the day in her Theosophical literature.

Here is her quote: "...if he was an initiate of either the Pythagorean Essenes, the Chaldean Magi, or the Egyptian Priests, then the doctrine taught by him was but a portion of the *'Secret Doctrine'* taught by the Pagan hierophants to the few select adepts admitted within the sacred adyts." [1]

If we are to listen to the Biblical Christian teachings of today, we are led to believe Jesus is the only begotten Son of God and unique as the only one revealing the true revelations of God. But it is clear in reviewing the history of the secret mysteries of pagan religions as revealed by Madame Blavatsky, Jesus is but one of many Avatars and his teaching was a continuation of the ancient mysteries of secret doctrines of bygone eras.

It is interesting to note that the *Egyptian Book of the Dead*, which is carved in bas-relief on some of the ancient Egyptian monuments, references the belief in the Immortality of the Soul and articulates the very phrasing, "The Day of Judgement," identical to the phrasing that is presented in the *New Testament.*

This said, in no way does it minimize Jesus' stature or his teachings. Jesus is recognized in many traditions to be a great Light, a moral beacon in the world, as are many of the teachings in the *Bible*. Count Saint Germain states many times in his commentaries through Reverend Rhinehart's mediumship that he takes Jesus Christ as his Lord and Savior! That alone, in our estimation, gives Jesus' consciousness Godly import.

The Masters have indicated, through the lessons dispensed through Reverend Rhinehart's mediumship, that Jesus directs many of their activities and studies from their secret abode in Shambhala. So, regardless of whether or not Jesus' teachings are unique in themselves, he is honored in Shambhala as a great leader and personage.

Jesus' ministry brought forward the Path of the heart and a deeper understanding of forgiveness. His ministry shifted the *Old Testament* or *Torah* "an eye for an eye" teaching to one of opening people's minds to a new understanding of morality and the Path to God.

He said, *"Divine Love is the Way. It is only through Divine Love that one establishes true understanding."*

Jesus goes on to advise us to take the pains to be diligent and intent in our earnestness in order to fully understand the Self. In this way, the great Light of God will eventually reveal itself. He encourages us to create our lives such that when we look back, we will not find ourselves lacking any quality of good, and we will rest in knowing God is our Strength, God is our Peace, and God is our Joy. Jesus explains it is through Divine Love we shall find the Way to Conscious

Immortality of the Soul. And as we are all aware, Jesus' main teaching guides us to understanding true Divine Love.

"Do unto others as you would have them do unto you."
Matthew 7:12 KJB

Madame Blavatsky interprets the word "Christos" to mean "Way" or the "Path." When a disciple addressed his Master, the Master would say: *"Thou art the Path."* After Jesus became the Christos, he said, *"I am the Way."* The Voice of the Silence, by Blavatsky, says, *"Thou cans't travel on the Path until thou hast become that Path itself."*

Madame Blavatsky again alludes to this notion when she spoke to her students, *"Do not follow me; follow the Path I show."* She further advised, *"Do not follow my personality; follow the Christos-principle within yourselves. It is the only 'Light on the Path' which really exists."* [2]

In other words, trust in yourself, trust in your highest Self, to assist you in finding the Way. Jesus is not saying to follow his person, but to follow the Light of the Christ dwelling within, just as he exemplifies.

Back in the seventies, a Holy Communion Séance in Aquarian Foundation's Mother Church in Seattle lends credence to these thoughts. This séance speaks to the sacred relationship we have with the inner world of our heart. The Masters have indicated the entire world exists in our heart alone; if true, it would be advantageous for us to enliven our attunement to the true nature of our heart, to see it anew, and listen more deeply to its inner promptings.

The following is one chela's experience of this séance. All the usual scientific conditions were in place as Reverend Rhinehart went into trance:

"From out of the Holy of Holies, Master Jesus manifested in blackout conditions under the red-light illuminating the séance environment. He presented himself in an ectoplasmic gauze, giving his consciousness physical substance and form. Once fully manifested, he gave a lesson on the *'Sacred Stones of the Heart.'* Then seemingly out of nowhere, an inner illumination lit up his heart area from within his chest cavity, shining out to the world his sacred beating heart. Each beat illumined its magnificent presence, each pulse emanating eternal, enduring Love. A startling Holy presence bathed the gathering, accelerating the Light until an upliftment filled all present with stunning awe."

Without speaking, Jesus advised us to investigate our mysterious heart to know the Self. Notice, he does not illuminate his brain. Here he is pointing to the Way, the Way to the Kingdom of God, emphasizing that the Way lies beyond the rational mind and opens its secrets to a person who listens to the heart and its wisdom. The Way is for those who dare venture beyond the constructs of worldly existence and the constraints of the mind.

Many in the New Age have turned away from the *Bible* because of Church corruption, the lack of moral discrimination of ministers, and a loss of belief in various passages. But as we've mentioned, the Masters often referenced the *Bible*, illuminating passages paying tribute to Christ. The following passages illustrate the miracles Jesus demonstrated to validate the Truth of his teachings, solidifying his stature as an Avatar.

> *"And if Christ be not risen then is our preaching vain*
> *and your faith is also vain."*
> 2 Corinthians 15:14 KJB

This part of 1 Corinthians speaks to the Christ being risen, indicating if there is no resurrection from the dead (ego), then the Christ has not risen. To rise into the Christ Light, the Masters suggest, as does this verse, to let go of the ego, die to the personality. This wisdom is reminiscent of what Krishna tells Arjuna in the *Bhagavad Gita* and illustrates how sacred wisdom crosses religious traditions.

SEASONS OF THE SOUL

"For him whose self (ego) has been conquered by the Self (Soul or Christ Self), the Self is the friend of the self; but verily, the Self behaves inimically, as an enemy, toward the self that is not subdued." [3]

Many of us require an experience of something extraordinary to believe a reality exists beyond our carnal perceptions. Duality is the only reality we permit to exist through our vehicles of perception. (If I can't see it, it doesn't exist!) The miracles demonstrated in the *Bible* illustrate there is more going on than meets the eye. The supernormal quality of miracles serves to give credence to Spiritual teachings and to bolster our Faith.

The following passages shine the light on some of the miracles brought forth through Jesus' ministry with the assistance of the Divine Hierarchy, providing credence and power to his teachings.

St. John 2:2-11 KJB

Here is Jesus at a marriage ceremony in Cana of Galilee when he turns water into wine:

"And both Jesus was called and his disciples, to the marriage,

And when they wanted wine, the mother of Jesus saith unto him, They have no wine.

Jesus saith unto her, Woman, what have I to do with thee? Mine hour is not yet come.

His mother saith unto the servants, Whatsoever he saith unto you, do it.

And there were set there six waterpots of stone, after the manner of the purifying of the Jews, containing two or three firkins apiece.

Jesus saith unto them, Fill the waterpots with water. And they filled them up to the brim.

And he saith unto them, Draw out now, and bear unto the governor of the feast. And they bare it.

When the ruler of the feast had tasted the water that was made wine, and knew not whence it was: (but the servants which drew the water knew;) the governor of the feast called the bridegroom,

And saith unto him, Every man at the beginning doth set forth good wine; and when men have well drunk, then that which is worse: but thou hast kept the good wine until now.

This beginning of miracles did Jesus in Cana of Galilee, and manifested forth his glory; and his disciples believed on him."

Matthew 14:14-21 KJB

In Matthew, Jesus feeds the multitudes and heals the sick.

"And Jesus went forth, and saw a great multitude, and was moved with compassion toward them, and he healed their sick.

And when it was evening, his disciples came to him saying, This is a desert place, and the time is now past; send the multitudes away, that they may go into the villages, and buy themselves victuals.

But Jesus said unto them, They need not depart; give ye them to eat.

And they said unto him, We have here but five loaves, and two fishes.

He said, Bring them hither to me.

And he commanded the multitude to sit down on the grass, and took the five loaves and the two fishes, and looking up to heaven, he blessed, and brake, and gave the loaves to his disciples, and the disciples to the multitude.

And they did all eat, and were filled: and they took up of the fragments that remained twelve baskets full.

And those who had eaten were about five thousand men, beside women and children."

One of the most revered miracles of Jesus' ministry is the resurrection. Here are two passages illustrating different aspects of the event:

Luke 24:1-5

"Now upon the first day of the week very early in the morning, they came unto the sepulchre, bringing spices which they had prepared, and certain others with them.

And they found the stone rolled away from the sepulchre.

And they entered in, and found not the body of the Lord Jesus.

And it came to pass, as they were much perplexed thereabout, behold, two men stood by them in shining garments:

And they were afraid, and bowed down their faces to the earth, they said unto them, Why seek ye the living among the dead?

He is not here, but is risen: remember how he spake unto you when he was yet in Galilee..."

John 2:19-22 KJB

Here, Jesus describes his resurrection:

"Jesus answered and said unto them, Destroy this temple, and in three days I will raise it up.

Then said the Jews, forty and six years was this temple in building, and wilt thou rear it up in three days?

But he spake of the temple of his body.

When therefore he was risen from the dead, his disciples remembered that he had said this unto them; and they believed the scripture, and the word which Jesus had said."

There are myths in other cultures and traditions describing saints and Avatars such as Osiris, Odin, and Ganesh, to name a few, enacting their resurrection, but we find no other proof in the historical records with the same credibility as that of Jesus.

TWENTY-EIGHT

BUDDHA
483 BCE — 400 BCE

G AUTAMA BUDDHA LIVED SOMEWHERE BETWEEN THE SIXTH and Fourth centuries BCE. He was born into a Royal family as Siddhartha Gautama, in Lumbini (Rupandehi District), located in present-day Nepal near the border of India. The Orientalists say there are five Wisdom Buddhas or five Dhyanis: Aksobhya, Amitabha, Amoghasiddhi, Ratnasambhava, and Vairocana, representing specific meditative states that are transformative aspects of consciousness. They are the icons of Mahayana Buddhism, the "Celestial" Buddhas that give rise to a human Buddha incarnating into Earth as a worldly manifestation of the eternal Dhyani prototypes. Each manifestation enlivens a different aspect of enlightened consciousness, assisting us in Spiritual transformation. With this understanding, we can determine there have been many manifestations of Buddha over the centuries and Gautama Buddha is but one of these Divine manifestations.

Buddha's teachings appeared during provocative philosophical challenges between the traditional schools of Vedic orthodoxy, Jainism, materialism, and various ascetic traditions. His rejection of the caste system's exclusivity of sacred Spiritual knowledge for the Brahmans alone was considered revolutionary.

At his birth, seers prophesied that the son of King Suddhodana and Queen Maya would have an extraordinary life. They predicted that Siddhartha would become a great ruler or a remarkable Spiritual leader. The king wanted his son to follow in his footsteps as a great king, so he did his best to shield Siddhartha from religious teachings and incidents of human suffering, providing Siddhartha with extravagant privilege and a diverse education. When Siddhartha turned sixteen, the king arranged a marriage between Siddhartha and Princess Yasodhara. Soon she gave birth to a son, Rahula. Siddhartha spent years living happily as a prince in Kapilvastu (now a district in Nepal) with his every desire met.

At twenty-nine, he ventured out and encountered the harsh realities of the world. He was appalled to learn of the frequency of sickness, suffering, and death. This realization upturned his world. He perceived human life was characterized by impermanence and uncertainty, a striking contrast to his royal upbringing. Devastated by these realizations, he rose in the middle of the night, left his wife, son, and family, cut his hair, and abandoned his royal garments for a modest white robe. This act has often been referred to as the "Great Renunciation," where he rejected his lot to pursue a Spiritual path. Immediately, he searched out enlightened teachers in an attempt to gain a deeper understanding of suffering.

He practiced under several teachers, mastering their teachings, but still he felt unsatisfied and continued to seek what he thought to be the ultimate truth. His pursuit eventually led him to join a group of companions who were determined to take their austerities further, depriving themselves of food and practicing self-mortification, to once and for all put their sinful natures to death.

One day, while following this plan, Siddhartha collapsed by a river. A girl named Sujata revived him, giving him milk and rice pudding. At this point, he began rethinking his course. Eventually, he decided the concentrated focus of meditation to be the middle Path and he moved away from extreme asceticism, leaving his companions behind.

He now realized the extreme teachings of self-denial were fraught with heartache and unnecessary suffering, so he shifted his full attention to the middle-ground, which he eventually called the "Eightfold Path." He sat under the Bodhi Tree in meditation, where he vowed to stay until he found the Truth.

Forty-nine days he sat, and upon the full moon of Taurus of the Wesak Festival, at the age of thirty-five, his body filled with radiant light, freeing him from ignorance and limitation. During those days, he realized his true nature, attaining enlightenment and becoming the Buddha.

At this time, he gained deep insights into what he called the "Four Noble Truths." He determined life was an endless cycle of rebirth, suffering, and dying again and again and again. Death was nothing but the changing of the physical body for a Spiritual body, at which point the Soul birthed again to a whole new experience, forwarding its karma to the new body. This pattern repeated itself until the self finally lifted into full Self Awareness.

The Eightfold Path can be visualized as a wheel consisting of eight spokes depicting the interconnected principles for Spiritual and personal development. The wheel presents the means to confront inevitable suffering and finally extinguish it by attaining Spiritual Enlightenment, freeing the mind of ignorance, attachment, and aversion.

THE EIGHTFOLD PATH

WISDOM FACTORS:
Right Understanding/Right View

- Comprehending the Four Noble Truths.
- Seeing the world as it is rather than how we believe it to be or want it to be.
- Recognizing impermanence and interconnectedness.

- The Eightfold Path should not be considered a linear progression, but an interconnected, holistic approach to Spiritual and ethical unfoldment.
- Developing insights into the causes of suffering.

Right Intent

- Having persistence and passion for the journey. Passion is a necessary ingredient for the climb that arises from the heart.
- Cultivating compassionate states of mind.
- Eliminating harmful thoughts.
- Developing the intentions of kindness, compassion, and renunciation of harmful cravings.

ETHICAL CONDUCT FACTORS:

Right Speech

- Right speech connects the heart and mind, bringing awareness to communicating in ways that unite, heal dissension, and foster compassionate action.
- Speaking truthfully.
- Avoiding harmful, divisive speech and gossip.
- Practicing kind communication.

Right Action

- Living with integrity in such a way that we do unto others the way we would want them to do unto us. We do unto the Earth in the same manner, living ethically.
- Maintaining healthy relationships.
- Refraining from actions that cause harm.

Right Livelihood

- Making sure a person's work supports and fosters the truths of the Spiritual Path. Our daily work should respect all life, promoting equality for all. Work should be done in an ethical manner.

- Maintaining a balance between professional and Spiritual life.

MENTAL DISCIPLINE FACTORS:
Right Effort

- Right effort amounts to holding positive thought that is backed by focused action and executed with an attitude of cheerful determination.
- Developing correct concentration and awareness.
- Maintaining mental discipline fosters insight and clarity.

Right Mindfulness

- Strive to be undistracted in the moment. Being completely focused in the moment allows us to best accomplish the goal. Here we are not excluding the world, but attentive to whatever arises with an even mind. In this way, we become aware of old patterns that inhibit the success of our present actions.
- Develop awareness at all levels of being: bodily, mentally, emotionally, astrally, vibrationally, Spiritually, and monadically.

Right Concentration

- Turn the mind to focus on the object desired. An uncluttered mind can achieve what it focuses on. Train the mind to remain focused. This implies we choose a direction or goal that is worthy of our attention and aligned with our Spiritual Path.
- Achieve mental clarity.
- Develop deep meditative states and inner stillness.

As in other Spiritual traditions, there has been a tight hold on occult knowledge. For centuries before Siddhartha became a Buddha, the *Vedas* were kept in the exclusive possession of the temple Brahmans. No one could access the knowledge outside the sacred Brahman caste. After Gautama studied the entire Brahmanical wisdom contained in the *Rahasya* and the *Upanishad,* he traveled to the snowy Himalayas to learn from the "Teachers of Life," dwelling therein. In comparing the two bodies of knowledge, the Brahman's *Vedas* and the wisdom of the "Teachers of Life," he discovered little difference between them. Given this awareness, Gautama determined this wisdom should be made available to more than the Brahman caste and decided to popularize the knowledge. [1]

Once Siddhartha became the Buddha, he was known as Shakya-muni Buddha. The name Shakyamuni is Sanskrit and Siddhartha was born a prince in the Shakya Clan. The Shakya are said to have been descendants of an ancient Vedic sage named Gautama Maharishi. This is where his family got the name Gautama.

As with Jesus and Krishna, many miracles surrounded Buddha's life. Here are a few examples from the *"Fifteen Days of Miracles"* attended by 80,000 Buddhists and 85,000 Hindus. The stories handed down render many different versions of Buddha's miracles, but the general gist is similar. There are depictions of these miracles carved on the stupas within Buddhist monasteries in the *Gandara* style of art and created in the rock-cut caves of the 5th and 6th centuries in Western India.

The story of the *"Fifteen Days of Miracles"* stems from the zeal of six seemingly great Hindu teachers representing the six schools of Hindu thought. They challenged Buddha to a competition to see who could manifest the greatest miracles. The heretical, resentful teachers petitioned King Bimbisara, the ruler of Rajagriha, to present the competition, but that petition was laughed out of the king's court. Finally, after many attempts, the six Hindu teachers persuaded the King to promote the competition, inviting Buddha to participate. The Buddha, knowing his participation could benefit the spreading of wisdom, accepted the invitation.

On the first day, Buddha held his toothpick in his hand, then placed it on the ground where it instantly turned into a fragrant wish-fulfilling tree, decorated with delicious fruit and jewels, much like the Christmas Tree in the West. Each day of the contest, Buddha continued to manifest amazing miracles. Once he established his Spiritual credentials, he began teaching, opening minds to new wisdom. Many of the listeners later became his followers.

Buddha graced Reverend Rhinehart's mediumship on several occasions. It is rare when an Avatar manifests in physical form after passing into Spirit. The following is a séance from the mid-seventies in the Ilikai Hotel, at Boat Harbor, Honolulu. Steve and two other chelas are in attendance. The séance took place in a single-story, small bedroom apartment with a balcony facing a beautiful ocean view. A make-shift cabinet installed in the bathtub of the apartment's small, pure white bathroom acted as the Holy of Holies for the séance. Seated in a chair in the bathtub, Reverend Rhinehart conducted the séance from behind the violet cloth enclosure with the usual fraud-proof séance conditions in place, including duct tape sealing his mouth shut. This is Steve's description of the séance:

"Once Reverend Rhinehart entered the trance state, a being presenting an ectoplasmic form emerged from behind the violet cloth curtain. He stepped out of the bathtub, then walked down the apartment's short hall, across the brownish carpet of the upscale apartment to where we were seated in the living room. His long white robe flowed to the ground. He presented no slight figure, as standing before us was a broad-shouldered man, maybe six-feet-six tall, possessing huge hands and fingers. He identified himself as Lord Gautama Buddha. Positioned less than two feet away, I could see the entire phenomenon unfold clearly in my sight. I attempted to glance at his facial features, but they were indistinguishable, shielded by a hood covering his head. As he moved past us, his white ectoplasmic robe brushed against my skin and I could easily detect the material of his robe to be very physical. Then a strong voice spoke from the ectoplasmic form, addressing many subjects and discussing Big Daddy Bray, a Huna teacher on the Big Island of Hawaii. Eventually, he gave certain predictions concerning possible wars. When he finished speaking, he asked one of us to come forward to retrieve the sacred stones apported in his hands during his talk. The sacred stones were real physical stones, so you can understand the ectoplasmic form had to have physical properties to be able to hold the stones, yet it was unlike any flesh and blood form with which I was familiar. Strange indeed!

"Upon viewing the phenomenon, I experienced an inner excitement. I had witnessed other physical phenomena, but this was the first time I witnessed physical ectoplasmic materialization of an Ascended Master. Soon Buddha returned to the Holy of Holies in the bathroom and subsequently Reverend Rhinehart walked out into the living room where we could see the duct tape still stretched across his mouth, assuring everyone present the voices we heard were not his, but genuine physical phenomenon."

This brief summary provides us with some history and a contemporary event that demonstrates Buddha's lasting influence. His appearance through Reverend Rhinehart (Master Kumara) speaks to his continual commitment and service to humanity.

TWENTY-NINE

KRISHNA
3228 BCE — 3102 BCE

K RISHNA LIVED APPROXIMATELY 3228 BCE — 3102 BCE. WE know the Mahabharata War took place in 3162 BCE, where his discourse with Arjuna in the *Bhagavad Gita* occurred. It is estimated by many that the *Bhagavad Gita* is the most revered of the Hindu scriptures and its discourse has endeared Krishna to many of the Hindu faith. It is declared to be the essence of the four ponderous *Vedas*. Krishna is considered the eighth incarnation of the Hindu god Vishnu, the supreme God of Vaishnavism. There are three supreme deities in Hinduism which are referred to as the Trimurti: Brahma, the creator principle; Vishnu, the preserver principle; and Shiva, the destroyer principle. Vishnu is the protector of the dharma.

Krishna played an instrumental role in shifting his contemporary Spiritual culture away from rigid *Vedic* study to the Bhakti practice of love, devotional chanting, and loving action. History reveals many Bhakti Cults that flourished during Krishna's incarnation, and the descriptions of the Gopis' (milkmaidens) devotion exemplify this notion.

The *Bhagavad Gita* directs our attention to Krishna's message, pointing to the way of righteous, dutiful action, elimination of all mistaken identity, and meditation for Divine Communion and God-Realization. He worked with joy ever-radiating through his Soul, carrying a veritable paradise wherever he went. There were many saintly ascetics and prophets of renunciation living in the woods during his day, but it was Sri Krishna who elucidated Divinity, living his life as a Christ while simultaneously performing his duties as a noble king.

His life was not a demonstration of the renunciation of action, but rather a renunciation of the desire for the fruits of action. Krishna demonstrated it is not necessary to abandon the responsibilities of material life. According to Krishna, the dilemma of Spiritual practice and earthly living is solved when we bring God here, where he has placed us.

Krishna entered this plane as a blue-skinned boy and an avid prankster. He was adored by the Gopis who flocked around him, as hypnotic melodies wafted from his enchanting flute. The Gopis danced ecstatically, passionately flaunting their devotion, each thinking Krishna danced only with her. Krishna replicated himself such that each maiden believed he reveled with her alone. Some have misconstrued Krishna's dalliances with the Gopis as carnal attractions, but the symbolism is solely meant to illustrate the unity of Spirit and Nature. The miracles surrounding Krishna are fantastical, unbelievable in our times; myth, magic, or miracle? But there is no question the man, Krishna, existed. The following are a couple of mythic tales, alluded to by Paramahansa Yogananda, surrounding Krishna's legacy of miracles:

Krishna's uncle, Kansa, thought Krishna to be his enemy after receiving a prophecy that the eighth child of his sister and brother-in-law, Devaki and Vasudeva, would kill him. In fear for his life, the evil Kansa imprisoned Devaki and Vasudeva, killing each of their children, one after the other, at birth. But miraculously, Krishna escaped Kansa's devilish plans and curiously incarnated in prison and subsequently spirited away. Like Jesus, Krishna entered life with a death decree. Kansa sent demon after demon in pursuit. The demon Trinivarta became a whirlwind, swooping up Krishna into himself and carrying him away in hopes of tossing Krishna to his death. But Krishna increased his weight such that he became prohibitively heavy, to such an extent the demon couldn't move. Consequently, the demon fell to the ground and died.

(It should be noted the titles "Christ" and "Krishna" have the same Spiritual connotations, Jesus the Christ and Yadava the Krishna. Yadava is a family name for Krishna. These titles identify the state of consciousness of two illuminated beings and their incarnate oneness with the consciousness of God.)

In another oft-related miracle, the people of Vrindavan were facing a torrential storm, potentially washing away their village. Apprehension filled the village. Lord Krishna lifted the mountain Govardhana with his little finger so the entire village, including all the cattle, could take refuge under the mountain.

This story, also related by Paramahansa Yogananda, reveals an aspect of Krishna's ineffable, unknowable nature:

Krishna lived by the river Yamuna in Brindaban. The Gopis were fond of bringing him fresh curds, his favorite food. One time when the banks were flooded, the devotees' curd offerings could not be delivered to their Master on the other side. Vyasa, an enlightened Krishna devotee, sat next to the river, his eyes gleaming with the intoxication of Krishna.

Believing in Vyasa's divine power, the Gopis enlisted his help. Vyasa said, *"You want to give all the cheese to Krishna? What about poor me?"* So the Gopis placed the curd offering before Vyasa. He ate, and ate, and ate. The Gopis began to worry that there would be none left for Krishna.

Then Vyasa rose and said to the torrential river, *"Yamuna, if I did not eat anything, then divide and part!"* The Gopis thought, "How precocious!" Vyasa's words appeared quite facetious. However, the Yamuna immediately separated into two walls of water, providing a miraculous floor of dry land between the two walls. The astonished Gopis entered the path, quickly reaching the other shore.

Once ashore, the Gopis did not find Krishna there to meet them as usual but found him fast asleep. When they awakened him, he looked uninterested in the cheese. The Gopis said, *"Master, do you not crave the curds today?"*

Krishna smiled sleepily, *"Oh, that fellow Vyasa, on the riverbank, has already fed me an over-abundance of cheese!"*

But the crown jewel of Krishna's life is his interaction with Arjuna in the *Bhagavad Gita*. Here, he reveals the practice of shedding the false images and conversations of the self, the misidentifications we all have, which tend to inhibit us from seeing the Self. He emphasizes that to realize our true nature, beyond all shadows of doubt, can be obtained through the practice of yoga.

In essence, it is transforming the little self into the Divine Self. It is the lifting of the physical ego, the body-identified self, the active consciousness in man, into Unity with the Soul. The battle that unfolds in the *Gita* represents the battle between the senses (worldly struggles) and the unchanging Eternal Soul. Arjuna's chariot is properly placed between the distorted tendencies of the mind and the discriminative tendencies of the Soul.

In time, we recognize that, throughout Krishna's dialogue with Arjuna, he had been preparing Arjuna for the ultimate truth wherein he displays the magnificence of his Divine Nature. When it occurs, Arjuna is wonderstruck; the radiance of ten thousand suns appears before his gaze. Krishna then bestows Arjuna with divine sight, erasing all lingering doubts. From that point forward, Arjuna stops his resistance and follows Krishna's lead. Here is Arjuna's experience, giving us a glimpse into Krishna's being:

"Arjuna saw the multifarious, marvelous Presence of the Deity, infinite in forms, shining in every direction of space, omnipotence all-

pervading, adorned with countless celestial robes and garlands and ornaments, upraising heavenly weapons, fragrant with every lovely essence, His mouth and eyes everywhere! If a thousand suns appeared simultaneously in the sky, their light might dimly resemble the splendor of the Omnific Being!" [1]

Because of the glorious depictions of Krishna's sublime nature, many, especially in the East, have worshiped Krishna as a personality. They limit their conceptions of God to images. But Krishna is unmanifest and doesn't assume embodiment. His state is unchangeable and unutterable. Yogananda further suggests that devotees who have temporary visions of lesser deities in meditation do not realize that these forms are merely manifestations of unmanifested Spirit. They are concentrating on finite forms of the Infinite God and their minds limit its Infinite Nature.

The *Bhagavad Gita* suggests that we forget not God's omnipotence, and focus on the invisible impersonal God:

Verse 52: To Arjun*a*, Krishna spoke, *"The Blessed Lord said: Very difficult it is to behold, as thou hast done, the Vision Universal! Even the gods ever yearn to see it."*

Verses 53-54: *"But it is not unveiled through one's penance or scriptural lore or gift-giving or formal worship. O Scorcher of the Sense-Foes (Arjuna)! only by undivided devotion (comingling by yoga all thoughts in One Divine Perception) may I be seen as thou hast beheld Me in My Cosmic Form, and recognized in reality, and finally embraced in Oneness!"*

Verse 55: *"He who works for Me alone, who makes Me his goal, who lovingly surrenders himself to Me, who is nonattached (to My delusive cosmic-dream worlds), who bears ill will toward none (beholding Me in all)—he enters My being, O Arjuna!"* [2]

THIRTY
MUHAMMAD
570 CE — 632 CE

T HE PROPHET MUHAMMAD FOLLOWS IN THE LINE OF MIDDLE
Eastern Prophets starting from Abraham, to Moses, to Jesus,
all teaching monotheistic beliefs. Unlike Avatars Jesus and Buddha,
Muhammad grew up in one of the most powerful, respected tribes
in Mecca, the Quraysh of the Clan Hashim, but he was not royalty.
In fact, his family was poor. His father passed before he was born. At
six, his mother passed, leaving him in the care of his grandfather who
passed when Muhammad was eight. Muhammad is finally left to the
responsibility of his uncle, Abu Talib, who becomes the head of the
Hashim Clan.

Mecca's power stemmed from being at the intersection of several
trade routes and the Quraysh were some of the most successful
merchants controlling the trade routes from Yemen, through Saudi
Arabia, to Syria. In early life, Muhammad worked in camel caravans for
his uncle, where he became familiar with the commercial trade routes
to Syria, the Mediterranean, and India. During this time, he earned a
reputation for honesty due to his trustworthy nature. Then Khadija,
a wealthy widow, hired him to guide her caravans safely to Syria. In
time, they fell in love and married. She bore him two sons and four
daughters, even though she was around forty when they married.

Common during this age, Mecca acted as home to many venerated polytheistic cults. In the temples of Mecca, people worshipped the idols of the various cults in an attempt to ensure the safe passage of goods along the trade routes crisscrossing the Arabian Peninsula. Occasionally, Muhammad took time to visit the sacred sites around Mecca. One time, while mediating in a cave on Mount Jabal-al-Nour, Archangel Gabriel manifested right before him, presenting Muhammad with golden engraved tablets inscribed with the teachings of God—the *Holy Qur'an*. Some say Muhammad felt disturbed by the revelations so much he kept them to himself for several years. The first to believe in his revelations turned out to be his wife, Khadija, who reassured him to be undisturbed.

One evening, when Muhammad was asleep, the Archangel Gabriel led him on a Spiritual journey. In the Spirit Realms, Muhammad mounted the heavenly steed Buraq, traveled from the Ka'ba in Mecca, then to the farthest mosque, which many believe to be Al-Aqsa Mosque in Jerusalem. There he prayed with the Prophets Abraham, Moses, and Jesus, ascending to the skies where Archangel Gabriel led him through Paradise and Hell, ultimately coming face-to-face with God. At which point, Muhammed returned to Earth to spread the message of the *Qur'an* and the Islamic Faith.

Professing Islamic Faith was a dangerous prospect in those days. Muhammad's message of one God directly confronted the dogmatic thinking of the day. At first, Muhammad was protected by his uncle Abu Talib, but when Abu Talib died, his other uncle, Abu Lahab, assumed leadership of the Hashim Clan, dropping Muhammad's protection. Subsequently, his task became a challenge, fraught with daring escapes, battles, and emigration to other locales. But Muhammad kept true to his commitment, spreading the Islamic Word. He led many different successful pilgrimages, to Mecca, to Khaybar, and one as far as the Syrian border. He passed away after his return to Medina in 632 CE.

There is a Spiritual link between Muhammad and Reverend Rhinehart. Several times during Reverend Rhinehart's ministry, Archangel Gabriel presented himself, giving lessons. It appears that Divine Intelligence found similar qualities in Muhammad and Reverend Rhinehart. Both possessed special attributes, warranting Archangel Gabriel to trust them in delivering messages of Light that would alter the consciousness of their times. As we have noted, it is rare for an Archangel to manifest through a medium.

During the 1975 International Inter-Galactic Banquet held in the Olympic Hotel in Seattle, Washington, five hundred people witnessed the flesh and blood manifestation of Archangel Gabriel through Reverend Rhinehart's mediumship. Never before has such a stunning demonstration of Spiritual phenomenon from the Spirit World occurred. Here is Steve Young's firsthand account:

"Prior to the séance phenomenon, David, my fellow policeman in the Honolulu Police Department and I checked out the séance cabinet. We crawled on our hands and knees to be certain no trap doors, wires, or confederates could assist the medium. We patted down the cloth of the Holy of Holies, attempting to detect any wires or foreign objects. Our thorough search proved the cabinet to be one hundred percent clean, and we announced to the audience there were no means to fake any resulting phenomenon, especially the phenomenon of a fully materialized being. Reverend Rhinehart wore a dark suit, which he also wore during the séance. But before the séance began, we witnessed Reverend Rhinehart stripping off his clothing to stand before us totally naked. We ran our fingers through his hair, under his armpits. He lifted his testicles and bent over, spreading his buttocks for our inspection. David and I were thoroughly convinced no hidden objects were on the body of Reverend Rhinehart and we announced our report to the audience.

"The curtain of the Holy of Holies was pulled back and I saw the entranced Reverend Rhinehart sitting in the cabinet chair. A white cord of ectoplasm flowed from his mouth, extending to a materialized being standing a few steps away, clothed in a white robe. The being stepped about five feet away from the cabinet into full white light, still attached to Reverend Rhinehart by a white cord from where he was sitting in the cabinet. I saw the medium and the flesh and blood manifestation simultaneously; it was evident they were two distinctly different beings. The entity identified himself as Archangel Gabriel. Archangel Gabriel appeared as a young male with dark brown hair, a dark mustache, and a goatee. He allowed photographs to be taken; it was declared to be the first time in the history of Spiritualism that a picture of an Ascended Being was photographed while being attached by a white cord to the medium. (This picture can be found in the book, *Photographing the Spirit World*, by Cyril Permutt, on page 173.)

"Archangel Gabriel delivered his Revelation to the audience. Upon the conclusion of his talk, his white robe fell to the ground and he and his body vanished into a pool of ectoplasm on the floor."

Archangel Gabriel tells us the wording used in the teachings brought to Muhammad was specific to the people of the time. For example, the message to not eat the flesh of swine was pertinent to the Middle East during Muhammad's day, not meant to be carried forward into the present age. The admonition to not eat uncooked pork is obvious today, as we know it rapidly spreads disease. The words chosen to be brought through the consciousness of any Avatar are designed to fit the vocabularies and lifestyles of the presiding people on the planet.

When Gabriel first came to Muhammad, he spoke often of beautiful heaven-like settings, where the afterlife flowed with abundant sparkling streams, was populated by plentiful, beautiful maidens, and shade trees flourished to rest the weary. In Muhammad's time, local springs of water were considered the highest and most desirable of blessings, but if Archangel Gabriel manifested in an Age where the people's desires were different, his vocabulary would have been specific to the tastes of that culture.

On one occasion, Archangel Gabriel came through Reverend Rhinehart's mediumship to present the verses of *The Cloaked One* out of the *Holy Qur'an* to illustrate the nature of God's consciousness and how it manifested during Muhammad's day. The immediate import communicated a warning to the people. During this particular séance, Archangel Gabriel comes back through Reverend Rhinehart's mediumship to reemphasize the warning and how the message would be couched differently for a contemporary audience.

Let's take a moment to explore the vocabulary Archangel Gabriel brought to Muhammad in the *Sacred Qur'an*, specifically Chapter Seventy-Four called, *The Cloaked One.* We can attempt to feel his words as though we were living in the Middle East during Muhammad's time. By comparing his words to those Jesus used in the *Holy Bible*, we can see they have a different cultural flavor, yet move the reader to contemplate similar notions and ideas. How might these words shift or transpose to meet the needs of our times? Why did Gabriel choose to relate the verses of *The Cloaked One* to a contemporary audience? Here are the words Gabriel brought to Muhammad:

"In the name of Allah, the compassionate and the merciful, you Muhammad, who are wrapped up in your vestment,

"Rise and deliver thy warning, magnify your Lord,

"Cleanse your garment and keep away from all pollution.

"Bestow no favors where you expect in return more than you have given.

"Be patient for your Lord's sake.

"The day when the trumpets sound shall be a day of woe and anguish for the unbelievers.

"Leave to me the man whom I created and endowed with vast riches and thriving children.

"I have made his progress smooth and comfortable, yet he hopes for more.

"But because he has stubbornly denied our revelations, I will lay on him mounting torment.

"He pondered and he schemed, confound him how he schemed, confound him how he schemed.

"He looked around, frowning and leering, then he turned away in scornful pride and said, 'This is nothing more than borrowed magic, the words of a mere mortal.'

"I will surely cast him into the fire of hell.

"Would that you know what the fire of hell is made, it leaves nothing, it spares no one, it burns the skins of men.

"It is guarded by Nineteen Keepers.

"We have appointed none but Angels to guard the fire and fixed their number only as a trial among the unbelievers.

"So to those to whom the scriptures were given may arrive at certainty, and the true believers strengthened in their faith, with no doubt left for the believers, even then the infidels and hypocrites may say, 'What could Allah mean by this?'

"Thus Allah misleads whom he will, and guides whom he pleases.

"None knows the warriors of your Lord but Himself.

"This is no more than an admonition to mankind.

"Know by the moon, by the retreating light, to those who would march on and those who would remain behind, each soul is the hostage of its own deeds.

"Those on the right hand will in their gardens ask the sinners, 'What has brought you into hell?'

"They will reply, 'We never prayed or fed the hungry, we engaged in vain disputes and denied the day of reckoning till death at last overtook us.'

"No intercessor's plea shall save them.

"Why then do they turn away from this reminder like frightened asses from a lion?

"Indeed, each one of them demands a scripture of his own, spread out before him.

"No, they have no fear of the hereafter.

"This is an admonition, let him who will, take heed, but none takes heed but by the will of Allah.

"He is the spring of goodness and forgiveness."

How might we reword the Seventy-Fourth Chapter, *The Cloaked One,* so contemporary people grasp the concepts more readily? What is the meaning the Avatar is presenting?

First, let's ask who is *The Cloaked One*? Is it Gabriel's consciousness? Or, does the voice represent that which remains "cloaked" in our consciousness as the Self—the God existing within?

The following is one approximation of how Archangel Gabriel might transpose his words for the contemporary person in today's age: Here is our interpretation:

In the name of Allah, the compassionate, the merciful, the one and only God, feel the essence of God's consciousness radiating perfect wisdom.

You, Keith, you Steve, and Marilou, you Abdul, you Giety, and you Monica and Bill, you Jose, Ivan, and Yoshi, and you Gary, each and every one of you, raise and give warning. Cleanse yourself, and give out no favors where you are expecting more than you have given in return.

Make the Spiritual Light evident here on Earth.

Don't concern yourself with others' lives and riches. I have given comfort and riches and yet people still wish for more. Leave to God-Consciousness their path. Translate the Spiritual into the physical so all may see.

Many have stubbornly denied our revelations, they pondered and they schemed, oh how they schemed! The day is coming when the non-believers will anguish. The Light will manifest karmic retribution, bringing physical disasters, a day of woe to the non-believers is coming, but without evil intent, manifesting as Natural Law.

Each soul is the hostage of its action.

The unbeliever resisted when the warnings came to Noah; they disregarded our revelations to Muhammad and turned away in righteous pride.

They will say these words are the devilry of a magician, no more than the prattling of a mortal, a deluded medium.

They suggest our words are not from Allah.

The scriptures were given so there would be no doubt among the true believers and their faith would be strengthened.

There will be none to save them. They will be cast into a Hell of their own making, overseen by the Lords of Karma.

They will argue and contemplate, but there will be a flame, a revelation of the Self, whose message will leave one in torment. But know the Spirit of the Divine seeks to mislead no one and only seeks to guide everyone towards God-Awareness.

Each demands to be recognized by God with a personal set of laws, while constantly being lost in debate and criticism. We are teaching the consciousness of Allah and Eternal Love through mediums and the physical phenomena of the miracles of God. Take heed of God's prophecies!

But none takes heed but by the will of Allah.

Some may feel Archangel Gabriel's revelation is harsh and uncompromising, but isn't it often those who feel the deepest love and most compassion who are the ones delivering that which seems most distasteful, but honest? The message from Chapter Seventy-Four, *The Cloaked One*, is relentless and to the point, but not unlike many of the Ascended Beings' revelations, no matter the religion. Muhammad was presented with a challenging mission given the superstitions and biases of his culture. We often feel our lives are challenging but nothing in comparison to the tests an Avatar faces, where his sacrifices and heartaches are rarely acknowledged.

Though difficult to hear at times, the Masters have but one intent and that is to guide humankind's evolution. If we find ourselves in reaction to the content in *The Cloaked One*, or possibly scoffing as an atheist may, we could inquire within as to the reason, or we may revisit the message at a later date.

THIRTY-ONE

KUMARA
REVEREND KEITH MILTON RHINEHART
April 1, 1936 — April 29, 1999

P REVIOUSLY, WE WROTE A BRIEF BIOGRAPHY OF REVEREND Rhinehart, so we won't repeat it here. But as we mentioned, few in our culture have an awareness of him. We can hear a skeptical audience exclaim, *"How can he possibly be an Avatar? Who is he? Why haven't we heard of him?"*

One of the main reasons we are scribing this manuscript is to bring public awareness to the works and life of Keith Milton Rhinehart, or as he became endearingly known to the members of the Church he founded, Aquarian Foundation, "Master Kumara." Like most Avatars, Master Kumara was a man of his time, *yet coming from the future.*

Ascended Master Intelligence through Reverend Rhinehart's adept mediumship gave us Spiritual teachings from the Heart and Mind of God that spanned over forty-four years. These teachings illuminated the consciousness and character behind the most evolved beings in the universe, the Ascended Masters, Archangels, and Dhyan Chohans (The overseers of the knowledge of the Tree of Good and Evil.) Never in the history of Spiritualism has there been a more scientifically tested medium, nor one who produced the miraculous, genuine, physical phenomena that Reverend Rhinehart materialized. (One reference being the Japanese testing conducted in *"The Fraud-Proof Chair"* described in Reverend Rhinehart's introductory biography in Chapter Three.)

Other physical phenomenon mediums have been investigated throughout history, corroborating similar Spiritual phenomena as the phenomena produced by Reverend Rhinehart. Daniel Dunglas Home and Florence Cook are two mediums who produced physical phenomena in the late nineteenth century. Sir William Crookes thoroughly investigated both of them and they are written about in Sir Arthur Conan Doyle's book, *The History of Spiritualism*. These are two of the more noteworthy mediums the Masters reference. But none provide the irrefutable evidence surrounding the extensive body of work produced by Reverend Rhinehart. Nor have their phenomena risen to the same caliber of Eternal Wisdom presented by the Ascended Masters.

Archangel Gabriel refers to the extraordinary quality of Reverend Rhinehart's mediumship, commenting during a Holy Communion Séance that he has not encountered another medium on Earth who has delivered Master Intelligence with the degree of mental and Spiritual clarity as that of Reverend Rhinehart. He went on to indicate the Masters have been able to push the buttons, so to speak, in Reverend Rhinehart's brain in such a way as to communicate knowledge and concepts never before possible. Additionally, Gabriel states they were able to withdraw Spiritual substance from Reverend Rhinehart's body to produce unparalleled physical phenomenon.

Before Reverend Rhinehart started Aquarian Foundation back in 1955, he was visited by the Ascended Master Mahatma El Morya who guided Madame Blavatsky in the creation and workings of the Theosophical Society. El Morya asked Reverend Rhinehart if he would be willing to start a Church, to become the mouthpiece for the lessons of the Ascended Masters. Reverend Rhinehart agreed.

In November of 1975, after twenty years of serving as the representative for the Ascended Masters, Reverend Rhinehart was honored at the momentous **International Inter-Galactic Banquet, Holy Communion Convention** in Seattle, Washington. The Masters conducted an initiation, anointing Keith Milton Rhinehart as the "World Avatar of the New Age." In the presence of an audience of five hundred delegates from around the world, Sanat Kumara, the oldest living being, existing at the subtlest level of form, stated, *"This is my beloved son in whom I am well pleased."*

From this point forward and throughout the Convention, many of the miracles of the *Bible* were duplicated. Participants witnessed the changing of water into wine, the stigmata phenomenon appearing on the forehead and palms of Reverend Rhinehart, apportation of sacred gemstones prophesied in Revelation 2:17 KJB, and ectoplasmic materialization of Masters who presented Spiritual lessons. During the Convention, healings also occurred.

The following is a quote from Marilou McIntyre's book, *Life is Forever — Get Used to It*. She attended the 1975 Convention and addressed many of the events that transpired, and her account is one of the best testimonies of the Masters' declaration regarding the legitimacy of Reverend Rhinehart's Avatarship:

"I couldn't sleep the night before the beginning of the convention. The day arrived October 31, 1975. The worldwide delegates and congregants were registering for the sacred event at the fine Olympic Hotel in downtown Seattle, Washington. What an exciting day. The sun was shining, unusual for Seattle, and people from all over the world were crowding in to participate in this once-in-a-lifetime happening. It was exhilarating meeting old friends and making new ones as we mingled together. What followed was a whirlwind of incredible demonstrations of psychic readings during the daytime meetings, films of movie stars, and popular, well-known luminaries of the time being interviewed by Reverend Rhinehart about their views of spiritualism, humanity, and life after death, among other subjects. We saw films of Mrs. Aldous Huxley of Hollywood; Dr. Aly Rady, PhD, a university professor; Youssef Wahbi, a celebrated Egyptian movie star; Prime Minister Alexander Mackenzie of Canada; and Arthur Ford, a famous medium. And these were a few we had the opportunity to see…

"The program announced that at 10:00 A.M., November 2, there would be a trance lecture and demonstration of physical phenomenon through KMR (Keith Milton Rhinehart) by Master Jesus entitled, *'The Second Coming of Christ.'* Nothing could have kept me away.

"Test conditions and examinations were being conducted on the medium by attending police officers, Steve Young and David Silverstein, both of Hawaii, who would be guarding the cabinet throughout the séance as the room filled with people. A hush filled over the room, and from the cabinet, we were asked to sing the "God Chant" to amalgamate and heighten the energies for the following phenomenon. Shortly, we heard a voice booming from the cabinet that introduced himself as Jesus the Christ of Nazareth. You could have heard a pin drop, except for the few gasps of air from many. Then he called out a few names, mine among them, and gave us permission to come to the railing in front of the stage with cameras. He instructed us he would tell us when we could snap flash pictures. Only when we were told should we take pictures. We promised to comply with his request. Again, a hush fell on the room in anticipation.

"Jesus started his lecture by saying, *"Verily, verily I say unto you,"* and he explained he would always use that phrase to verify it was truly himself manifesting. The Avatar of the Piscean Age began to tell us of his mission on Earth to transmute concepts of a fearful God from the Judaic era to a loving God. He spoke of how religions and Spiritual concepts had been perverted because of greed and the desire to control the people through the abusive power of the priesthoods and Spiritual leaders.

"The lecture that followed hit deep into the core of my being and released many misconceptions about religion and its purpose. He went on to say his mother was not a virgin. His conception was like everyone else who entered the Earth Plane. That was like a sock to the solar plexus. People could no longer excuse themselves for being imperfect. Jesus came into the world just like the rest of us. This is how he demonstrated that right action and living a life of love and harmlessness bring a soul back to God realization and eternal life. An example for all of us, and something we should do, as we learn from him.

"So, Jesus was born as everyone else and faced the same trials and tribulations, overcoming everything. He never intended that people would think he could forgive their sins (errors) and then they would be like new. Everyone, he explained, is responsible for what they put into action. That is why harmlessness and loving God are the key to immortality. He closed by explaining that he allowed himself to be crucified to fulfill the prophecies of the Old Testament so the multitudes would recognize he was chosen by God to help humanity wake up, be responsible, and be loving. His ultimate physical ascension proved that even flesh is incorporeal, beyond corruption, if one lives a life as he did. This means anyone can reverse the aging process, overcome disease, release limitations, and master physically if he or she chooses.

"Then he told us it was time to take pictures. The six of us readied our cameras and focused on the curtains of the cabinet. There was a rustling sound; he stepped out, fully flesh and blood materialized. Flashes snapped in a flurry. I was so surprised; I dropped my camera, a little Brownie Kodak. We then took our seats, and the shiny image before us welcomed everyone with a voice like honey. Love emanated from him and enveloped all. He then asked the police guards to get some bowls or containers, as he was about to demonstrate a miracle for us. Jesus said we are all from the same source, and the same blood flows through our veins. He was leaving some of his blood to mix with ours, helping us to realize we are one. I thought blood was going to start gushing out of him. He went on to explain the apports he was bringing through now were created from his solidified blood, nothing man-made.

"We were told to get ready to take more pictures. Back to the rail we went. As I looked through the lens, the master opened both of his hands, and red-faceted stones the size of a nickel came pouring out. The guards quickly tried to catch them in the containers they held. Cameras flashed, stones poured, it was otherworldly. Finally, the apportation stopped. Buckets were filled with the red apports. Once again, Jesus spoke. I paraphrase; the reason he brought so many apports through was to assure the skeptic there were too many to have been inside the medium's body prior to the phenomenon, refuting the argument that maybe they were regurgitated. Besides that, we saw them coming out of openings in the palms of his hands. He admonished those with eyes to see and ears to hear to acknowledge the wonder of this experience and grow from it...

"The room remained completely silent except for the sound of those weeping. We all felt we had been touched by the heart and mind of God, never to be the same. We sang a few hymns until the medium signaled he was ready to be untied from his chair and the tape removed from his mouth. The police guards entered the cabinet, untied him, and helped him from the room. No one moved. We were still trying to compute what we had just heard and witnessed, and how to relate to what we had experienced. Finally, the room started to clear, and we started talking about the next event to attend.

"That evening, a séance with the adept medium Keith Rhinehart, and with the only known black physical phenomenon medium in the world, Mona Ndzekeli (known as Mama Mona to her followers), who would attempt materialization phenomenon. It started at 8:00 pm and people started lining up at 7:30 pm, so anxious to get a good seat. The room was filled with hundreds from around the world in hopes of seeing something spectacular.

"There were two Holy of Holies erected on the stage. One was for Rev. Rhinehart, and the other for Mama Mona. Before the séance, the mediums had been examined internally and externally by the same two police officers from the morning séance. Investigators searched the surrounding areas and armed security guards and scientific researchers stationed themselves at all entrances and exits to the room. They kept close vigil, policing the room during the séance. The lights were always on to illuminate the entire room at all times. I knew this was really going to be a special event with all this security to make sure no one entered or left after the séance started, to allay any suspicion that fraud was being perpetrated. Each medium entered his/her respective cabinet, and the séance, in full light, began.

"The first thing we heard through Reverend Rhinehart was the Spirit Guide again giving permission for the named people to use infrared and white-flash cameras. This meant I could sit in the front row. I realized how lucky I was as the event began to unfold. We were told to get ready to take pictures. From KMR's cabinet stepped a magnificent being in flesh and blood, clothed in shining raiment, as spoken of in the *Holy Bible*. His entire presence radiated light visible to the naked eye. He was magnificent. A beatific smile broke across his face, radiating love to all. He told us he was an archangel from the higher planes of existence come to help present the Avatar of the New Age for the planet, who would help accelerate evolution. This would be the last avatar for the planet, and the event has been planned for over five hundred years in the etheric levels of existence. Finally, the time was at hand, he said humanity had earned the right for new Spiritual guidance by a designated divine person.

"Archangels, he said, oversee development of the planet and its inhabitants. He prophesied planet Earth would evolve to be the most advanced planet and civilization in our planetary system. It was evolving daily to eventually be the center of incredible intelligence and the greatest compassion ever created. Peace on Earth will be a reality and will lead other civilizations in their evolutionary process. The United States was to lead other countries into right action, and the planet Earth was to lead other planets into perfection. The next being to appear would announce the identity of whom they speak and provide definite evidence of his genuineness. Then he started disappearing from the bottom of his robe up, floating in the air. The last to disappear was his turban-wrapped head.

"The cabinet curtain opened again and out stepped another materialized being, with a small, neat beard and brilliant eyes radiating to us. It was breathtaking. Spiritual love and power exuded from his being to envelope all present. With a voice like music, he spoke to us about the coming age and evolution of humanity. It transported me, it seemed, to another dimension with his words of hope and reality. So much so that I can barely remember consciously what he said at first, except I know it made me feel safe and excited about things to come. Then I had to consciously focus on the present, as we were being asked to take our positions for pictures.

"He told us to get ready for pictures because what was about to happen must be preserved for history. For the most skeptical among us, he was going to verify the truth of his coming pronouncement. He was going to apport from Sanat Kumara, the oldest living soul in the universe and the overseer of the universe, some sacred objects from his private collection in Shambhala, the ascended masters' hidden retreat in the Himalayas. Then almost immediately, brilliant, large, yellow, faceted stones started materializing from his robes, hands, hair, and even thin air. They were huge, some the size of baseballs and all intricately faceted. I have never seen anything so beautiful. They kept coming and coming. Cameras were flashing; people were on their feet, straining to see. Right in front of my eyes, some of the stones grew in size after being apported. Still, they kept coming. It was like they floated to the floor. None were chipped, they landed softly. That alone was amazing.

"When the apport phenomenon finished, the Archangel directed Steve and David, the policemen guarding the cabinet, to check the inside after the séance for more yellow stones.

"Then he gave a message from Sanat Kumara, stating these stones had never been seen outside of Shambhala before. He allowed them to be materialized here and now because he too was verifying the great personage to lead civilization, the Last Avatar for the Planet. Greetings were given from space beings, Lords of Karma, Council of Nine, and Spirit Guides and Masters throughout the galaxy. The archangel went on to explain over one hundred pounds of sacred objects had been brought through. The large amount should prove they came from a source outside of the medium, as there was no way he could have secreted one hundred pounds of anything inside or outside himself. This should satisfy all skeptics here and in the future.

"The illuminated being stepped up to the curtain of the sacred Holy of Holies and drew it back so I could see the medium sitting in his chair as well as the materialized cosmic being in front of him. We were told to watch closely the area between the medium and him and be ready to take pictures. I strained to focus on that area. Much to my astonishment, there developed heat waves between them. Gradually, the waves became denser until my eyes could not believe what they saw. A shimmering silver cord was flowing from the adept-medium to the fully formed, majestic being. When I regained my senses, I started snapping pictures as fast as possible. This would be the picture of the century, if not all time. You've heard it said, 'One picture is worth a thousand words.' Never before was there a picture of any medium showing the connection between themself and the materialization. This was a picture of a thousand words.

"He announced he was the same Archangel who appeared to Mary and proclaimed the coming birth of Jesus the Christ for that age. He said on this occasion, he is presenting to the multitudes the Christ of the Aquarian Age and proving he is inseparable from divine cosmic essence by the link of the umbilical cord of life. He said, 'When the pictures are developed, they will provide the world with empirical evidence of the millennium. Eternity on camera, divine ascension in flesh and blood, splendor beyond death.'

"He then introduced the entranced medium as their chosen one, whose Spiritual name is Master Christos Logos Kumara, meaning cosmic light to the world, the New World Avatar. He brought our attention to the fact that the medium's initials, KMR, had always vibrated the energy of KuMaRa, but only now were we aware of that. This externalization and announcement that we were experiencing had been in the planning process for over five hundred years in the Spiritual or inner planes before humanity was ready and able to receive the information.

"The curtain dropped closed, and the flesh and blood of the cosmic materialization melted into a pool of ectoplasm in front of the cabinet. Those who came to see something spectacular experienced far more than they could have imagined. It was earthshaking and momentous for all time."[1]

Many additional incidents occurred through Reverend Rhinehart's mediumship, further establishing credence to Master Sanat Kumara's declaration that Master Kumara (Reverend Keith Milton Rhinehart) was indeed the Avatar of the New Age. For example, on an extremely rare occasion, Sanat Kumara, through Reverend Rhinehart's adept mediumship, demonstrates a form of Spirit materialization called "*etherealization.*" It is much different from ectoplasmic materialization that is often used by Ascended Masters to take on a physical form.

This séance occurred in a rented room in the Ilikai Hotel in Honolulu, Hawaii that Steve attended in the late 1970s. Here is Steve's description of what transpired:

"Many local members of the Church were present on this day. The séance unfolded under the precautions of red-light conditions, so everyone could see the phenomenon and the medium could be protected from the harmful rays of full-spectrum light.

"The séance began with a meditation, then evolved into our singing of inspirational songs to build up the group energies for the enhancement of the medium's mediumistic abilities. In time, a Being entranced Reverend Rhinehart from within a make-shift violet-clothed Holy of Holies cabinet set up in front of the room. Hidden within the cloth enclosure, the Being addressed the audience, introducing himself as Lord Sanat Kumara. He stated he intended to demonstrate a rare form of materialization called etheric manifestation. Subsequently, he stepped out of the cabinet into the red light barely illuminating the room.

"I could tell immediately this occasion was not one of the usual Spiritual manifestations we were accustomed to seeing. A translucent blue-luminous form took shape before us, constantly moving, almost dancing in space, brimming with bounding, shimmering energy. Since the materialization was etheric in form, no physical form resembling a human being ever materialized. As I watched, the scintillating, luminous form swayed in constant motion. I have never encountered such an amazing Light and never have seen it again. While seated in the front row, in close proximity to the phenomenon, I heard a clear human voice speak out from the translucent, luminous motion, presenting a revelatory teaching. Once delivered, the luminous materialization returned to the Holy of Holies.

"I felt humbled and honored to witness such a special event. I imagined the event could be compared to the phenomenon of the burning bush Moses encountered in the wilderness."

Here is the line in the *Book of Exodus* in the *Bible* referencing the *"Burning Bush"* so we might draw comparisons:

Exodus 3:2 KJB

"...and the bush burned with fire, yet the bush was not consumed, and the voice of God spoke out from within the bush."

"It is difficult to assess if the Light was exactly the same, but clearly there are similarities with the voice speaking from within the manifesting luminous Light."

The following is another momentous séance witnessed by Steve during the 1975 Convention attesting to Reverend Rhinehart's fulfillment of Avatarship:

"I experienced another miracle of the *Bible* during a séance in the seventies. At the séance, Lord Jesus entranced Reverend Rhinehart. I stood no more than three feet away from Reverend Rhinehart when I heard Jesus say, *'Steve, would you like to feel my blood?'* Overwhelmed, my heart pounded like crazy, and I answered in the affirmative. Jesus then reached out and grabbed my right hand, placing three of my fingers upon the Stigmata wound inflicted into his forehead. I not only felt the wetness of his lifeblood upon his forehead, but I observed the Stigmata puncture wounds on his palms as well.

"Several hours later, Reverend Rhinehart reappeared for another public appearance. Those in attendance observed the Stigmata wounds were no longer present, attesting to the fact the physical phenomenon was indeed genuine."

Reverend Rhinehart not only produced the miraculous, but he exhibited exemplary human attributes as well. Tireless in his commitment to the Ascended Masters, his service to the chelas consumed him to a fault.

I, Gary, once had the occasion to spend quality time around one of the leaders from the Church in San Francisco who enjoyed many wonderful years of service with Reverend Rhinehart in Seattle. Cecelia related a story describing a morning she and Reverend Rhinehart spent together at the parsonage in Seattle before the start of Sunday Service:

On this particular morning, she and Reverend Rhinehart were full of pizzazz, having great fun working and playing together, creating a Church project. As a result, she felt extremely chummy and close to Reverend Rhinehart that morning. They continued in this chummy manner as they drove to the Church, laughing and carrying on, but when they arrived and Reverend Rhinehart passed through the front doors of the Chapel, she instantly turned invisible to his eyes. It was as though he didn't even know her. She felt shocked! Once he stepped into the full service of the membership, addressing the needs of each person and situation, he stepped out of his individual personality and into a Universal Masterly role.

Was Keith Milton Rhinehart always living in his Avatarship? Each of us will have to make that determination for ourselves, as an authority for our own truth. But suffice it to say, Reverend Rhinehart didn't allow societal limitations to curb his appetite for life. So many bound by the dogmas of yesteryear may struggle with the eccentricities of his life, yet there can be no dispute about the physical miracles he demonstrated. They are unparalleled in the current age, and when physical phenomena occurred through his adept mediumship, directed and controlled by the Ascended Masters of Light, he was fully of the Light, communicating the word of God as the Avatar of the New Age.

At times, an Avatar can be disguised as an extremely ordinary, or what some might judge, an unsaintly person. It's often the case that few recognize an Avatar's sainthood until years after he has attained the Avatar mantle. This might seem strange, but it allows the Master to execute his mission without the burden of adoring throngs or interference by the naive and intolerant.

We suspect, after time passes, this will be the case with Reverend Keith Milton Rhinehart. His dedication to the Church and its members, service to the Masters, immense sacrifices, love in action, and the production of novel, and in many cases, controversial dispensations of Light, will ultimately find world recognition.

Each Avatar generally has a message with which they are noted. One of the main messages Master Kumara delivered to his followers and the world speaks to how he led his life, *"Love thy Self as thy God."* Or, we could say: *the most sublime Master of all is the God Self within!*

THIRTY-TWO

THE SOUL MATE AND TWIN RAY EXPERIENCE – ETERNAL HARMONICS

Lᴇᴛ's ᴛᴀᴋᴇ ᴀɴ ᴇxᴄᴜʀsɪᴏɴ ɪɴᴛᴏ ᴛʜᴇ Sᴇᴀsᴏɴs ᴏғ ᴛʜᴇ Hᴇᴀʀᴛ. We might start by asking who doesn't want to find a soul mate? Since our first Valentine's Day, most of us have been looking for that special someone, the mythical shining knight right out of the Courts of Camelot or that irresistible woman who captures our immediate attention! We have been seduced by a culture designed around the mystique of finding true Love. From glamorous advertisements to passionate romantic stories in the classical vein of Romeo and Juliet, Dr. Zhivago, Cinderella, Beauty and the Beast, or more contemporary examples such as Casa Blanca, Ghost, Titanic, and Pretty Woman, our heartstrings are tugged every which way. Many people in their early adult years are on the prowl, incessantly trolling for that ideal person, the one who will pay attention to them more than anyone else, serve them like royalty. But no matter the passion, once we have found the perfect soul mate, the outcome doesn't always follow the theme of Beauty and the Beast. There are many Romeos and Juliets, Casa Blancas or Dr. Zhivagos where love goes unconsummated.

We find history replete with famous couples who are flirting with the notion of soul mates. Some are more notorious and tragic than pure, and each is uniquely different and in many ways, archetypal. Some fulfill our images of glamour and glitter. Some are deeply loving, devotional couples, while others find artistic or career collaboration their focus. Some are engrossed in transforming the world stage, and still others create a distraction with their antics, providing a release of personal and societal tensions.

The following are well-known couples. We might feel into the essence of each of these couples. Which relationship is most like ours? What energies do they embody? What is their public persona? Is there a public, glossy, maybe superficial level and then a private, more mystical, archetypal level of their love? Each captures a flavor of the soul mate experience, hinting at enduring Love. A few of these will bring a smile to your face, some a sense of joy and fulfillment, others a piercing pang, reminding us that human love isn't always silky smooth or everlasting.

Here is the list in no particular order: there is Master Odyssa and Lady Master Rasha of Atlantean fame; Shiva and Shakti; Osiris and Isis; Dr. Robert John Kensington and Suzie (Reverend Rhinehart's cabinet guides living on the Spirit side of life); Sir Lancelot and Lady Guinevere; Tristan and Isolde; Romeo and Juliette; the protagonists of the Ramayana, Rama and Sita; Mark Anthony and Cleopatra; Vikings, Ragnar Lothbrok and Lagertha; East Indian royalty, Shah Jahan and Mumtaz Mahal; Queen Victoria and Prince Albert; Abraham Lincoln and Mary Todd Lincoln; Pierre Curie and Maria Sklodowska (Madame Curie); Gertrude Stein and Alice B. Toklas; Edith and Archie in the TV series, *All in the Family*; Diego Rivera and Frida Kahlo; notorious outlaws Bonnie and Clyde; Ralph and Alice on the TV series "The Honeymooners"; the comic characters, Popeye and Olive Oyl; Kathrine Hepburn and Spencer Tracy; John Kennedy and Jacqueline Bouvier Kennedy; Desi Arnaz and Lucille Ball; Superman and Lois Lane; Martin Luther King and Loretta Scott King; George Takei and Brad Altman; and John Lennon and Yoko Ono—to name but a few.

We could easily write a chapter on each of these relationships, delving into the unique qualities of their love, devotion, and sacrifices, but we readily experience poignant emotions in just hearing their names. Are they all soul mates? We can't say—obviously not in many cases, but on one account, we can say without reservation that Master Odyssa's and Lady Master Rasha's love is Eternal. They speak of their love through Reverend Rhinehart's mediumship, describing their feelings and outlining what criteria fulfill the requirements of genuine soul mates. As an aside, Master Odyssa and Lady Master Rasha lived on the physical continent of Atlantis in the Capital Queen City. Master Odyssa is known for his teachings regarding the Titans and Atlans, the beings who first established Atlantis, populating the Northern regions of Earth after migrating from distant star systems. Odyssa was a guide for Jesus, accompanying him during his initiation in the King's Chamber in the Great Pyramid in Egypt.

In exploring the love of soul mates, a question arises regarding the distinctions of love on the Spiritual and physical levels, a question the Ascended Masters find compelling. They ask: Can we genuinely love God with all our heart, all our mind, and all our soul without loving our mate with the same intensity of heart, mind, body, and soul? Is Eternal Love not operating on all levels of consciousness, not just on the emotional level? Can we create a happy marriage without concentrating our relationship on a mutual love of God, while honoring the sanctity of all life? Does not Love, like life, continue, forever generating union after union filled with beauty, truth, and justice in the physical and the Spirit Worlds? Is it not God who is bringing us the Love experience as we attempt to create happiness for another? If we find these thoughts compelling, we might ask: who is it with whom we may want to spend Eternity? Who is it with whom we would want to give and receive without expectation; that is, give unconditionally, and likewise receive without guilt? These are the final questions the Ascended Masters ask those who seek a soul mate.

Is our soul mate always obvious? A match made in heaven, or are there inherent challenges lurking around the corner? What personal growth or events may have transpired since the last connection in a past life? Can a couple find their polarities have drifted far apart?

Here is an excerpt from Marilou McIntyre's book, *Life Is Forever— Get Used to It*, where she interacts with her Master Teacher in a private session through Reverend Rhinehart's mediumship regarding soul mates:

"When I first heard of soul mates, I wanted mine. Not having had many loving experiences—except as a mother, of course—I yearned for melding with another and experiencing utopia. That's what I thought soul mates were about. That was my initial impression of soul mate love. As the years went on, the desire grew stronger. One day in the '70s, a handsome young man, twenty years my junior, named Brent came to the Foundation (Church). As the months passed, we became acquainted and really enjoyed each other. My inner self said, 'Too bad he's so young, I could go for him.' In those days, women didn't get younger men, only men got younger women.

"One evening, Brent confided in me that the first time he saw me, he thought I was his soul mate. We both laughed nervously, and I said that was nice to say, but I really doubted it. I promised myself I would think about it, however. Often, when I'd see him, he'd ask me what I thought about being his soul mate. It put me in such a quandary that I decided to have a private (session) with my master, who works with a band of masters led by St. Germain for answers.

"I sat in the blackened séance room with Reverend Rhinehart, entranced in the cabinet, waiting for my teacher to come through him to hopefully answer my questions. To my surprise, the red light came on and my teacher stepped out of the cabinet fully materialized. He stood over six feet tall and was clothed in a white robe and hood. He lovingly addressed me and said he had come to help me regarding my soul mate. He went on to say soul mates often meet but are not at the same level of development. Perhaps mine was a camel in the Sahara Desert. He chuckled and said it was possible. He materialized out of thin air a beautifully crafted gold ring with a large pink laser ruby stone and three small diamonds on the sides set in gold. My master told me St. Germain personally created it for me. It was blessed for soul mates and twin rays (two people of the same consciousness on three [Odyssa states four] of the seven levels of our existence). The levels are physical, astral, emotional, mental, etheric, Spiritual, and soul. It was given to me to wear and meditate with, and I was to return in six months for another private (session). I was disappointed he just wouldn't tell me who my soul mate was. Apparently, a natural law prevents masters from interfering in a person's karma. If this were karmic, I suppose I had some healing to do before I could know. I was thankful I received a sacred object to help me.

"I continued to see Brent. We grew very close, but I still didn't know. We had many things in common. We shared the same love of beauty, music, spirituality, and mental curiosity. We could be twin rays because we had three spiritual bodies in harmony, but soul mates? Six months passed, and I went for another private (session). Master St. Germaine materialized this time. I knew this right away as he looked just like the pictures I had seen of him. He discussed some very private things with me.

"Then he asked, 'Do you still want to know about your soul mate, even if he is a camel in the Sahara?' I excitedly said yes and asked for the name. He said he was surprised that I had no doubt or fear, but acknowledged it was better to know than not to know. After a short exchange with me, he verified that Brent was my soul mate. I was aghast. I wasn't sure that was what I wanted to hear. Was I ready to handle the age and cultural differences between us? Time will tell." [1]

Even with Marilou's sincere interest, questions and doubts arise. In many ways, it could be said finding our way back to our soul mate is analogous to finding our way back to God. There are similar difficulties, similar challenges the ego faces in the interweaving of the feminine and masculine energies. Here we face the integration of the blessing of opposites, where sacrifices and loyalty are often challenges. Are we going to be subservient or willful? A shifting must occur in our listening to that of the heart rather than the mind. However, with success, we find there are similar joys in finding God and in finding a soul mate!

We must acknowledge even though many are looking for a soul mate, some prefer different lifestyle choices than one involving a soul mate in the traditional sense. Some find happiness in celibacy, some in polygamy, or lifestyles such as devotion to a cause rather than a mate. We each are moving through different phases of Spiritual development and evolution. If we can observe others' choices around relationships with no judgment, we honor the freedom of choice and align with the Principle of Natural Law.

How can we say what is best for another? The Masters indicate that simply because we find great happiness in mating or perhaps in celibacy, a preference should not be forced upon another. But the Masters do feel compelled to offer a teaching based on their observations of inhabited planets and thousands of years of witnessing all types of relationships. What they share is quite simple. *They say to love is more favorable than not to love.* To love a special person in a personal way is preferable over not loving, and it is better to be loved in some special way than not to be loved.

With this stated, we might ask: "Is a soul mate relationship always heterosexual?" Absolutely not! The Masters intimate there are seven different types of sexuality and any one of these expressions of sexuality can constitute a soul mate relationship. There is homosexual love, lesbian love, asexual love, transexual love, celibate love, and androgynous love—all of which can bring enduring, eternal Love. We must end our dogmatic, prudish, ignorant definitions of love, which, until recently, society has narrowly defined as heterosexual relationships!

As we look around at our friends and associates, we find many are already united in a loving relationship, but not all are prepared for a love relationship or are even interested. As much as we'd like to think otherwise, the love experience is not free of its inherent difficulties. A relationship can be looked at like an adventure and what adventure isn't peppered with challenges, unsuspected turns, and even heartache? But again, even so, the Masters' perspective remains; *It is better to love than not to love!* And for those who want to encounter the best marriage has to offer, they suggest that it is through monogamous love that we find the most happiness. But as always, we remain the authority for our own truth in this domain, like all others. With this said, finding a soul mate, like any relationship, isn't an automatic ticket to a blissful love experience. Every successful relationship takes effort, empathy, and kindness.

Now we come to the question on many people's minds: how do we find a soul mate or a twin ray? In the West, we are free to select our partner, but in other parts of the world, such as India, mates are often selected by the family. Surprisingly, these unions are often very compatible and happy. Gratefully, in the West, we have been afforded a choice. In Marilou's passage, she speaks to the concept of being in harmony or vibrating with a mate on various levels of consciousness. This understanding alone is a good guide in selecting a mate.

The Masters indicate, to experience a twin ray relationship, a couple needs to have at least four of their seven bodies of consciousness in tune with each other. Again, the levels are: physical, emotional, mental, astral, vibrational, Spiritual, and monadic. Of all the bodies, one of the most critical bodies is the physical body. It is not imperative for a couple to be in harmony on the physical level, but in most cases, it makes for a happier marriage. Soul mates have at least four and usually more of their bodies in tune with each other—often all seven. Master Odyssa and Lady Master Rasha revealed that they have all seven bodies in harmony with one another. They are not inhabiting a physical body at this point in their evolution but exist in the Seventh Realm of Consciousness (the seventh plane of the seventh sphere surrounding our planet), experiencing a Spiritual Union or a type of Spiritual intercourse at the highest level of life. Filled with a love of God and a love of humanity, Master Odyssa imagines Lady Rasha as the essence of Beauty, Love, Kindness, and Goodness. With their levels of consciousness perfected, in exquisite harmony, he exclaims their relationship is an extremely happy one, where they mutually experience Joy Eternal.

The Masters suggest to eventually unite with a soul mate, vibrating in harmony on all seven levels of consciousness, brings about the greatest possible happiness, especially considering all the potentially millions of persons who could be a twin ray. We might ask: What does it mean for a couple to attune to each other on each of these seven levels of consciousness? What is the outcome of an experience in attuning with someone on just one level of consciousness? How many levels are you in harmony with your mate?

Here is one person's experience when first meeting a soul mate, where they were in harmony on all seven levels of consciousness:

"I was with a group of students sitting in a design showroom in San Francisco, waiting for our furniture tour to start. As I waited, in walked a man whom I had never seen before. He was a bit older than the rest of the students and not a part of our class. Looking at him, to my surprise, I instantly experienced knowing him better than anybody I have ever known without us uttering a word. There was a visual transmission that hit me head-on, and I felt something undefinably deep within. We didn't speak that day, nor for months. Eventually, we met in a class, chatting briefly, but only in passing. The last day of classes passed and we still had not connected. I was sure I would never see him again, as I planned to return to Burma in the coming weeks and likely would not return to the States. To my delight, at the last possible moment, on the evening of our final student gathering, he asked me out. We immediately clicked. There were challenges, but we eventually moved in together, married, and have thoroughly savored thirty-seven years together!"

THIRTY-THREE

FINDING LOVE WITH A SOUL MATE THE SEVEN LEVELS OF CONSCIOUSNESS

I T SEEMS IT IS DESTINY FOR SOUL MATES TO CROSS PATHS AT LEAST once in a lifetime, as the ending story in Chapter 32 illustrates—the most improbable circumstances unfold, presenting the opportunity. However, it is not a given they will mesh, or experience exceptional rapport and genuine Love. Generally, soul mates have been together many lifetimes, some grow closer and closer. Others have fomented tumultuous experiences, presenting difficult karma to resolve, forcing their polarities further apart. The possibility certainly exists for a grand ride. But the Masters suggest the first question we should consider in selecting a mate is: "Would I, or the one I am fancying, enjoy an intimate sexual relationship or is neither of us interested in this type of a relationship?" This question is one of the keys to understanding the ancient wisdom of marriage that plays a significant role in determining a choice.

In addition to sexual intimacy, harmonizing intimately on the various levels of consciousness is vital and allows a couple to evolve as soul mates. Let's familiarize ourselves with the seven bodies of consciousness the Masters articulate so we might broaden our understanding of how to tune into a mate:

PHYSICAL LEVEL OF CONSCIOUSNESS (Vehicle of Perception)

We will start with the physical body, which is the most obvious and easiest to identify out of the seven bodies. Harmony on the physical level finds that each mate experiences a yearning, excitement, and fulfillment in the sexual realm,;there is sexual compatibility and happiness. If there is not compatibility in the sexual area, then it would benefit the couple to reach out to teachers or classes in the field. Some couples imagine eliminating sex from their marriage is a way to Spiritualize their marriage. If sex is strictly viewed as a hedonistic, animalistic, lustful act, then we might understand their point. St. Germaine implies removing sex from a marriage is analogous to striking harmony from music, often resulting in the disruption of a couple's emotional and Spiritual harmony. The sexual union is not only a physical act, but is a mystical, ecstatic, Spiritual act, reminiscent of the Tantric traditions of liberation in the East.

EMOTIONAL LEVEL OF CONSCIOUSNESS (Vehicle of Perception)

On the emotional level, bodies are harmonious with one another when the couple experiences a great warmth and tenderness towards one another. They experience similar emotional responses to stimuli from internal and external phenomena. For example, if both look at a sunset or listen to a concert and experience totally dissimilar emotional responses, they are not likely to be in emotional rapport.

MENTAL LEVEL OF CONSCIOUSNESS (Vehicle of Perception)

If a couple connects on the mental level, holding similar beliefs and values, their minds process and analyze in similar ways. It doesn't matter if their beliefs are true or not. A person's beliefs are the root cause behind his or her behavior, and if these beliefs are at odds in primary areas of life, it will more often than not lead to a marriage that is no more than a casual or distant union. When key values are out of alignment, the coupling is in jeopardy and likely incompatible.

ASTRAL LEVEL OF CONSCIOUSNESS (Vehicle of Perception)

For the astral bodies to be attuned, we find there is fulfillment in the realm of dreams. If we sexually fantasize about other mates in the dream state, we might attempt to attune to our mate at a deeper level, such as working to engage in more meaningful ways during daily life. To find genuine harmony on the astral level, a couple experiences enjoyable intimacy in the dreamscape, as well as in the more mundane aspects of life.

SPIRITUAL LEVEL OF CONSCIOUSNESS (Vehicle of Perception)

Regarding the Spiritual body, Spiritual harmony exists when couples experience similar religious or Spiritual feelings and beliefs, and they feel a sense of mutual religious ecstasy. When the Spiritual bodies are aligned, a couple will feel an effortless Spiritual affinity, respond similarly to religious inspiration, while believing their marriage is founded in the sight of God. Mates who do not feel there is anything sacred about their marriage are usually a couple not in attunement on the Spiritual level.

VIBRATIONAL LEVEL OF CONSCIOUSNESS (Vehicle of Perception)

At the vibrational level of consciousness, harmonious compatibility exists when there is a feeling of closeness, even when the couple is not communicating verbally or physically close. No matter the physical proximity, the couple doesn't experience a distance or boredom with their mate simply because they are not talking or physically engaged. The vibrational body operates on abstract levels. It is mythic and symbolic in nature, and experiences transpire on archetypal levels where superheroes and epic tales live. The vibrational body is difficult for some to understand, so we will share one person's dream experience to illustrate the closeness and intertwining that occurs at the vibrational level:

In this dream, we believe the roles could be interchanging, either one could have acted out the other's role as the experience is recorded in the soul body. The episode is emblematic of how deep the Love flows, how intricate the tapestry weaves, and how far-reaching the experience travels between our different levels of consciousness.

"In my dream, I found myself running away from a group of soldiers chasing me. I tried to blend in by slipping from group to group in this particular city. In my attempt to blend in with a certain group, somehow, people discovered I was a wanted woman. As a result of this discovery, I left the group.

"Two to three people in the group sympathized with me and became my followers. As we moved about from group to group, I picked up more followers along the way. Simultaneously, the soldiers chasing me grew in numbers.

"I had a mission: I was looking for a man who had been imprisoned in a high-security dungeon. The circumstances were precarious, but I would not be deterred. Finally, after a long search, we found the person for whom I was searching. When we first saw him, he didn't even look human; he had ears like those of a bat, a gnarly tail, reddish-brown, gray skin, flashing fangs, and sharp teeth. Honestly, a downright ugly creature, hulking, over six feet tall. Even though ugly and vicious-looking, his eyes radiated a gentle, soft demeanor.

"Gazing at him, BAM! I abruptly realized this creature was my soul mate! Now I knew I had to break him free. While attempting to smuggle him out of the prison, we were discovered. We ran, then realized we must protect him, so we all circled him and continued running through the streets in a huddle-like formation.

"Somehow, I don't know how, we all ended up in a wooden cart, surrounded by the soldiers shouting and screaming profanities at us. They drew their weapons, moving ever closer and closer. I felt certain we were all going to die. Right then, the creature began to transform. The bat-like outer layer started to deteriorate, sloughing off like a chrysalis. A bright light slowly emanated from within him. Then, he sprouted two huge white wings, and his skin turned translucent and glowed. Taller and taller he grew, nine to ten feet tall. As we watched, he morphed into a glorious angel, even more than an angel, I believe an Archangel. He scooped us all up with a flap of his wings and we ascended, escaping the soldiers and leaving the people behind."

SOUL LEVEL OF CONSCIOUSNESS – MONADIC (Vehicle of Perception)

Finally, let's view the soul body. The soul body stores all past life-times, past experiences, marriages, and life streams. The soul body is commonly referred to as the monadic body of consciousness, and most often sound asleep in people. To have attunement on this level, each mate usually has had similar past-life experiences, generating a parallel level of knowledge and Spiritual consciousness. If there is no attunement at the soul level, past-life experiences have taken separate, dissimilar paths, resulting in a lack of common feeling, lack of closeness, and lack of wisdom existing on the other levels of consciousness.

When the monadic level of consciousness awakens, the light turns on and the soul remembers where it's been, who it's been, its mates, and where it is going. With the mutual dawning of this level of awareness, soul mates recognize the sexual act is a mysterious act, igniting the Spirit and soul, not simply a function of creation. Attuning at the soul level is the quest to unravel the mysteries of the Self, the mysteries of existence. When we open up at this level of consciousness, we can find happiness with whomever life sends our way.

To understand more fully the rapport experienced between soul mates, we might explore how Life Force first emerges from the Elysian Fields at the beginning of life expression. Without this knowledge, the notion of soul mates can seem unlikely, but life's beginnings provide clarity.

In the beginning, there exists Life Forces, where life expression presents itself both in form and matter. In this model, the Masters indicate that "Form" is physically intangible, the essence of creation. It represents an abstract principle separate from a physical vehicle and is considered the positive polarity. "Matter" would be the physical expression representing the negative polarity. There exists a continuous process of creation issuing from these two polarities of life, "Form" and "Matter." These two elements seek whatever expression may be available in a given Kingdom.

When the Force of Life emerges from a physical vortex phenomenon in outer space, it may come into being through the Mineral Kingdom, the Plant Kingdom, or the Animal Kingdom. Each Kingdom's purpose and function is to evolve life forms. A Life Force may first enter into the Mineral Kingdom, then develop and evolve to the Plant Kingdom, and then to the Animal Kingdom. In some cases, an expression of life evolves solely in one Kingdom. In such a case, the entity evolves into a great Nature Spirit in the Mineral Kingdom, but it is most common that the entity eventually seeks the Plant Kingdom, then evolves into the Animal Kingdom. In the initial development of an entity in any Kingdom, the entity begins life as part of a group-soul and is not self-aware.

The physical form of any entity has polarity—the yin and yang, the negative and the positive. At some point in an entity's evolution from the Mineral to the Plant to the Animal Kingdom, the entity becomes self-aware. Right at this exact juncture, a point of individuality emerges and a separation occurs from the group soul.

Here begins the conscious point of evolution—**I exist, as such, I am aware I exist**. At this moment, a division of polarities transpires into the masculine and the feminine; this is the separation that creates the expression of soul mates. At first, it is an inner division representing only behavior differences rather than physical characteristics. But as the being evolves towards humanness, a physical division happens between the feminine and the masculine aspects, separating into two separate entities. At this point, they divide again, so both the feminine and the masculine forms contain each of the polarities. This division completes the physical birth of soul mates.

In this example, we can observe both polarities contain the common ground of past experiences vibrating through their consciousness. This history accounts for the compatibility of the eventual reunion. Of course, this explanation is a simplified, a Cliff Notes version, but it gives us the basic understanding of how soul mates evolved.

In returning to the physical life experiences of soul mates and twin rays, we can understand, like any relationship developing over years of marriage or togetherness, some may come to feel their husband, wife, or mate is not attentive enough. We've all seen relationships devolve into boring routine patterns. Master Odyssa indicates the answer for most of these issues is to become the type of mate who seeks to please, rather than being the one expecting to be pleased. Odyssa suggests we take the time to find joy in the beautiful qualities of a mate, making the effort to exemplify in ourselves the qualities we want to see in our mate. We could ask ourselves, how can we best fulfill the needs of our mate? How might we relate to our mate in new, exciting, imaginative ways? If anyone can bring happiness into the marriage, it has to be us! If we accept the dissatisfying consequences that develop in a marriage, knowing we once were happy, then we can choose once again to be happy, to be a loving, demonstrative, kind person. In other words, both parties commit to doing whatever they can to please their mates.

Master Odyssa exudes that no greater Joy does he experience than when God's presence beams upon him, shining through Lady Rasha. When Divine Love streams through her consciousness, he feels an intimacy he experiences through no other. It is this communion that makes the couple almost one—yet still separate. Odyssa finds that Love is the one Eternal link existing between man and God, and that

Love is glorified when we Love that specific person and are Loved in return. So, like Odyssa, when we Love without reservation, Love without inhibition, and Love without limitation, then the experience of Loving that special someone moves us closer to God! A flowing into one another, the motion of life ever growing and expanding.

Some young souls may think there is greater happiness in the excitement of being free from attachment to anyone. Yet, Master Odyssa alludes to the fact that he has lived many, many lives and witnessed millions of relationships. The security and inner peace he finds in a soul mate or twin ray relationship is preferred over the rambunctious excitement of a lusting, hustling life. The happiness present in the warmth of tuning to God, family, and loved ones is greater than all other happiness. Through this enduring, exhilarating happiness, in his union with Lady Rasha, Odyssa experiences a relationship founded in Eternity, and it is Eternity that makes the difference!

To conclude, we'd like to present a few comments the Masters have made about Love. They suggest we experience many kinds of love, personal and impersonal. One of the most common versions of personal love is the Love for God. But in many instances, we find this type of love is no more than the love of desiring or the love of possessing. This love of desiring and possessing is satisfied when what has been wanted is possessed. In this type of love, once we gain the desirable object, the intensity of love ceases. If we pause for a moment, we realize that we have created an untenable desire, a conditional form of love, as God is never possessed.

To desire, to want, and to possess are human characteristic we all recognize and often enact. In wanting something so desirable, we have felt an intense emotion, a passion, which we often label as "Love." It could be desiring something, someone, or Godliness. Most often, this wanting cannot be characterized as pleasurable, only as intense. If our desire is for a mate, it behooves us to make the act a conscious

Love for union and unity; that is, an attempt to make it a Love for the sole expression of Love and for the beauty and pleasure of loving and not for possession. If it is for an object loved, then it should be loved for the pleasure of having love toward the object, and again, for the beauty and pleasure of loving, not for receiving some type of blessing in return. In this kind of Love, there exists a distinction that will shift the understanding of Love into a higher vibration, bringing a union that frees us from the limiting types of love most people attempt to find.

It is through practicing the joy of this more evolved standard of Love that we tune to God. Love is the expression and power that extends man beyond his animal nature into his higher Superconscious Self. It is through the enactment of this Love that we witness the unknowable, the God of and beyond Nature, expressing within each self, his full glory.

THIRTY-FOUR

SACRED GEMSTONES OF THE BIBLE
RESERVOIRS OF MYSTIQUE AND MANNA

W E WILL OPEN WITH STEVE'S EXPERIENCE OF THE MASTERS' apportation of a spectacular, sacred gemstone and his experiences with the apportation process over the years:

"I'm at the Ilikai Hotel in Honolulu, sitting in the living room of a Church member's home with a couple of other members present. Reverend Rhinehart is in trance behind a make-shift curtain cabinet replicating the Holy of Holies in the apartment's small bathroom. Suzie, Reverend Rhinehart's cabinet guide, is the first to speak through the trumpet on this day, though soon St. Germaine takes charge of the trumpet booming out inspirational personal messages. Despite sitting in the living room quite a distance from the bathroom, the messages are perfectly clear due to the increased volume produced by the projection of his voice through the trumpet.

"Then I heard Saint Germaine say, *'Steve, look to the carpet a couple of feet in front of you.'* As I look, a shimmering light-like force field appears at the floor, incredibly vibrant, similar to what one sees from the heat rising off the tarmac on a hot summer day, but much more scintillating. My first thought is, *'Wow! This is just like a scene out of Star Trek!'* While St. Germaine continues talking, a portion of the shimmering light starts to congeal, becoming more and more solidified until the shimmering light slowly fades, and what remains is a solid gemstone, solid to the degree I can pick it up and hold it in my hand. The stone is magnificent, a large blue topaz I estimate to be in the neighborhood of a thousand carats, the size of a golf ball. I put it up to my eyes, it's perfectly translucent. I have seen quartz crystals and smoky topazes before, but nothing like this. It is simply stunning, resplendent light! St. Germaine says the stone was de-apported from an apartment a couple of apartments away and re-apported into the living room before us.

"I am reminded in my personal collection of apported sacred objects some have inexplicably disappeared—then months, sometimes even years later, reappeared. I don't know exactly why, but my imagination concludes the object is being reprogrammed and imbued with additional blessings by the Masters, only to reappear when the new energies become useful in my life. One such object was a favorite ring my father gave me before his passing. Although not an apport, the ring held special meaning and disappeared from my apartment one day. It went missing for years. One morning, I was showering at the Kaneohe Police Station, where I'd been assigned to work as a detective. Over the beating spray of the shower, I heard a loud noise coming from the direction of my locker, a few feet away. Exiting the shower, I went to my locker and lifting the locker's clasp, I swung open the door. There on the floor of my locker lay my Father's ring! Startled, I couldn't believe it—my sentimental keepsake had returned. Immediately, I realized the clanking noise I heard was the sound of the ring crashing to the floor of my locker. I felt so elated!"

Why don't the Ascended Masters simply hand out sacred objects to all, since the objective is to uplift all of humanity? Why all the fuss and extra effort with the apportation phenomena? Is the arcane process necessary? We believe they are attempting to communicate that these objects stand beyond the mundane. They are not straight off the shelf from Macy's, Bloomingdale's, or Harrod's only to be stashed away in a jewelry box once they've been received. The Masters' intention is to create a vibration that uplifts awareness to evolve the soul. A sacred object is meant to be meditated upon. Many who experience the manifestation of sacred objects have been profoundly moved.

The Masters have spent thousands of years programming sacred objects of all shapes and sizes, at times expending hundreds of hours focusing concise thought forms into a single object's molecular structure, diligently preparing a new dispensation of Manna in such a fashion unprecedented in recorded history. They want to assure, to the extent possible, the objects are seen as sacred, that they are earned by Spiritual attunement and sacrifice, and are paid the proper respect.

The *Bible's* verse in Revelation speaks to this truth, revealing the plan to gift encapsulated vessels of Light to those who overcome. Each stone is a repository, acting as a tome of wisdom, mystery, and love, a veritable Spiritual powerhouse of Revelation.

Reverend Rhinehart is the only medium who has brought forth these sacred stones in such numbers it confounds the mind. But when we understand the purpose, we realize the manifestations of these Spiritual treasures have not happened out of the blue, nor have they been casual, incidental events. They represent a grand vision the Divine Hierarchy designed to shift the consciousness of humanity.

Here again is the *Revelation* verse in the *Bible* portending what was to come. This statement by John, the author of *Revelation* written in 95 CE, reveals the Hierarchy's plan more than two thousand years ago.

Revelation 2:17 KJB

"He that hath an ear, let him hear what the Spirit saith unto the churches; To him that overcometh will I give to eat of the hidden manna, and will give him a white stone, and in the stone a new name written, which no man knoweth saving he that receiveth it."

Why has it taken so many years for this Biblical verse to come before the public's attention? Why has this verse slipped past the attention of the clergy and never been addressed or interpreted in all these years? Popes, priests, ministers, and laymen of all stripes have interpreted and expounded on every line of the *Bible* ad nauseam, but not one has addressed this verse. Might we suggest the verse wasn't relevant until Reverend Rhinehart brought forth the blessed white stones. Now that Steve Young has Spiritually attuned to the verse, giving the stones further historical and Spiritual significance, maybe Christianity will begin to inquire and consider Steve's insight.

In terms of the interpretation, what does it point toward? There could be varying understandings. Here is one version to consider:

To those who open their hearts and minds to Spirit, making some manner of sacrifice, Spirit will present a gift of a white stone, and in that stone their name is written, and the wisdom therein is only accessed by the one who "overcometh."

To deepen our understanding of sacred gemstones, or any object considered sacred, we can gain a measure of clarity from St. Germaine's comment when he declared certain passages to be "Holy Writ" in *The Great Book of Jewels,* by Ernst A. and Jean Heiniger. The following quote is one such passage that furthers our insight into objects considered unique and sacred:

"The sacred is distinct from the magical and the symbolic.

"To have faith in an object — for example, to wear an amulet for protection — is to live within a magic circle.

"To see a sign of wisdom in the structure, form, and color of an object, and to link it with immaterial truths, is to confer on it a symbolic role.

"To evoke, by means of a symbolic object, the presence of another is to cross the threshold of the sacred. This implies a tangible link with the unique, and the object becomes sacred." [1]

This passage presents a way to interpret the apported stones manifesting through Reverend Rhinehart's mediumship. With the presentation of these sacred stones, Spirit demonstrates the desire and commitment to work with humanity on a one-to-one basis, bestowing those who receive these stones with pure thought forms of wisdom, imagination, and protection. Many who have received these sacred stones have encountered unusually powerful Spiritual experiences. There are numerous examples. Here is one I, Gary, experienced.

"This particular evening, I received a sacred object called the *'Stigmata Stone.'* Visually, it was a half inch in diameter, of blood-red faceted glass, in the shape of a four-sided gemstone. While gently fondling its surface, it so captivated me, I decided to tape the Stone to my third eye at bedtime.

"During sleep, I experienced a lucid dream more real than any physical experience I've encountered in my life. In the dream, I sat cross-legged on the wooden floor of a rather large auditorium. Packed to capacity, off to my left in the auditorium, an incredibly beautiful woman wove a graceful ballet movement through the crowd. Her beauty was such I became fascinated, completely fixating upon her. She glided closer and closer, with every movement lacing the attentive crowd together, eventually passing right by me.

At that moment, I recognized the woman as my mother. Stunned, in disbelief, I continued following her every move. She continued to dance her pirouettes through the audience for a time, then assumed a chair at the front of the auditorium. To my surprise, the crowd rose en masse from the floor, creating a darshan-like line to pay their respects. One by one, each person stepped forward, inching their way towards the seated woman.

"Out of respect, I joined the crowd, feeling somewhat strange knowing my mother was the one whom I approached. When I reached the front of the line, I realized the woman was no longer my mother, but St. Teresa!

"I froze! Standing in awe of her powerful, beautiful presence, I felt spellbound and not sure of how to proceed. I continued moving forward, and once standing before her, I felt an overwhelming urge to kiss her. When I leaned in to kiss, she moved her head off to the side, so I moved to the other side once more, attempting to kiss her. Again, she moved her head to avoid me.

"Somewhat miffed, I still felt this deep connection. Suddenly, in a wave of fluidic motion, she spread open her arms and loins, wrapping her legs and arms around me, kissing me in a full, nearly sexual embrace. Immediately, a blasting ecstatic, Spiritual energy shot through my entire body, activating every nerve. It felt so intense, if I didn't disengage, I would blow to smithereens! It might be compared to receiving a whopping bolt of electricity! Right at the height of the blast, the powerful bond miraculously released. With this, the dream concluded.

"It is known in the Order of Carmelite circles, St. Teresa of Avila displayed the Stigmata phenomenon, but at the time of my experience, I was unaware of her history with the Stigmata phenomenon. Later, the following morning, when I described my dream to my roommate, she told me of St. Teresa's religious ecstasy, her levitation episodes, and the stigmata phenomenon. This shocked me, for this experience emphatically dramatized the Masters' thought forms programmed into the 'Stigmata Stone' which I had taped to my forehead.

"I have experienced many powerful life experiences through sports, sex, leadership, and meetings with fascinating Spiritual people, but this dream experience touched me deeper than any. Although receiving Shaktipat from Baba Muktananda was powerful, this dream was exceedingly more powerful. (Shaktipat is an act of grace imparted from a guru, where a Spiritual transmission of energy can awaken the kundalini energy of the recipient.)

"I found it such a blessing to receive an object imbued with the thought forms from the most advanced, loving, intelligent beings in the universe. To know I was in communion and working with the Masters gave me great joy."

It is unfortunate to note that at this juncture, so few have attuned to the vibrations of the sacred objects. We suspect and truly hope future generations become more attuned, seeking out these remarkable stones of Light more enthusiastically. Do we stretch too far in subscribing sacredness to these apports? Here is another comment by the authors of *The Great Book of Jewels* on ascribing sacredness to an object.

"No object — precious or otherwise — is sacred of itself; it becomes so by the faith and love with which men surround it and by which it acts as a bridge between the divine and the human." [2]

And in a slightly different vein, yet still opening insights on the value of objects which have been considered sacred, we again turn to *The Great Book of Jewels:*

"Very early in their history, Christian communities preserved relics of the saints, not so much in memory of them as people or as personalities, but more for the profound belief and precious testimony to which they had consecrated their lives." [3]

THIRTY-FIVE

BIBLICAL AND CONTEMPORARY SIGNIFICANCE OF GEMSTONES

I T MAY BE SURPRISING TO FIND THAT COMMUNION WITH GEM-stones has been active for millennia, as we find gemstones referenced in the *Bible* over 1700 times. The following are examples of verses in the *Bible* illustrating sacred stones aren't necessarily novel:

Exodus 28:15 KJB

And the Lord spake unto Moses:

"And thou shalt make the breastplate of judgment with cunning work; after the work of the Ephod thou shalt make it; of gold, of blue, and of purple, and of scarlet, and of twined linen, shalt thou make it."

Exodus 28:17-20 KJB

"And thou shalt set in it settings of stones, even four rows of stones: the first row shall be a sardius, a topaz, and a carbuncle: this shall be the first row.

And the second row shall be an emerald, a sapphire, and a diamond.

And the third row a ligure, an agate, and an amethyst.

And the fourth row a beryl, and an onyx, and a jasper; they shall be set in gold in their inclosing.

"And the stones shall be with the names of the children of Israel, twelve, according to their names, like the engravings of a signet: every one with his name shall they be according to the twelve tribes."

Exodus 28:30 KJB

"And thou shalt put in the breastplate of judgement the Urim and the Thummim; and they shall be upon Aaron's heart, when he goeth in before the Lord: and Aaron shall bear the judgement of the children of Israel upon his heart before the Lord continually."

In these verses, we discover gemstones being utilized for judgment. As we've noted, the *Bible* admonishes us against divination. Because of misinterpretations and misinformation delivered through passages in the *Bible* (Deuteronomy 18:10 KJB) and promulgated by the Christian clergy, we find conflicting understanding regarding the stones of the *Bible*. Ironically, assumptions that divinations through stones are evil have been deliberately promoted by the Church. Again, this assures the Church's Biblical scripture remains the mainstay of Revelation, negating the possibility that contemporary revelation is alive and relevant in Spiritual discourse and evolution.

These passages, in the Old Testament, describing the stones in High Priest Aaron's breastplate, such as the Urim and Thummim (stones used to interpret and amplify wisdom imparted by Spirit), indicate that these stones were meant to be used by Aaron in the act of judgment. This is in itself divination.

The Ascended Masters specifically refer to the Urim and the Thummim as tools intended to access and interpret Divine Wisdom. These stones enhance the Light of God pouring through to a priest from Spirit. A priest, such as Aaron, acts as an intermediary, sitting in the Holy of Holies, communing with Spirit. There is a play of polarities between the Urim and Thummim. Urim—feminine (odic, receptive) and Thummim—masculine (actinic, projecting). The stones interact to signal to a mediumistic priest streams of intelligence.

We continue to discover references to gemstones in the visions of St. John of the Isle of Patmos. In Revelation, he points to the significance of gemstones and their future role in the New Jerusalem.

Unfortunately, the New Jerusalem is an enigma for many and interpreted in a multitude of ways, from an actual physical city, a new heaven and earth, to an eternal state.

Here are the references to the New Jerusalem in *Revelation*, followed by Ascended Master Zoser's experiences of St. John's vision regarding his perplexing mention of gemstones. Master Zoser, the Pharaoh of Step Pyramid notoriety, refers to St. John's visions through Reverend Rhinehart's mediumship:

Revelation 21:2 KJB

"And I John, saw the holy city, New Jerusalem coming down from God out of heaven, prepared as a bride adorned for her husband."

Revelation 21:19 KJB

"And the foundations of the wall of the city were garnished with all manner of precious stones. The first foundation was jasper; the second, sapphire; the third, a chalcedony; the fourth, an emerald; the fifth, a sardonyx; the sixth, Sardius; the seventh, chrysolyte; the eighth, beryl; the ninth, a topaz; the tenth, chrysoprasus; the eleventh, a jacinth; the twelfth, an amethyst."

Why mention gemstones? What is the purpose? Clearly, the chroniclers of the *Bible* felt the precious and semi-precious gemstones in St. John's visions were important enough to emphasize. Was it mostly to highlight the beauty, social status, and grandeur of the New Jerusalem, or was something far grander and significant at play?

If we take a moment to travel back to ancient times, we find jewels were used to adorn, sexually attract, and portray wealth and rank in society. In Medieval and Renaissance European times, society was divided by costume and jewelry; those with the gumption to wear jewelry above their station in life were met with sumptuary regulations and taxes.

To understand St. John's visions, we must trespass beyond these somewhat shallow, societal functions to where jewels served purposes beyond the superficial. Here, jewels play instrumental roles for those attuned to the signals beaming down from on high. It has always been the mystics, the priests, and the royalty who possessed the ear to hear, and the eye to see, seeking out the stones of divination for guidance and communion with Spirit. One such person was St. John.

So, who was St. John? How did he happen to write the *Book of Revelation*? An ardent believer in Jesus, St. John became a leader of considerable importance within the new movement, called "The Way." In his time, this alone created danger as worship of Artemis was the norm. For John, refusing to recognize Emperor Domitian's (81 CE–96 CE) divinity proved even more egregious, earning him an expulsion from the Roman city of Ephesus.

He was exiled to the damp, rat-infested caves of Patmos, a Greek isle, and delivered there by a large galley ship manned by slaves. In the cold, darkened, cramped caves, he experienced a series of visions, a profound communion with God recorded in the *Book of Revelation*.

St. John looked on as his visions unraveled, reporting back exactly what he saw to his personal scribe. Through Reverend Rhinehart's mediumship, Master Zoser relates that he, too, had similar visions as those of St. John regarding gemstones.

In Zoser's inner experiences, with eyes closed, he saw a myriad of gemstones careening through the skies, clusters of crystals, diamonds, and sapphires flying helter-skelter in every direction. In his vision, majestic full-spectrum rainbows arched through the heavens, transforming into grand complex geometric patterns of light and color.

He asked himself, *Where might these images be originating? Are they from my intellect? No! No, he was not contemplating such things!* Then he dropped deeper and deeper into reflection. Bam! Crystals and diamonds exploded through his vision! The patterns continued to bend and bow into a pastiche of fluctuating images.

Later, while contemplating this experience, he realized his perceptions came from a meditative state. He had not imbibed any substances, so he knew his mind had not been superficially altered (like Huxley or McKenna in contemporary times). He viewed from deep within, experiencing something nearly primeval, possibly akin to experiences gained through ancient tribal practices. Feelings of awe filled him while the mystery confounded him. He asked himself again, *Where do these images originate? Is someone directing them other than me?* He looked, but he saw no instruments of Light, no God, or lesser Gods! Zoser then turned to his heart, gazing at the universes and worlds therein.

Spontaneously, he realized he was observing, yet not conceiving these visions and images. So why did he continue to envision temples of jewels, Christs, wizards, and suns exploding into profusions of geometric patterns?

Zoser searched his emotional body, his astral body, his Spiritual body, he could not discover the source. He sat in a state of meditation, asking for God's communion. He realized an energy was flowing through him, but his questions continued. *From where did this energy come? And from where did the visions of St. John of Patmos come?*

To Zoser, it felt primeval; a kind of cellular energy existed where all the moons, stars, heavens, and hells issued, past the mind, free of emotions, beyond the physical, coming from an ancient, primeval source. Then it finally dawned on Master Zoser, the visions arose from the symbolic fields of memory perceived through the vibrational body (one of the seven vehicles of consciousness), where mathematical abstracts reside, where the exquisite beauty of gems of Light burst forth.

He was communing with symbolic, pure abstracts, the primeval energies issuing forth from God. With his insight, Zoser understood what transpired on the Isle of Patmos—Divine Revelation! St. John had directly perceived through his vibrational body pure abstractions of Light. It is here where mental constructs dissolve and Plato's geometric abstracts come to life as real as any physical object. Through the vibrational body, pure Spiritual revelation arises in the heart.

Zoser discovered, as did St. John, the sacred gemstones that St. John describes in the *Bible* were a form of sacrament, where grace opens communion between the finite and infinite worlds, fulfilling man's age-old quest to commune directly with God and the Infinite. Herein lies the answer to the question of why all the references to gemstones were written into the *Bible*. Simply stated, they assist in opening the gates to pure visions of the Divine! They are the window into the origins of creation.

The sacred stones manifesting through Reverend Rhinehart's mediumship demonstrate we have evolved from the Piscean Age into the Age of Aquarius, progressing from one form of communion with Spirit to another. In the Piscean Age of Christendom, many followed the old Essenes' practice, which Jesus partook, the communion drawing upon bread and wine. Jesus said, *"Take, eat, this is my body— take this cup and drink, this is my blood."* This exercised a symbolic practice of ancient wisdom whereby one could relate to the pain experienced by Jesus on the cross. It allowed practitioners to eclipse the pain of their times, the misery doled out by the rulers of the day, and to make contact with the greatest King of all—God!

As we enact rituals, what do we feel? Do we feel deep, eternal Love, profound, ever-lasting Peace, revelatory insight? Do we feel bathed in the all-pervasive Light? Although a ritual may be the same, each of us may have a completely different experience. In the Piscean Age, the Essenes' practice was to feel their Divinity through ritual. They interacted with the Vegetable Kingdom, using wheat and grapes as the active elements in their ritual.

Now we move into the Age of Aquarius, where communion exists on the streets of the New Jerusalem, paved with glistening gemstones of Light. In our New Jerusalem, we symbolically and Spiritually interact with the Mineral Kingdom. Earth's minerals provide Spiritual revelations beaming in from a crystalline source, emanating from the tiniest diamond to the largest star we circumnavigate, our Sun, the God-given source of Light that has brought about our existence. In this Age, we drink from the Manna emanating from the crystalline clusters, feasting upon the Light of a New Dawn, filling ourselves with pure abstractions of beauty, truth, and justice, the splendor of God's Light!

We'd like to conclude this chapter with a few stories of contemporary examples of how sacred stones have interacted with different chelas, providing protection and prophecy. The following story was revealed to Steve by the leader of the Miami Beach branch of the Church. The leader, Marilou, a loving, trusted, and honest Church leader, speaks to the protective power imbued in some of the sacred objects:

"I traveled to South Africa on a mission for the Ascended Masters. One night in Johannesburg, I was approached by two robbers attempting to accost me. Just as they were about to grab my valuables, they ran off in a frightful scramble. Immensely relieved, I happened to look down at my chest to the sacred breastplate draped around my neck. To my great surprise, I observed that this inanimate object was now electric, radiating, sending out beams of Light! Apparently, it so alarmed the robbers, off they ran, scared out of their wits."

The following story by me, Gary, speaks to the prophetic blessings imbued in the molecular structure of an object and how they lie dormant until the magic moment:

"Around 1989, a good friend of mine decided to leave the Church. He acquired a large collection of sacred objects over the years of his participation in the Church. When he left, he gifted me several sacred objects blessed by the Masters. I was delighted. One object proved quite curious. It was a very small, insignificant, faceted, amber droplet, one-quarter inch in length, a sleeper to be sure. It looked like a trinket that might fall out of a Cracker Jack box. He told me it held a special connection with the police officer Steve Young. At the time, I felt mostly repelled by cops and found little interest in it. Knowing nothing of Steve at the time, I saw no connection, but out of respect, I accepted the gift.

"In the coming years of participation in the Church, I noticed the Masters were always questioning if Steve was present at the séances. Then I became aware of Steve's significant role as a Board Member in the Church. It still baffled me as to why I had been gifted this object.

"Maybe eight years after receiving the sacred object, I had the occasion to meet Steve in Miami Beach at an Aquarian Psychic Fair. To my surprise, we kind of hit it off, even though my take on cops hadn't changed. Little by little, Steve and I became friends, in time realizing we had the same fondness and devotion for the Masters' teachings. Eventually, we talked of writing a book. Our conversations meandered all over the place for over ten years, and finally, in 2021, we got serious and decided to write *Seasons of the Soul.* So, after this experience, I never underestimate the power imbued into an object blessed by the Masters!"

One of Reverend Rhinehart's main missions was to provide Earth's people access to these sacred stones of Light. But few knew the rigor and sacrifices he assumed to fulfill his mission. During special séances, untold pounds and pounds of sacred breast plates and faceted stones were apported through Reverend Rhinehart's gaping mouth and tissue, some ripping open exit points in his flesh, leaving behind permanent wounds and scar tissue.

The following episode, told by Steve Young, provides a small glimpse of the ordeals Reverend Rhinehart gracefully faced in providing humanity with the Sacred Stones:

"One afternoon, I was in the parking lot of the Ilikai Hotel in Honolulu, walking towards my car, accompanied by Reverend Rhinehart. Along the way, Reverend Rhinehart stops and begins a protracted hacking, so loud passersby stop to gawk in concern. The hacking continues louder and louder until Reverend Rhinehart finally turns and says he has an apport stuck in his throat. When I look closer to inspect his throat area, I see a lump of about one-half inch in diameter, raising the skin on his throat a quarter of an inch up. Even with forceful hacking, Reverend Rhinehart failed to dislodge the apport from his throat. His obvious discomfort concerned me, but I felt at a loss for what to do.

"I didn't know if this episode represented a common occurrence, but Reverend Rhinehart once told me he experienced severe pain at the exit points where apports departed his body, often leaving scar tissue in his chest, facial areas, or arms. The Ascended Masters have commented that a half hour to one hour of physical phenomenon (apportation of sacred stones or physical materialization of Spirits) could be considered equivalent to forty hours of manual labor digging ditches. After a long séance, Reverend Rhinehart could be bedridden for days.

"Another comment once made by the Ascended Masters alerted me to what they faced in dealing with Earth's vibration. When taking on a materialized physical form, they felt as though they endured something similar to wearing a coat of armor weighing three thousand pounds. From this comment, we can get a sense of the sacrifices Reverend Rhinehart confronted in fulfilling his earthly mission."

And so, the world over, gems take on something more meaningful than what simply meets the eye, something more than a beautiful birthstone, more than a signet, and more than a nuptial engagement extolling *"diamonds are forever."* For the Ascended Masters, their purpose is clear; jewels and sacred objects are used to guide and protect humanity and, without a doubt, are an instrumental part of their dispensation of Light. This knowledge, evidenced through Reverend Rhinehart's adept physical phenomenon mediumship, is foreordained in Steve's recounting of the reference to the "white stones" which he discovered in Revelation 2:17, related in Chapter 5, "Becoming Our Own Authority for Truth."

THIRTY-SIX

HISTORICAL CROWNS AND RINGS ROYAL AND MYSTICAL GEMSTONES

I N THIS CHAPTER, WE EXPLORE THE MYSTERY AND ATTRACTION OF unique gemstones in history. Some intuitively sense an attraction to gems without knowing why. We would suggest certain gems radiate a vibration that people feel but cannot describe. This attraction helps to explain why rare, splendid gemstones have so captured man's imagination.

On occasion, we know more about these stones from grandiose writings tucked away in the vaults and dusty chambers of antiquity than we know from actually viewing the physical jewels. Many majestic specimens have been lost in the plunder of conquest or pilfered as much for their mystical power as their staggering value.

One of the most sublime expressions of adornment, symbolic of all ceremonial ornamentation, and highly sought after, is captured in a royal golden crown where exquisite jewels radiate. If we reflect, as medieval minds discerned, we can determine how such relics were used as a mediatory power between the Earthly and the Spiritual Realms. At their highest level, these examples of ancient splendor played a mystical role, and at their lowest, a magical role. Let's look to the *Bible* for insight and a historical perspective on the role of royal ornamentation:

Revelation 4:4 KJB

"And round about the throne were four and twenty seats: and upon the seats I saw four and twenty elders sitting clothed in white raiment; and they had on their heads crowns of gold."

Revelation 4:5 KJB

"And out of the throne proceeded lightnings and thunderings and voices: and there were seven lamps of fire burning before the throne, which are the seven Spirits of God."

There are several historical crowns still in existence, providing physical testimony and recorded history which the Masters point to as "Holy Writ." These jeweled crowns symbolize the mystical power of previous emperors and renowned saints. Here are a few such crowns giving us a pictorial sense of how Spirit worked through royalty and saints, shifting the consciousness of the times, as described by the Heinigers in *The Great Book of Jewels:*

"The gold crown of the Holy Roman Empire still survives in the Schatzkammer in Vienna as witness to the ceremonial magnificence with which the Ottonian Emperors (German Dynasty 919–1024 CE) surrounded themselves, anxious to assert themselves as the true heirs of Charlemagne and the Caesars. The crown is composed of eight arched plaques enriched with filigree and set with precious stones—sapphires, rubies, emeralds, and pearls, and decorated with cloisonné enamel in imitation of Byzantine cloisonné enamel. The crown's design is modeled on that of a Byzantine imperial crown, and as on Byzantine crowns, the central plaque is surmounted by a cross that is also set with gems and pearls. The subject of the enameled plaques, four in all, is Christ as Lord of the World. Above the figure of Christ, the inscription reminds kings that it is through Him that they reign..." [1]

The crown symbolizes more than a connection to Spirit, as it represents an admonition from on high that, after a coronation, whoever wears this ceremonial regalia must acknowledge God as the source of all influence and power. They must rule justly, with wisdom. It is thought the crown now residing in Vienna was made for the coronation of Emperor Otto the Great in Rome in 962. He was crowned Western Emperor by Pope John XII and is credited with fostering culture and learning in the so-called Ottonian Renaissance, which inspired important intellectual and architectural development.

Here is another passage the Ascended Masters thought worthy of declaring "Holy Writ." Again, described by the Heinigers:

"The great reliquary statue of St. Foy at Conques (France), a wooden figure covered with sheets of gold and silver, also wears a crown, together with the pieces of ceremonial jewelry that late-tenth-century France thought proper for the image of a greatly venerated saint. Her crown is a closed one, consisting of a circlet and two arches of jointed plaques with fleurs-de-lis between, set with antique cameos, pearls, and gems." [2]

The St. Foy crown is modest compared to many of the Holy Roman and Byzantine Empires. It is adorned with uncut stones in the typical styling of the Middle Ages. The reliquary statue of St. Foy represents a martyr (Saint Faith) who was persecuted under Maximian's persecution of the Christians in Gaul. At the time of her martyrdom, she was a twelve-year-old child. Arrested, she refused to surrender, never wavering from her faith, no matter the cost. Once beheaded, word spread of the great miracle cures and visions occurring around her relics. Believers thought the possession of her body would bring salvation to their country and redemption to their people. She was enshrined in a church within Agen until monks of Conques successfully confiscated her remains, returning them to Conques in hopes of generating more funds and a more powerful Spiritual vibration in their Church. Indeed, St. Foy attracted hundreds of Medieval Christians to her reliquary in Conques, where the pilgrims donated an abundance of precious gems to adorn her golden skirt.

Another noted crown of history representing both temporal and Spiritual power was a closed crown rather than an open one like that of Byzantine Empresses. It presents an oriental splendor of sparkling rubies, emeralds, turquoise, pearls, and gold with niello. Again, the Heinigers write:

"There still survives a crown that gives some idea of a Byzantine crown of this type, the celebrated crown of St. Stephen, the Holy Crown of Hungary, traditionally said to have been sent by the Pope to King Stephen." [3]

St. Stephen (997–1038 CE) was the first King of Hungary and Transleithania or Transylvania. Born a pagan, he was baptized at age ten, and throughout his reign, he encouraged the spread of Christianity. Pope Sylvester II recognized the sovereignty of his territory and supported St. Stephen's endeavors. King St. Stephen worked to put his nation (Austria-Hungary) on a sound moral footing, suppressing blasphemy, adultery, murder, and public crime. Under his rule, Hungary enjoyed a period of genuine peace, becoming the destination of choice for pilgrims and merchants of Western Europe en route to the Holy Land.

King St. Stephen's crown was moved to a variety of safekeeping locations following his death. Interestingly, during the U.S.—Russia Cold War, the crown of King St. Stephen was kept in a vault in Fort Knox, Kentucky, to protect it from confiscation by the Russians. President Carter returned the crown to Hungary in 1978.

Rings throughout history have played a role in gently reminding the wearer of a commitment to God, the beloved, or to Self. Like crowns, rings have been ascribed mystical, protective, and healing powers in legends and lore. Rings, blessed by the Ascended Masters, open the finger and wrist chakras to more powerfully transmit Spiritual healing. Guardian Angels often employ rings to protect their earthly subjects, as the ring allows a connecting link between the guardian and the person wearing the ring. Here are some interesting references illustrating the mystery surrounding rings of power in the group mind of humanity:

According to George Frederick Kunz in his book *Rings for the Finger* (1917), one of the earliest references to rings incorporating gemstones is by the Roman, Pliny the Elder. In Pliny's comprehensive books titled *The Natural History*, published 77-79 AD, Pliny covered many topics and based his discussion on the origin of gemstones set into rings by drawing on both mythical characters and historical figures. In one of the mythical Greek fables, Pliny relates that the Titan God, Prometheus, impiously dared to steal fire from heaven for mortal man. He became doomed by Jupiter to be chained to a rock in the Caucasus Mountains for thirty thousand years while vultures swooped in to feed on his liver. However, Jupiter eventually relented, freeing Prometheus. To remind Prometheus of his violation, it was ordained this Titan must wear a link from his chain on one of his fingers as a ring. In the ring was set a fragment of the rock to which he had been chained.

The Papal rings worn by the higher ecclesiastics of the Roman and Greek Churches are regarded with a special reverence and power. The most noted is the *"Fisherman's Ring"* worn by the Pope. This ring features a bas-relief of Saint Peter, who was a *Fisher of Men*. The ring was used as a signet until 1842 to seal official documents for the Pope. The usage of these types of rings worn by cardinals, bishops, and abbots dates back to the early history of Christianity. [4]

And in the *Bible*:

Genesis 41:42 KJB

"And Pharaoh took off his ring from his hand, and put it upon Joseph's hand, and arrayed him in vestures of fine linen, and put a gold chain about his neck... and he made him ruler over the land of Egypt."

SEASONS OF THE SOUL

St. Germaine, through Reverend Rhinehart's mediumship, occasionally refers to the time Catherine de Medici, Queen of France from 1547 to 1559, imprisoned him in Italy. Arch enemies, she coveted the power she perceived residing in his rings. Once incarcerated in her chateau's dungeon, she visited his chamber, insisting he hand over his rings. He flatly refused. Mercilessly, she chopped off his fingers, confiscating his sacred rings. Later, he grew back his fingers, eventually recapturing his rings.

St. Germaine often exclaimed, *"There's magic in dem rings, there's mystery in dem rings, hi-ho the merry o' there's power in dem rings!"*

Many other rings are featured in literature, but none more enchanted than the one called *"Precious"* by Gollum in the highly successful trilogy of J.R.R. Tolkien's *The Lord of the Rings*. There is a magical ring described by Plato in one of his stories that likely inspired Tolkien's work. It's called the *Ring of Gyges*.

Plato's story tells of a shepherd called Gyges who seeks refuge from a storm following an earthquake. In the cave where he sought protection for his flock, Gyges spots a corpse not looking quite human, apparently dislodged by the earthquake. There on its finger is a ring. Gyges finds when he slips the ring over his finger, he takes on a cloak of invisibility. Upon discovering this quality, he returns to the palace where he courts the wife of the king. After successfully wooing her, Gyges dons his ring of invisibility to kill the king. He then became the King of Lydia. The similarities to *"Precious"* are obvious.

Years back, I, Gary, came across a magnificent ring in Scotland purported to have come from Atlantis.

The story goes that upon the fall of Atlantis, the ring reappeared in Egypt, then traveled to Tibet, where Lamas reset it in a traditional Tibetan setting. Finally, the ring traveled West to Scotland. It is the largest ring I have ever seen! It covered three fingers, featuring an enormous, richly colored turquoise cabochon (A polished, convex dome-shaped gemstone, unfaceted). Legend describes the ring as a symbol of the seat of Spiritual power. Wherever the ring resided, the current height of Spiritual power reigned. Knowing of the ring's past residencies, from Atlantis to the West, we can follow the history of Spiritual power on Earth.

In returning to gemstones, we notice that Life Force shines through certain stones more than others, attracting avid interest, building a renowned communion between the Mineral Kingdom and Mankind where legend and romance converge. Over the years, the Ascended Masters have alluded to some precious stones with curious histories. Like a person with a celebrated resume, they travel Earth's byways from one fiefdom to the next, radiating their power, slipping through the hands of the prestigious, often assuming new monikers as they change owners.

The Heinigers describe a few of the more illustrious diamonds the world has known.

Shah Diamond – 88.7 Carats, Yellowish

The **Shah** is inscribed with much of its history right on its surface. The first inscription tells us the owner was Burhan Nizam Shah II in 1591, the ruler of Ahmednagar, India. The second inscription records the stone to be in the possession of the builder of the Taj Mahal, Shah Jahan. And the third reads Fath Ali Shah Qajar, 1739, who inherited the stone. In 1829, the Russian ambassador to Persia was assassinated in Tehran. In atonement, the **Shah** was presented to Tsar Nicholas I, becoming part of the Russian crown jewels, avoiding a war. The **Shah** is now part of Russia's treasury of diamonds in the Kremlin.

Kohinoor Diamond – 108.93 Carats, Colorless

Sources say the **Kohinoor** was found in the Godavari River in central India some four thousand years ago. It eventually fell into the hands of the Rajas of Malwa and then passed to Baber, who founded the

Mughal Dynasty in 1526. It then became one of the most prized possessions of the Mughal Emperors. It passed from ruler to ruler through the subcontinent of India for many centuries. In 1739, Nadir Shah of Persia invaded India and confiscated all the Mughal treasures except for the great **Kohinoor.**

One of the women in Emperor Nadir Shah's harem told the Shah that the Mughal Emperor hid the great **Kohinoor Diamond** in his turban. The conqueror then invited the defeated emperor to a feast, where, as a gesture of friendship, he offered to exchange turbans with the conquered emperor. The Mogul Emperor had no choice but to agree. Later in the privacy of his tent, Nadir Shah unrolled the turban, and the great gem fell out into his hands. Nadir Shah exclaimed, *"Kohinoor!"* (Mountain of Light)

The gem continued in the Persian dynasty, but there were numerous attempts made to gain its ownership. It attracted tremendous greed, violence, deception, provoking madness, and was feared to be cursed. After the Sikh wars, it was taken by the East India Company as part of the indemnity levied in 1849 and subsequently presented to Queen Victoria. It has been worn in the coronations in the English court. In 1911, the jewel was placed in a crown made for Queen Mary and later in another crown made for Queen Elizabeth. It is now on view, residing in the Tower of London. The tradition associated with the gem states that, *"who so ever owns the diamond will rule the world, but possessing it is dangerous for anyone but a woman."*

Regent Diamond – 140.54 Carats, Colorless

The **Regent** is considered one of the world's finest diamonds, sporting a fascinating, well-documented history. Found in India in the Seventeenth century, the **Regent** was smuggled to the coast beneath the bandages of self-inflicted wounds of the finder. Despite the concealment, the owner was murdered by an English sea captain who sold the stone to a Parsi trader. Then, in 1702, the diamond was sold to Thomas Pitt, Governor of Madras. Pitt sent it home to England, where it was cut into a cushion-shaped brilliant, taking on the name of Pitt. In 1717, Pitt sold the diamond to Phillipe, Duke of Orleans, the Regent of France. Louis XV wore it at his coronations in 1722. The diamond was frequently worn by Marie Antoinette, two generations later. In 1792, the diamond was stolen along with the **French Blue (Hope Diamond)**, but unlike the other jewels that were stolen, it was recovered and given as security for a war loan and eventually redeemed five years later.

When Napoleon Bonaparte was crowned Emperor of France in 1804, he carried the great **Regent Diamond** in the hilt of his sword. Later, it moved to Austria, but then back to France, where Charles X wore the **Regent** at his coronation in 1825. In 1887, the French crown jewels were sold at auction, all but the Regent, which was exhibited at the Louvre.

Hope Diamond – 45.52 Carats, Fancy Dark Grayish Blue

The most famous, or should we say the most notorious, of all diamonds is the **Hope Diamond**. Upon investigation of the **Hope Diamond**, it appears evil intent is at play. The Masters, aware of the **Hope's** vibration, programmed a stone for positive, transformative effects, transmuting the evil in the stone, transmitting wisdom into the world. A gemstone is a blank slate in and of itself, but once programmed, it houses the intent of the programmer and pulses out those vibrations into the world. But as we know, what can be positively programmed can also be negatively programmed in the wrong hands.

Here is some history of the darker side of the **Hope Diamond** as described by the Heinigers:

"The **Hope**—the diamond of misfortune.

"This great blue diamond is perhaps the most notorious gem in history. It has left behind a trail of so many unlucky owners that it has been popularly supposed to be cursed.

"The **Hope** was mined in India, and the 112-carat gem was brought to France in 1668. It was said that a curse resided in it, for a thief was reputed to have stolen the diamond from the eye of a statue of the Hindu goddess Sita, wife of Rama.

"Tavernier, who brought the gem from India to France, sold it to Louis XIV, who had it cut into a 67-carat heart-shaped stone and named it the *Blue Diamond of the Crown*. Tavernier is said to have been killed by wild dogs on his next trip to India.

"Louis XVI and Marie Antoinette inherited the *French Blue*, as it was popularly known. In 1792, about the time of their executions, the *French Blue* was stolen from the Garde-Meuble together with all of the French crown jewels. Some of the gems taken in this robbery were recovered, but not the *Blue Diamond of the Crown*.

"It is intriguing to note that a gem resembling the **Hope** is worn by Queen Moria Louisa of Spain in a portrait painted by Goya in 1800. There are reports that the stone *French Blue* was recut to its present size by Wilhelm Fals, a Dutch diamond cutter. Fals is said to have died of grief after his son, Hendrick, stole the gem from him. Hendrick, in turn, committed suicide.

"In 1830, there appeared in London a 44.5 carat deep blue, oval-cut diamond the gem experts agreed was the *French Blue*, recut to conceal its identity. Henry Hope bought it, and since then, it has been known as the **Hope Diamond**.

"The **Hope** moved on. An Eastern European prince gave it to an actress of the Folies Bergére only a few months before an army revolt toppled him from his throne in 1909.

"Evalyn Walsh McLean, a wealthy and eccentric American social figure, bought the **Hope Diamond** in 1911. Her son was killed in an automobile accident, her husband died in a mental hospital, and her daughter died in 1946 of an overdose of sleeping pills.

"After Mrs. McLean's death in 1947, New York jeweler Harry Winston purchased her jewels, including the **Hope**. He gave the gem to the Smithsonian Institution in Washington, D.C. in 1958, no doubt with a certain sense of relief. Coincidence or not, the diamond seems to have left enormous trouble in its train." [5]

Just as we have found the *Bible* to hold a rich history illuminating the mysteries of gems, so it is with the *Ramayana* and *Mahabharata* in *Vedic* lore. We can find similar references popping up in the religious texts of the *Torah*, the *Koran*, and Pagan sources, each alluding to the import of sacred gemstones, so let's go East and see the magnificent examples of gemstones sprinkled through a few of the sacred texts.

In the *Ramayana*, found in the third book, the *Aranya Khanda*, the sage Agastya meets Sri Rama in the Dandaka Forest. Sri Rama gifts Agastya a divine bow inlaid with gold and bejeweled with gems designed by Vishvakarma. (Another identical bow is known as the "Brahmadatta," which Brahma once gave to Vishnu.) What is the meaning of the bow being encrusted with gems? Is it ornamentation? To some extent, yes, but we would place a greater emphasis on the concept that its creator wanted to remind the owner to only draw the bow when attuned to God. Before taking aim, ask to be divinely guided and pray that any foe meet with Divine Justice. And may any arrow finding its target burn off the karmic debt of the felled.

There is a gorgeous, large, historical emerald recently reset within an aigrette (a fan-like display of jewels) by Cartier, depicting deities from the *Ramayana*. It could be considered a Hindu version of the breastplate, similar to Aaron's breastplate. In a like manner, the aigrette performs as an intermediary element connecting its wearer to Spirit. It is worn around the neck over the breast to ensure all inspiration originates from the heart and mind of God, and whoever wears the breastplate shall be divinely protected. There are carved scenes on this 380.898 carat gem depicting Rama, the Avatar, and his consort Sita, along with Hanuman, a devotee of Rama who is venerated in India for his humility, fearlessness, mental acuity, and enlightenment.

The Black Stone in Mecca

We cannot end the discussion on sacred stones without speaking to the **Black Stone** in Mecca, Saudi Arabia, revered by Muslims. The devoted believe the **Black Stone** was sent to Earth from heaven through Archangel Gabriel. To this day, its history is shrouded in mystery. Muslins believe Adam was the first human being to receive the stone from God. Legend says the stone was hidden on a mountain for many years until Gabriel brought it to the Prophet Abraham. It is believed the Prophet Muhammad once kissed the stone, so Muslims attempt to at least once in their lifetime make a trip to the Ka'aba (building that houses the **Black Stone**), to perform the "Hajj Pilgrimage Ritual," attempting to kiss the stone. Once at the Ka'aba, they perform the ritual of circling the Ka'aba seven times, reciting a prayer from the *Qur'an* in the name of God.

Many say the stone is a meteorite with supernormal powers, but no one has inspected or analyzed its structure, so that remains unknown. If we return to the quote from *The Great Book of Jewels*, we can see the power of the Muslim's faith at play:

"To evoke, by means of a symbolic object, the presence of another is to cross the threshold of the sacred. This implies a tangible link with the unique, and the object becomes sacred."

THIRTY-SEVEN

THE FORMATION OF GEMSTONES NATURAL AND THE SACRED

G ENUINE GEMSTONES ARE TRULY FREAKS OF NATURE! THEY ARE rare, beautiful, difficult to come by, and so unique people have rightfully ascribed supernormal attributes to their creation.

Humankind, from its earliest beginnings, has courted a love affair with stones. Early man was first attracted to the pebbles found by the riverside, picking them up to admire their beauty, rubbing the treasures in their hands. Like people today, they likely delighted in the puzzle of their sparkle, color, and mystery. With their fascination, man soon crafted the stones into forms of human adornment.

To start to understand some of the qualities of gemstones, let's dig into one of the most remarkable of all gemstones, diamonds. What are the forces lying behind their creation? Many think diamonds are formed from coal squeezed at extremely high pressures; however, this is false according to gemologists. Most semi-precious stones are formed within the Earth's crust at about the depth of thirty-two feet, but diamonds form at around one hundred and twenty-eight feet to five hundred and twelve feet below the surface of the Earth, deep in the mantle. They are eventually transported to the surface by explosive magmatic eruptions. During a volcanic eruption, the magma rises fast from the mantle to the surface crust, forming and carrying along diamonds for the ride in rocks called kimberlite.

Diamonds grow from carbon-bearing fluids in the mantle. These fluids migrate and flow through the cracks in rocks. As the fluid percolates through rock material, changes in pressure, temperature, or composition can cause carbon to crystallize out of the fluid, creating a solid form. Scientists have realized many of the minerals found in diamonds first originated in the Earth's crust and were then carried into the mantle by tectonic plate movement called subduction. Elements like blue boron are deposited in the mantle, triggering diamond growth. Through inclusions formed in the diamond, there are naturally occurring radioactive isotopes which can be dated, telling us diamond formation can originate from 90 million to 4.5 billion years ago.[1]

So, when you behold a complex faceted diamond, what might you comprehend? First, a mineral creation of God, fashioned into existence by the great beings of the Devic Kingdom. These are evolved intelligences, as we mentioned in Chapter Thirty-Two on Soul Mates. The Life-Force of these beings foregoes the usual evolutionary progression to other Kingdoms, evolving within the Mineral Kingdom, developing into great Mineral Devic Spirits.

Once the crystallized mineral is discovered by man, a lapidarist skillfully spends five to ten hours faceting a beautiful stone. In the case of special gemstones, intricate faceting requires many more hours of careful, tedious, concentrated skill. In creating an object that is considered sacred, there is the additional step by the Masters, whereby they program wisdom into the molecular structure of the stone.

So, if you are in the possession of a sacred object, the possibility exists for you to sense a strong communion with God, the Mineral Kingdom, the Masters, and Man. Through their collaboration, they bring into existence one of the most coveted objects in man's world, a sacred object, billions of years in the making!

If we analyze the formation of a sacred object programmed by an Ascended Master, we notice that the faceting and polishing of the stone increase the intensity and clarity of the thought vibration placed within. Additionally, the color, shape, and symbolism of an object influence its vibration, its specific communication, and its mission. Some objects are designed to be person-specific, others are more focused on a worldly mission.

The exquisite apported stone that materialized before Steve wasn't brought forth primarily to present a beautiful specimen of nature, but to present an object that crosses into sacred territory. As the Heinigers infer, the object becomes a bridge through which Spirit interacts with humanity.

The Masters suggest that sacred objects act as beacons of revelatory light, pulsing and beaming out new thought, forging the promise of a more highly evolved civilization, while raising humankind to greater heights of consciousness. The objects are not conscious in themselves, but more alive than one might imagine. In essence, they are veritable, encapsulated crystalline vessels pumping out eternal wisdom and transformation available to those fortunate enough to tune into such an object.

It is interesting to note that during his lifetime, Reverend Rhinehart scoured the planet collecting unique mineral specimens, amassing a world-class mineral collection. Each specimen is a work of Devic artisanship, a magnificent example of pure mathematical precision, all housed in crystalline structures. As the Avatar of the Aquarian Age, Reverend Rhinehart instinctively attuned to gems, knowing they would play a significant role in human evolution.

It must be stated that a common mineral in and of itself doesn't contain specific thought forms of healing, although a sensitive person may perceive incidental thoughts that have haphazardly been captured in the molecular structure. To rely on a mineral for a healing or a cure can be a dangerous, misguided undertaking. But when Master

Intelligence intervenes, attuning to a particular mineral's attributes, imbuing the crystals with pure thought forms, the results can be most insightful and rewarding.

Through Reverend Rhinehart's mediumistic attunement, we find there are vibrations innately contained within different minerals, such as Silicon Carbide, which opens the mind to new awareness of creation, or where Jasperite discerns truth from falsehoods, or how Sphalerite improves the ability to see distinctions in colors. The Mineral Kingdom to which Reverend Rhinehart was attuned presented a phantasmagoria, a kaleidoscopic rendering of endless symbolic abstractions.

Welcome to the New Jerusalem of the Age of Aquarius, where God's Manna lies resident within sacred crystalline structures, giving us opportunities to see gemstones in a whole new Light.

THIRTY-EIGHT

GOD
I AM – YHWH – BRAHMA – SOURCE

"IN THE BEGINNING GOD CREATED THE HEAVEN AND THE EARTH. *And the Earth was without form and void; and darkness was upon the face of the deep. And the Spirit of God moved upon the face of the waters. And God said, Let there be light: and there was light. And God saw the light, that it was good.*" Genesis — 1:1-4 KJB

In the *Genesis* passage, the Masters infer that God represents the allegorical symbol for the Divine—the Eternal Absolute Reality. Here God remains forever the same, unchanged. In this statement, *"And the Spirit of God moves upon the face of the waters,"* we are not informed there is a time for which creation began, as God IS already existing. There is no reference to before or after, no beginning, and no ending.

If we are to understand the first lines in the creation allegory in the *Book of Genesis*, we must use our imaginations! The Masters suggest since we are the extensions of God/Cosmic Mind and part of its functioning and ability to think, we possess the ability to create our own understanding.

Genesis does not say the Earth had form and was void, but says the Earth was without form and void. Our imagination must kick in here and reach past the concreteness of our current existence and grasp the Infinite Dimensions beyond our physical reality.

In this way, we may come to understand the space where all things burst forth from the plane of Infinite Dimension, a place where all is in motion. We might say creation springs into existence through the Natural Laws of Infinite Motion. This Motion animates life and flows through the inanimate creations as well. This force courses through galaxies, rocks, trees, clouds, and all living things.

Following this allegory, we must assume that all things first emerge from darkness; what we might call the "Womb of the Great Earth" or the "Womb of Creation." According to the Masters, everything that is, first existed latent in the darkness. The "Heaven" *Genesis* describes is an allegorical representation of the consciousness of God. It is a symbol of the fluidic nature of life in all its manifestations, not just the physical. The allegorical reference to "Earth" refers to planes of consciousness to which humans incarnate from the Spirit Realms. We would suggest to strictly limit God to physical or even Spiritual manifestations is missing the multi-dimensional nature of the Divine.

In this interpretation, God acts as a chimera, where we discern God is moving everywhere and cannot be worshipped in any single form. In fact, some say the God we know from Christianity was invented to assign all the unknown causes of phenomena which man has either admired or feared, but never understood. The Masters claim they have awareness of the causes existing behind phenomena within and without our Solar System, and they clearly state there is no God nor Gods behind such phenomena pressing the buttons or pulling the switches.

In listening to many Masters discuss the nature of God, without exception, Ascended Masters like Count St. Germaine, Koot Hoomi Lal Singh, Elijah, Jesus, Odyssa, Space Master Clarion, and others refer to God as ineffable. God simply IS, has always been, and shall forever be. They allude to God as all and everything, comprising existence and non-existence alike. They state God has never been seen by a human being and they will not be cajoled into saying God is a being or that God is a personal Divinity answering our questions.

They will not intimate that God is a thinking, conscious God, or that God is aware of our presence. God is indescribable, undefinable, unchangeable, and unbound by man's endless attempts to give God dimension, personality, and wonderful super-human attributes. No matter how persistent humans are in ascribing an anthropomorphic identity to God, the Masters will not bend their experience and understanding to fit man's limited awareness and understanding.

If we look to the Burning Bush in Exodus 3:14 KJB we arrive at the closest definition of God to which the Masters would subscribe. Moses posed a question to the illuminating presence,

"Who should I say with whom I spoke," and the presence said,

"Tell them, I AM WHO I AM."

"I Am That I Am" clearly alludes to a notion that God is indescribable, not a thing looking like this, or that, something beginning at a certain time or ending someday. God is the force and presence behind all creative power, always in motion, moving equally through one phenomenon after another into Infinity.

If this is true, we might ask where the concept of Faith fits into such an understanding. Can we have faith in things we can't describe or define? Can we have faith in things we do not know? Can we justify that kind of Faith? If God is beyond our ability to grasp, can Faith still bring about miracles, happiness, and Divine understanding? We think most can say their Faith in God has ultimately brought about much good, even miracles. So Faith is a force unto itself. We can look to Matthew 15:21-28 KJB, where the Faith the Gentile woman displayed proved fruitful:

"Then Jesus went thence and departed into the coast of Tyre and Sidon.

And behold, a woman of Canaan came out of the same coasts, and

cried unto him, saying, Have mercy on me, O Lord, thou son of David; my daughter is grievously vexed with a devil.

But he answered her not a word. And his disciples came and besought him, saying, Send her away; for she crieth after us.

But he answered and said, I am not sent but unto the lost sheep of the house of Israel.

Then came she and worshipped him, saying Lord, help me.

But he answered and said, It is not meet to take the children's bread, and to cast it to the dogs.

And she said, Truth Lord: yet the dogs eat of the crumbs which fall from their masters' table.

Then Jesus answered and said unto her, 'O woman, great is thy faith: be it unto thee even as thou wilt.' And her daughter was made whole from that very hour."

This event demonstrates Jesus believed Faith in God is real and can be justified. But can Faith be called upon when we have received true understanding, knowing our Faith in the personal God we once imagined is unfounded? The Masters say, "YES!" We may still have Faith in the power of God without declaring God is a thinking God or a personal God. God just IS and as such, exists!

Master Koot Hoomi Lal Singh, who is the overseer of the Yellow Ray of the intellect, illustrates on several occasions the futility of attempting to create mental constructs regarding the nature of God. In one comment, he indicates there are only two things we can say nothing about and through pure logic come to a surprising conclusion. He infers we can say nothing about the true nature of God, and we can say nothing about nothingness itself; so, Koot Hoomi reasons, since God and nothingness are intrinsically the same, God must be nothing and nonexistent!

We can determine the confusion that arises in attempting to articulate the nature of God through the mental body alone. Creating mental constructs through pure logic and language leads to untenable results, which the Masters find somewhat absurd and whimsical. All mental constructs live within the reasoning of the construct itself and prove invalid when explored from other vehicles of awareness, such as the Spiritual or vibrational bodies. Through the Spiritual body, awareness spontaneously occurs. No mental translation is required. Here, pure knowingness and awareness arise.

If we are to assume God is a thinking, intelligent being, what would that imply? Thinking implies analyzing and composing ideas. Inventions promulgate change, both in creation and destruction. And if we were to imply God is intelligent, are we not saying God possesses thinking attributes, which again suggests change? These attributes contradict God's eternal, infinite, unchanging nature. The Masters imply God is Power, God is Truth, God is Wisdom, God is Perfection, and God is Energy. If these absolutes are true, doesn't this imply God transcends what we call thinking? In the end, we must acknowledge God eludes man's insistent efforts to anthropomorphize God's nature.

The mind is a great tool, but only one vehicle through which we perceive and interact with reality. The mind does not render a comprehensive understanding of God, or, for that matter, even the physical world. The human mind wants to identify, categorize, and pin down everything in the universe according to its limited vision.

Our human tendencies find no reliable ground when exploring the nature of God. So where can we gain a deeper understanding? Barring direct awareness and mystical revelation, it appears futile. But for a moment, let's travel to Java and visit a sacred site that may give us a roundabout insight.

Set against the spectacular backdrop of the Menorah Mountain Range in central Java, Borobudur, a 9th Century Mahayana Buddhist temple, sits perched above a sparse verdant jungle growth. Walking the grounds of this magnificent temple, we can glimpse a metaphor of the power and glory of God. On the temple grounds sit five hundred and four carved stone Buddhas, each encased in a stupa, a stone dome-like architectural structure. Each of the stupas is perforated with a series of diamond-shaped openings. When we attempt to view the entire Buddha at once, no matter how vain our attempt to see the Buddha, it proves hopeless! We can only view through a single perforation at a time, allowing us to see but a smidgeon of the entire Buddha.

And so it is with God. We can merely glimpse a fraction of the power and revelation of God, as God's image is impossible to grasp in its entirety. If perchance we miraculously stumble into perceiving God's full image, God's omnipotence would obliterate our ability to integrate the magnitude of God's magnificence. If we were to attempt to spy through the perforations of Borobudur's stupas, stretch a perforation wider and wider in hopes of illuminating the meaning of the ineffable, what visions might we behold?

The exalted ones allude to God as Transcendental Light manifesting as Cosmic Mind; therefore, what we see is that every one of us is an extension of Cosmic Mind, an aspect of its activity, but not its cause. This inward experience eclipses a single definition. According to the Masters, as we are one with all humanity, we fulfill the Cosmic Mind's capacity to think, to express, to be. We are its very nutrients, its substance of thought, telepathically radiating out to all through space and dimension.

If perhaps we allow ourselves to inhabit Cosmic Mind unrestrained, fulfilling its function in a physical human form, what do we imagine would transpire? We might ask, how does God function in our world? How does God interact with the diversity of humanity? Who is graced by God? The Masters emphasize that each must eventually come to experience all ways of Truth, Life, and Light, no matter our station, our religion, or our ethnicity.

Without exception, Divine Power manifests to all, as the rain falls equally upon the just and the unjust alike. To say it bluntly, God bestows no special favors on anyone! Heath, wealth, truth, error, and ignorance fall upon all of us!

We might also ask how God works and functions. Has God ever worked in the world without working through someone or something? For us to engage God, we must create an opening in such a way as to allow God to work through us. One way this manifests is through healing. But for a healing to transpire, we must allow God to move through us, unrestricted. If we hold the person for whom we intend God to heal, to our personal characterizations of them, then we chain this person to our limitations of what is possible. Some ask, can a person stop drinking, heal a previous trauma, or heal from a debilitating illness?

Nothing is impossible when we believe. So, if we are holding someone to their current state, we must release the bondage of any thought we may hold and let God work through us without limitation.

Although they seldom make headlines, miracles are ongoing in contemporary times as they were in Judaic times. No Church can claim to possess or demonstrate the power of Almighty God's miracles more than any other. No country is more deserving of miracles than another. Miracles are occurring at Lourdes and many religious shrines in India, just as they have occurred through Reverend Rhinehart and Aquarian Foundation.

Must we be perfect and unblemished to direct a Spiritual healing? The Masters suggest sorrow is a part of life and is often symbolized by clouds in a Spiritual context. We may think we must be untainted by emotions, such as sorrow, to enact Spiritual healings or miraculous deeds. But even Jesus experienced the clouds of sorrow, illustrating that the only one who is perfect is the Father residing within. The Masters accept this truth, allowing imperfections to exist without judgment. With this understanding, the Father's Love will flow unrestrained through the healer even in the presence of human imperfections.

We have discussed the inability to define God's qualities and character. Is this idea a recent concept put forth by the Ascended Masters through Reverend Rhinehart's mediumship or a notion from Pagan times? We would point to the fact that throughout history, Earth's mystery schools have expressed this awareness and conception of God. But it is not solely the mystery schools' knowledge, as it is alluded to in Judaism as well.

YHWH, the Hebrew God, is mentioned throughout the Torah. What is the word YHWH and how is YHWH pronounced? It has no vowels, so it defies pronunciation! It consists of the Hebrew consonants of Yod, Heh, Waw, and Heh, which is known as the tetragrammaton. The word suggests that God is unspeakable, ineffable, and indescribable. Some have come up with a pronunciation and have added consonants, making it more easily pronounced, but in so doing, they disregard the original intent of its abstract ineffable nature. "Yahweh" is a commonly used version, allowing for easier pronunciation, but again, this representation ignores the original intent.

What does YHWH mean? It can be translated to mean: I Am That I Am. This was the Hebrew name revealed to Moses in Exodus. The Masters say, when we tune in to this "I Am," we will know the "I Am" that has always been, and discover it penetrates all activities and thought forms coming from our being. The "I Am" is the water nourishing a thirsting soul. The "I Am" radiates equally everywhere and to everyone, remaining changeless under all conditions, through war and peace, sickness and health, and even as "the rich get richer and the poor get poorer."

When we attune perfectly to the "I Am" presence, we become an affirmation of Infinite Light and Love. We animate the "I Am." At the moment of this awareness, we are no longer speaking the affirmation, but we embody the affirmation, becoming the enactment of Light and Love. In this awareness, we cease trying to become better or different, as the voice of the "I Am" presence moves us, and moves through us, without effort.

Many define YHWH as Source, the creator of all and everything. In the Hebrew concept of YHWH, we honor the creator. The God of creation is symbolized in Hinduism with the God, Lord Brahma. Hinduism perceives all cosmic phenomena to be the work of the Hindu Trimurthis or Trinity: Brahma (the creator), Vishnu (the preserver), and Shiva (the destroyer).

In Hinduism, Brahma was the first to emerge from the primal waters as differentiated consciousness. He is not created by someone or something else; he emerges from himself. Brahma is the Supreme Spirit, the Universal Self, or the Cosmic Egg. The image of Brahma is depicted with four heads and four arms and hands. We could go into the symbolism behind the depiction, but it furthers the concept that God manifests in some type of form, contrary to the Masters' thought of a formless, ineffable God. So we will leave it at Brahma is the God of creation, similar to the Hebraic God YHWH.

Many of Christian faith and other faiths may be skeptical of the Masters' explanations and experiences of God. If we revisit the grounds of Borobudur, peering through the stupa's 40,000 perforations in an attempt to view the nature of Buddha, we quickly grasp that God's entire nature cannot be apprehended, only partially glimpsed. We can then perceive the futility of man's efforts to describe God in human terms or expound upon the fathomless rooms of God's glorious mansion.

Although we may not be able to perceive God's full nature, the Masters state *God is Real* and experienced through Spiritual communion. However, despite filling many pages in an attempt to articulate and define God, we circle back to our original statement: *God is ineffable,* and as Master Koot Hoomi Lal Singh suggested, *something we can say nothing about!*

THIRTY-NINE

PRAYER

P RAYER CAN BE A DIFFICULT SUBJECT BECAUSE OF THE WIDE variety of approaches practiced in different faiths throughout history. If we browse through the ages surveying countless religions and Spiritual practices, we can conclude few have unlocked the true mysteries, opening the secrets of prayer. Why? Because prayer demands we leave timidness behind and venture into territory that terrifies the ego. The objective of prayer is never fulfilled by those who refuse to enter uncharted terrain. Some ancient religions, shamanic practices, and mystery schools are founded on superstitions or dogmatic, biased thinking, while others have gone the distance and uncovered genuine Spiritual magic.

Most orthodox religions believe prayer is a communication with God, a supplication where we humbly seek God's goodwill or favor. The intent of the communication varies, but most prayers, aside from the praises of God, are petitions whereby the petitioner asks God to fulfill Spiritual, emotional, or physical needs, sometimes in exchange for a sacrifice. Another common plea consists of an outreach to heal the world or cure personal afflictions, where the petitioner assures God of acceptance, no matter the outcome. But subliminally, even openly at times, there is the thought God's business is answering prayers and the petitioner's thought goes something like this:

"Heal me, God, help me pay off my debts, fill me with Your power and I will faithfully serve You the rest of my life! I promise to make sacrifices. I'll give up vodka! I'll give up my adulterous ways! I'll donate twenty dollars to the Church every week!"

Often, the request amounts to something most would consider nearly impossible in return for a trifling. In attempting to barter, the petitioner is reaching out to a force, an omnipotent being, to achieve results with abilities they don't believe they themselves possess. Rarely, according to the Masters, does this kind of prayer get results. Unfortunately, those who engage in such pleas often lose faith in God because their prayers go unanswered. The Masters contend that a prayer answered is answered by a conscious entity (a Master, a Saint, or a Spiritual being) existing outside the petitioner. Or, by one of the petitioner's own minds (subconscious, superconscious, or conscious).

Before inquiring deeper, let's identify some of the most common types of prayer and the wide range of intentions behind prayer:

PETITION

Asking for God's help through prayers of intercession is a familiar form of petition. Here, the petitioner is not generally concerned with personal needs, but with the needs of others. The petitioner intercedes, asking for God's mercy to be directed to healing a friend, to stop a war, or for assistance in some endeavor. Saint Teresa of Ávila employed this type of prayer with great success. We will review her inspiring story in the coming pages.

REBUKING EVIL

Prayers of petition may include rebuking evil, *"Deliver us from evil."* This prayer confronts the evil within and the evil without by transmuting darkness into Light. There can be a danger here, which is good to observe. In zealousness to eliminate something seen as negative in another person, the person directing the prayer could be addressing a personal pet peeve they perceive in another. While the intention is good, the perception of the person praying may be misguided. This misperception behind the intent of the prayer may fall short of aligning with Divine Principle or moral code and therefore, create the possibility of generating negative karma for the person praying. Rebuking evil and negativity should remain an attempt to eliminate that which harms society, a person, or oneself.

PRAISE

In liturgies and Masses, there are prayers of adoration and praise where God's greatness is humbly recognized, and when we acknowledge our dependence upon God in all things. "In God We Trust." Personal faith falls into this category. This form of prayer can take on a yearning, a deep, consuming desire to return God's grace.

FORGIVENESS THROUGH CONFESSION

In the Catholic tradition, there are prayers requesting God's forgiveness of sin: *"Forgive us our trespasses as we forgive those who trespass against us."* This approach to prayer is a heartfelt *"coming to Jesus moment,"* where we seek a cleansing, soliciting forgiveness through an acknowledgement that we have failed to measure up to our perceived standard of God's morality, or a promise to ourselves. It's a confession, often through an intermediary to God: *"Holy Mary, Mother of God..."* It is an act of honest vulnerability, like standing buck-naked before God and declaring a willingness to repent and reform. For some, it is a personal bargaining that if they do certain penance, they will receive a less harsh judgment.

A prayer of confession can take the form of a public statement in a personal growth training, an admission to a priest, or a sincere private act. Confession is an unburdening, a cleansing, whereby we can start anew, free of our sins. There is much confusion around sin, as it is a loaded word with tons of societal baggage. It is good to keep in mind the Golden Rule regarding perceived sin: *"Do unto others as you would have them do unto you."*

Ultimately, the Masters state there is only one violation of the moral code, and that is the violation of the Golden Rule. Every other so-called moral infraction, if indeed it is an infraction, is but a deviation from the Golden Rule.

UNITY WITH GOD

The prayers of Spiritual practice found in many different religions are an attempt to experience unity with God. These are prayers affirming that every breath creates oneness with God. They are prayers of devotion to the Almighty, an affirmation that the I Am presence directs every thought. Often, there is a seeking, a sincere yearning for oneness with God, where we aspire for complete obedience to God's will, a dissolving of the ego into union, selflessness in service to God. St. Teresa of Ávila exemplifies this practice throughout her life.

As a generalization, Western traditions are more mental in their approach to finding unity with God, whereas the Eastern traditions of devotional chanting tend to be more heart-centered in nature. So, prayer for unity with God is the mental or emotional reflection upon that which is Holy.

THANKSGIVING

Maybe the most common prayer is one of thanksgiving. In giving thanks, we articulate our heartfelt gratitude for the blessings and gifts received in life. There is an acknowledgement there is something larger than the self which is present and operating in our lives and attending to our needs. We shower immense gratitude upon the universe, friends, or Source, acknowledging such blessings. We are all familiar with these types of prayers around food, gracious friends, and sudden arrivals of unexpected gifts, whether they are physical or Spiritual.

PROTECTION

Finally, we all send prayers of protection for our children, friends, family, and worldly events. We ask God to seal our loved ones in protective shields, guarding them against any possible misfortune. This prayer might be considered an overlap with prayers for rebuking evil, but it is more preventative in intent.

Most of the afore-mentioned forms of prayer are petitions seeking assistance from something beyond ourselves to intercede on our behalf. But as we will discover, the Masters suggest each prayer can be approached in a more impactful manner with a shift in understanding. They say prayer doesn't start with wanting to heal someone in pain or to correct the ills of the world. Prayer starts with a sincere relationship with God and the clarity of our thoughts. Without this, manifesting the object of prayer becomes somewhat remote.

The types of prayers we have discussed are reasonable places to begin our development in prayer, but fall short as a powerful practice for this reason: The Masters infer prayer is *more than a private communion with an external God or a supplication to the Infinite.* Although these forms of prayer are partially effective, there exists a deeper, more dynamic practice. So, we might ask the Masters how we can faithfully interact with these initial ideas, yet take them to new depths of understanding.

Yes, there are many examples of individuals and prayer groups accounting for healings through Faith and prayer, but the Masters imply these are isolated healings and generally one-off situations. We must ask what resides behind a faith cure, a mesmerism process, or any healing. There may be a more mature level where prayer can be replicated in a scientific manner, shedding the label of "miracle."

In this Chapter, we will elaborate on some of the keys we think are important in understanding and enacting genuine prayer. First, we must realize that no matter what is given by a priest, a prayer practitioner, or a Master, that alone will not bring about the fulfillment of prayer.

Development is never delivered on a platter! It is incumbent upon the student to develop the final steps of the fulfillment of prayer through inner realizations. Prayer, like any learned skill, must be continually practiced and fine-tuned. Knowledge from the Tree of Knowledge can be imparted, but the rest of the journey is up to the student! As humans, we want to know exactly how to do something, we want someone to show us the way, we want each step to be outlined like the specifications on the floor plans to a building, or we feel lost. But from time immemorial, the force of mystical wisdom has been grasped through the development of inner awareness. It comes about differently for each chela. It is always individual.

The force, once experienced, is then directed in a unique manner by the practitioner. Unfortunately, there is no exact map to arrive at this awareness. According to the Masters, one of the main reasons for people's inability to manifest the objective of their prayers is that the understanding of Spiritual abstracts, or forces, such as Love, Truth, and Faith, has lost much of their power over time. The majority of us no longer experience the true meaning of these words. The meanings have been diluted, adulterated, and often never fully understood from the start. As a result, the transformational force empowering prayer is lost and must be reimagined through new creative powers. The Masters remind us that this power comes from awareness and personal discovery and is further developed from there.

If we look at the word "bless," we will find it is a terrific example of this phenomenon regarding the loss of original understanding. "Bless" is a word tossed about extremely casually in our society today; so much so, its meaning has become rather obscure. Someone sneezes and people say, "Bless you!" Someone performs an act of kindness and people say, "Bless you!" Someone falls sick and people say, "Bless you!" Others often say, "Bless your enemies!" What is the meaning behind blessing someone? "Bless" at one time was used as a powerful sacred force in the mystery schools in both Eastern and Western religions. Once it became publicly used, the word began to defuse and lose its power.

The following is the meaning of "bless" as practiced by the Siddhas in India: *To Bless was an act of transmitting a power and awakening that power within another. It is called Shaktipat by the Siddhas. In the West, the Essenes enacted a similar Spiritual practice, whereby, through Grace, an infusion of power awakened the devotee to the presence of God.*

There is a vitality, an energy awakened within the person that has been blessed. A blessing is not casual, but a deliberate giving, a gift moving from one to another. It is something felt. We can feel Shaktipat when it occurs. If we revisit the scene in the *Bible* where a woman who had been bleeding for twelve years touched the hem of Jesus' cloak and was healed, we see the enactment of this type of blessing. It is Virtue that flowed from Jesus, and the woman was healed!

In mystery schools, a blessing takes many different forms as the chela passes through initiations. Many students have felt the touch of a Master as in Shaktipat, but it doesn't have to be a physical touch. It could come in the form of a dream where the Master lays a hand on the chela and the blessing passes from the Master to the chela. One of the last blessings an initiate experiences is the crucifixion. This is not necessarily the dying on a cross, but an event of extreme testing where the chela masters the body.

John the Baptist (not to be confused with St. John, the writer of the *Book of Revelation*) delivered a form of initiation in the Jordan River. During the baptism, there was a clear intention of both John and the participants to receive a cleansing of the Spirit. A purification ensued, renewing the devotee and opening the heart, mind, and soul to the new energies that would be forthcoming. The Masters imply that this understanding of baptism has lost its meaning in the ceremonies of churches today. An important element of baptism is that the person being baptized is Spiritually prepared, consciously wanting a Spiritual cleansing, and is eager to shift their consciousness toward a more Spiritually oriented life. To simply get baptized by a minister or priest because it is the family tradition or your Church recommends getting baptized, in the Masters' eyes, has little lasting significance.

This chapter has been intended to raise our Spiritual consciousness to a new understanding of prayer, moving beyond traditional approaches to prayer. Genuine, effective prayer entails more than simply reaching out to God; there is a rigorous practice of developing new awareness so our prayers may be more intentional, powerful, Spiritually guided, and fruitful.

FORTY

THE MYSTERY OF SCIENTIFIC PRAYER
MARY BAKER EDDY 1821 – 1910

MARY BAKER EDDY, THE FOUNDER OF THE CHRISTIAN SCIENCE Church, is one who resolved herself to unlocking the mystery behind prayer and healing. Reverend Rhinehart revealed on several occasions his admiration of Mary Baker Eddy's life, especially the rigor she demonstrated in her pursuit of the science of Divine Healing. Through her study, she discovered her personal key. Let's start by investigating Mary Baker Eddy's thoughts on scientific prayer.

Mary's study intensified after a severe fall in 1866, which threatened her well-being. To address her health, she reached out to the *New Testament* and experienced a Spiritual illumination that brought immediate physical recovery, Spiritual authority, and power. Most of us would have given profound gratitude to God, claiming a miracle occurred, then returned to our normal day-to-day activities. But Mrs. Eddy wanted to know the mechanics behind her healing. She sensed something and wanted to know intimately the force with which she was healed. She spent the next nine years studying the *Bible*, applying what she learned to healing people in her community, while developing a teaching protocol that culminated in 1875 with the publication of *Science and Health*. After years of further refinement, she added the words to the title with *"Keys to the Scriptures"* in

1883. Later in her publication, *Retrospection and Introspection*, she emphasized the metaphysical science she discovered through intense study of Biblical scripture, which she eventually coined, "Christian Science."

The miracles she once imagined to be supernormal were now divinely natural, the enactment of Divine Law, repeatable and scientific! With her new understanding, she claimed prayer was not a petitioning of God to take away an illness; nor did it rely on specific formulas, but rested in unequivocal faith and moral discipline. Prayer, she realized, is nothing more than an acknowledgement of Jesus' promise that all who exercise this understanding have the power to heal! The following statements by Jesus reflect this promise:

"I and my Father are one." John 10:30 KJB

"Be ye therefore perfect, even as your Father which is in Heaven is perfect." Matthew 5:48 KJB

"Verily, verily, I say unto you: He that believeth on me, the works that I do shall he do also; and greater works than these shall he do; because I go unto my Father." John 14:12 KJB

Who is the "I" that is referred to in these statements? It is not the personal "I," the self, with which Jesus is referring. Mrs. Eddy states this "I" is unreal. It is the "I" that is the Godself, which is Real and whom Jesus is referring to! It is the Self residing in the heart. This is the "I" that executes the work! It is the "I" that delivers on Jesus' promise, the one illuminating the shortcomings of the lower self. The real "I," she states, is Eternal and Real; whereas, the personality "I" is temporal and unreal. Simply put by Mrs. Eddy, Spirit is Reality, and matter is unreality.

Mary says for twenty years she toiled away, in an attempt to trace all physical effects back to a mental cause. In late 1866, she gained what she classified as "scientific certainty" that all causation was actually issuing from Mind and every effect strictly a mental phenomenon.

After her illumination, the scriptures possessed a new tongue and she grasped their true Spiritual meaning. She called God "Immortal Mind." She describes "mortal mind" as that which sins, suffers, and dies. Mary says she learned the physical senses testify falsely, that the five physical senses are witnesses only to matter, which is unreal and as such, they are inadequate to form a proper conception of Infinite Mind. She says St. John illuminated us on this concept with his statement, *"If I bear witness of myself, my witness is not true."* John 5:31 KJB

Jesus never questioned those whom he healed as to their disease. To him, the body had no efficacy. He simply enacted the supremacy of Spirit over matter. By refusing to drink the vinegar and gall to remedy the torture of the Crucifixion, he demonstrated his obedience to God's Laws: Spirit Real, body unreal; Crucifixion, the final conquest over the illusion of the body.

Mary continually practiced deepening her acquaintance with God, looking to God to guide her every thought and every deed. She says every thought must be Spiritualized to come to a greater understanding of Spirit. Every thought must be grappled with until it is honest, unselfish, and pure. Our over-reliance upon material things shifts to a constant inquiry into Spirit if we are looking for Truth. In healing, it is Mind that reconstructs the body, nothing else. Its revelation is scientific, not haphazard, but the fulfillment of Principle.

Mary says many have a belief in an illusion she calls sin; this belief must be faced head-on and mastered. She classifies illness, sin, and death as illusions and each a hypothetical claim in error. To eliminate error, we open our eyes to all illusive and subtle forms of error and the reality beyond form. Christian Science claims sickness is a belief based on fear. Perfect Love eliminates all fear.[1]

After Mary's new understanding, she preached, taught, and healed around her community for free. One time, the Lyceum Club, at

Westerly, Rhode Island, called her requesting she give a speech at the club. Upon her arrival, the hostess revealed the next-door neighbor, a fairly young woman, was bedridden and dying. Mary asked if she could visit the woman. The hostess accompanied Mary to the invalid's home, explaining physicians long ago gave up on the woman.

Mary stood by the woman's side for about fifteen minutes, and then the woman rose out of bed, got dressed, and carried on in good health. Upon leaving, Mary passed through an adjacent room where she witnessed the clothes prepared for the woman's burial. Later, she discovered the lady's condition stemmed from an operation at the birth of her last child, after which the doctors proclaimed the woman would never deliver another. Following the healing, the woman gave birth to a twelve-pound babe, exclaiming she never suffered so little giving birth.

Mary's scientific demonstration so disturbed the local clergy they discontinued allowing her to speak in their Church. But speak she did in many Churches! Folks walked in on crutches and walked out with their crutches resting upon their shoulders, while others came sick and left disease-free simply by listening to her sermon.

There is one last testimony we would like to relate regarding Mary Baker Eddy's healings. In this vignette, she states that one Sunday during a church service, she detected a strong soprano voice floating up above the choir, a vibrant and sympathetic voice that caught her ear. Upon the end of the service, two ladies pushed their way through the congregation up to the platform. The mother, sobbing profusely with tears of joy, gathered herself and exclaimed, *"Did you hear my daughter sing? She has not sung since she left the choir due to consumption! When she entered the Church an hour ago, she was unable to speak a loud word. Now she is healed!"*[2]

FORTY-ONE

MYSTICISM OF PRAYER
SAINT TERESA OF ÁVILA 1515 – 1582

T HERE ARE OTHER REMARKABLE EXAMPLES OF THE POWER of prayer throughout history, as in the case of St. Teresa of Ávila. Teresa lived in the Sixteenth Century, steeped in the Catholic tradition. She entered the convent, taking the Carmelite habit of the Incarnation at Ávila in Castile at age twenty-one, asserting her betrothal to the Lord. Over time, she progressed in contemplation and prayer, eventually founding a Carmelite convent. She traveled for twenty years, traversing Spain, enduring great hardships, while reforming the Carmelite Order. As a Carmelite mystic, she founded seventeen convents. Forty years after her death, she was canonized by Pope Gregory X.

In Teresa's early home life, she learned to pray with devotion to her Lady, Mary, the Mother of Jesus. Upon entering the convent, she spent her days in solitude, confessing frequently, and sitting in prayer—earnestly attempting to anchor the presence of Jesus in her heart. Teresa's prayer developed by beginning her prayers with inspirational reading. This focused her mind beyond the trials of personal life. As recorded in her diaries, slowly God began to fulfill her prayer requests by granting favors such as restoring someone's sight, removing another's intolerable pain and disease, and delivering souls who wandered astray from God's company.

This one story sums up Teresa's state of mind in approaching healing. In the *Life of Saint Teresa of Ávila By Herself,* Teresa relates one of the nuns living in her convent suffered from a painful stomach disease, one which horrified all the other nuns. For Teresa's part, rather than becoming frightened, she only envied the Sister's patience. Teresa prayed for God to send her any sickness He well pleased, providing He sent her the patience with which to deal with the affliction. To Teresa, anything transitory seemed of small account, no fear of any disease ruffled her because her soul was focused on the Eternal.

Teresa's prayers were answered within two years when she contracted a disease, not the same one that took the nun's life, but no less difficult and painful to bear. She suffered great torments, finally experiencing a severe attack, leaving her insensible for nearly four days. Rites of the Sacrament of Extreme Unction were performed. The Sisters believed death to be a certainty every minute of every hour. For a day-and-a-half, an open grave lay awaiting her body. When she recovered, Teresa claimed had it not been for her confession regarding the ways in which she offended God, He would not have brought her back from the dead.

As we mused over her account from the standpoint of 2025, we sensed her early prayer work arose from the need to absolve her guilt issuing from her self-professed wickedness. But through her sincere prayer and profound Love, she demonstrated a commitment to repay the Lord for bestowing such great favors upon her, proving herself so pure even her self-loathing didn't prevent the grace of God's Natural Law.

Although she attained sainthood, experiencing visions of the heights of Heaven and depths of Hell, we believe her practice strayed from the path of prayer and healing that the Ascended Masters teach. Praying for illness to repay God for sins, or taking on another's illness as penitence, is not required to manifest healing and God's grace.

The Sixteenth Century in the Catholic Church portrayed Spiritual practice as a time of vivid visions, confessors and confessions, sin, penitence, and martyrs. It was under these constraints Teresa carved out her path, highly successful, but clearly not reflective of the Spiritual ideology of many teachings in the New Age.

In view of the countless raptures, visions of Jesus, and so-called miracles of prayer, we will take a moment to investigate Teresa's comments as we believe they could prove useful in aiding us in the challenges of practicing contemporary prayer. Her comments may call to mind the type of prayer coming from a devout Catholic, but nevertheless her ascent opens insights for anyone seeking unity with God.

If we delve into her autobiography, we find she applied herself diligently with unwavering faith and selflessness in the service of the Lord. She exhorts through the power of prayer, that which she saw with the eyes of the body was such a mockery, compared to that which she saw with the eyes of the Soul. God's gifts of ecstatic visions marked the beginning of her living Love of God.

He guided her through nearly twenty years, under the difficulties and constant stress of reforming the Carmelite Order. She says, though all of us are always in the presence of God, those who practice the power of prayer are in His presence, in a different way, as they are aware He is watching, while others forget He sees them. This awareness steadied her through her constant challenges.

St. Teresa believed words were not necessary for prayer, all that was needed was the will to Love. She says we are first a servant of Love when we follow the way of prayer. Most have a fear of being servile, which, according to Teresa, translates to a fear of God. When we let go of who we think we are, then *"I and the Father are one"* becomes a reality. (John 10:30 KJB) We think we are giving of ourselves completely when we are only partially giving; rarely do we manage to give up the self to completely give. It is the work of shedding our identification with the body and its consuming desires that makes wholehearted giving possible.

Teresa suggests her practice of prayer is analogous to creating a garden for the pleasure of the Lord. It is solely a labor of Love to which one commits. She says, Be glad to have the opportunity to work in the garden. Embrace the labor without resistance, for your labor is never in vain. With long perseverance in prayer, God does not fail to reward. Teresa assures us as we work, God stands by, providing the water to nourish the garden, bringing favors so as not to allow any trial to deprive us of Eternal Blessings.

She discerned four stages of prayer in the ascent of the Soul to God. She draws upon the allegory of watering and growing a garden so we might understand her process in the practice of prayer. The following are her stages of development using the allegory of the garden: **The First Water** — **Dipping of the Bucket,** *Mental Prayer and Meditation;* **The Second Water** — **The Water Wheel,** *the Prayer of Quiet;* **The Third Water** — **The River,** *Total Absorption in God;* **The Fourth Water** — **The Rain,** *Ecstatic Consciousness.*

Teresa claims in the initial stage of prayer, **The First Water**, it is wise to detach from every type of pleasure. To some this means bearing the cross, but we would suggest this is an overly negative connotation and it doesn't have to be burdensome. Instead, it can represent a form of release: a release from personal victimization; a release from neediness; a release into a soaring freedom of Spirit!

She begins elaborating on **The First Water** of *Mental and Meditative Prayer,* outlining the challenges that plague the beginner. There exists the temptation to believe devotion is a severe practice where we can't be cheerful or ever indulge in recreation. She says devotion is not shattered if we relax for a moment to enjoy ourselves. We must maintain discretion, though, not allowing overconfidence to lead us astray by over-indulging in desires. This observance is most necessary until we establish ourselves in virtue. By proceeding humbly throughout our devotional practice, the Lord is a friend and lover of the courageous souls who put their trust and efforts in Him. Teresa claims she could do nothing of herself and found admiration in St. Augustine's statement, *"Give me what You ordain, and ordain what You will."* (St. Augustine's Confessions)

In terms of a burden, we ask, did Jesus experience the cross as a burden? Through Reverend Rhinehart, the Masters say, *"Yes"* and *"No!" "Yes"*, there was physical, excruciating pain. Spiritually, *"No,"* the Crucifixion was a blessing, the opportunity to finally conquer the illusion of the body. It is the ego that finds the cross burdensome, as it fears that which destroys its comfort. Teresa says to be unafraid of the work, because the Lord helps to carry the load when we are fully committed. With full commitment, Love does the work, and the experience of burden dissolves! No work done in a humble state leaves a distaste in the soul, but as we draw nearer and nearer to God, humility lays the groundwork.

Even demonstrating great devotion, Teresa became frustrated with her lack of humility at times, insisting over and over it is this foible that blocked her advancement on the path of prayer. She says humility is best attained when we withdraw our attention from the body and the self, focusing on the Spirit, while putting worldly anxieties aside, trusting without reservation that our needs will be met. By embracing this wisdom, freedom of Spirit comes forth in an unsuspecting manner. It is not for everyone, especially those with families and vocations where others are relying on them to provide in a worldly manner. But for those committed to prayer, this approach serves well.

Another burden Teresa experienced was numerous health issues challenging her commitment. When she abandoned her need for comfort, her health turned for the better. Many unknowingly use health to hold them back from full immersion, in this way, the ego controls the advancement in prayer. Teresa says we should not be frightened by our own thoughts and doubts at the beginning of prayer because fears inhibit our commitment. In the beginning, middle, and end, it is but you and God working together in the garden of Love. All else is a distraction.

In the **First Waters**, often beginners in their zeal to be virtuous are tempted to see the faults of others. Teresa says the security of the Soul lies in its ability to cease being anxious regarding others. It is better to be concerned with watching ourselves and pleasing God. It is a good practice, no matter what stage of prayer we are practicing, to never neglect self-examination. No Soul advances so far as to not require this element of self-knowledge. Teresa states that in prayer, good intentions for others are a mistake. She has experienced this herself and often witnessed it in others. The mind is best set on looking at the virtues and good qualities in others while asking for God's grace in dealing with ourselves. If we focus an overactive mind on meditating on the Passion or the greatness of God, then God leads us to more supernormal ways. As another remedy, we might ask, what of the pains that Jesus suffered? Who was it that suffered? And can we summon the Love and understanding with which he suffered his ordeal?

Having labored intensely in the beginning stages, we move into the **Second Water**, where drawing the water for the garden takes on a different dimension, *Prayer of Quiet*. The gardener now draws more water with less effort, finding increasing rest in the process. A quiet fills us, bringing greater peace of mind and Spirit. Grace draws closer and closer, revealing itself more clearly and the soul now savors the new pleasure. Here, the will is so occupied that it is taken captive, consenting wholly to becoming God's prisoner. There remains no liberty to Love anyone but God. Tears are now tears of Joy as the labor finds less weariness in the *Prayer of Quietude*. The Soul is rising,

rising from its animal instincts and compulsions, receiving intimations of the exceeding joys of Heaven. Virtue is imparted and God begins communing with the Soul. The Soul arriving in this state begins to lose interest in Earthly delights—the riches, the honors, and estates, as they are so inferior to the newfound satisfaction. This is true Joy, a content that is pleasurable and satisfying.

Teresa says experiencing this state comes at the pleasure of the Lord, and no matter how many austerities we adopt, it is only through the Lord that Joy continues. She is uncertain how to articulate this satisfaction or whence it comes, indicating many things demand learning, but learning does not address how it comes on or how it's maintained. This state simply must be experienced by the gardener. There is nothing to read, nor is there anything to do, as little exists that explains the state. But here the splendor of the garden's fragrance fills the Soul. Here we find service to God by simply walking in the garden. Yet the Soul still has much to do to gain full understanding.

Many souls venture into this stage of prayer, but few advance beyond it. Since there is such joy and repose, most hesitate to advance, fearing they might lose what they have worked so hard to attain. Teresa says just as this state was attained by the blessing of the Lord, so is it maintained by the blessing of the Lord. But by-and-by, the will calls back the intellect and memory, and alas, challenges arise. At this juncture, Teresa recalls her own weaknesses and admonishes us to keep ourselves in high esteem and on the path of prayer, even though it's rocky.

Many come to loathe the path of faith that got them to the point of peace, but the practice must continue. There comes a greediness for the sweetness once experienced, and we try in every way to rekindle the sweetness, but in so doing, we only douse the Spiritual flame we've been nourishing in the garden. Even so, a tiny spark of God still rests within. This tiny spark is God's signpost. In due course, it will again throw out its mighty flame. Residing in God's light, we see He will not abandon us if we keep to the path of faith without cessation.

When these times come, Teresa says to stay quiet, do not amass piles of rationale as to why we don't deserve that which we have received. Instead, keep the intellect quiet, pay it no heed, as it only distracts and causes commotion. If we cave to the mind's seemingly great learned arguments, we extinguish the Light. Return to prayer and praise the goodness of God. Trust the favors God has blessed us with, know they are true, and rebuke the notion they are mere delusions. Know God is with us and therefore we can choose to be loving and grateful.

Moving into Teresa's **The Third Water**, *Total Absorption in God*, she talks of the changes in the garden—how God is now by her side, watering. The Lord is pleased to be her assistant, moreover, He is the gardener Himself. God is merging with Teresa. The gardener is now drenched in sweetness to such an extent the delights are rendering her, as Teresa, powerless to carry on in a normal fashion. The gardener is dying to the world and finding great Joy in the death of all worldly things.

Teresa says the Soul knows not whether to laugh or weep as there exists a sort of heavenly paradox where true wisdom is now acquired effortlessly. At this stage, where an uptick of profound experiences unfolds, Teresa fails to fully understand. As a result, she declines further commentary, feeling there is not complete union of her faculties. That is, her intellect becomes of little use, while her awareness determines she clearly has entered a more advanced Spiritual stage. She claims there exists an intoxication, a bewilderment she didn't understand and yet felt, without question, to be the workings of God.

For Teresa, it's like the flowers in her garden bloomed and sent out a delightful fragrance. The task at hand is to enjoy the pleasure and delight in the fragrance. This takes a measure of courage, as in so doing it seems the Soul may just up and leave the body!

The wisdom she attempted to gain over the last twenty years through endless intellectual effort has departed in but a moment. It's as if the fruit ripened, and the gardener is seemingly sustained by the garden alone. The virtues are grander than ever as the gardener has simply consented to God's grace while rejoicing in their captivity.

As the mystic, Teresa describes prayer as a process of courting and realizing her union with God—the process of fully shedding the ego, where the two transform as One. In **The Fourth Water**, *Ecstasy Consciousness,* Teresa says there are no terms to define the *Divine Union of Mind, Soul, and Spirit as One.* She explains it is as though a flame leaps high out of the fire, although seemingly separate, it is not a different thing than the fire itself.

The raising of the Spirit into union with God comes with Heavenly Love, but for Teresa this union is not the same as the elevation that takes place within the union. She says a small flame and a large flame are both fire, but a large flame will melt a piece of iron more rapidly than the smaller one. She expounds, the flame pours from the virtue of obedience, the greater the obedience to God, the greater the favor.

The gardener sees the falling rain nourishing the garden when least expected, stating it often pours after long mental prayer. Within this bliss, it is useless to attempt bodily activities. The eyes cannot perceive, and the ears lack understanding. All physical attributes vanish; all to maximize the bliss. When we perceive we are in the presence of God, there is a sense that God is ALWAYS close at hand. Teresa asks the Lord what is understood in this state of prayer? How is the Soul occupied? The Lord replies, *"It dissolves utterly my daughter, to rest more and more in Me. It is no longer itself that lives; it is I. As it cannot comprehend what it understands, it understands by not understanding."*[1]

Though Teresa's accomplishments are inspirational and profound, she makes many statements counter to how the Ascended Masters address the practice of prayer. Her approach projects a sense of guilt in being human, lamenting the machinations of the self. It appears to be her way of shedding the ego, slaying her inner demons, but its severity lacks respect and acceptance of herself and her process. She continually refers to herself as stupid, wicked, and miserable, saying we must recognize our unworthiness, claiming she is slack in her ability to serve and doesn't deserve what she's been afforded:

"O my Creator, do not pour so precious a liquid into so broken a vessel. For you have seen already how often I spill it."[2]

Throughout her Spiritual and self-revelations, her Spiritual development is obvious, but her extreme distaste for herself is overbearing. Understandable, though, as she was so steeped in the Catholic traditions of her era. She lived in a world where self-loathing, guilt, and damning sin were the norm, where nuns relied on confessors as superiors who admonished them to observe reprimands and recommendations.

As we have mentioned, and as the Masters make clear, a practice of relying on superiors is not a Spiritual solution. The steps of prayer are particular to each person. No one practice fits all, save faith and perseverance. We believe if alive today, St. Teresa's conversation around prayer and her self-characterizations would be much different, more akin to simply returning to faith and prayer without damning herself for indulging in what she considered a sinful thought. Possibly, simply directing more kindness towards herself.

FORTY-TWO

THE POWER OF PRAYER AND AFFIRMATION

B OTH St. Teresa and Mary Baker Eddy attained profound success in rejecting the form of the body as real, determining it to be an illusion. This is a Truth acknowledged by the Ascended Masters, but as we have mentioned, a partial Truth, and if we look to the Ascended Masters' commentary, we find a secondary Truth revealed.

Reviewing the Chapter on the Ascended Masters, we'll remember accounts of Masters who attained Physical Immortality. In so doing, they raised their bodily vibration to a rate whereby physical substance possessed the same vibration as Spiritual substance. As a result, that which was physical became Physically Immortal, or what we could call *Spiritualized physical material rendered Immortal!* There are many Masters in different Spiritual traditions throughout the world who state the body and physical world are illusions, but it is the Ascended Masters who give voice to the Reality of Physical Immortality.

Let's now turn to investigate the Masters' concepts and thoughts behind prayer and affirmation. What is an affirmation or a prayer but creation springing from the cradle of our consciousness. It starts with Jesus' statement, *"I and the Father are One."* To be effective in formulating affirmations, we must know an affirmation comes from the Illumination of the Father. A prayer created in the mind does not have the Power of a prayer created in the heart. If we are still, existing in the heart, we need not fret over the wording of an affirmation, as all worries originate in the mind. If we rest in the heart, we will source the Power from which effective affirmations arise. Looking for a Power beyond the Self is believing in an unreality! We therefore must have faith that Power resides within us and can be expressed through prayers and affirmations.

The fulfillment of affirmations is based on what the Masters refer to as control of the "Inner World" or "Inner Reality." This Inner Reality is the Living God. The Masters tell us to feel it on a deep emotional level, letting the Power move through us. All Good and Love and Truth exist within this Power, and when it comes from within the heart, it manifests in the fulfillment of an affirmation. When the Power is expressed as Goodness and Love, there arises Eternal Joy! The Masters contend that when we feel the Power of Truth, we become one with the Father. Here, there is Unity! The presence of the Living God fills us. With this Unity, we are aligned with perfection, radiating the Christ within.

The creation of an affirmation requires some necessary prerequisites. When we create an affirmation, we must own it! Put our stamp of originality upon it! Let the creative God express itself, knowing we and God are one with every fiber of our being. We begin by releasing all doubts from the mind. St. Teresa encourages us to have faith in the stillness and peace of Reality. There is no need for searching or discovery. An affirmation is the call of the Christ within. The Masters direct us to feel the words radiating from the stillness of the heart and declare that they come from the Power of the consuming God within. This is the ground from which magic arises and miracles occur. No person can get us there. We must enter this sacred ground through our Faith and Love, with the absolute, Spiritual knowing that we and the Father are one!

The act of affirming or praying creates a gift moving from one to another, similar to the idea of the blessing of Shaktipat. The Masters remind us to feel gratitude for being given the opportunity to interact in this experience of life. As we state an affirmation, a transfer of energy is put into motion, and with the knowledge of the power behind its expression, we are moving from superstition to what Mary Baker Eddy would call repeatable Divine Law, knowing that all is in Perfect Order.

When we form a prayer or affirmation, it is an emphatic statement of our Truth. There is no request or plea to a Force outside the Self! In effect, we are making a command for the fulfillment of Divine Principle through ourselves as Divine Beings. From this understanding, an enactment of the Cosmic Power streams forth from the conscious mind now acting as one with the Father. The two are linked. This union with the higher Self is the mover, the creator, and the fulfiller of prayers and affirmations.

With this understanding, let's form some affirmations. The Masters suggest that we feel the Power and presence of the living God within— the *I Am that I Am.* We begin by entering the Magical Power of Mind and Spirit! By creating our own affirmations from our individualized consciousness and saying them three times, we establish their Power. In this way, our affirmation becomes a statement of devotion to God.

Here are some examples of affirmations along the lines of the Masters' instructions:

+ The Power of God comes from within

+ I and the Power of God are One

+ God's Light and Love radiate from my heart

+ All goodness radiates from my heart

+ In my perfect stillness, I know the Truth

+ I create, create, create from this Truth

- My Truth is sweeping the world
- It consumes all humanity with perfect Love
- Through the Power of Love, the world is at Peace
- Where there is Peace and Love, no war can exist
- I declare all are lifting into God
- God, God, God, my every breath is God
- Through the Power, I am free, free, free
- I give of myself, affirming life, decreeing God's Light brings perfect Peace

The key is not what is spoken. It is not in the form or process. It is what is felt during the formation and repetition of affirmations!

The Masters ask, as you read the affirmations, what did you feel? Did you feel the Power of the Ecstasy St. Teresa felt in *The Fourth Water of prayer?* The Masters say to let that Power and energy animate our affirmations.

In addition, the Masters' caution, when we direct this Power towards personal health, personal fulfillment, protection, world peace, or whatever our imagination creates, we must keep in mind the Golden Rule so as not to violate any person's rights.

Here are some examples of affirmations to address a health concern:

- God's Power is ever present in my being
- God's force is the Light
- I magnify the Light now, now, now
- I direct this all-consuming Light to my mother (spouse, relative, or friend)
- I focus the Light on the cancer in her stomach
- The Light burns away every atom, molecule, and tissue of cancer
- The damaged tissue is replaced by perfect Christ cellular tissue
- My mother is restored and rejuvenated in the Light of God

- My mother has perfect health now, now, now

- I am grateful for the healing Light of God

Following the sincere effort to send affirmations, it is good to rest in knowing that virtue has gone forth and our faith has made the difference.

We must keep in mind that thoughts are things operating on all levels of our being. They are real, tangible forces put into motion.

So the Masters suggest, do not casually approach affirmations, looking for a quick moment to do our good deed for the day. It is best to take time out from our routine and give of ourselves. In this way, we can rejoice in being an Emissary of Light.

When we send affirmations to another, our affirmations are engaging with the physical, mental, astral, emotional, vibrational, Spiritual, and monadic bodies of the person to whom we are sending healing. Results can manifest in any one of these various bodies, so they may not be obvious on the physical level. We can be grateful the Power lies within us, and we have been given the opportunity to humbly send sacred energies. There should be no concern about immediate results, as healing may manifest sometime down the road.

FORTY-THREE

DEATH
AND AFTERLIFE

U TTER PANDEMONIUM BREAKS OUT ON THE TITANIC AS THE
bow of the "Wonder of the Twentieth Century" tilts skyward,
pitilessly descending into the icy depths of the North Atlantic Ocean.
William Stead, a passenger and London newspaper editor, finds himself in full-on panic, fighting for his life. An animated suspense ensues.
He muses, just where is he? Then he recognizes several friends who
passed earlier and realizes he has joined them in Spirit. With this
awareness, he finds death to be but a stepping from one room into
another.

Unexpectedly, as he scans the room, he finds the appointments
shockingly similar. Once his distress subsides, he reaches out to
assist those frightened by the trauma, who are very much in need of
emotional assistance. Throughout the episode, he experiences only a
marginal separation from his final demise, as he still exists so close to
Earth he could witness all the chaos unfolding.

The aforementioned experience is gleaned from the book *The Blue
Island*, communicated by William T. Stead, who passed on the sinking
of the Titanic, April 15, 1912. These thoughts are related through the
automatic writing of William Pardoe in the presence of Estelle Stead,
William's daughter. An ardent believer in Spiritualism, William Stead,

spearheaded investigative journalism. At the time of his death, he was in transit to establish a psychic clearing house in New York City for cataloguing genuine psychic experiences.

The Masters refer to *The Blue Island* as one of the best references to understanding the immediate events occurring after death, as well as gaining clarity into the Spirit Realms. But Stead's thoughts regarding his death experience are in stark contrast to the immediate death events described in *The Tibetan Book of the Dead*, which is considered by many, especially in the East, the primary textbook regarding the science of dying.

Let's take a moment to investigate the *Tibetan Book of the Dead*, or *Bardo Thödol*, as written in the Tibetan language. If the book were simply folklore or hypothetical conjecture, it would be easy to dismiss, but the book is considered a key to understanding the innermost recesses of the human mind by Swiss psychiatrist and psychoanalyst Dr. Carl Jung and a legitimate guide to liberation from the standpoint of *Tibetan Mahayana Buddhism*. There exist comparisons with the *Egyptian Book of the Dead*, where some claim they both originate culturally from similar ground and use nearly identical funeral rites. What we know for sure is the *Bardo Thödol* descends from the highest snowy ranges of Tibet, where the elusive, ghostly Himalayan Snow Leopard makes its home; Tibetan Lamas present passages from the book at a person's passing, and Timothy Leary redesigned the book as a guidebook for an acid trip!

The *Bardo Thödol* was translated into the English language by Walter Evans-Wentz, who called it the *Tibetan Book of the Dead*. According to Donald Lopez, an acclaimed Buddhist scholar, the book is not Tibetan, not a book for that matter, nor about death, and is much more American than Tibetan, owing much debt to Madame Blavatsky, since Evans-Wentz was a great admirer of Blavatsky. From our read, Lopez took offense with Blavatsky's association with Spiritualism and questioned the validity of her accounts.

Historians say the *Bardo Thödol* was written in approximately 800 CE by Padmasambhava, also known as Guru Rimpoche, the Indian founder of the Nyingma school of Tibetan Buddhism, the original and oldest of the four branches of Tibetan Buddhism. The *Bardo Thödol* was first introduced to the West by Madam Blavatsky and the Theosophical *"Mahatma Letters,"* not Evans-Wentz. The late Lama Kazi Dawa-Samdup believes that Blavatsky was intimately familiar with Lamaistic Teachings, and he claimed she was an initiate with knowledge on the subject.

If we are to side-step Lopez's comments, which some feel are biased, and assume the book presents valid ideas about death, we would say the *Tibetan Book of the Dead* represents a viable guide for vulnerable sojourners. It attempts to ease the anxiety of the dying process as we move through unfamiliar terrain into the other world.

The word Bardo translates literally to mean "between two" and refers to the time between death and rebirth. At first glance, it acts as a treatise on the art of dying; secondly, it instructs trusted Spiritual teachers and loved ones on how to guide and console those passing by presenting instructions to recite to their loved one at the time of passing; and thirdly, it outlines the experiences the deceased may face in the intermediate period following death and how best to negotiate what they are confronting.

The purpose, the crux, of the entire book is to awaken the dreamer into Reality by illuminating the limbo terrain existing between death and rebirth. Instructions act as guides at each Bardo stage to guide the deceased through the changing phenomena of the Bardo states, and if followed, assist in liberating them into the Clear Light, eliminating the need to once again experience rebirth.

The *Bardo Thödol* explains that after death, there are three Bardo states. The first is called the *Chikhai Bardo*, occurring at the moment of death, where the deceased may be unaware of passing. In this first

Bardo, the Clear Light dawns, revealing the primordial purity of the transitional state. This is the state most conducive to awakening the deceased to the Pure Reality of the Clear Light. It is radiant, shining, and thrilling, our true nature! With this recognition, we are liberated and don't devolve back into physical form, which some consider the second death.

According to *Mahayana Buddhism*, most are unable to hold onto the transcendental state of the Clear Light as it is karmically obscured, so they transit into the second Bardo, called the *Chönyid Bardo*. This is the transitional state whereby the deceased faces hallucinations, projections based on the deceased's consciousness and karma. The deeper our attachment, the more unsettling and harrowing the images.

The *Chönyid Bardo* goes into these states in some detail, describing the peaceful and wrathful deities the dying person may face. Generally, the deceased first encounters peaceful deities that are more feeling-oriented—heart-born. If they realize these visions are issuing from their own psychology, they are set free into Reality; if not, their karma presents more wrathful, ghoulish reflections, eventually triggering the rebirth process. It must be noted, as the Masters suggest, although these apparitions appear real, there are no heavens or hells other than the mental content within the deceased's psychology. The visions are hallucinations, no matter how real they may appear. This, the *Bardo Thödal* repeatedly, emphatically states.

The last Bardo, the *Sidpa Bardo*, is the state where reincarnation happens if the Clear Light is not recognized. As such, the deceased begins to descend into sexual fantasies, leading back to seeking a womb. This entire encounter, unraveling in the limbo state from death to rebirth, is said to take forty-nine days as outlined in the *Tibetan Book of the Dead*. But in listening to the Ancient Ones, through Reverend Rhinehart's mediumship, we hear the stay can be extended much longer.

The Bardo descriptions and the Masters' thoughts both likely have merit, but we would reiterate that the consciousness of the deceased determines the nature of the experience. The enlightened experience the Clear Light; the partially enlightened and unenlightened would likely not, so their immediate experiences would not necessarily resemble each other in content nor length of stay.

Dr. Carl Jung is recognized as one of the early Westerners to become a fan of the *Tibetan Book of the Dead*. He said the book represented the psychological states of the dying person's mind, indicating the *Chönyid Bardo* is the reality of thought, fantasies that take on real form. Jung goes on to say the entire book is created out of the archetypal content of man's unconscious, the data of psychic experience. Each of the five *Dhyani Buddhas* the deceased confronts on its downward cycle through the *Chönyid Bardo* is no more than psychological data. To Jung, even though the deceased is now in the Spirit Realms, ultimately, all is psychological content. In somewhat of a contrast, the Masters discuss seven different vehicles of consciousness with which we perceive, the mind being only one, whether we are in the physical or Spirit.

The question becomes, can we "know" without the use of the mind? Can the death experience be held within one of our other vehicles of consciousness without mental interpretation? If so, the death experience would differ for each individual based on their level of consciousness.

If we revisit William Stead's death experience, along with many stories of NDEs (Near Death Experiences), and statements made by the Ancient Ones, we believe the *Thödal Bardo/Tibetan Book of the Dead* gives us an Eastern perspective. We would suggest it is culturally biased, or more correctly, culture-specific, especially in terms of the nature of visionary images confronted in the *Chönyid Bardo* state. True, the wisdom comes to us from wise, enlightened Tibetan lamas, but still living lamas, not from Masters who have overcome the life/death cycle.

A Hindu, a Catholic, a Muslim, or an Aborigine would likely confront different imagery. It is our belief the *Bardo Thödol* should be used as a guideline that opens the mind to possibilities that may arise at death. The Masters infer the emphasis is on confronting the nature of our Mind as an evidential truth. If we refer to *The Mahatma Letters,* the most important message regarding death is that what we hold in the mind and heart at the time of death will determine our experience. The Master Koot Hoomi suggests this vision is either the bliss or woe fashioning our future.

Picking up from where we left off with William Stead's death experience, we continue to discern a different type of experience than we find elaborated in the *Tibetan Book of the Dead*:

The Titanic continued sinking as time rolled on until hundreds of bodies drifted aimlessly in the frigid Atlantic waters—dead! Yet as Stead watched, hundreds of souls elevated through the air, alive—yes, ALIVE! He noticed they felt incensed at their inability to save their treasures. Despair quickly arose—what of their loved ones back home? What was to come? Were they about to see their God? Would there be a punishment? What, what, what... ?

Then, according to Stead, in one extraordinary motion, the entire scene leapt to a completely different locale. The deceased were tossed through the air at high speed, but so gently no insecurity stirred. The sense of time escaped, but they could see from afar a beautiful land abounding with Light. It seemed to be a place for those who passed suddenly. For those unsettled spirits, the place became a respite to recapture their emotional and mental equilibrium. Surprisingly, all appeared quite physical, not unlike the world they left. Upon their arrival, they met old friends and relatives from earthly life, seamlessly parting ways with the folks from the Titanic.[1]

As you can gather, this "Titanic death experience" is not the frightening apparitions outlined by the Lamas, but more akin to what we might expect of someone passing who had experienced life from the vantage of living in the West. Many feel the afterlife is a total mystery, unknowable no matter what, but we have found if we are curious enough, this is not the case. To grasp it fully, admittedly a stretch, but knowledge is out there for those who are motivated. Many NDEs give us a glimpse of the immediate events transpiring after death. Over nine million NDEs have been reported in the United States alone. Some report after seeing an overpowering Light and feeling a wonderful peace, they return to their bodies experiencing significant changes in their lives. Others describe Spiritual awakenings, or the lack of fearing death, or perhaps renewed appreciation of life. But it is through scientifically tested mediums such as Reverend Rhinehart that we have the opportunity to attain trusted, real insights into the death experience and beyond.

Through Reverend Rhinehart's mediumship, the Masters give us an understanding of the physical, astral, emotional, and mental terrains in the land of Spirit. One of the first things they discuss is the nature of thought. As we know from *Thought Forms*, by Annie Besant and C.W. Leadbeater, thoughts are things that are profoundly evident in the Spirit World. They create distinct and visible forms in the astral plane, influencing the Spiritual world. We can't shift identities like a chameleon according to our capricious impulses.

In Spirit, all true emotions and thoughts are revealed in colorful, etheric emanations radiating from our consciousness, floating close to our astral bodies. Our actual thoughts are stamped on our foreheads, so to speak. Here, no hidden agendas are possible. The good, the bad, and the unspeakable are lit up right there for all to see. Unscrupulous thoughts like self-pity, hate, and vengeance, if not curbed and mastered, eventually lead to rebirth, according to the Masters.

In the Spirit Realms, there exists perpetual Light, constantly dawning on the new arrivals. Once in Spirit, the deceased looks down upon the discarded body, feeling freed from old identities, free to create anew. Without the encumbrance of the physical body, the Spirit senses the time has come to explore the inner self. This self confronts shocking revelations when first viewing its undisguised emotions and thoughts. But no matter how impure, no matter how unforgivable the supposed sins, the Spirit realizes there exists the possibility of a new beginning, fresh, free from past identity, free from earthly enslaving, dominating powers, free from all limitations.

In Spirit, there is no Heaven and there is no Hell. In the Spirit Realms, Heaven and Hell are notions carried from Earth, or imaginings created there. The slate begins clean in the Spirit Realms. Even the most accomplished new arrivals set out to cleanse themselves, for now is the time to see with eyes born of innocence and purity, experience all the surrounding beauty in the new environment, untainted from the past. Old, worn-out beliefs are washed away. No longer do influences from our past religions, education, and family prejudices dominate our thinking. By shedding the past, we discover the Spiritual Self nested deep within.

The Masters tell us that once awareness dawns in the "Great White Spirit Land," we may find ourselves traveling on a river of Light. On the riverbank, we find old friends and family gathered to welcome us home. After the rejoicing, we are guided to a plane of consciousness prepared for our arrival based on our thoughts and deeds generated upon the Earth Plane. In short, we are guided to the Schools of Transcendentalism, a realm where we find new educational opportunities and extended senses well beyond our past five senses on Earth.

Though true freedom is reachable, some only wish to engage in their familiar rituals and routines, whether it be Catholics, Protestants, Muslims, Buddhists, American Indians, Aboriginals, or African tribes. Feeling comfortable doesn't come easily for all, and a sense of fear may arise. In such cases, we may end up roaming the lower Astral Planes or finding ourselves drawn back to the familiarity of our corpse. Death's foreboding sting evaporates, though, when we allow the attachment to past distinctions to dissolve.

The Masters send their love, but if the new arrivals are to progress, they must open to the nature of their new reality. They must follow their guides into the Light and Spirit Schools of Learning, ignoring the religious or cultural constraints that pertain only to their former Earthly beliefs.

William Stead reflects that once the deceased become residents in the Spirit Realms, many think the new inhabitants possess a key to unleashing all wisdom and knowledge. Suddenly, they are the wisest of the wise, omnipotent, capable of seeing with total clarity into the future and past.

Numerous queries were put to Stead regarding this idea. Now viewing from the vantage of Spirit, he implies the change from the physical to Spirit doesn't instantly render a person a part of the Eternal Deity. We are not necessarily more knowledgeable about the eternal questions, nor the tantalizing follies. The mysteries aren't immediately available, but open slowly to those who persist. That revealed, once in Spirit, we can generally see somewhat farther down the road, possessing a bit more knowledge than the average Earthly resident. [2]

Others query, if the afterlife is so marvelous, why do we exist in this world of stand-up comedy and tragic heartbreak? Why do we struggle so? What's keeping us from simply entering the "Great White Spirit Land" at will?

The Ancient Ones imply if we use our Earthly existence in an expansive manner, feeling into our hearts, we can discover this great land residing beyond the veil, even while in the body. Whether we find ourselves living in the body or in Spirit, on whatever plane, it is good to remind ourselves these new experiences are all phases of consciousness, each opening new awareness.

It must be noted that many, while in the body experiencing extreme emotional or physical pain, attempt to run from their hardships, thinking that in death they can magically escape. The Masters say this is not the case; we must face our hardship either while on the Earth or in the afterlife. (This is addressed further in Chapter 46, Suicide and Assisted Death.) Still others feel death is a fearsome prospect, but as William Stead suggests, it is as basic as stepping from one room to another. After death, the next breath is simply of Spirit.

FORTY-FOUR

NEWCOMERS TO
THE SPIRIT REALMS

A RRIVING IN THE AFTERLIFE CAN BE SOMEWHAT STARTLING
TO some. The Masters tell a story about a tour for new arrivals
recently killed in war. To acclimate the newcomers to the Astral
Realms, the Masters first guided the deceased soldiers through some of
the Astral Hospitals. The men were frankly astonished, commenting,
"Why do hospitals exist here? Damn, our bodies were obliterated,
abandoned, a total wreck, yet we are not laid up in these hospitals."
The Ancient Ones explained that a deceased person attached to pain,
hatred, circumstance, or sickness carries those afflictions into the
Spirit Realms, ending up in Astral Hospitals, a transitory stage for
healing. The Masters used this tour as a guide for the soldiers to help
them better understand the nature of the afterlife.

The Masters explain that the Spirit World is not a hideout or a
quick escape route from whatever torments us. They suggest if we
let go of the clinging and grasping, we will find the silence of God's
eternal heartbeat. In this way, we move with the currents of life that
God thrusts upon us. No matter the comedy nor the tragedy we
have endured on Earth, the hereafter is not somewhere out there,
but rather, always breathing through us. One moment dies into
another and another. Each inhalation is an expansive aliveness, each

exhalation is a contracting, death of sorts. This life-death cycle repeats itself throughout our lives, regardless of our situation, relationships, or locale. We have all moved in and out of our bodies from time immemorial. When death is at hand, the Soul who has experienced the personality's death countless times finds the terrain surprisingly familiar! By living life to its fullest, we will live death to its fullest!

As the Masters emphasize, all Life is a learning. Whether in the Spiritual or physical side of life, learning is a constant. That is why, once we land on the "White Shores" of the Spirit Realm, and the rejoicing with our loved ones comes to a close, we are led by our guides into the teaching halls where we learn to adjust to the Spirit World.

At this point, new arrivals in resistance don't move on until adjusted. Those who are struggling, in resistance to flowing with the situation, are often the ones who passed while young and restless. They could be suicides, the victims of abrupt accidents without warning, and other sudden and violent ends. Some are paralyzed, waiting for Clarion's call to blare and for Jesus to ceremoniously escort them to Heaven. These are usually the most resistant and stubborn, refusing to follow their guides. These spirits may move to another part of the Astral World, according to the dictates of their consciousness.

However, most newcomers, along with some who first resisted and are now sufficiently adjusted, enter the Halls of Learning. The majority are elderly, closely resembling how they looked when in the body. There exists in these halls an odd hodgepodge of characters, all of whom are determined to integrate into the Spirit World.

According to the Ancient Ones, once the new arrivals have been introduced to the Spirit World, they find the trees, flowers, and skies quite similar to those on Earth. Many sights and sounds seem familiar, even though at first they may have difficulty grounding themselves in their new surroundings. Their guides appear to slip in and out of the scene and events happen in less than a predictable fashion.

Some are feeling exuberant, bursting at the seams, ready to jump in. Those who have recently adjusted, such as the sick, are feeling quite renewed. Those who lost limbs are once again functioning perfectly, restored to normal. For many, there is the sense they are genuinely reborn, birthed anew into the Spiritual Realms! The time is upon them to let go of past loved ones and move into the adventures awaiting. In life, we each possess different levels of understanding, awareness, and insights, this is the same experience in the Spirit Realms.

Most religious doctrines, ancient texts, and the Masters agree that where a person ends up in terms of the spheres and planes of existence in the Spirit Realms is ultimately determined by actions and attainments while on Earth. Despite each of us possessing an astral body, once comfortably established in Spirit, it is quickly discovered the use of the astral body is noticeably different; now we find we can shift locations with the use of the mind! It may be awkward, but with instruction, we learn how to improve these abilities. Our bodies, astral, emotional, mental, vibrational, Spiritual, monadic, are real, but most are still limited in use and under the direction of their guides.

This process can be extremely disturbing to some. There are those who simply can't adjust, and they are guided back to the previous locales where they first landed, while others who are supremely disturbed move back into proximity to the Earthly homes they left behind. But in every case, all arrivals are urged to leave the past behind and move forward, extricating themselves from their past identities—no matter how famous, how loved, or how insignificant they may have felt.

The newcomers eventually find new awareness creeping in. For instance, time is unusual, appearing to almost stop, and events seem most strange. Slowly, old friends begin to appear mixed in with new acquaintances as though the newcomer stopped off at an old, frequented pub, only to find the unfamiliar now dominating the scene!

However, it is consciousness that has mostly changed, and the guides assure the new arrivals that there's no way around that fact.

As learning increases, clairaudience and clairvoyance play a much bigger role in the moment-to-moment experiences, opening previously unknown abilities. In time, there exists a knowing similar to the knowing experienced in deep meditation but issuing from newly acquired organs. New arrivals may begin seeing all sides of an object at once, or see the object from the inside out. New colors, sounds, and smells arise, bringing unexpected excitement. Communication is more extrasensory and non-verbal. Eventually, the newcomer refines the ability to send deeper experiential events to another on a variety of sensory levels, all transpiring through newly developed organs not formerly possessed on Earth.

As the new arrivals evolve, education becomes more profound. They freely chose courses to their liking, evolving at their own speed. If it is all too much, a new arrival can move back into a relationship with those who feel similarly. This may mean moving into cities and situations that accommodate a person's comfort levels within the Spirit Realm.

For the most part, anything is open to the newcomers except something that would inhibit Spiritual growth. Little by little, the new arrivals begin to develop a love and passion for Spiritual life, Spiritual thought, meditation, and Spiritual Love, a love expressed without a reward other than that of Love itself. New concepts will be faced, humbling the most intellectual and religiously inclined. The Ancient Ones admonish us to accept the strangeness of it all, bizarre though it may be, not looking back, trusting and following the guides. Welcome to the Spirit Realms!

FORTY-FIVE

PLANES OF HABITATION

NOW THAT WE HAVE GOTTEN A FEEL FOR WHAT IT'S LIKE TO arrive in the "Great White Land," let's investigate its neighborhoods, characteristics, and distinctions. Madame Blavatsky refers to these places as "The Spheres and Planes of Habitation and Existence." The Spirit World is simply a different dimension from the physical world. Some call it the afterlife or Heaven. We suspect you'll find it decidedly different from the worldly concepts where cherubs frolic, lounging in cloud-like amphitheaters, plucking guilted harps, wafting out boring, melodic sounds, while sporting the goofiest of grins. Most assuredly, it is a much more diverse multiverse than any idyllic, paradisiacal land one might initially fancy. What are these planes of consciousness that we inhabit here and after death? Madame Blavatsky states in her Theosophical writings there is a seven-fold nature of man which is reflective of the seven-fold nature of the universe; man being the microcosm of the greater macrocosm—as above, so below.

Many assume that once we arrive in Spirit, we are anchored in one plane of consciousness at a time, maybe the mental or emotional plane. In reality, we may be partly involved in all the levels of consciousness in one form or another. The plane that is primary for us is the plane that designates our level of consciousness. When we are physical, it is our physical existence that usually dominates, but we can exist in mental and emotional bodies of consciousness simultaneously. Some of us sense that we live in a sort of delicate balance, operating on all levels at once. This is certainly possible, but to find ultimate balance in them all, we must have balanced the Seventh Sphere of Consciousness. This is the terrain of the Masters, and rare.

The Ancient Ones delineate the situation this way: Surrounding the Earth Plane are seven spheres of habitation, each sphere is divided into seven planes, and each of these seven planes is again divided into seven sub-planes. 7 spheres x 7 planes = 49 levels x 7 sub-planes = 343 total planes of habitation or possible locales of existence. Immediately, one can determine this depiction is not a classical Greek rendition of Hades, or a lush tropical island inhabited by scantily clad women, seductively gyrating the hula, as imagined by some. No, it is a complex cosmic stratosphere accommodating every imaginable version of consciousness.

The seven major planes lie next to each other in varying stages of manifestation within every human being, within every group, and within every civilization. The Mind of each individual contains all levels of consciousness, all potentiality lies within, as does the potentiality of all good and all evil. Each individual is in constant motion, searching, attempting to expand and discover these levels of consciousness hidden within. The purpose of life is to find the life expression of these various levels of consciousness in all its possible manifestations, constantly expanding awareness while traversing through the manifestations of the seven spheres of consciousness.

As we've mentioned, the state of consciousness at the time of death determines the newcomer's plane of consciousness, or entry point into the Spirit planes after casting off the physical body. It might not appear this way, but each of us exists on different levels of consciousness. We exist in different states of awareness even though we may be functioning side-by-side, happily married, brother and sister, or compatible work associates. Planes of consciousness can be compared to levels of understanding, not necessarily places or specific locations, so they cannot be nailed down as such. Two planes, though similar, are not necessarily in close proximity. It is not like the intersection of Haight and Ashbury, Rodeo and Wilshire, or the crossroads of some medieval marketplace. The Spirit World is another dimension, much different than the physical dimension. As a different dimension, we wouldn't use the same type of language to describe it as we would use to describe the physical dimension of Earth. It simply is a place unto itself!

Some say the seven spheres that surround every planet of the entire universe have one sphere circumscribing the other, one circling the other, expanding outward until we reach seven spheres. Living in the physical, viewing from Earth, we would see seven bands, the final band extending infinitely until it merges with the seventh band of another planetary system. Others contend that one sphere with all its associated planes lies above the next, then the next sphere lies above the previous sphere and so on. This is the way in which the Masters visualize it, though it is only a close approximation. Each band is not only physical to a degree, but represents a change in consciousness, a change in awareness and understanding. In the Spirit World, we might visualize the seven spheres of consciousness as intertwined, existing in what we could call a general area surrounding or interpenetrating the planet. If we were to bring to mind the popular Lava Lamps of the sixties, we could grasp how two different elements, oil and water, interact with each other and yet remain separate and distinctly different, though existing right next to each other. We might imagine these different levels in this way. Throughout these levels of understanding, beings are in sync with the other inhabitants who possess similar levels of understanding; they all function in the same or a very similar vibration, making them more or less compatible.

As mentioned, we each possess a primary base of consciousness underlying our understanding, underlying all the other levels of consciousness within us, forming our foundation. If we are primarily a loving person, it colors our existence; likewise, if we are primarily mental in our makeup, this becomes the foundation that drives our consciousness, establishing in general terms the sphere and plane of habitation where we exist in the Spirit World. Surprisingly, each plane has its negative and positive aspects of manifestation. So, let's move into an exploration of the different levels and characteristics found in the various planes of consciousness.

THE PHYSICAL / ASTRAL PLANE OF CONSCIOUSNESS

The Ancient Ones indicate no plane of consciousness is better than another. Each level has a base level and each level has a masterly level. Once in Spirit, we find ourselves inhabiting these levels and evolving through them as our souls develop. A level existing in its highest form of perfection is good. The levels are only different from one another in that they manifest different aspects or characteristics of a particular plane of consciousness.

In the primary level of life—the first level, or the Physical Plane of Consciousness, it is the *Physical World* that grabs our attention: flesh, bones, and blood; concrete manifestations are what matter. Existing on this level, we find the intellect, emotions, intuition, and Spiritual understanding have little persuasion because there is mostly a strong attunement with nature. Living in harmony with our physical surroundings creates wonderment and fulfillment. It matters not if the culture is industrialized or savage; the beauty of nature and its diversity is what captures us on the Physical Plane. If we find objects of nature attracting us, we are likely existing in the primary Physical Level of Consciousness. Delightful bouquets, majestic mountains, ice cream decadence, athletic exhilaration, and wild fields of flaming

Lupine and Indian Paintbrush are likely fascinations. But there are some distinct differences between living in the physical and living in the Spiritual. Living in the physical body, we must bathe and care for the needs of the body. In Spirit, we cleanse the mind rather than the body. Thoughts accumulate around us like a trail of debris and build up in our wake. While in Spirit, we create a practice of cleansing that which collects around us.

The Astral Plane is lumped in with the Physical Realm because all physical reality is first created on the Astral Level of Consciousness. The Astral Level exists in the immediate spirit level of consciousness surrounding the Earth. It has its seasons, its trees, its rivers, buildings, and cities similar to the Earth Plane. The Astral Level is the first level humans pass through after death, and can be experienced as very physical. Just as William Stead described, death is the act of moving from one room to another, one level to another, the Physical to the Astral!

The Astral is situated between the Earth and the higher planes. It is the Astral Planes where one is cleansed of Earthly attachments and crutches, a sort of purgatory where desires are greatly magnified. This realm is referred to by the Greeks as Hades or the Underworld, Purgatory by the Catholics, and the Astral Plane by the mediæval alchemists. We readily associate the Tibetan Bardo levels with the Astral. Some of us spend years languishing in the lower Astral, especially those who are attached to Earthly delights. We, who remain in the lower Astral, are often referred to as Earth-bound. Once we release our attachments, we rise to higher levels of the Astral Realms of the afterlife. Here, nature is still the most important element. We would like to note the length of stay before taking on a new incarnation varies. For instance, a Tibetan Lama can reincarnate almost immediately, but typically, an average stay in the afterlife is for a period of two hundred Earth years, according to the Masters.

THE ETHERIC PLANE OF CONSCIOUSNESS

The Second Level of Consciousness is referred to as the Etheric Plane. For those of us existing on this plane, Karma Yoga (service) is the primary level of consciousness. Here, understanding the *Power of Action* is paramount; doing for others and doing for ourselves through action. A powerful desire to create dominates the mindset if our primary foundation is the Etheric Plane. In the process of bringing something into form, the key is manifesting our vision through using the forces of nature. Hobbyists, oriental carpet weavers, builders, and jewelers may be found in this domain, to name a few.

THE EMOTIONAL PLANE OF CONSCIOUSNESS

Those of us who function primarily on the Emotional Level of Consciousness live to *Emote*. We seek the pleasures of love, the thrill of the chase, or any dramatic endeavor; diametrically, we can exhibit a complete lack of emotion. Generally speaking, *Desire* rules the Emotional Level of Consciousness. As a result, we think in personal ways, love in personal ways, and feel in personal ways. Desires can have either a positive or a negative, or even a disastrous effect. When we desire in a negative way, those desires are expressed as possessiveness, jealousy, and fear, etc. In the positive sense, we operate from the base of love, understanding, patience, and admiration.

The entertainment industry often attracts those on the Emotional Level of Consciousness. Those in the humanitarian fields: health care workers, psychologists, and teachers, exhibit a deep sense of observation and caring. As observed by the Masters, most of Earth's inhabitants live their lives from the Emotional Level of Consciousness and consequently may reside on the emotional plane in the Spirit World. If we have mastered the emotional level, we don't experience great fear, hate, prejudice, anger, or any of the pernicious emotions.

THE MENTAL PLANE OF CONSCIOUSNESS

This is the Fourth Plane, the level where the *Intellect* captures our attention. Logic and reason dominate our consciousness on this level. Those of us existing on this level revel in thought, we love to learn, to analyze, and to know. These are scientists, computer programmers, and researchers who enjoy thinking and reading more than anything. Librarians, statisticians, and mathematicians jam the corridors of this plane of existence. Those existing primarily on the mental level don't necessarily like to feel emotionally, get sweaty and physical, or experience intense desire.

THE INTUITIVE OR VIBRATIONAL PLANE OF CONSCIOUSNESS

The Vibrational Level of Consciousness is designated as the Fifth Level of Consciousness. On this level of consciousness, the focus is to know, to feel, to understand the *Living Esssence* of things. Existing on the Vibrational Plane, we constantly reach out to understand our affinity with God, with Truth, and everything that we experience. While residing here, we search into a reality lying just behind the form of things.

The Essence Plane or Vibrational Plane is known as the Plane where things are not what they appear to be. By reaching out, we can suddenly understand the causation, the vibration of a given situation, what's really going on beyond the five senses. We spontaneously act in life, becoming strongly intuitive. There is a proclivity towards mysticism, possessing an intuitive sense for unraveling the mysteries shrouded behind the phenomena of the universe.

Like the other Planes, the Vibrational Plane has its negative and positive aspects. On the negative side, we do not exert a great deal of thought; we rely mostly on intuitive skills. We live from moment to moment, intuitively bouncing from situation to situation on a somewhat superficial level. If this is the main viewpoint of consciousness, it will color all the other levels from which we operate.

In the higher manifestations of the Vibrational Plane, we might be involved in the healing arts. At even deeper levels, we are intent on knowing the *Essence of Being*. This is the level of consciousness where the desire for mastery beyond intellectual constructs takes root. We begin to undergo a transformation whereby we spontaneously accept our responsibilities, our emotional experiences, and effortlessly acquire new intellectual and Spiritual ground. Our past resistances fall away. We don't necessarily stop desiring to be creative, stop our love affair with nature, or stop experiencing good and negative emotions. But we do start reflecting deeper into the essence of each situation, that thing which exists beyond the surface, the causation which finds its oneness and unity with the world. By functioning with the intent to know the oneness of all things, we interact in life primarily from the intuitive, within the Vibrational Level of Consciousness.

THE SPIRITUAL PLANE OF CONSCIOUSNESS

This is the Sixth Level of Consciousness. Our existence on this level is primarily engaged with *Religious and Spiritual* experiences. We want to get to the bottom of things at a Spiritual level. Although somewhat surprising, even the Spiritual Plane displays higher and lower aspects. Not all inhabiting the Spiritual Planes of Consciousness necessarily have an evolved picture of life. We can simultaneously be living in the Astral while existing in the Sixth Level of Consciousness. In the lower imperfect manifestations, ideas regarding religious beliefs are expressed in a dogmatic, limited fashion. Fundamentalism and rigid thought find their home in this neighborhood. Here lives the minister who passionately delivers a sermon on family values, then fornicates with a married choir member in the back room after his sermon. Unfortunately, as we have found in life, some of the most hypocritical behavior manifests in the Spiritual and devotional domains. But variation must exist! If all of us were the same in our interests and actions, many existing in this, or any realm, would go bonkers in short order. This is another area of consciousness where Earthly attachments tend to keep some of us earthbound after passing.

In the higher levels of the Spiritual Planes of Consciousness, we are reaching out to God, finding the non-emotional, non-intellectual, and more beautiful, compelling aspects of life. The intention is to gain an understanding of the unknown, the supernormal, the infinite. If mystical oneness is approached, a level of mastery allows us to expand into other dimensions of consciousness. At this level, we find value in gathering up the irrational, otherworldly, supernormal experiences and organizing them into religions and Spiritual groups. This is the level where consciousness demonstrates agape Love, Love existing beyond personal identification. It is Christlike, beyond emotions, beyond thought, radiating a purity that envelops all we encounter.

THE SOUL OR MONADIC PLANE OF CONSCIOUSNESS

Within the Soul Plane, we find the most complex and difficult to grasp level of consciousness. This is the level of the *Monadic Being*, existing in perfection, beyond emotion, thought, or experience. If we travel to the Mustang District in Nepal, perusing the ancient Sky Caves of yesteryear or wandering today's streets of Varanasi, Kathmandu, or Rishikesh in the East, we will discover some of the mendicants and sadhus who dwell on the Soul Plane of Consciousness. They are extraordinary, uncommon beings free from all dogma, free from all emotion, free from all thought, and free from everything discussed throughout the first six levels of consciousness. These beings inhabit the Seventh Level of Consciousness. Here, consciousness, the Soul or Monad, is the most conscious aspect of our being. By existing here, it's possible to observe the motion of it all, the expansion and growth through involution and evolution, as well as the process of the Monad consciously moving into individualization. On this level, the Soul takes command, the permanent, immutable *I AM that I AM.*

Here we emerge as a Soul, then a body. Our Immortality dons a personality. Yet, despite being in an exalted state, like the other planes, there exists a negative expression of the Soul Sphere of Consciousness.

It's called insanity! In its negative state of expression, schizophrenia and psychosis overwhelm us. Normal thoughts, emotions, and desires are mostly void. This state is difficult to express, but it closely resembles the irrational. Those of us living in the West often perceive the Tantric Ascetics, naked Nagas, and the colorful, sandalwood-slathered Sadhus, alms bowl in hand, as teetering on the fringe of madness; yet, in fact, they are symbolic of the consciousness of the Soul Body.

The Soul Plane of Consciousness can seem almost unfeeling and distant but in its most exalted, sublime state, it is the Monadic/Soul of life. It lives, understands, feels, and fully knows the personality side of us, it is the side that is at all times conscious. Yet it doesn't think or feel the way the personality thinks or feels. The Monadic (Soul) self doesn't know the dizzying heights of love or the sinking depths of fear and despair, but when perfected, it remains calm in all its aspects. When not perfected, it comes across as totally irresponsible, not functioning well with the rest of the world, and socially inappropriate. It is the one who knows without thought, just knows without trying to know. It is the very essence of the Divine Observer, undiluted by thought. We might compare it to **The Fourth Water,** *Ecstasy Consciousness* in St. Teresa's analogy of the garden in the cultivation of prayer. To the intellect, it is incomprehensible, an unintelligible mystery. It is the undisturbed radiant being witnessing through the personality. It has been described as higher super-consciousness, capable of gazing freely upon all lifetimes, upon all emotions, upon all experiences, and simply allowing the motion of it all to exist.

The Monad has no negative thought or emotional response to anything that comes its way; it just absorbs the essence of everything that a person thinks, feels, or does. This is the Buddha in all its glory. If we experience something ecstatic, generating happiness, the Monad looks on and simply radiates a loving vibration and just is. This is the Master essence within the highest plane of consciousness, the rarest of rare in human experience.

For each personality, these various levels of consciousness will appear prominent at times. To determine on which plane we might fall can be a tall order, but if we examine the foundation beneath our intent, that will assist us in determining the plane of existence where we might reside.

FORTY-SIX

SUICIDE AND ASSISTED DEATH

S UICIDE CAN FLASH THROUGH PEOPLE'S MINDS WHEN THINGS get dire and we feel vulnerable, when it appears we have no alternatives. If we tune into the contemporary commentary on suicide, we can hear a rush of new beliefs. They are indicative of the wide range of differing Spiritual beliefs we find in our ever-changing world. In some circles, we can hear, *"If God is all forgiving, all loving, why wouldn't He embrace the one who committed suicide in the same manner He accepted anyone who passed? Forgiveness is His way! It matters not the act!"* Or, as the British occultist Aleister Crowley (1875-1947) states, *"Do what thou wilt is the Law!"*

Then there are those who say eternal condemnation awaits those who take their own lives. We may hear others say, *"It's their body, and they have a right to do with it as they please."* For others who commit suicide, some assume they have been overtaken by Satan or have been subjected to a flurry of Satanic lies and pressured to commit suicide. Being of weak will, or succumbing to unbearable stress, or acting under Satan's persuasion, they willingly leave their uncertain futures. These are but a few reasons for such dire actions. However, based on Master Intelligence, we may view these reasons as unfortunately misinformed. Let's listen to what Master Intelligence has to say on the subject. Some of us might find their commentary surprising.

Lady Rasha lived and mastered in the days of Atlantis, and now resides on the Seventh Plane of the Seventh Sphere, the most elevated sphere of existence. When I first heard her query during a séance, I must admit I was shaken and left in a quandary. She posed a question, asking chelas to answer for themselves. Here is what we remember Lady Rasha querying through Reverend Rhinehart's mediumship:

Two men are facing a survival ordeal. One man lies weakened and near certain death, the other slightly stronger. If the stronger of the two believes he had the possibility of going on to perform great accomplishments for humanity, would it be the correct moral decision for the stronger man to take the weakened man's life, surviving by consuming the weakened man's flesh?

The dilemma rises fast, confronting our deepest moral understanding. What would the best answer be? There are many cases throughout history where this very scenario occurred, likely with varying results. What do you think Lady Rasha unequivocally stated? Here is her response:

No human has the right to extinguish the Christ Light existing within another human being's body, no matter the circumstance, no matter how illustrious or grand the survivor's future deeds may be. It is God's decision and God's alone.

Is there an exception to the rule? That is for each of us to decide. From the enlightened consciousness of Lady Master Rasha, taking another's life or taking our own, falls under the moral law forbidding us to extinguish the sacred Christ Light resident within a human heart.

Inherent in her question exists the additional question: Do we have the moral right to assist another at the request of a medically terminal person? In other words, is assisted suicide a compassionate moral option? Is euthanasia a moral option? How do we justify these activities even as many States are passing legislation legalizing what is often referred to as "death with dignity and compassion?"

There is an incident in the *Bible* where Saul, who has been brutally wounded, commands a fellow soldier to run him through with his own sword. Saul's fear is he will be killed by an enemy who is not circumcised, and in killing him, the soldier will be ridiculing Saul's religious beliefs. The soldier is terrified by Saul's request and refuses. Saul then falls on his own sword. Is there dignity and honor here? Who stands upon the higher moral ground, Saul or the soldier?

A death, that might be compared to Saul's code of honor, is well-known under Bushido Law, where a Samurai warrior takes his own life with the act of hara-kiri or seppuku. This is a ritualistic act of death whereby the Samurai takes his life by disembowelment with his sword. It is excruciatingly painful and was once considered an exemplary display of character in Japan. In this act, a samurai's courage, self-control, and willful resolve lead him to enact seppuku voluntarily following the death of his lord or master, or as an act of atonement regarding shame or dishonor. Do we consider this moral? And is this a death with dignity and honor, or does Lady Rasha's admonition still stand?

Here is another perspective on this inquiry. In a question-and-answer session between A.P. Sinnett and Master Koot Hoomi Lal Sing (both well-known in Theosophical circles) and recorded in the book, *The Mahatma Letters to A.P. Sinnett*, Koot Hoomi addresses suicide. He surprises us by saying:

"...not so fast! We must ask what the implications are with such an act? Does someone simply move on from the unresolved complications driving them to suicide, or are there extenuating circumstances we should consider?"

Here is Koot Hoomi's reasoning:

"...there is another kind of 'Spirits,' we have lost sight of — the suicides and those killed by accident. ...Well, this class is the one the French Spiritualists call 'les Esprits souffrants.' They are an exception to the rule, as the suicide (victims) have to remain within the Earth's attraction, and in its atmosphere, the Kama-Loka (land of intense desires), till the

very last moment of what would have been the natural duration of their lives. In other words, that particular wave of life-evolution must run on to its shore.[1]

If we address assisted suicides with the same level of discernment we've gained from the wisdom of the Spirit World, we readily comprehend the complications. Add to this commentary once made by Count Saint Germaine and the issue escalates. He once shared a story regarding a man suffering from horrendous pain. He poses this comment:

If the man suffering had just waited a few more hours, enduring his pain without taking his life, he would have died naturally and avoided the necessity to incarnate once again.

From our limited vantage, we simply do not know the full ramifications of our actions; however, as the Masters have openly shared, the doorway to unlocking the mysteries of life often opens through suffering! Difficult to process, we know, but that is their testimony.

So yes, who doesn't want to take away another's pain? But when we come from the viewpoint of the ego, we generally operate from ignorance with a limited understanding of the larger picture. In assisting another's death, we are accomplices in extinguishing the Christ Light from the body. In so doing, we risk personal karma. Also, the person whose life has been taken is then faced with living out their original life's duration in the Kama-Loka. Is there evil at play here? What are the real consequences of taking actions that facilitate death?

The push in our contemporary society to legalize assisted suicides must be reviewed by each and every heart before taking such actions. Is there a right answer? Maybe not, but at the minimum, we hope the Masters' commentary provides a basis for contemplation.

These Masters' thoughts are only meant as guidelines to assist us in making the best decision in each circumstance. Again, we are our own authority for Truth and must decide within our own hearts how best to deal with this difficult dilemma.

FORTY-SEVEN

PALLIATIVE CARE
ENDING LIFE WITH DIGNITY

WITH OUR PAST DISCUSSIONS ON DEATH, IT WOULD BE REMISS not to address the final stages of life. Most would agree dying and death are not the scary parts. It's the suffering that terrifies us! We know there are record numbers of people living in chronic pain and dying in less than optimum situations. What can we do? How do we avoid such conditions in our own lives and deaths? How do we die with dignity, without regret, when facing dire circumstances? What is most important to the one dying and to the one providing care? How do we prevent missing a precious opportunity to be alive at the time of another's crisis?

It is my experience, Gary, after shepherding several family members through the death process, that those dying do not want to burden their loved ones with their hardship. When my wife was dying, she kept saying, *"Don't worry, Gary, I'm going to be ok!"* It didn't matter how much pain she was enduring, all she wanted was for me not to suffer with her. Then, on the other hand, the caregiver's intent is to reduce the level of discomfort and create the most comfortable physical, emotional, and Spiritual environment possible.

Although hospitals try, the hospital is generally not the optimum environment for the end of life. By necessity, they are sterile, cold environments, where drugs are the compassion of choice. Hospital liability and financial incentives restrict the hospital environment. Although drugs can be appropriate in certain situations, most of us would say we don't want to enter the death experience in a morphine induced state when it's avoidable. Drugs are disorienting and create handicaps for the one negotiating the first moments of entering the Spirit Planes.

I oversaw my wife's passing in a hospital. Fortunately, we had a nurse who responded to my requests, moderately spacing the morphine treatments rather than dosing every hour. I considered us lucky, but I would not recommend facing death in a hospital if there is another choice.

I have heard some say that providing the senses with sensory stimulation helps the dying to deal with their circumstances. They believe it creates a distraction, or some level of comfort. Tasting or smelling chocolate chip cookies or brownies pleases some. This may be true but during my wife's last days, she was not interested in experiencing any smells, especially of food, nor pulling the blinds up to see the glorious mountains, hearing any music, or experiencing my touch. She wanted to be silent, completely present in her own experience. I sensed my simply being there, witnessing as a compassionate companion, was what she wanted.

I suspect each person is completely different depending on their illness and personality. I feel it is incumbent on the caregiver to be inquisitive and sensitive enough to intuitively reach out to find the most compassionate environment and method of care for the person experiencing the last stages of life. I do not believe one method or approach fits all, and the best one can do is to adopt a mindful state of awareness while attending to the needs of the person. But we can't go wrong, in my opinion, if we stay alive to each moment, maintaining a compassionate heart while commanding our entire being to be in service. We may not have answers but asking ourselves what is the best thing to do in this moment comes from the mindset of not knowing, while doing our best.

I remember when my mother was within days of passing and she had become bed-bound and hopelessly restless. Her mental faculties for the most part were lost, and she desperately wanted to get out of bed and walk; walk anywhere, just get up and go. My wife and I asked her where she wanted to go, and she said without hesitation she wanted to go to Paris. I said to myself, 'Mom! Damn, you're dying, how the Hell are we going to go to Paris?' But then I paused and asked myself how I could get Mom to Paris? So I said, *"Ok, Mom, get your suitcases, we're going to take the train to Paris."*

"Really, Gary? Ok, I'll get them."

"Do you have everything you need, Mom? Got your tickets?"

"Yes, yes, they're right here, Gary." And with that, we softly shook the hospital bed, rattling it like a powerful locomotive rumbling out of the station.

"Choo, Chooooooo!" And off we went! It didn't matter that the train couldn't cross the Atlantic! We were on our way and Mom was excited out of her mind. We just kept rattling the hospital bed every so often and over the hills and valleys we rolled.

"Are we almost there? Boy, this is a long trip!"

"Paris is a long way away, Mom. We're getting closer, just hang in there, it won't be long now."

Well, we rattled and jangled the bed for over an hour with Mom continuously inquiring when we were going to arrive, but eventually she fell peacefully asleep and we soothed another of her uncomfortable moments.

So, with a little imagination and compassionate love, you can do the impossible if you are present and willing to serve no matter what. If you do, you will midwife your loved one into the Spirit World successfully!

Hospice, in general, is a good source to use for end-of-life care, as the primary concern is keeping the patient comfortable throughout the entire process. Hospice nurses are attending to life, not death, and so there exists a dignity that is not often present with other methods. Hospice even brings bona fide doctors into our homes so we can be confident our loved one is receiving professional care when it comes to the dosage of Morphine, Haldol, or the dressing of wounds, etc. Hospice is just a phone call away if it's an emergency, and I found them very responsive. I used Hospice once and flew on my own once. I was glad I used Hospice with my mother and glad I attended to my wife alone. Each situation is different, and we must be comfortable with what we choose.

There's one rather technical issue we would like to address regarding the body that has passed. The silver cord that extends from the umbilical cord area of the body to the Astral body can stay attached for thirty-six hours after death. To avoid any unnecessary discomfort or pain to the one who has passed, it is advisable to refrain from any post-mortem activities until thirty-six hours have passed. Most mortuaries will accommodate you with this request.

FORTY-EIGHT

THE PHYSICAL DEATHS
OF AVATARS

Tᴴɪꜱ ᴄʜᴀᴘᴛᴇʀ ʀᴇᴠɪᴇᴡꜱ ᴛʜᴇ ᴇɴᴅ ꜱᴄᴇɴᴀʀɪᴏꜱ ᴏꜰ ᴛʜᴇ ᴘʜʏꜱɪᴄᴀʟ life of a few well-known Avatars. At death, Avatars may choose Physical Immortality or Spiritual Immortality. If they choose Physical Immortality, they might reside in Shambhala. If they choose Spiritual Immortality, they would reside in the subtlest plane of the Spiritual Realms around a given planet.

Some of the Ascended Beings discussed in this chapter will be quite familiar, others more obscure. Each Avatar's story is based on Spiritual agreements made before taking birth. This could include the mission, the personal karma, and even the group karma existing at the time of birth. As we have previously discussed, the nature of an Avatar's passing is generally pre-ordained to advance humanity's evolution in some manner, bringing forward a new dispensation of Light.

In this segment, we will give a testimony from a chela who was present during Reverend Rhinehart's (Master Kumara's) last days. Each is unique and couched in the trappings of the day.

Osiris

Through Reverend Rhinehart's mediumship, we learned that the death of Osiris (approx. 3150 BCE), the divine king who ruled all of

Egypt, was an unusual passing and marked by vengeance similar to the incidents surrounding Jesus' death. But in Osiris' case, it was decidedly more personal, based on the jealousy of his younger brother Seth (Set). Osiris, firstborn of the Gods, Geb (God of the Earth), and Nut (Goddess of the Sky) became a popular king, well respected for his wisdom and benevolence. Seth harbored a thirst for power, resenting the admiration Osiris received from the masses.

To seek revenge and gain power, the treacherous Seth set up a party with the idea of gifting a coffin (highly valued and prohibitively expensive during this period) to the guest who perfectly fit in the coffin. Seth fashioned a beautifully decorated coffin, attracting many to the party. Each who attended sat in the coffin hoping it would be theirs, but none fit as the coffin had been specifically designed to fit Osiris. After all failed, Seth cajoled Osiris into trying. Once in the coffin, Seth slammed the lid shut and threw the coffin into the River Nile, where Osiris drowned.

Egyptian mythology elaborates the rest of the story in this manner: To ensure Osiris never resurrected, Seth retrieved the body, cut it into pieces and dispersed it throughout Egypt. He tossed the phallus into the Nile. When Isis, wife and sister of Osiris, discovered Seth's treachery, she set out to retrieve Osiris's body parts. Once all the parts were retrieved, minus the phallus, she reassembled the body, performing powerful rituals to bring him back to life. Incomprehensibly, she succeeded! Osiris resurrected temporarily, long enough for them to conceive their son Horus, who became the legitimate heir to the throne, all to Seth's dismay. Quite amazing, since Osiris' phallus was never found.

Krishna

We have to look to the *Mahabharata* during the Kurukshetra War to pinpoint the events leading to Krishna's death. Gandhari was a princess and the wife of Dhritrashtra of the Kauravas Clan in the epic. At this time, the Kauravas were the primary antagonists in the Kurukshetra War. Gandhari and Dhritrashtra lost hundreds of their sons in the war, and Krishna came to meet them, giving his sympathies. Gandhari was incensed with Krishna, insisting he could have prevented the war if he so chose. She cursed him, shouting there would be no peace or prosperity in his kingdom, and after thirty-six years, he would die along with every member of Krishna's royal Yadavas Clan. After Gandhari finished, Krishna said, *"So be it!"*

Thirty-six years later, Krishna and the Yadavas Clan were celebrating a festival when a dispute broke out, generating much bravado over who was the most powerful, gallant warrior. It escalated to the point where they started killing each other. Krishna stepped in to stop the fight to no avail. It continued until all perished. Krishna escaped into a dense forest to meditate under a Pipal tree, propping his left leg over his right. In the forest, a hunter named Jara saw Krishna move his leg. Thinking a deer moved in the forest, he shot his deadly arrow, striking the bottom of Krishna's foot. Shocked, Jara prayed for Lord Krishna's forgiveness. Lord Krishna said, *"Whatever has happened has happened as per my wish."*

Krishna goes on to explain that in his previous birth, he incarnated as Rama during the Treta Yuga (second of the four yugas in a Yuga Cycle), and he killed King Vail from behind; now he reaped the same from Jara, who was King Vail in his previous incarnation. So we find, even the Ruler of the Universe faces the same Laws of Karma.

Buddha

Buddha's passing in relation to the other Avatars was low-key. He lived to the old age of eighty and passed surrounded by a large group of disciples. His death took place in Kushinagara, India (486-483 BCE), where he took the great state beyond Nirvana, Mahaparinirvana, freed from the cycle of birth, death, and suffering. It is said Buddha's last meal was prepared by Cunda, a metalworker. Although it was determined that the food was not poisonous, it was still considered the catalyst for his death. According to legend, the Buddha departed while lying on his right side as depicted in many sculptures throughout the Orient, giving one final instruction to his devotees, *"Be a Light upon yourselves,"* firmly placing responsibility upon the individual to free themselves from delusion.

Jesus

"A little while, and you no longer are going to see Me; and again in a little while, and you will see Me." John 16:16-23 KJB

This statement by Jesus foretells his absolute knowing of the details surrounding the completion of his mission enacted through the crucifixion and resurrection. Let's not fool ourselves, Jesus' crucifixion was agonizing, excruciating pain, but there is no gift from God in which he felt more gratitude. He endured the trauma of Hell and still rose. To believe he cried out on the cross, *"Why hast thou forsaken me,"* represents the most enshrined fallacy in the *Bible*, according to the Masters. Actually, this statement encapsulates man's misunderstanding, the ignorance of the ego's attachment to form, the ego's fear of existing in a world without enduring Love. The crucifixion is the last initiation to be completed in the final victory over the attachment to the body. Some call it a price to be paid, but we would call it more akin to an attachment to be shed. For Jesus, it was the Passion ending with the crucifixion; for others, it may take on a myriad of different forms; yet in each case, it is the final victory of the soul over the ensnarement of the ego and the body.

While Jesus hung upon the cross, it is claimed his twelve disciples were not amongst the crowd, having abandoned him. There is some dispute about this account but suffice it to say he was abandoned at his arrest, despite the disciples' earlier declarations of loyalty. (Mark 14:50 KJB) However, none were more devoted than Mother Mary,

Mary Magdalene, and Mary, John's mother, who were all present at the crucifixion. Each never wavered in their faith, experiencing the full meaning of the Passion. And who were the first to meet him after his resurrection from the tomb? The three Marys, according to the Ascended Masters.

Thereafter, Jesus appeared before his disciples in the darkened Upper Room in the Cenacle. This place, in the southern part of Old Jerusalem on Mount Zion, is where they had participated in the Last Supper and where the disciples stayed when in Jerusalem. There, Jesus displayed his wounds on his hands and feet, proving he was of flesh and blood. He then reminded them of what he foretold, saying everything that was written in the Law of Moses would be fulfilled. *"The Christ will suffer and rise from the dead on the third day."* Luke 24:46 KJB

Keith Milton Rhinehart (Kumara)

Here is what a devoted chela observed at the passing of Reverend Rhinehart, Master Kumara:

"I am gathered with a group of students who have traveled from different locales to assist Reverend Rhinehart during his last days. He has been battling an illness for several years, experiencing severe pain. He is in his last days.

"In these latter days, he ate little. During this time, he began delivering lessons that were extremely heart-wrenching to hear, detailing the injustices he witnessed throughout his lifetime. At this point, his pain turned acute, nearly unbearable.

"Many difficult feelings pressed upon me during this trying period. Most present experienced the privilege of witnessing first-hand phenomenal Spiritual occurrences, receiving proof and evidence through the Reverend's adept Spiritual mediumship, their loved ones still existed in the Spirit planes of life, some even having close relations physically materialize in their presence.

SEASONS OF THE SOUL

"In their appreciation, they promised to support Reverend Rhinehart's work in every way possible. Did they? I have my reservations—going as far as to suggest, from my observations, there were hurtful betrayals and insensitive requests. It brings to mind Peter's three betrayals of Jesus that Jesus prophesied would occur before the cock crowed. Painful!

"On the night of April 30, 1999, I witnessed Reverend Rhinehart surrounded by Master Beings inhabiting the Spiritual Planes. As I looked, I could distinctly feel their presence. Reverend Rhinehart sat uncomfortably in a chair, but without complaint. One by one, I psychically saw his six bodies of consciousness separate and lift out of his physical vehicle and drift into the arms of the Ascended Masters. I say six, as his seventh body already existed in Shambhala.

"Reverend Rhinehart was my beloved friend and minister since 1970. Watching these events shook me to the core, provoking uncontrollable tears, without question, the saddest time of my life. I felt I failed him—I felt we all failed him! I loved him so! He changed my life like no one else, but not only mine; he changed the lives of thousands, giving absolute proof of continued existence beyond the grave, alleviating many people's fears. He cared for every single member of the Church beyond what they ever imagined. Anyone in need pulled on his heartstrings.

"Once while working in the Church's library, I stepped outside to find him sitting on the front steps of the Church, deep in thought over a lady he knew. He revealed the woman was hurting for funds. Her husband had once been incarcerated, leaving her challenged to feed her children. Earlier, Reverend Rhinehart had set up a charitable fund, separate from the Church, so families like hers could receive assistance. Such a compassionate man, he couldn't say no to any sincere person in need.

"During his last hours, many were attempting to chant but I could see he just wanted silence, to experience his own inner peace

without disruption. He brought us wisdom to negotiate life, but in his last moments, we were so insensitive we couldn't accommodate his needs by responding with the wisdom that he had taught. After his last breath, we called the officials to verify he passed from this mortal plane. Immediately thereafter, all the students began to bicker and complain like a room full of chaotic school children."

As we have mentioned, the time of an Avatar's death is usually preordained, but there is much speculation regarding the time of most people's death. Some say we don't die before or after our time and that is generally true. But the Ancient Ones say although death can be ordained, it is somewhat rare, and in general, there is no absolute time of death. The actions, reactions, causes, and effects of life play the biggest role in the time of death. We must also consider the fact that life can be extended through genuine Spiritual healing, as has been demonstrated by healers throughout history, such as Jesus, Mary Baker Eddy, St. Teresa, Keith Milton Rhinehart, and innumerable others.

FORTY-NINE

PROPHECY "MY BOWL OF WATER DOTH REVEAL TO ME"

P ROPHECY IS A SUBJECT FILLED WITH SURPRISE AND INTRIGUE like no other. A good prophet dips into a cosmic sea, reaching unsuspected mystery, a mystery in terms of both *time* and *chance*. Some think prophecy is a scientific fact, and others say it's science fiction. We will explore a multitude of forms of prophecy throughout this chapter in an attempt to determine whether prophecies resonate as fact or fiction.

What is prophecy but packets of information synapsing from the random to the specific? Prophecies emerge from Spirit to be gleaned by prophets, from the Greater Now to the now. They are then interpreted and delivered to the world by prophets such as the Oracle at Delphi, Mother Shipton, Reverend Rhinehart, Nostradamus, St. John of the *Bible*, Edgar Cayce, or some lesser known but Spiritually gifted persons. When we get curious about dissecting the fundamentals of prophecy, it unmasks the nature of reality like few other phenomena. In prophecy, a medium steps onto irrational ground, trespassing the constrictions of time, not looking to determine what event might logically follow another. A prophecy supersedes the logical mind to shine the Light on that which spontaneously arises from the gaze of the prophet.

The *Bible* calls it a revelation—a miracle of knowledge. Others call it an inner vision or voice. But whatever we call it, it is not a rational, logical process connected in some way to what is previously known. In fact, it leaps beyond the known into new dimensions, shattering delusions of mind, of heart, and conceptions of the world. Many consider it to be a supernormal endeavor relying on pre-cognitive and religious faculties. It matters not whether the medium is a shaman in Africa, a prophet from Biblical times, or a Spirit communicator in modern Spiritualism; history illustrates genuine prophetic utterances do occur. The names of those whose predictions materialize with regularity pass from lips to lips, and those who are exemplary are anointed as prophets. Those prophets who are truly extraordinary, blessed by the Divine, originate our religious traditions.

Even though a prophecy may spring from the seemingly irrational, it must have some relationship with that which is. In other words, if the possibility exists to prophesy a future event, then there must be some relationship to that which already exists; and if so, then the possibility exists that a future event may similarly cause a present event just as a past event has caused a future event. If this statement is true, it throws us into a state of paradoxical mayhem where we no longer know just where we exist in a given timeline. What is up and what is down? If we are to find our way through this conundrum, we must refrain from placing our faith in *time*, believing another way will be revealed, guiding us out of the confusing paradox.

Given that *time* is the element in question, we might ask what the truth is about *time*. The Masters suggest the truth is that *time*, as we know it, exists as a relative experience. In terms of our lives and the universe we inhabit, the Masters say *time* is an illusion. Our worldly *time* is created by a covenant written as an "Earthly Agreement." We use *time* to keep track of our lives, and as a relative experience, we manipulate it to our convenience. We stretch it, cut it, save it, rush it, shrink it, dread it, and highly value it in different circumstances. The Masters agree that all of our experiences of growth, both physically and mentally, rely on *time*; yet, as an absolute, *time* is but an illusion. Given this understanding of time, a prophet's ability to prophesize future events becomes more plausible.

If we can agree prophecy is a truth, then it begs the question: Is there predestiny or is there free will? Are there events etched into an eternal clock in the space-time continuum that can't be altered, perhaps events such as the Second World War or who we may marry? If predestiny exists, does this violate some of the basic concepts of free will, whereby the choice between right and wrong is overridden by predestiny? If so, it would be impossible to change the outcome of an event through actions. On the other hand, if we assume nothing of a supernormal nature can interfere with free will, then it stands to reason the future cannot be prophesied. Again, we come to an intersection. Can a prophet genuinely see what the future will bring, or have we all been hoodwinked?

Master Odyssa, whom we previously introduced in Chapter 33 in our discussion on Soul Mates, assures us, *Yes! Absolutely! The future can indeed be prophesied!* Allowing his statement to stand spins us into a quandary as to the workings of the universe. Are we operating under free will or predestination? Odyssa posits that just because predestiny is in operation doesn't mean free will has been eliminated. But paradoxically, there is truth to both sides of the coin. Predestination reveals truth, as does free will. There are two elements acting like different rapids cascading into the stream called Life. They simply occupy different positions in the rapids. It may be considered a confusing stream, but there are those among us from time immemorial who have been able to dip into this stream and prophesize the future.

Some refer to this phenomenon as divination, a communing with higher intelligence. When we look to higher intelligence, we look to a source that has no preferences, no prejudices. In doing so, we freely open ourselves to the unknown.

Prophecy can have a frisky tendency to rip holes into the fabric of our world, leaving many in disbelief with wounded egos. For instance, where do you go when you hear a medium declare the CIA created Jonestown as an experiment to study cults, or Princess Di was murdered on a directive from the Queen, or Hitler escaped to South America alive? And on a more personal level, what if you were informed that during a previous life, you were responsible for much of the dogmatic thinking pervading the Catholic Church? Each statement, whether it is personal, social, or worldly, represents a daring leap, startling our understanding of the accepted or known narrative.

If we are attached to the world existing as we believe it, statements such as these can prove unacceptable. Fear arises in some as we fight to maintain the status quo. Assessing the role of prophecy, we find it tends to strike the ego right where it's attached, where it clings the most. At times, the ego feels a need to strike back and, in so doing, inadvertently enters the sea of genuine prophecy!

Prophecy is a study that challenges much of Western Civilization's physical construction of reality. Quantum mechanics, which has been destabilizing the Western World's concepts of reality for many decades, is now fast shedding new light on the mystery behind the mechanics of prophecy. What we once believed to be hardcore postulates defining the concrete physical world are now considered by quantum physics to be highly flawed. It is no longer far-fetched to state that the future can influence the past, black can be white, and the present moment exists in a completely different model of *time* from what we originally imagined.

This new understanding helps us to fathom how a man such as Nostradamus can gaze into his metallic-like glass bowl and predict with some level of poetic accuracy what may occur five hundred to a thousand years into the future. Here are his predictions concerning Nagasaki, Hiroshima, and the French Revolution:

> *"Near the gates and within the two cities*
> *There will be two scourges, the likes of which have never been seen,*
> *Famine within plague, people put out by steel,*
> *Crying to the great immortal God for relief."*
>
> > Century 2, Quatrain 6
> > Nostradamus — 1555/Europe

> *"From the enslaved people's songs, chants, and requests*
> *For Princes and Lords captives in the prisons.*
> *In the future, such by headless idiots*
> *Will be received as divine utterances."*
>
> > Century 1, Quatrain 14
> > Nostradamus — 1555/Europe

Not only could Nostradamus see these types of visions, but the soothsayer Mother Shipton, living in a woodland cave and shunned by society, predicted some of the most historic events to ever take place in Europe. Here are her prophecies on the French Revolution and the Second World War:

> *"Three times shall lovely sunny France be led to play a bloody dance. Before the people shall be free, three tyrant rulers she shall see."*

> *"In nineteen hundred and twenty-six built houses of straw and sticks. For them shall mighty wars be planned, And fire and swords shall sweep the land."* Mother Shipton —1560/Europe

Although uncanny predictions for their time, these examples illustrate prophecy is not necessarily precise, but demonstrate, with a bit of imagination, some prophets can project nearly five hundred years into the future and snatch out of thin air provocative events closely mimicking the events of a future day. Unfortunately, we must admit that some have translated some of Nostradamus' quatrains in an extremely loose manner with the intent to enhance the validity of the quatrain. There is no excuse for this. We believe Nostradamus' work stands on its own; he was renowned in his day for his accuracy of more current events. Projecting five hundred years into the future, we might expect that our imaginations must expand to a degree when interpreting Nostradamus' quatrains.

Let's return to Einstein's quantum physics to gain further understanding from a scientific perspective. In quantum physics, an electron is both particle and wave. Wave-particle duality is an example of superpositions, demonstrating that a quantum particle can exist in multiple states at once and in multiple locations, just like predestination can exist right along with free will, both interweaving in the same stream. It's a paradox, and all paradoxes are both confounding and explanatory. Knowing that a quantum object can exist in multiple states and places at once, an electron is both here and there. It is not until an observer sees the electron that it settles down in one location. The observer plays a key role in determining the electron's final location. Similarly, the gifted prophet seemingly exists in two timelines at once, seeing present time and predestination at once, whereas the ungifted is tethered to a united concept of *time* and sees but the normal continuation of events.

It is through prophecy that new knowledge and wisdom beyond the mundane machinations of the common man are revealed. They shine out like a neon flash, uplifting those who suspend their beliefs long enough to embrace a different vision. There exists a wide variety of different types of prophecy. From primitive to modern societies, practices of divination have taken on far-ranging and unique forms. Many forms involve some element of *chance* where the process interacts with what Carl Jung characterized as synchronicity. This is the coincidence of two unrelated events that have intertwined, creating a meaningful connection between the individual's mind and the material world. In this manner, *chance* becomes an active element in prophesying.

One practice, involving the element of *chance* that captured the early Germanic and Viking peoples, was the use of Runes. Runes are small stones carved with inscriptions on their surfaces. The word "Rune" is denoted as an alphabet letter. The stones are randomly tossed to predict the future. These people believed the verbalization of the inscription on the Rune made the inscription a part of the fabric of their reality. To the Vikings, the inscriptions possessed the power to create reality!

While holding a question in mind, a Viking tossed the Runes. The Runes landing face up acted as an oracle, presenting an answer. On a deeper level, the Vikings believed Runes meant a whisper, secret, or mystery, and the Rune held the inherent powers of speech. When cast, they facilitated a communication between Invisible Powers and Mankind. These ancient peoples believed the Runes to be a potent means of altering or redirecting fate through the process of *chance*. Others might suggest the Runes trigger a mystical process by which the subconscious mind communicates with the conscious mind, revealing what is unknown to the conscious mind.

Many cultures around the world utilize *chance* as well, holding similar beliefs to the Vikings. The Turkish/Arabic cultures activate the powers of *chance* by reading the patterns of coffee grinds remaining at the bottom of a cup of coffee. The oriental cultures read tea leaves; the Mediterranean cultures read wine sediments. All are considered the practice of Tasseography. In China, people threw bones (Scapulimancy). In ancient Greek and Roman Times, they read spilled entrails or sacrificial offerings (Hieromancy) as divination. Countless other cultures used sacred books (Bibliomancy) such as the *Bible*, the *Qur'an*, the *Vedas*, and the *Mahabharata* to divine the future.

One method of prophesying the Masters highly respect and frequently select to give prophecies to mystery school students, is the use of the *I Ching* or *Book of Changes*. Similarities exist with the Runes, but the *I Ching* is far more detailed in its conception of innumerable probabilities. Its origins go back to mythical antiquity, and it is one of the five classic books of Confucianism (2 BCE). Confucius and Lao Tzu used the *I Ching* to consult the cosmos, stating it to be one of their main sources of inspiration.

Not only did the *I Ching* influence Chinese philosophy, but the creation of Chinese sciences drew from the wisdom as well. Boiling the *I Ching* down to its simplest form, it is an oracle functioning by means of the principles of *chance*. In our modern era, many famous people have been influenced by the *I Ching*, including the poet Allen Ginsberg, musician John Cage, Danish physicist Niels Bohr, the German mathematician Gottfried Wilhelm Leibniz, the contemporary choreographer Merce Cunningham, and author Philip K. Dick. Herman Hesse's novel *The Glass Bead Game* revolved around the principles of the *I Ching*, and Terence McKenna's *Novelty Theory* found inspiration there.

Of all the contemporaries who found meaning in the *Book of Changes*, psychiatrist Carl Jung became its biggest admirer and most vocal advocate. Since the Masters have given importance to the *I Ching*, we thought exploring Carl Jung's thoughts outlined in his foreword to Richard Wilhelm's translation of the *I Ching* might be of value.

Knowing Western science draws on the laws of causality for its underpinnings, Jung is a surprising choice to write the foreword to Wilhelm's translation of the *I Ching*. However, Jung states that the axioms of causality, the relationship between cause and effect, are a statistical truth but not an absolute. The Oriental mind views the world through direct observation of Nature. What the Chinese notice is that Nature is either partially or totally interfered with by *chance*. Nature conforming to specific laws is almost the exception rather than the rule. Jung states the Chinese mind is mostly preoccupied with the *chance* aspect of events rather than cause and effect. What we term as coincident, the Chinese highly value, and what the Westerner reveres as causality goes practically unnoticed by the Chinese.

For the Chinese, the coincidences comprising a chain of events are part of the components making up a given moment, connected through a person's psychic state. They believe there is a direct relationship between a person's psychic perceptions and the events transpiring around them in *space* and *time*. So it could be said, from a Chinese perspective, at any given moment, an observation of the physical universe is as much subjective as it is causal.

Does this sound familiar? As we've noted, the modern science of quantum physics is proving that events in the world follow a psycho-physical model. Here we find similarities to the Chinese belief in how a person's psychic state directly influences the events in life. Given this understanding, they developed an oracle procedure, the *I Ching*, where they drew from the randomness of *chance*.

To create an oracle based on this understanding, the Chinese used the tossing of coins or yarrow sticks, incorporating *chance* as an active ingredient in the oracle procedure. Through tossing coins, they built trigrams comprised of straight lines (*Yang*) and broken lines (*Yin*). When two trigrams were combined, they formed a hexagram. Considering all the possible combinations of the trigrams forming the hexagrams, sixty-four hexagrams evolved. In effect, the sixty-four different hexagrams are equivalent to a causal explanation of the events we might experience in life. Everything that could happen in Heaven and on Earth was represented in the sixty-four hexagrams.

With this writing, it is not our intent to elaborate on the mechanics and history regarding the formation of the trigrams and hexagrams. (If you are not familiar with the *Book of Changes*, you are encouraged to do further research.)

Given the understanding that the *I Ching* becomes personified when asking a question, we thought we could ask the *I Ching* a question to get a feel of the Spiritual agencies at work and determine if the *I Ching* produces a meaningful answer to our question. We will ask the *I Ching*, "What will be the import of the book, *Seasons of the Soul?*" What follows is the hexagram the *I Ching* produced, along with the commentary, when I threw three ancient Chinese coins six times, producing solid *yang* lines and broken *yin* lines:

HEXAGRAM 51: CHEN / THE AROUSING
(Shock, Thunder) No changing lines.

The Hexagram Chen represents the eldest son, who seizes rule with energy and power. A Yang line develops below two Yin lines and presses upward forcibly. This movement is so violent that it arouses terror. It is symbolized by thunder, which bursts forth from the Earth, and by its shock, causes fear and trembling.

THE JUDGEMENT

Shock brings success.
Shock comes – oh, oh!
Laughing words – ha, ha!
The shock terrifies for a hundred miles,
And he does not let fall the sacrificial spoon and chalice.

The shock that comes from the manifestations of God within the depths of the Earth makes man afraid, but this fear of God is good, for joy and merriment can follow upon it.

When a man has learned within his heart what fear and trembling mean, he is safeguarded against any terror produced by outside influences. Let the thunder roll and spread terror a hundred miles around: he remains so composed and reverent in Spirit that the sacrificial rite is not interrupted. This is the Spirit that must animate leaders and rulers of men – a profound inner seriousness from which all outer terrors glance off harmlessly.

THE IMAGE

Thunder repeated: the image of SHOCK.
Thus in fear and trembling
The superior man sets his life in order
And examines himself.
The shock of continuing thunder brings fear and trembling.
The superior man is always filled with reverence at the manifestation of God; he sets his life in order and searches his heart,
lest it harbor any secret opposition to the will of God. Thus reverence is the foundation of true culture.[1]

The element of Shock is often a tactic the Masters employ, and the *I Ching* appears to hit the mark as it points towards success from an arousal issuing forth from God. With the searching within our hearts, we get our houses in order and drop any concealed opposition to the will of God. Amazing! The oracle clearly has touched upon our intent.

As an observation, we could say Spiritual agencies, acting mysteriously, account for the coin toss, manifesting a meaningful answer, presenting events that follow a psycho/physical model. It is these Spiritual powers that form the living soul of the *I Ching*, allowing the practitioner to access a spring pouring forth from the living waters of life.

In Jung's estimation, it is a valid method of consulting the unconscious mind, bringing to light answers to questions the conscious

mind seeks. In using the *I Ching*, we avoid tripping over our "if…
then…" mental-causality or prejudices, and the oracle becomes
personified without our mental interference. Jung believes the thought
placed in the *I Ching* by the old Masters is of far greater value than the
philosophical prejudices held by the Western mind.

The role of prophecy plays an important part in every religion,
and the Masters encourage us to explore the ideas of prophecy and
determine for ourselves whether it is fact or fiction. We trust this
chapter brings a measure of clarity. We might look to what the *I Ching*
prophesied in our example; through a level of shock, we are aroused to
a point of reverence for God. It is our sincere hope that the Masters'
wisdom presented in *Seasons of the Soul* inspires a more profound
understanding of God and a deeper understanding of ourselves.

FIFTY

PROPHECY
REVEREND KEITH MILTON RHINEHART

R EVEREND RHINEHART FREQUENTLY DEMONSTRATED THE GIFT
of prophecy in different parts of the world during his 44-year
career. Through his adept mediumship, Dr. Robert John Kensington
and Comte de Saint Germain communicated most of the prophecies.
The purpose of their prophecies wasn't to impress people with
outrageous personal predictions, but to uplift people's awareness of
themselves, and on the bigger stage, to expose the hidden agendas
around international events.

On occasion, the Masters shed light on the mechanics behind the
prophecy process. For example, they often explained the dynamics
behind a prophecy by using the metaphor of sitting on the rooftop of a
moving train. From the rooftop, a person gained a decided advantage,
seeing far ahead in all directions; whereby, those sitting in the carriage
could only see out the window for a short distance. What is apparent
through this analogy is that we can easily discern the advantage of
seeing over short spans of time, but seeing into the future five hundred
years is another matter. Precision and accuracy seem to fall off the
farther we reach into the future. To accomplish prophecies of this
order, it is not a passive, meditative process, but an active outreaching.
The Masters encourage people who are attempting prophecy to reach

out, stretching and expanding their awareness (from the rooftop) with absolute faith, knowing the infinite will meet them. It is a focusing process where we concentrate our mind on receiving information by confidently projecting ourselves.

Over the years, Dr. Kensington and St. Germaine presented countless prophecies to sitters and, through telephone hookups, to the various branches of the Church. Here are a couple of personal prophecies directed to Steve and to me.

One evening, Steve experienced a curious prediction from St. Germaine through Reverend Rhinehart's adept mediumship. Events transpired in grand proportions. The following is Steve's testimony:

"I'm at a well-known Hawaiian female singer's home in Honolulu with a group of people. The singer participated as a member of the Church years before there was an official Branch of Aquarian Foundation in Honolulu. Reverend Rhinehart was present this evening. The gathering amounted to a casual get-together, not intended to be a presentation of phenomena. The evening moved along as many parties do when, suddenly, Reverend Rhinehart became animated and jumped in front of the living room sofa, displaying lively enthusiasm towards me. He said, *'St. Germaine is here! He is saying, When you get home, Steve, check under your bedroom pillow and report back what you find.'* I said, *'I will.'*

"After leaving the gathering, we went straight home. Before entering, I checked the entire house for any signs of forced entry at the windows and doors, and I found none. My wife and I walked directly to our bedroom—again, we saw no signs of entry. I went to our bed and lifted my pillow. Underneath, an envelope had been placed in which I found six airplane tickets to Seattle. My heart raced—Incredible! Just as St. Germaine predicated! Apparently, a runner in the outer world purchased these tickets and the Masters apported them under my pillow.

"I'd never traveled to the mainland but as excited as we were to arrive in Seattle, we decided to make a quick detour and visit Disneyland, to the thrill of my children. Once in Seattle, we stayed at the personal home of Reverend Rhinehart, where we continued to witness interesting events.

"One that captured my interest was a demonstration the Count gave after entrancing Reverend Rhinehart. The Count had a large mineral collection and possessed great knowledge. On this day, he illustrated when a clear topaz was placed under the heat of a fire he lit in the fireplace, the heat markedly changed the color of the topaz. Then, a bit later, he changed a citrine into a smoky topaz by placing it under heat—interesting!

"On Sunday, we were invited to attend the Church's Sunday Service. This Sunday entailed an evening church service with approximately fifty people in attendance. Once seated, I noticed a certain awe come over the audience, then I got a hint of Suzie's perfume wafting through the chapel and understood the awe. Suzie's perfume was strong and unmistakable. (Suzie was one of Reverend Rhinehart's cabinet guides, along with Dr. Robert John Kensington, her soul mate.) I interpreted the perfume as a sign that the Spirit side of the evening arrived, and the proceedings were set to begin. Shortly, a volunteer came up to the cabinet to assist in setting up the scientific test conditions for the séance. The volunteer tied Reverend Rhinehart's arms and legs, restricting any movement, and then taped his mouth shut. In time, some fifty Ascended Masters astonished me, materializing one by one in the ectoplasm withdrawn from the Reverend's body, each introducing themselves and giving us their blessings. We witnessed a staggering pageantry of enlightened beings parading before us! At one point, the legendary Hawaiian musician, Alfred Apaka, materialized and sang a song dedicated to my wife and children! His songs are still heard on the radio in Hawaii today. To have Alfred Apaka honor my family in this manner was overwhelming!

"The phenomena continued, when subsequently St. Paul manifested his upper body right in front of us, with no facial features—strange, but often consistent with ectoplasmic phenomena. Eventually, Madame Pele materialized, famous in Hawaii as the Volcano Goddess. Huge presence! Stories circulate there have been reports of people picking up Madame Pele along a roadside on the island of Oahu. When they happened to gaze in the rearview mirror, they got a shock—she vanished completely. According to local legend, this occurrence indicated a volcanic eruption was imminent.

"In addition, Queen Liliuokalani materialized on this evening, the beloved last Queen of Hawaii before the U.S. Military forcefully took over the island. Then King Kamehameha the Great materialized, bringing messages and blessings. To close, Queen Liliuokalani sang Aloha Oe in Hawaiian to my four children. We felt extremely touched, as did all who were present. How could we have been more lovingly embraced? It became exceedingly obvious that much of the evening's proceedings were designed around myself and my family to honor our first presence in the Mother Church. Reflecting, I realize the Masters were welcoming me into the fold in recognition of the role I would play as a Board member of the Church for nineteen years. My gratitude for the Masters' love during this unforgettable evening has never diminished. With this, the séance came to an end.

"At the conclusion, the same volunteer came up to the séance cabinet and confirmed the tape covering Reverend Rhinehart's mouth was still intact, assuring the audience the materializations we witnessed were genuine.

"By the end of the séance, Reverend Rhinehart was totally exhausted. He slept for two to three days after the extensive display put on by the World of Spirit. It is interesting to note that the Spirit World claims that one hour of physical phenomena, of the order in which we witnessed, was equivalent to working forty hours of hard labor.

This séance took likely three to four hours, so you can comprehend the sacrifice Reverend Rhinehart makes for every physical phenomena event."

The following is another testimony by me, Gary. Reverend Rhinehart is entranced, and the precise accuracy of this prophecy I found remarkable!

"In 1998, I was in attendance during a worldwide telephone hookup call in San Francisco. Reverend Rhinehart communicated from an unknown location. Dr. Robert John Kensington, who entranced Reverend Rhinehart, presented me with a prophecy claiming, *'In two weeks, you will get a call in the morning. The caller will offer you a job, and it is up to you whether you want to accept the job or not.'*

"In exactly two weeks from the time of the prophecy, I got a call in the morning from a man with whom I was unfamiliar, offering me an excellent opportunity to do a project for his client in the famous Pacific Heights District of San Francisco. I was asked to design a rooftop garden for a home once owned by the owner of the San Francisco Giants. Within a short period after the call, I signed a contract at a wage higher than I had ever received before. I was shocked by the exacting accuracy of the prophecy, one fulfilled by a man whom I had never met!"

Now we would like to present a flavor of the Masters' messages given regarding the world. The predictions are not meant to cause fear, only alert people to the forces at play in the world and take precautions if that is deemed appropriate. The following prophecy statements are listed in no particular order. The predictions cover an eclectic range of topics from the Spiritual to schemes behind world events to pop culture. To date, we must note some were spot on, some never materialized, some aroused provocative eternal implications, and others that are simply superficial novelty comments about society, maybe even considered gossip by some. Others are not so tame, even shocking, rocking our current beliefs, upending the powers-that-be narratives of the world. As always, you are your own authority for truth. If the prophecies conflict with your understanding, do your own research or put the comment on a shelf and let it simmer.

Keep in mind, Reverend Rhinehart passed on April 29th, 1999. Most of the listed messages came through in the seventies, eighties, and nineties, so some may sound familiar. When the date is known, it will be provided. A prophecy, according to the Masters, is not dependent upon a linear sequence of time. For the Masters, the Past, Future, and Now exist simultaneously; prophecy can speak to any one of these time frames, but the time frame may be somewhat off. At times, the Masters' messages might seem to be opinions or simple statements, but the Masters' intent is always to make the audience think about implications not yet considered and how those implications might impact our lives; here are some of their prophecies over the years:

- Jesus never said, "Sell all you have and give it to the poor."
- The Red Sea never parted.
- 1997: Princess Diana was murdered; her death was not an accident. (Diana believed she would die young, thinking they would kill her in a helicopter or car accident. She was aware she had many enemies. Dodi Fayed's father, Mohamed Fayed, has not accepted the official cause of their deaths and says he is certain they were murdered.)
- The last Pope was murdered.
- Doris Duke was murdered, and her baby, whom she gave birth to in 1940, her heir, was killed within 24 hours of birth. (A court-appointed investigator, Richard H. Kuh, concluded that her doctor caused her death with an intentional fatal overdose of morphine. New York Times, April 1995. Additionally, one of Miss Duke's private nurses claimed Mr. Lafferty [Former butler and executor of Miss Duke's estate] conspired to kill Miss Duke along with others.)
- Onassis' son, Alexander Onassis, was killed. (*The New York Times* states his death was caused by a plane crash at the Athens Airport with subsequent brain hemorrhaging.)

Prophecy – Reverend Keith Milton Rhinehart

- It is not uncommon for heirs to be murdered.

- 10-23-1976: I have seen a vision of buildings all over New York City falling, huge towers collapsing. (This was St. Germaine's vision communicated through Reverend Rhinehart's mediumship. On 9-11-2001, the twin towers of the World Trade Center were attacked by airplanes, and the business complex in New York City fell to the ground along with other buildings.)

- 1996: The things that limit humans are the speed of light, life spans, and the tyranny of administrators.

- We are living on the prison planet of the universe, completely enslaved from cradle to the grave.

- Do not start wars by creating things that lead to wars and oppression. The things that lead to wars are a lack of genuine justice, lies, and gossip.

- Lord Dowding of the Royal Air Force was responsible for winning the Battle of Britain, completely changing the direction of WWII, leading to the defeat of Hitler.

- War is created to stimulate the economy.

- There is a desire by some in the Middle East for an atomic war, just to fulfill prophecy.

Zechariah 14:12 KJB

"And this shall be the plague with which the LORD will strike all the peoples that wage war against Jerusalem: their flesh will rot while they are still standing on their feet, their eyes will rot in their sockets, and their tongues will rot in their mouths."

- 1987: George Bush will attempt to take over the president's duties–he's run by his wife. (George Herbert Bush was Vice President under President Ronald Reagan's presidency (1981-1989) at the time of this prophecy, and became president from 2001 to 2009. There are some, author Roger Stone, among others, who believe George Herbert Bush was behind the 1981 assassination attempt of President Reagan.)

- 1998: Huge numbers of people murdered. Border towns between Texas and Mexico: young Blacks, Latinos, and people with darker skin are sought, especially in Texas. The kidnapping must stop! Latinos fighting to get into the U.S. are murdered, then rushed to the emergency room, where their organs are removed and delivered to the wealthy! (August 26, 2022, Jennie Taer, investigative reporter, reports a Central American trafficker says cartels are harvesting children's organs as part of their illicit cross-border operations, making great profits selling to wealthy people across the globe who are purchasing the organs through unauthorized clinics.)

- **1998: The secret government is planning the destruction of churches.** (If true, this follows in the footsteps of the Bolsheviks, who tried to destroy the Russian Orthodox Church, calling it the "opiate of the masses". In 2023, the Christian advocacy organization reported that the "Hostility Against Churches" report showed hostility on the rise. A recent Family Research Council report in 2023 identified 436 incidents against churches.)

- **1998: Why should that which is legal without money changing hands suddenly turn illegal once money changes hands?**

- We have been deprived of true justice. The corrupt must be brought to justice—when they are found guilty, they must be sent to a penitentiary for five to ten years rather than being allowed to dodge their sentence. Evil is in the most personable leaders of our world.

- Bring pressure to the oppressors to the fullest extent that you can; otherwise, injustice will continue.

- **1987: A famous alleged psychic surgeon will be arrested.** (John of God, an alleged Brazilian psychic surgeon, was arrested on charges of sexual exploitation on Dec. 12th, 2018. On July 10th, 2023, he was sentenced to 370 years for heinous sexual crimes against victims who sought his Spiritual help.)

- The human race has been greatly stunted by people with money and politics.

- **1999: Many top officials laugh as they know they can be taken away to secret underground sites at any time, which are located in Colorado and under the Pentagon, to name but a couple of locations.** (There is an underground base in Cheyenne Mountain, Colorado, built for NORAD.)

- Heads of Corporations shouldn't have salaries more than thirty to forty times that of an employee.

- Tons of gold were dropped into the market on the unsuspecting public to lower the price. (There are numerous examples of this phenomenon; one happened on January 6, 2014. After the market rallied over $15.00 for the price of gold in the European and Asian markets, the price of gold suddenly plunged $35.00 in a span of less than sixty seconds, where 12,000 contracts traded, equal to more than 10% of the total day's volume.)

- 1999: Japan and Britain are in danger of sinking.

- There is an analogy between Catholicism's tyranny over the masses and the scientific and media's tyranny over the people of today.

- Watch the program "V Series," a 1984 science fiction TV series–where lizard people are taking over. Already happening! Politicians are lizard people. (Several sources confirm this statement, saying the Draco and the Abraxas reptilian races have interbred with humans, but there is no extraordinary evidence, so they remain at the level of rumor. H. P. Blavatsky in *The Secret Doctrine Volume II* discusses several alien races that have inhabited Earth.)

- Eventually, court cases will be brought against the establishment. (Sovereign immunity is granted to the states in the Eleventh Amendment, and no provision in the Constitution expressly grants federal immunity, but at this point, all cases brought against the United States Government fall under the doctrine of sovereign immunity, which is drawn from pre-Founding English Law. But as we have seen, there have been many cases brought against Trump who could be seen as an agent of the elite establishment.)

- Jim Jones was a CIA agent, and the Peoples' Temple Agricultural Project, in Jonestown, is a CIA cult experiment. Not all the devotees died from consumption of the cyanide punch, but were injected with poison from hypodermic needles or shot in cold blood. (The Guyana government's top pathologist, Dr. Leslie Mootoo, told the *Chicago Tribune* he believed murder, not suicide, was responsible for more than 700 of the 911 persons who died at the Peoples' Temple in Jonestown, Guyana. The report from Dr. Mootoo, medical examiner and first doctor on the scene of the tragedy, indicated he found the victims with injection wounds in their upper arms in an area where it is virtually impossible for a person to self-administer a shot. Dr. Mootoo even found a two-year-old child with an injection wound in his arm. Jim Jones was not found with injection marks, but with a gunshot wound to his head.)

- It is a crime when the freedom of the press only supports those in power and enslaves the people. The press must be free but also responsible and accountable to the people. The media has hurt minorities, especially minority religions.

- Don't remove incentives for doctors and the gifted, but there should be limitations.

- AIDS is not a virus; it is a retrovirus. The supposed virus doesn't cause AIDS, but AIDS is caused by a collection of different diseases acquired through a deficient, compromised immune system. (Inventing the AIDS Virus, Dr. Peter Duesberg. This is a good reference book for AIDS; Dr. Duesberg elaborates on the causes of AIDS, the Masters supported Duesberg's book and work.)

- Dr. Charles Richet and Albert von Schrenck-Notzing, through Reverend Rhinehart's mediumship, say the AIDS virus is "Hokum". (Dr. Richet, 1850 to 1935, was a French physiologist and immunologist who won the Nobel Prize in 1913 for coining the term anaphylaxis and Von Schrenck-Notzing, 1862 to 1929, was a German physician, psychiatrist, and noted psychical researcher.)

- Mid-Eighties, Dr. Fauci is corrupt. He stole all of the French virologist, Luc Montagnier's research and gave it to Dr. Gallo, who claimed he discovered it himself. Both men worked for NIH; they are corrupt and should be incarcerated. (This prophecy came out in the early eighties, around the outbreak of AIDS. [Oct. 6th, 2008, heard on: *All Things Considered*, by Richard Knox. "This year's medical Nobel ends decades of speculation about who would win the everlasting credit for discovering HIV, the deadliest virus of our time. The surprise is not that French researchers Francoise Barré-Sinoussi and Luc Montagnier won the Nobel, but that American Robert Gallo did not share in it."])

- AIDS deliberately targeted the gay community.

- Penile implants have ruined the lives of many men.

- Right after the Iraqi War began (March 20, 2003), Dr. Kensington pre-dicted the war would last for twenty-something years. (The Iraq War started in March 2003. The U.S. declared an end to the war in Iraq on December 15, 2011. In 2024, the U.S. still had roughly 2,500 troops in Iraq amid public calls from the Iraqi government for the U.S. to withdraw its troops–CNN)

- **1987: A Major earthquake hit Iran, killing thousands.** (A 5.7 magnitude earthquake hit Iran on Sept. 7th, 1987, not sure of the death toll)

- **1999: Coastline will be different. Most of California and Oregon will be gone.**

- **1999: There is a group planning to explode a nuclear warhead—the Islamic people will be blamed.**

- **1999: A nuclear warhead will be exploded in the next two years. Do not blame the people of Islam; the media will attempt to blame them.** (Chemical analysis done by the DOE Sandia on the World Trade Center site identified the chemical/radiation footprint or fingerprint of the warheads based on samples taken after 9/11 of the fallout at ground zero. Nuclear weapons used at ground zero are confirmed from multiple sources. [Nuclear 9/11 Revealed, by Gordon Duff, Senior Editor, one of the top global intelligence specialists] The Islamic people were blamed for the attack by the media with no reference to nuclear devices.)

- **Off the coast of Okinawa, there exist various species of fish that can change gender almost at will. The process takes up to ten days.** (Apparently, there are fish in the Caribbean that also change their sex. How does this information impact the morality of transgenderism?)

- **1997: There are seven sexes in the universe that already exist on our planet.**

- **Crop circle information was fed to UFO magazines by the CIA.** (How we interpret this statement is the crop circles are made by humans on earth possessing technology possibly created from reverse-engineered alien technology.)

- **UFOs are everywhere on the surface of the Earth.**

- **Life on Mars will be proven; simple forms are existing on the surface of the planet.**

- **The Mars' surface has an abundance of limonite.** (Limonite is a somewhat amorphous earthy mass and has a variable composition, but often contains significant amounts of hydrated iron oxide, indicating the presence of water.)

- There will be an influx of the birth of people on Earth with six fingers or toes, they are from the planet Telegra.

- Some Tibetans reincarnate within minutes of passing; most people stay in the afterlife for two hundred years.

- The Dalai Lama reincarnated instantly. (Gedun Gyatso was recognized and confirmed as the reincarnation of Gedun Drub in the Fifteenth Century – no mention of instantaneous birth–soon after, the Dalai Lama Institution was established. For more than six hundred years since Gedun Drub, a series of unmistakable reincarnations have been acknowledged in the lineage of the Dalai Lama.)

- Incredible change for the better will take place one day.

- Continually improve your ability to articulate ideas.

- Eventually, we will have a Master Race, but by then, there will be moral control. We will all have beautiful bodies that each will find attractive.

- All spirits are not good, nor are all aliens good.

- New Age groups and Spiritualism are attracting hatred from the far right.

- The Black Stone, sacred to the Muslims, arrived in Muhammad's presence.

- Don Johnson becomes a rock singer.

- 1996, In fifty thousand years, interstellar travel will be conquered.

The Masters pointed out several instances in the *Bible* that referred to prophecies, showing the efficacy of prophecy demonstrated in the *Bible*. The following are two examples:

John 1:45 KJB

"...We have found him, of whom Moses in the law, and the prophets, did write, Jesus of Nazareth, the son of Joseph."

Mark 14:55-72 KJB

"And the chief priests and all the council sought for witness against Jesus to put him to death; and found none.

For many bare false witness against him, but their witness agreed not together.

And there arose certain, and bare false witness against him, saying We heard him say, I will destroy this temple that is made with hands, and within three days I will build another made without hands.

But neither so did their witness agree together.

And the chief priest stood up in the midst, and asked Jesus, saying, Answerest thou nothing? what is it which these witness against thee?

But he held his peace, and answered nothing. Again the high priest asked him, and said unto him, Art thou the Christ, the Son of the Blessed?

And Jesus said I am: and ye shall see the Son of man sitting on the hand of power, and coming in the clouds of heaven.

Then the high priest rent his clothes, and saith, What need we any further witnesses?

Ye have heard the blasphemy: what think ye? And they all condemned him to be guilty of death.

And some began to spit on him, and to cover his face, and to buffet him, and to say unto him, Prophecy: and the servants did strike him with the palms of their hands.

And as Peter was beneath in the palace, there cometh one of the maids of the high priest:

And when she saw Peter warming himself, she looked upon him, and said, And thou also was with Jesus of Nazareth.

But he denied saying, I know not, neither understand I what thou sayest. And he went out into the porch; and the cock crew.

And the maid saw him again, and began to say to them that stood by, This is one of them.

And he denied it again. And a little after, they that stood by said again to Peter, surely thou art a Galilean, and thy speech agreeth thereto.

But he began to curse and to swear, saying, I know not this man of whom ye speak.

And the second time the cock crew. And Peter called to mind the word that Jesus said unto him, Before the cock crew twice, thou shalt deny me thrice. And when he thought thereon, he wept."

This has been merely a glimpse; there were hundreds and hundreds of prophecies delivered by Reverend Rhinehart. We believe we can determine they are fairly precise and of high caliber, demonstrating evidential prophecy is alive in contemporary times and not limited to only phenomena from historical prophets, including those in the *Bible*.

FIFTY-ONE

PROPHECY
THE VALUE OF ALLEGORY
MONICA SZU-WHITNEY

P ROPHECY IS NOT ONLY MEANT TO PREDICT AND ILLUMINATE, but to foster encouragement for people to investigate the patterns of their lives and overcome negative influences. Many times, prophecy simply offers Hope, considered by some superfluous, but more often is invaluable, life-affirming, and uplifting. The Masters found allegorical stories highly effective in assisting chelas' Spiritual and personal growth. Allegory is used as a tool in the *Bible*, making the teachings more accessible. The allegorical form allows a sitter to view themself within particular situations through new perspectives. By not speaking directly to a situation, the allegories provide a recipient with the means to drop defenses and open their mind to new possibilities.

In this allegorical fashion, Monica Szu-Whitney (1956–2021), my wife, wove stories into her psychic readings, offering sitters transformational ways to view their circumstances in search of Healing and Hope. We wouldn't call Monica a prophetess in the traditional sense, but through her mediumship, she presents a teaching that is not confrontational nor overly personal for a vulnerable sitter.

In many ways, Monica's tales could be compared to the oral folk stories compiled by the Brothers Grimm. In these tales, the storyteller weaves inspirational, allegorical stories such as *Cinderella, Little Red Riding Hood,* and *Tom Thumb,* which enlivened our childhood.

The following is one allegorical story Monica presented to a woman suffering from Lyme's Syndrome and Multiple Sclerosis, inspiring the woman to carry on. Monica viewed the images on her inner screen and relayed the story in rapid fashion, spinning the thread in five minutes or less. Isis is the Spirit-Guide who directed Monica's work with psychic messages and prophecy:

The Lava Pit

There exists before me a huge lava pit-like depression descending maybe a half mile into the Earth. At the center of the vast pit exists a pond with a beautiful fountain flowing sparkling, fresh water. There are three paths leading to the fountain. One path is overgrown with thick, gnarly branches presenting nasty thorns. Sharp jagged rocks project into the second path, making passage extremely precarious. Possibly even less inviting is the third path, thronging with dirty, smelly lepers covered in dark blankets concealing their bandaged faces, hands, and feet, all riddled with disease.

In my gaze is a weak, sickly woman pulling a cart and wanting to retrieve water from the pond. She solicits people to help her pass through the thorny path, hiring strong men to clear the branches with machetes, but the branches prove so hard and thick that the blades don't make a dent. Failing, she proceeds to the second path, again hiring men in an attempt to bulldoze the jagged rocks blocking her way, but once again the effort proves of no use as the rocks are so deeply entrenched, they are unmovable.

Finally, she decides the third path is the only legitimate option. Again, she hires people, insisting they remove the lepers, but the lepers are so repugnant the helpers balk, refusing the task. With this, she notices the lepers have extended their hands towards her. She instructs those hired to give them golden coins. The lepers stare blankly at the golden coins, throwing them to the wind. With their hands, they gesture to their mouths as if to say, *"We're hungry!"* Instantly, the woman is alone facing the lepers. Not knowing what to do, she attempts to simply walk past them, but they won't allow her passage, again gesturing to their mouths.

Exasperated, she spots a large apple tree filled with apples. This makes her happy. She is thirsty and plucks a few apples to appease her thirst. Because she is sickly, she is unable to eat solid food, so she sucks the juice out of an apple. She takes one taste, but it tastes so horrid she spits it out. Looking back at the lepers, surprisingly, they seem to want the apples. She picks more apples for the lepers. One by one, they eat the apples; their faces light up as if the apples are the most delicious food they've ever eaten. After eating, they back away from the path, allowing her to proceed.

Even so, the path continues to present an arduous course. She goes back to the tree, picking all the fruit she can get her hands on, loading her cart with apples for the remaining lepers. With each apple given, the path opens further. Soon, all kinds of people stand before her. There are rich people, poor people, young and old, sad people, happy people, distraught people, and people of every ethnic group. She keeps passing out her apples and the path keeps opening and opening. As she moves down the path, she starts to hug everyone, smiling, talking, and giving words of encouragement despite feeling extremely tired and laboring to pull her cart. Her eyes fill with unbridled compassion and love as she struggles on.

Little by little, the woman's load gets lighter. By the time she is halfway to the fountain, the apples are gone. She looks up and there are still hordes of people crowding the path. Just as she feels exceedingly discouraged, a couple comes up to her asking what she is doing. She points to the fountain, saying, *"I'm trying to get to the fountain. I'm parched and thirsty."*

They say, *"There exists another way."* They led her to an underground passage through a large tunnel. With their guidance, she finally arrives at the prized fountain. In front of the fountain stands a wooden gate. Even on her tippytoes, she can't see what lies behind the gate. The couple stops at the gate, indicating this is as far as they can take her; for the remainder of the journey, she must proceed alone.

The woman sighs, her skin is dried and full of boils, she's completely exhausted, but happy as she knows her goal is close at hand. She swings open the gate, taking a couple of steps. Right where she thought the fountain existed lies the remains of a pond, bone-dry! In place of the fountain, a waterless mound of dirt spreads out. In every direction she looks, the landscape is desolate and dry. But right on top of the dried-up mound, a single apple is perched. She approaches the mound and picks up the apple. She recalls how bitter and sour the apples tasted. Instinctively, without hesitation, she takes a bite. It is so sweet she can't believe it! Suddenly, water spurts out of the apple, filling the dried-up pond.

With that, the entire area begins to grow lush vegetation. Water lilies, lotus blossoms, and colorful flowers spring to life. She drinks the water, pouring it all over her body. Her dry skin and boils vanish, and she finds herself floating face up in the pond. Suddenly, Master Jesus is present, holding her securely in the water, then Master Buddha visits, and finally Master Babaji gives his blessings. Eventually, she is floating alone, but now floating in absolute, ecstatic bliss!

The woman for whom this allegory was directed appeared to find Hope as she related to many of these symbolic images, but we have no way of assessing the influence it had on her life.

FIFTY-TWO

PROPHECY
NOTEWORTHY PROPHETS

THE MASTERS ARE FOND OF HIGHLIGHTING A FEW SELECT prophets throughout history. These have demonstrated the genuine gift of prophecy. Mother Shipton, Nostradamus, and Edgar Cayce, along with a few prophets from the *Bible*, captured the Masters' attention. Each of these prophets, at one time or another, communicated through Reverend Rhinehart's mediumship. Most people interested in Spiritual history are familiar with Nostradamus and Edgar Cayce, but few are familiar with Mother Shipton; therefore, we will introduce Mother Shipton first:

MOTHER SHIPTON 1488-1561

Ursula Southeil, also known as Mother Shipton, lived in the reign of King Henry VIII of England. Ursula began life on a dark, stormy night in the Knaresborough woodland. Her mother, a homely fifteen-year-old girl, Agatha, refused to name the father; consequently, Ursula became shunned as a child. Agatha was accused of witchcraft, not uncommon in early Medieval Europe. Soon, people viciously attacked Ursula, slinging derogatory epithets claiming the child possessed a wretched, crooked nose, a twisted, deformed body, and a witch-like countenance just like her mother. Both mother and daughter were ostracized as pariahs.

So, life began for little Ursula in a cave, poor and destitute with her young mother, pushed to the fringes of society. With no means, Agatha relied on the Nature Kingdom for sustenance near the banks of the River Nidd.

At the age of two, Ursula's plight came to the attention of the local abbot of Beverly, who found a family to take Ursula, but not Agatha. Unfortunately, Agatha died a few years after their separation, never reuniting with Ursula.

Because of Ursula's unusual appearance and behavior, the townspeople never failed to taunt and ridicule her. Eventually, the child found great solace in the forest near the cave where she was born, developing a wonderful rapport with the fauna and flora of the woodlands.

As she grew older, she concocted potions and healing remedies. The townspeople took notice, inquiring about her remedies. During this time, she ingratiated herself with the community and happened to meet a carpenter from York, named Tobias Shipton. To everyone's surprise, they married. Shortly thereafter, Ursula's gift of prophecy started to blossom.

One day, a neighbor woman declared that some of her clothing had been stolen from her home. The next day, a woman went strolling through town singing, *"I stole my neighbor's smock and coat, I am a thief!"* Subsequently, she shamelessly handed the garments over to Ursula. Unusual events such as this regularly swirled around Ursula, creating her growing mystique.

A few years into their marriage, Tobias died. Once again, Ursula became ostracized and retreated back to the woods. Here she practiced her skills as an herbalist.

During this time, odd premonitions arose in Ursula's mind. She bravely declared her visions and became known as Mother Shipton. Initially, her premonitions predicted only local affairs. But as time passed, she announced grander and grander predictions having greater ramifications.

One of Mother Shipton's early local predictions described the destruction of the local Trinity Church, declaring that in the night, the highest stone in the Church would become the lowest stone on the bridge. Not long thereafter, a violent storm fell upon the town, taking down the Trinity Church's steeple and crashing it into the bridge. Stunned, the townsfolk spread the news of the prediction beyond the local community. In time, even King Henry VIII referenced Mother Shipton, in a letter to the Duke of Norfolk, naming her the Witch of York.

In another incident, the famous diarist, Samuel Pepys, gives an account of the Great Fire of London, where he included specific details after hearing the Royal Family discuss Mother Shipton's prediction of the fire.

She made numerous predictions that included famous people such as King Henry VIII and his main adviser, Cardinal Thomas Wolsey. Discussed in a pamphlet in 1641, she foresaw Thomas Wolsey's fate after failing to secure the annulment of Henry's marriage to Catherine of Aragon. Mother Shipton predicted Wolsey would take a journey between London and York, but he would never reach his destination. He supposedly died of natural causes during his journey, before he arrived at York.

With her titillating predictions of the famous, Mother Shipton's stature was elevated to dizzying heights for a person originally relegated to the fringes of society. She died at the age of seventy-three, remembered fondly.

Her fame gave rise to the archetypal witch featuring the tortured body, crooked nose, and strange behavior often depicted in the movies and cartoons. Few know these witch-like characters were modeled after Mother Shipton!

NOSTRADAMUS 1503-1556

Despite Mother Shipton's prophecies stunning her contemporaries, prophecy, barring the *Bible*, is most often associated with the legendary Nostradamus. Born Michael de Nostredame, December 14, 1503, his name was Latinized to Nostradamus. A French physician, astrologer, alchemist, and apothecary, he earned high respect as a learned man early in life, and with the publishing of the book *Les Prophéties* (1555), his fame spread quickly throughout France. The book contains a collection of 942 poetic quatrains predicting future events spanning 1555 CE to 3797 CE.

Because of his nuanced use of languages, his prophecies have been subject to endless interpretations, misinterpretations, insane ridicule, and attacks insinuating his work to be the product of the Devil. We can now determine many of his prophesies didn't come to pass, others were never understood, but many materialized in his day, enough to gain the attention of King Henry II and his Queen Catherine de' Medici, where the predictions were all the rage of the French Court. Of the many great personages admiring Nostradamus, Queen Catherine de' Medici became his greatest advocate. Henry II didn't hold the same devotion, yet here is Nostradamus' provocative prophecy concerning the King, (Century 1, Verse 35):

> *"The young lion will overcome the older one,*
> *On the field of combat in a single battle;*
> *He will pierce his eyes through a golden cage,*
> *Two wounds made one, then he dies a cruel death."*

As predicted, one day King Henry II (older lion) lined up to joust Gabriel, comte de Montgomery (young lion) during the summer of 1559. The joust occurred at an event to celebrate the King's daughter's upcoming wedding. With the final jousting pass, Montgomery's lance tilted upwards, bursting through the king's visor (piercing his eyes through a golden cage) and splintering. The splinters from the lance entered the King's eye, throat, and temple. Even with the best efforts of the King's surgeons, Henry experienced agonizing pain, finally dying a cruel death eleven days later.

The Black Plague initially swept through France in 1347 and occasionally reoccurred for the next 200 years. Early in Nostradamus' life, just after failing to receive his doctor's license, the Black Plague reoccurred in Montpellier in Southern France. Nostradamus decided to abandon the pursuit of his Doctorate, feeling the need to attend to the afflicted with the hopes of making use of his newly acquired knowledge.

Due to his unusual confidence and unflinching courage in the face of unimaginable circumstances, Nostradamus proved to be medically and psychologically sound, creating remarkable success with a variety of his remedies. Later, in 1544 in Provence, he again served the victims of the ever-worsening plague.

Throughout his diary, he wrote about many details of his work; one of his most interesting entries included a report of the use of a rose pill formula he created. He notes, those who took the pills lived, those who didn't died. His colleagues bled and practiced physicking their patients, but Nostradamus refrained, opting to utilize his skill as an apothecary.

We believe some of his early inner promptings were in the pharmaceutical arena, which set him apart from the ordinary physician. He concocted this formula to save many patients and himself:

- Sawdust from the greenest Cyprus, 1 oz.
- Iris of Florence, 6 oz.
- Cloves, 3 oz.
- Odorated Calamus, 3 drams
- Lign-aloes, 6 drams
- Three hundred to four hundred red roses plucked before dawn, pulverized, and mixed in with the above powder.

Once these ingredients were pressed into pills and lozenges, Nostradamus instructed his patients to keep the medicine in their mouths at all times. The pills generated such a terrific odor, Nostradamus claimed it eliminated bad breath, foul smells, and cleaned decaying teeth. He felt the pestilence was transmitted through foul air, and with the purified air created by the use of the lozenges, his patients were saved. [1]

For a period of three years, he experienced an idyllic life, enjoying his productive practice, family life, and intellectual stimulation, but when his beloved wife and child contracted what some believed to be the Black Death, he proved unable to save them. Devastated, losing the ones he loved the most, wanderlust overtook him, and he set out on a journey to add to his pharmaceutical knowledge. On this journey, it is said he experienced one of his first prophetic insights:

While in Italy, he saw a young Franciscan from Ancona coming towards him, named Felice Peretti. In passing, the emerging prophet put a knee to the ground devoutly as the ex-swine herder passed. When asked the reason for his unusual behavior, Nostradamus replied, *"I must submit myself and bend a knee before His Holiness."* In 1585, Cardinal Felice Peretti became Pope Sixtus V. [2]

Another similar experience took place during the same time period, hinting at the full blossoming of his gift for predictions:

Nostradamus, visiting with Monsieur and Madame de Florinville, was treating Madame Florinville's grandmother. One morning, Monsieur de Florinville and Nostradamus were out on a stroll around his chateau when they came across two little suckling pigs, one of which was white and the other black. For sport, Monsieur asked Nostradamus what would become of the piglets. Nostradamus replied, *"We will eat the black one and the wolf will eat the white one."*

Monsieur de Florinville, scheming to make the prophet a liar, secretly directed his cook to kill the white piglet and serve it for supper.

The chef killed the white pig and readied it for roasting on the spit, and then went out on an errand. In the meantime, a small wolf cub entered the spit area and feasted on the rump of the white piglet. When the cook returned, to his shock, he found the white piglet nearly devoured. To avoid disappointing his master, he killed the black pig and served it for supper since no one would know the difference.

Upon eating dinner, Monsieur boasted, "Well, sir, we are now eating the white pig and no wolf will touch it here."

Nostradamus exclaimed, *"I do not believe it! It is the black one that is on our table."*

To get to the truth of the matter, Monsieur called the chef, who confessed to the accident, exclaiming Nostradamus was correct! The black piglet had been the one served for supper. [3]

EDGAR CAYCE 1877-1945

In his day, Cayce demonstrated precognitive perception, presenting an array of prophecies on medical topics from halitosis to spirit-possession, reincarnation, wisdom, and ancient civilizations. Through Reverend Rhinehart's adept mediumship, Mr. Cayce states he had been working with the Aquarian Foundation since its inception, providing several lectures, one of which spoke of the ancient continent of Atlantis. Cayce infers that during Atlantean times, there were many miraculous healings, and the Atlanteans employed methods of aerial transportation patterned after the movement of planetary bodies rather than that of birds. He discussed how these methods didn't burn toxic, polluting fuels like today's vehicles.

Cayce, called the "Sleeping Prophet," delivered readings from a trance-state, diagnosing illnesses, discussing wisdom, and the past lives of his sitters. In this state of universal consciousness or the super-conscious mind, he became extremely relaxed, giving uncanny responses to questions like: "What do I do for my arthritis? How were the pyramids of Egypt built? What is the purpose of my life?" The sessions were conducted by his wife, Gertrude and recorded by his secretary, Gladys Davis.

As a devout Christian, Cayce initially felt troubled by what he characterized as a mysterious voice speaking through him. Eventually, he realized the voice was of Good and coming from God. This voice prescribed and diagnosed remedies for thousands of diseased people for whom conventional medicine failed to assist. Cayce's remedies proved to be highly accurate and successful.

Cayce could perform his service remotely without seeing the person. Often, he only possessed the name or address of his patient when giving his reading. Cayce never studied biology or medicine, and after a reading, he referred to a doctor to understand the terminology he used in a diagnosis or prescription.

Prior to developing his gift, he made his living selling insurance and photography. Throughout his healin career, he never requested payment. His primary motivation and passion were to serve God, but on occasion, he accepted donations.

In Edgar Cayce's *Famous Black Book*, he reviews the innumerable remedies he prescribed, cataloguing a remarkable testimony to his gift, but his predictions and comments concerning the Great Pyramids and Atlantis captured popular imagination. The following descriptions are extrapolated from his comments:

The pyramids took one hundred years to construct and were started and completed during the time period of 10,490 BCE to 10,390 BCE. (Until recently, Egyptologists placed the Sphinx's construction at about 2,500 BCE, but new discoveries show erosion at the base attributed to ancient floods, suggesting both the Sphinx and the Pyramids were constructed much earlier, sometime around 10,000 BCE.)

In 1932, Cayce predicted there would be a discovery of a hidden chamber underneath the Sphinx's paw. Within the chamber, a Hall of Records full of information about Atlantis and the secrets of the Sphinx would be discovered by archeologists.

In 1997, seismological studies done by Joe Jahoda and Dr. Joseph Schor suggest there is indeed an empty space underneath the Sphinx, much like Cayce described. The space appeared to be sitting at a ninety-degree angle and way too precise to be created naturally. The researchers believed it was artificially created. They sought permission to excavate but were denied by Egyptian authorities.

We have explored a smorgasbord of different forms of prophecy. In most Spiritual circles, prophesying implies Biblical prophecy, but as we can see, prophecy has continued through others and Reverend Rhinehart. The Masters often advise us to heed the prophecies. First, we might ask ourselves what the Masters mean when they say to heed the prophecies. Is every prophecy carved in stone? No! Many prophecies, no matter the caliber of the prophet, never materialize. Clearly, the Masters don't intend for people to tremble in fear with every warning or prediction of disaster. Although it is easy to buy into the fear of dire predictions and dogma, all prophets predictions don't occur, or they happen long after we are gone.

So, are the Masters suggesting we submit ourselves to scripture? Again, we'd say a qualified, No! But we would venture to say they expect us to examine with intelligence and heart each prediction and be forewarned. We need to be proactive in endeavoring to understand the forces at play regarding the prophecy and probe into why Spirit might present such a prediction. Once we understand, we should act to make changes, or avoid making changes, as we are inwardly prompted.

Many Christians in their analysis suggest God has a plan, saying everything is foreordained by the Word of God. Can we embrace this stance? Some do, but this position feels overly rigid, not accounting for misinterpretation and misunderstanding.

If we return to our Chapter on God (Chapter 38), we discussed God not as a personal God, but that which IS, the I Am That I Am presence residing within each of us. Herein lies our ability to discern prophecy from the vantage of the Self and not from fear. We'd suggest this is a depiction of God inspiring us from within, prodding us to listen to our inner voice and avoid the misconceptions of the ego and making decisions from fear.

FIFTY-THREE

VIRTUE AND SOCIAL JUSTICE ASPIRING TO LIVE DIVINE PRINCIPLE

W E WOULD LIKE TO CONCLUDE SEASONS OF THE SOUL WITH the Masters' lucidity concerning one of humankind's greatest attributes, Virtue. Virtue, like love, truth, and blessings, is a word overused in our culture. As a result, we never fully grasp its implications, nor the manner in which it's attained. Virtue, for many, can be found in a list of ethical attributes like kindness, trust, and truthfulness. We use it to sculpt our character. But we would suggest it is much more than a placeholder in a list of honorable, character-building attributes. Those who truly possess it radiate a goodness, a Light, bringing comfort and healing to others.

The Masters imply that genuine Virtue eludes us until we discover the nobility of humility. It lives when we are free from the need to self-inflate our importance. Humility comes with hard-fought knocks and rigor. It is what Saint Teresa lamented she lacked, constantly battling her pride. When aspired to and attained, it is the redeeming quality to which our soul yearns, to establish the power of sincere Love, compassion, and transformative magic. Again, one of the best examples of the power and grace of Virtue comes to us from the *Bible*. Luke 8:46-47 KJB

"And Jesus said, somebody hath touched me for I perceive virtue has gone out of me. And when the woman saw that she was not hid, she came

trembling, and falling down before him, she declared unto him before all the people for what cause she had touched him, and how she was healed immediately."

We think we can assess from this example, Virtue is more than any one given quality. When Virtue is attained, it acts as a power, a hidden reservoir of goodness residing within the person who has mastered the life experience. This energy is transmitted, uplifting those who find themselves in its presence. How is this power cultivated? The following concepts are insights the Masters encourage us to adopt if we are to foster true Virtue:

- Love and Respect Thy Self, the Commandment of the New Age. If we don't Respect ourselves, how can we expect others to respect or follow our lead?

- Attempt to make the world Spiritually, socially, and environmentally, a better place because we dare not to be enslaved by others' evaluations and criticisms.

- Step beyond the consciousness of self-centeredness and shed the me-focus pattern.

- Live the Golden Rule without exception, "Do unto others as you would have them do unto you." The cultivation of morality is the Virtue that creates Mastery. Developing the discernment of what is right over what feels good.

- Don't allow human flaws to hamper the soaring eagle within.

- Rise above what we think, willingly questioning our intellectual position, and become excited to engage with other people's minds. Seek adversarial cross-pollination.

- Be ever-ready to consume and embrace more truth.

- Realize whatever sorrow, misfortune, or pain we experience or witness, therein lies a Virtue.

- Refrain from indulging in self-pity as it sets our personal evolution into retrograde.

- Focus on the home front rather than finding fault with others; in other words, in the face of difficulties, confront ourselves first.

- Make a habit of garnering enlightenment by questioning our intent, then question our questioning.

- Be aware of wandering too far inward; strive to achieve social justice by eradicating evil from within and without.

- Be inspired by the best in others rather than discouraged.

- Seek beyond victimhood regarding any circumstance; reach out for inspiration instead.

- Expose injustice wherever it lives, at whatever level it exists. Silence is tantamount to allegiance.

- Remember there is Virtue residing behind our faults; don't shrink from the power of Life in the face of defeat or faults. Practice the mantra of We Can, We Will, We Do!

- Transcend intolerance and disgust to find forgiveness.

- Live in such a way that our duty is our Joy and our Joy our duty.

- Be quick to acknowledge others' talents and character, giving praise whenever or wherever it is deserved.

- Commit to selfless Divine sacrifice. (It slays all dragons.)

- Foster the inward penetration of Light and an outward emanation of Virtue.

We could call this cultivation of Virtue an inward and outward quest for the Holy Grail, establishing ourselves on the path to discover the mystery beyond all mysteries—Immortality, whether it be Physical Immortality or Spiritual Immortality. But at times in our Spiritual search and practice, we can become overly enamored with Spiritual gifts and our Spiritual development, forgetting that Mastery lies in resolving our personal issues. In other words, it is wise to attempt to resolve the faults that block us from the next observation, the next inspiration, or the enactment of Virtue. So even in times of great exasperation, it is prudent to adhere to the pull of Virtue, holding its cultivation as the supreme pinnacle. For isn't our search to achieve the archetype of a Master, our deep yearning to be more Godly?

As we stoop to gather each of the feathers we scattered from the mountain top on our search for Truth and Virtue, might we believe that with each feather retrieved, we are assembling the angelic wings that set us free.

Again, we are our authority for truth! If the Masters' thoughts in this segment don't resonate with you, put these aspects of Virtue on the shelf, perhaps for later consideration.

On a more temporal note, there exist many worldly forces challenging our quest for Virtue. Socially, we encounter regular discourse surrounding survival and fears for the future. There's an underlying uneasiness hovering in the background regarding natural disasters, the grid going down, nuclear attacks, and political and social uncertainty. It is easy to feel paralyzed. What can we do to prepare for cataclysmic events? Basic Survival 101! It is not a difficult matter to buy first-aid supplies, long-term food storage, and survival supplies, so we are reasonably prepared for any event that might arise. For many, though, this preparation is not enough to put them at ease.

If we step back for a moment and establish a broader soul perspective, we realize eternity is a long, long time, and in this awareness, all Earth shall shift, change, and pass away. With this notion in mind, some of the best Spiritual guidelines we can embrace to establish a sense of peace and engender a deeper Spiritual Truth are meditation and the contemplation of the Biblical Psalm 23. It doesn't matter if it's in difficult times or difficult circumstances, meditation and the truth of Psalm 23 are always comforting. By embracing meditation and the message of Psalm 23, we stand in the Truth, leaning into the Faith of the still, small voice dwelling within:

"The Lord is my shepherd,
I shall not want.
He maketh me to lie down in
green pastures; He leadeth me beside the
still waters,
He restoreth my soul. He leadeth me
in paths of righteousness for His Name's sake.
Yea, though I walk in the shadow of
death, I will fear no evil for Thou art with me,
Thy rod and Thy staff they comfort me.
Thou preparest a table before me in the
presence of mine enemies; Thou anointest my
head with oil.
Surely, goodness and mercy shall follow me
all the days of my life, and I will dwell in the house
of the Lord forever."

In addition to potential cataclysmic events troubling our hearts, there exist unsettling issues between our government and the people. In looking for solutions to address the inequities in the balance of power between the people and government, a viable social pact is essential. The Masters direct our attention to the Bill of Rights in the United States Constitution as a model of social Virtue. If adhered to, it represents a legitimate path to success. Here are the Rights as outlined in the Bill of Rights within the United States Constitution.

People will have:

- ◆ Freedom of Speech
- ◆ Freedom of Religion
- ◆ Freedom of Assembly
- ◆ Right to Keep and Bear Arms

- No Person Shall Be Deprived of Life, Liberty, or Property Without Due Process of Law

- Right to a Speedy and Public Trial

- There Will Be No Unreasonable Search and Seizures

As Thomas Jefferson penned, these are inalienable Rights we each possess as sovereign individuals, Rights that can't be challenged nor violated, as much a part of us as the air we breathe—God given. We often take these Rights for granted, assuming our protection agencies are enforcing these sacred trusts. In reviewing the list of Rights, if we are honest, can we find one of these Rights that has not been violated over the last fifty years? Some may believe the Rights have been upheld, but if we analyze our government's actions at home and abroad, we would be hard-pressed to say the Bill of Rights' integrity has been preserved. Breaches of trust could be listed, but it would be exhaustive and likely divisive. Most would agree, however, we are at a low point in our trust of government.

As we have seen, the Masters believe our Spiritual practice and the garnering of Virtue doesn't stop within the confines of the temple but extends into the world. The liberty we enjoy, and expect our families to enjoy, depends on social justice and the fulfillment and preservation of these Rights. No one will maintain them but us! **Liberty exists only upon our insistence.** Disrespecting these rights whenever it serves the governmental agenda inevitably disrespects citizens and creates societal breakdown. We, the people, must demand the strict adherence to the social contract that the government promised to lawfully uphold! Let us not forget the government is in service to the people, not the people enslaved by the government.

For a moment, let's ask ourselves, what kind of world we live in? What do we imagine as the present realities? We welcome the wonderful stories of kindness and joy, such as the work of Doctors

Without Borders. But when events get a bit darker and we discover incidents we don't want to hear or believe, atrocities that run counter to our inalienable rights, how do we respond? Unfortunately, most are not overly surprised when they encounter moral infractions. Infractions like theft, lying, and infidelity abound. We need to ask ourselves, have we become anesthetized to the rampant breakdowns in our own society? Are we really aware how far we have strayed as a society from the Golden Rule and from our own Bill of Rights? We easily see what some may consider minor infractions, but what kind of behavior has escaped our moral code and the purview of the law?

What might we discover if we take a walkabout to examine the current events in our world? First, we'll drop into China, then stop at the Mexican border, observe the battlefields in Gaza and the Middle East, and finally move West:

In China, we discover recreational playgrounds throbbing every morning with folks practicing *Falun Gong* for Spiritual and health benefits. Inexplicably, on a morning in 1999, two to three fellow practitioners didn't show. They simply disappeared, never to practice again! They were swept away in a military raid and forced into government-run labor camps like Masanjia.

As planned by the Chinese government, doctors, many under threat, assembled an organ database of the inmates for elite buyers around the world. Once an order came over the internet, the recipient client was hustled to a Chinese hospital where unethical doctors sacrificed the *Falun Gong* practitioner's organs, snatching great profits for the military, middlemen, and hospitals, with no regard for the life of the *Falun Gong* practitioner. — **International Tribunal for Natural Justice, Testimony from *Falun Gong* practitioners and former Chinese "Live Organ" surgeon Enver Tothi.**

One prisoner, *Falun Gong* practitioner Sun Yi, wrote a letter exposing the horrors in the camps where many were savagely tortured with electric batons and submerged in cages for long periods of time. When this letter was discovered, a Canadian filmmaker created the documentary, *"Letters from Masanjia."* The film achieved wide acclaim and resulted in China apparently abolishing the labor camp system.

Arriving at the Mexican border, we discover that children seeking asylum often get separated from their guardians and whisked away by a wide range of criminal cartels. They end up in child trafficking rings, forced into labor camps, sacrificed in Satanic rituals, not to mention getting live organs robbed for transplants. The children are then left to die. — *Insight Crime*, **August 30, 2023.**

On the battlefields in the Middle East and Gaza, we find medical agents at the ready, armed with refrigeration units, scanning the dead to harvest the organs of the innocent. This war is operating as a literal life extension program for the elite, providing them with vital young kidneys, eyes, and livers. — **Agent M, Middle-Eastern Rogue Agent, February 2024**

Stopping briefly in Somalia, we find an emaciated child so starved he is a flaccid sack of bones. He is so weak he is unable to absorb any food and is languishing away in a hovel on barren dirt floors. A short distance away, a teenager wheels into his parents' villa in Saudi Arabia, flashing hundreds of sparkling diamonds the size of his thumbnail glued to the hood of his glitzy Mercedes-Benz. — **David Adair, Astrophysicist (Rocket Man)**

A quick trip to Europe, and we find a man who was brutally tortured physically and sexually in childhood. To cope, he psychically split away from his body to escape his Nazi hell. He is there, but not there. He had been so traumatized during childhood that he gladly chose to be the perpetrator of bullying and brutality in school, acting out his Nazi fantasies on his classmates. His inner Light and Love, gifted at birth, are wasted, buried deep in an internal freezer along with his hardened consciousness. Hate and anger consume him. All he can think of is brutally killing every human being he can get his hands on. As an adult, he lands the perfect job with elite bankers, where he spends his time gleefully funding staged wars for the benefit of banking cartels. He is so good at his work that the bankers know he is fully groomed for the last stage of development, the participation in human sacrifice during Satanic ritual ceremonies. He is rather self-satisfied, yet there exists a gnawing, undeniable anxiousness. He just can't shake the internal conflict. To alleviate the torment, he imagines his first act of love will be to kill himself, making the world a better place. — **Personal disclosure at the International Tribunal for Natural Justice. Inquiry into Human Trafficking, Ronald Bernard, Former Elite Banker**

Moving back to the United States, we watch as a mortician receives a dead body delivered to his parlor. The mortician quickly grabs his cell phone, calling all his contacts to pimp out the fresh body. He must rush, as the warmer the body, the higher his fee. — **Story related from a U.S. Police Officer.**

Relocating to another incident in the U.S., we drop in on a MK Ultra Monarch Project (CIA Division) mind-control victim's encounter. In her diary, *Trance Formation of America,* Cathy O'Brien relates a variety of incidents. For example:

To date, I have been to MacDill Air Force Base and Disney World for governmental/military mind-control programming. Today, I arrived at a hunting lodge near Greybull, Wyoming, to be prepared for "A Most Dangerous Game." There are variations on the game, but in this instance, I am stripped naked and sent out into the wilderness where I am hunted down and caught like an animal, never knowing whether I will be severely tortured, raped, killed, or all of the above. These aren't ordinary hunters, but elites, many from the United States government, names you would easily recognize.

We could easily go on and on, stopping in every country listing atrocity after atrocity, writing volumes, but you're likely already numb or nauseous, and it's too painful to continue. We must not overemphasize the negative, because the majority of worldwide citizens are ethical, God-loving human beings; yet, sadly, we must admit these inhumane acts are systemic in our world today.

This is a quick snapshot of the shadow side of the group mind, and we haven't even considered the devastating wars, the fraud, and the misuse of power, all organized and run by a small cadre of evil people. Isn't it time we activists stop pointing our fingers at the Satanists, the elites, and the pedophiles, attempting to rally the three-letter agencies to fix the problem? Damn! Too often, the agencies are the problem! It is we, the masses, who must act in unison from Love, Compassion, and Forgiveness to put an end to such inhumanity.

In the Spiritual Realm, although constructive, no amount of meditation will completely eradicate the pervasive suffering and criminality within every society. If we are to create genuine social justice, it is time to unite, one with the other; the Spiritual with the profane, the agnostics with believers, Christians, Buddhists, Muslims, and Jews, demanding in one voice, "NO MORE! NO MORE! NO MORE!"

These listed perversions are not reflections of who we are. But we must endeavor to ensure that the monsters are no longer allowed to dominate and terrorize our world. As the Masters suggest, we are the change for which we are looking! We must stand firm together, conscience to conscience, husband to wife, brother to sister, brother to brother, sister to sister, friend to friend, enemy to enemy, judge to judge, community to community, church to church, and country to country. A worldwide human uprising must ascend, where we stop the denial of our enslavement and begin acting as sovereign entities to put an end to criminality once and for all! We can no longer wait to become enlightened Bodhisattvas existing on some comfy Loka, safe and sound. Action is required! NOW! A new Humane Spirit must arise. The Spirit of the Golden Age is calling. The Masters exclaim, *"Listen and Awaken!"*

The transformational changes required won't manifest without some level of confrontation. We suspect many are reticent to engage in confrontation. Lord Sanat Kumara offers this about confrontation:

Where two individuals, two religions, two cultures, or two systems meet in an open battlefield of the sincere exchange of views, the results are not likely to be the destruction of either, but, to the contrary, the clarification and refinement of each by the enduring values of both.

We are a melting pot of diverse minority cultures, varying religious beliefs, and people of assorted handicaps. Can we honor and allow all to flourish? The evolution of consciousness and the evolution of society rely on the human heart and mind to birth new solutions reflecting empathy and compassion while engaging in adversarial confrontation.

In reflecting on moving forward in *Seasons of the Soul*, we each have three choices from which to choose regarding the Ascended Masters' thoughts. No choice is right or wrong. They simply reflect our consciousness in the *Seasons of our Soul*:

1. Spend time in denial, proving ourselves to be the exception to eons of the Ascended Masters' wisdom and experiences.

2. Do nothing. Stand pat, finding no reason to believe or disbelieve.

3. Spend time doing whatever it takes to prove or disprove to ourselves the legitimacy of the Masters' thoughts. Are they sincere in their efforts to reflect Truth and represent answers to eternal questions we all ponder?

We'd like to end with a séance in which Reverend Rhinehart is entranced by Comte de Saint Germaine, where he speaks to an aspect of Virtue not commonly associated with Virtue—Happiness. In closing the séance, the Count reminisced if he had but a brief moment to communicate only one message that would make the biggest difference in someone's life, what would he say? He said he wouldn't discuss karma, past lives, Immortality, nor love. No! He would speak to something much simpler and easier to grasp. He reflected:

No matter our circumstances, no matter our station in life, no matter whether we are living under the most extreme, untenable hardship or living high on the hog, we have a choice to be happy, or a choice to be imprisoned by our circumstances. It is always a choice! There is no way around it! It matters not whether we are imprisoned, handicapped, sick, working in an unpleasant job, have lost our beloved, or are married to a difficult mate; in choosing to be happy, we will create the best possible outcome for our immediate circumstances and radiate Light for our Soul. Saint Germaine suggests, **"Choose To Be Happy!"**

NOTES

Chapter Four
COMTE de SAINT GERMAINE – EIGHTEENTH CENTURY
1. William Bramley
   The Gods of Eden , Avon Book, 1989, Pages 259-270
2. Isabel Cooper-Oakley, Introduction Manly P. Hall,
   The Most Holy Trinosophia – *Comte de St. Germain*
   Phoenix Press, Los Angeles, 1933, Pages 8-17
3. Ibid.

Chapter Seven
THE LIVES OF THE ASCENDED MASTERS
1. Baird Spaulding
   Life and Teachings of the Masters of the Far East
   DeVorss & Company, 1924, Volume 1, Chapter I, Page 12
2. Ibid. Volume 2, Chapter VII, Pages 66-67
3. Ibid. Volume 1, Chapter II, Pages 15-18

Chapter Eight
CHELAS' INTERACTIONS WITH THE ASCENDED MASTERS
1. Transcribed and compiled by A.T. Barker
   The Mahatma Letters, To A.P. Sinnett
   Theosophical University Press, 1923, Pages 16-17

Chapter Nine
UNEXPECTED ENCOUNTERS WITH THE ASCENDED MASTERS
1. Baird Spaulding
   Life and Teachings of the Masters of the Far East
   DeVorss & Company, 1924, Volume 2, Chapter XIII,
   Pages 119-123
2. Ibid., Vol. 2, Chapter X, Pages 93-95

Chapter Sixteen
MEDIUMSHIP – TO CONSOLE AND COMFORT THE MOURNER
1. Laura Huxley
   This Timeless Moment
   Mercury House, 1968, Pages 324-327

Chapter Nineteen
MEDIUMSHIP – HISTORICAL SCIENTIFIC REFERENCES
1. Sir Arthur Conan Doyle
   History of Spiritualism
   Cassell and Company, 1926, Page 316
2. Ibid., Pages 174-176
3. Cyril Permutt
   Photographing the Spirit World
   Bath Press, Avon, 1983, Pages 172,173
4. Baron von Schrenck Notzing
   Phenomena of Materialisation:
   A Contribution to the Investigation of Mediumistic Teleplastics
   Translated by E.E. Fournier d'Albe
   Kegan Paul, Trench, Trubner & Co. LTD,
   E. P. Dutton & Co., London, 1923, Page 17

Chapter Twenty-Two
THOUGHT – DIVERSE AVENUES OF PERCEPTION
1. Annie Jacobsen
   The U.S. Military Believes People Have A Sixth Sense
   TIME, April 3, 2017

Chapter Twenty-Four
THE DILEMMA OF DUALITY
1. Paramahansa Yogananda
   God Talks with Arjuna, Bhagavad Gita
   Self-Realization Fellowship, 1995, Verses 5 & 6, Page 598

Chapter Twenty-Seven
JESUS
1. Helena Petrovna Blavatsky
   Isis Unveiled II
   Theosophical University Press, Pasadena, CA 1988, Page 94
2. *Theosophy Magazine*
   Jesus The Christ
   May and June, 1936
3. Paramahansa Yogananda
   God Talks with Arjuna, Bhagavad Gita
   Self-Realization Fellowship, 1995
   Verses 5 & 6, Page 598

Chapter Twenty-Eight
BUDDHA
1. Helena Petrovna Blavatsky
   Secret Doctrine
   Quest Books, 1888, Theosophical Publishing House,
   Vol. 1, Page 271

Chapter Twenty-Nine
KRISHNA
1. Paramahansa Yogananda
   God Talks With Arjuna, Bhagavad Gita
   Vision of Visions: The Lord Reveals His Cosmic Form
   Self-Realization Fellowship, 1995, Page 818, Verses 10-12,
2. Ibid., Page 835

Chapter Thirty-One
KUMARA, KEITH MILTON RHINEHART
1. Marilou McIntyre, DD
   Life is Forever—Get Used to It
   New Worlds Press, 2010, Pages 119-125

Chapter Thirty-Two
THE SOUL MATE AND TWIN RAY EXPERIENCE - ETERNAL HARMONICS
1. Marilou McIntyre, DD
   Life is Forever—Get Used to It
   New Worlds Press, 2010, Pages 103-104

Chapter Thirty-Four
SACRED GEMSTONES OF THE BIBLE - RESERVOIRS OF MYSTIQUE AND MANNA
1. Ernest A. and Jean Heiniger
   The Great Book of Jewels
   Publisher-Edita S.S. Lausanne, 1974, Page 177
2. Ibid., Page 178
3. Ibid., Page 179

Chapter Thirty-Six
HISTORICAL CROWNS AND RINGS - ROYAL MYSTICAL GEMSTONES
1. Ernest A. and Jean Heiniger
   The Great Book of Jewels
   Publisher, Edita S.S. Lausanne 1974, Pages 202-203

2. Ibid., Page 203
3. Ibid., Page 204
4. George Fredrick Kunz
   Rings for the Finger
   Dover Publishing, Inc., 1917
   Pages vii, 1-2
5. Ernest A. and Jean Heiniger
   The Great Book of Jewels
   Publisher, Edita S.S. Lausanne 1974
   Pages 286-287

Chapter Thirty-Seven
FORMATION OF GEMSTONES – NATURAL AND THE SACRED
1. Evan M. Smith, Gemological Society of America
   "How are Diamonds Formed?"
   Natural Diamonds, Online, 8-15-2022

Chapter Forty
THE MYSTERY OF SCIENTIFIC PRAYER – MARY BAKER EDDY
1. Mary Baker Eddy
   Retrospection and Introspection
   Published under the will of Mary Baker Eddy, Boston, 1891
   Page 28
2. Ibid., Page 40
3. Ibid., Page 16

Chapter Forty-One
MYSTICISM OF PRAYER – SAINT TERESA OF ÁVILA
1. *The Life of Saint Teresa of Ávila by Herself*
   Passed from hand to hand in 1565
   Translated by J.M. Cohen, Penguin Books, 1957
   Page 127
2. Ibid., Page 123

Chapter Forty-Three
DEATH AND AFTERLIFE
1. W.T. Stead, through the hand of Estelle Stead
   The Blue Island
   ESPress, Inc., 1940
2. Ibid.

Chapter Forty-Six
SUICIDE AND ASSISTED DEATH
1. Transcribed and compiled by A.T. Barker
   The Mahatma Letters, To A.P. Sinnett
   Theosophical University Press, Written 1880-1884,
   Published 1923, Page 109

Chapter Forty-Nine
PROPHECY – "My Bowl of Water Doth Reveal to Me"
1. The Richard Wilhelm Translation
   The I Ching
   Bollingen Series XIX, Princeton University Press, 1950
   Pages 197-200

Chapter Fifty-Two
PROPHECY – NOTEWORTHY PROPHETS
1. Edgar Leoni
   Nostradamus and His Prophecies
   Dover Publications Inc., 1961, Page 22
2. Ibid., Page 20
3. Ibid., Page 21

Acknowledgements

The authors first wish to thank Reverend Keith Milton Rhinehart without whose adept mediumship not a word would have been written. Additionally, we would like to extend our deep gratitude to the Ascended Masters and Archangels for their outreach to humanity imparting their Love, wisdom and devotion. We have brought to the printed page many concepts of the Masters and although it is impossible to list all the Masters we have listened to over the years we would like to mention the few who we have hi-lighted in the book. There is Master Jesus, Master Comte de Saint Germaine, Master Buddha, Master Krishna, Master Muhammad, Master Odyssa and Lady Master Rasha, Archangel Gabriel, Master Zoser, Master Koot Hoomi, Master Elijah, Master Emil, Master Clarion, Master Babaji, Master Yogananda, Lady Master Saint Teresa of Avila, and Lady Master Saint Therese of Lisieux.

Many have taken the time to work with us, contributing personal experiences greatly enlivening the book. We would like to express our appreciation to April Lee, Marilou McIntyre, Monica Szu-Whitney, Linda Dunn, Sheila Scoular, Vlasta Mozina, Craig Ramsell, Sarah Liles, Dulce Catalan, Joyce Keller, and many others who would prefer to remain anonymous.

Along the journey others have contributed in a number of ways with encouragement, reading, and critiques. We would like to acknowledge Yohanna Fogelberg, Vickie Matthews, Bill Vartnaw, Larry Matthews, Tawni Hill, Mariah Miller, and Mila Johansen.

Finally, we would like to shine the Light on Penelope Fox whose long hours, insights and intellectual rigor gave our text clarity and depth, making the book far more accessible to the reader.

About the Authors

GARY WHITNEY

Gary was born and grew up in Petaluma, California. He received his M.A. in Art from California State University, Chico, and a B.A. in Interior Design from San Jose State University. He taught art for several years at Quincy Junior/Senior High School in Northern California. In the eighties, he joined Aquarian Foundation, studying the Masters' teachings. During this period, he worked for several personal growth organizations and was active in the consciousness movement, working as a personal coach and teaching courses in the development of the imagination. Over the years, he has created businesses in the health food industry, graphic arts, and interior design. Gary is now writing. In 1999, he co-authored the book *Portals and Corridors* with his wife, Monica Szu-Whitney.

STEVE YOUNG

Steve was born and raised in Honolulu, Hawaii. He served in the Honolulu Police Department for 30 years in the Patrol, Traffic, and Criminal Investigation Divisions. He retired as a White-Collar Violent Crime Detective, Certified Fraud Examiner, and Certified Protection Professional. Steve became the ninth officer in the history of the Honolulu Police Department to receive the Honor of Valor Award after entering a burning building to save a woman's life. He joined Aquarian Foundation in 1973 and served on the Church's Board for nineteen years in different capacities until Reverend Rhinehart's passing. Reverend Rhinehart considered Steve a trusted confidant, his bodyguard and protector of the Church.